Triathlete magazine's

ESSENTIAL WEEK-BY-WEEK TRAINING GUIDE

Plans, Scheduling Tips, and Workout Goals for Triathletes of All Levels

MATT FITZGERALD

Author of *Triathlete Magazine's Complete Triathlon Book*

GRAND CENTRAL
Life & Style

NEW YORK · BOSTON

Neither this wellness program nor any other wellness program should be followed without first consulting a health care professional. If you have any special conditions requiring attention, you should consult with your health care professional regularly regarding possible modification of the program contained in this book.

Grand Central Life & Style
Hachette Book Group
237 Park Avenue
New York, NY 10017

www.HachetteBookGroup.com

Grand Central Life & Style is an imprint of Grand Central Publishing.
The Grand Central Life & Style name and logo are trademarks of Hachette Book Group, Inc.

Printed in the United States of America

First Edition: April 2006
10   9   8   7   6   5   4

Library of Congres Cataloging-in-Publication Data
Fitzgerald, Matt.
      Triathlete magazine's essential week-by-week training guide : plans, scheduling tips, and workout goals for triathletes of all levels / Matt Fitzgerald. —1st ed.
         p. cm.
      ISBN: 978-0-446-69676-0
         1. Triathlon—Training.   I. Title: Essential week-by-week training guide.
II. Triathlete.   III. Title.

GV1060.73.F583 2006
796.42'57—dc22

2005029233

Exercise photos by John Segesta
Book design and text composition by Ellen Gleeson

for my mother and father

Acknowledgments

I would like to express my deepest gratitude to the many people whose help and support made this book possible and better than it otherwise would have been. Most especially, I wish to thank Hunter Allen, Mark Allen, Dan Ambrosio, John Duke, Sally Edwards, Gear Fisher, Joe Friel, Christina Gandolfo, Paul Goldberg, Donavon Guyot, Rachel Joyce, Fernanda Keller, Michael Lovato, T. J. Murphy, Tim Noakes, Andrea Pedolsky, Lindsay Peters, Robert Portman, Jay Prasuhn, Lonna Ramirez, Dave Scott, John Segesta, Joanna Zeiger, my wife, Nataki, and my brothers, Sean and Josh.

Contents

Introduction

*T*his book is something of a sequel to *Triathlete Magazine's Complete Triathlon Book.* In writing that first book I made a strategic decision to include just one ready-made training plan: a 12-week sprint triathlon training plan for beginners. I just didn't have enough room to include a full array of training plans in addition to all of the other information on topics ranging from equipment to diet. So instead I included a chapter on how to design your own training plan using a few simple guidelines, which included that single ready-made plan for beginners.

Not everyone wants to design his or her own training plan, however. After the *Complete Triathlon Book* was published, I began to receive e-mails from readers who appreciated the do-it-yourself chapter but nevertheless wanted to know if I could provide them with a ready-made training plan. Before long it was clear to me that I would need to write this follow-up book, which contains no fewer than 42 triathlon training plans. There is a plan for every conceivable variety of triathlete in the following pages, from the absolute beginner to the elite veteran, and for every distance from sprints to Ironmans. You could develop from a beginner training for your first sprint triathlon to an elite veteran training for your first Ironman victory and not have to look outside this book for a suitable training plan. That ought to put a stop to all those e-mails!

Just kidding. Feel free to contact me if any questions arise as you progress through your training (fitwriter@hotmail.com). Until then, stick to the plan and enjoy the journey!

Chapter 1
IT STARTS WITH A PLAN

*T*his book is not like a novel, which you need to read from start to finish, without skipping anything. It's more like a big recipe book that you can and should use one recipe at a time. There are 40 complete training plans (plus a pair of off-season training plans) in these pages, at least one of which is a good fit for you today, given your current fitness level, schedule, and event goals. But of course you can't follow multiple training plans simultaneously. So the way to use this book is to choose the best plan for you, complete it, and then pick another, and so on.

This chapter, however, is required reading. Its purpose is to give you the information you'll need to choose the right training plans to follow and to get the most out of them. First I'd like to explain the key features shared by all of the plans in this book. Understanding the rationale behind each of these key features will help you assume greater control over your training. In my experience, triathletes train with more motivation and discipline, and therefore get better results, when they truly understand and believe in their system of training.

Key Training Plan Features
There are six key features of the training plans presented in this book that you should understand before you begin using them.

Balance
Each plan has a more or less even balance in the number of swim, bike, and run workouts scheduled every week. (Note that bike and run workouts are sometimes combined into "brick" workouts.) Most age-group triathletes tend to do more workouts in their favorite discipline,

which is almost always their strongest discipline. This is not the best way to improve as a triathlete, because you have the greatest potential for improvement in your weakest discipline, so it makes no sense to marginalize it.

On the other hand, some coaches advise triathletes to do the greatest number of workouts in their weakest discipline, precisely because it offers the greatest opportunity for improvement. I see nothing wrong with maintaining this sort of strategic imbalance for short periods of time, but in the long term triathletes who take this approach tend to lose fitness in their strongest discipline, which is also undesirable. By doing a roughly equal number of workouts in all three disciplines you get something close to the best of both worlds: You get stronger in each discipline and weaker in none.

There's an exception in some of my middle-level half-Ironman and Ironman training plans, which include three swim workouts versus four bike and four run workouts in a typical week. At these longer race distances the swim leg is proportionally shorter than the bike and the run legs as compared to shorter race distances. Triathletes who are trying to keep their total training volume relatively moderate in preparing for longer races can't do four workouts per week in each discipline. One of them has to give, and it makes the most sense that it's swimming.

Variation

One of the most common problems in the training of self-coached triathletes is a lack of variation in their workouts. They fall into a rut of doing basically the same few workouts over and over. But you'll get fitter faster if you challenge your body in a variety of different ways in your swimming, cycling, and running workouts. Each of the training plans in this program incorporates a diversity of workout types, which you'll learn about in the next chapter.

Three Phases

Each training plan is divided into three phases. First is the *base phase*. It features a gradually increasing volume of primarily moderate-intensity training to build aerobic fitness and endurance, limit the likelihood of injuries, and prepare your body for the tougher training to follow in the second phase of training—the *build phase*. It also includes judicious doses of high-intensity training to develop sport-specific strength and power and prepare your body for the high-intensity workouts of the build phase.

The challenging, high-intensity workouts added in the build phase increase your aerobic fitness and enhance your ability to resist fatigue at higher speeds of swimming, cycling, and running.

The final phase is the *peak phase*. In this phase the top training priority is workouts that are highly race-specific in their demands. The two main types of race-specific workouts are long swims, rides, runs, and brick workouts that prepare you to go the full distance on race day and somewhat shorter workouts performed at or near race intensity. The final week to two weeks of the peak phase is a "taper" period, in which your training load is steadily reduced to leave you rested and ready for maximum performance on race day.

Step Cycles

Step cycles are four-week blocks of training in which the second week is more challenging than the first, the third week is more challenging than the second, and the fourth week is a recovery week, in which training volume is reduced 10 to 20 percent. Training in step cycles is much better than training with less week-to-week variation in training volume. The incremental training increases in the first three weeks ensure that your fitness moves in a positive direction with minimal risk of injury or exhaustion. The recovery weeks taken every fourth week allow your body to fully absorb recent training and prepare for still more challenging training in the weeks to come.

One Rest Day per Week

Every single training plan in this book has one scheduled day of complete rest per week, from the Level 1 sprint plan all the way up to the Level 10 Ironman plan. Why? Because even if you're a noncompetitive beginner who plans to do only one short triathlon, you should exercise six days a week, for the sake of your health if not your performance. And even if you're a world-class veteran triathlete capable of handling the most punishing workout schedule, you'll still benefit from regularly scheduled rest as much as anyone else—maybe *more than* anyone else.

Tune-up Races

A peak race is a triathlon that you want to be optimally prepared for—fit and ready to produce your best performance. The whole reason training plans exist at all is to make peak races possible. Every training plan culminates in a peak race, and its job is to raise your fitness level as high as possible between now and then.

In addition to peak races, the training plans in this book also have scheduled tune-up races. The only exceptions are the sprint triathlon training plans, which are only 12 weeks long—a little too short to squeeze in a tune-up race. The Olympic-distance plans feature a sprint-distance tune-up race in Week 12. The half-Ironman training plans include a sprint-distance tune-up race at the end of Week 12 and an Olympic-distance tune-up race at the end of Week 16. The Ironman training plans feature a sprint-distance tune-up race at the end of Week 12, an Olympic-distance tune-up race at the end of Week 16, and a half-Ironman tune-up race at the end of Week 20.

There are three reasons to do tune-up races. First, they're great workouts. You just can't push yourself as hard in a regular training session as you can in a race. For this reason, the right tune-up race at the right time can boost your fitness better than any regular training session. Second, tune-up races provide valuable experience in such areas as transitions, race nutrition, and dealing with race discomfort, to help you race better the next time. Finally, tune-up races reward all of your hard work in training. It takes many weeks of sweat and sacrifice to achieve peak fitness. It's a shame to put in so much effort for just one competitive performance. Even though you might not be able to perform at quite as high a level in your tune-up races as you can in your peak race, you can still perform well enough to be proud and feel rewarded for your training.

Of course, the odds are not great that you will always be able to find accessible races of the prescribed distances taking place at the times I've scheduled them in these plans. Don't sweat it. The tune-up race schedules in these plans represent what I consider the ideal scenario. Do what you can to create a race schedule that matches up with the ideal, but don't worry if you have to shuffle things around a little. The principles that underlie the race schedules in my plans are as follow: (1) It's generally best to avoid racing in the base phase, if for no other reason than because you'll probably disappoint yourself; (2) it's best to schedule shorter races before longer races; and (3) it's best not to race too often (one or two races a month in the build and peak phases are plenty).

How to Get the Most Out of These Training Plans

There are 40 complete training plans evenly divided into four groups according to the distance of your peak race: sprint, Olympic-distance, half-Ironman, and Ironman. Not every triathlon fits these four formats exactly, but every triathlon loosely fits one of them. There is no official sprint format. The typical sprint features a swim of about 0.5 mile, a 12- or 13-mile bike leg, and a 3-mile run. The official Olympic-distance format is a 1.5-kilometer (0.93-mile) swim, a 40-kilometer (24.8-mile) bike leg, and a 10-kilometer (6.2-mile) run. The official half-Ironman distances are 1.2 miles, 56 miles, and 13.1 miles. The official Ironman distances are 2.4 miles, 112 miles, and 26.2 miles.

Before you choose a plan, choose a peak race—not merely a distance but an actual event of that distance. This event should be at least as many weeks in the future as the training plan is long. The sprint plans in this book are 12 weeks, the Olympic-distance plans are 16 weeks, the half-Ironman plans are 20 weeks, and the Ironman plans are 24 weeks. If you have a buffer of one or more weeks before you need to start your chosen plan, train sensibly in a way that prepares you for the workouts that Week 1 of the plan calls for. If there's less time between now and your peak race than the plans for that distance call for, then the training you've been doing had better look a lot like the weeks of my plan that you've missed!

Choosing the Right Plan

Within each peak race category the plans are ranged according to levels, 1 through 10. As you move up from Level 1 the number of weekly workouts increases, as do the average workout durations, the total weekly training volume, and the amount of high-intensity training.

To choose the appropriate level, look at the brief description of the plans at the beginning of each chapter. These previews provide a few words about whom the plan is a good fit for, plus information about the amount of training in the first week and in the peak training week (the second- or third-to-last week of the plan). Note that swim workouts are prescribed by distance (yards), whereas bike and run workouts are prescribed by time. It just makes more sense that way. In most cases, if you can handle Week 1 of a given plan now, you'll be able to handle the plan as a whole. However, there are exceptions. For example, if the training in Week 1 of a given plan is close to the maximum volume of training you've ever done, it's probably not a good plan for you unless you're a relative beginner and the plan in question is a lower-level sprint or Olympic-distance plan. Use common sense and don't bite off more than you can chew.

Because there are so many plans within each category, the differences between plans of adjacent levels are small. While this might make it a little harder to choose a plan, it also offers some flexibility that makes it much harder to choose the wrong plan. If, after completing a few weeks of a given plan, you begin to find the training unchallenging, feel free to begin subbing in some workouts from the next level up. Likewise, if you begin to feel overwhelmed by your chosen plan, drop down a level for some or all of your workouts. (Note that some workouts on some days are identical in plans of adjacent levels.)

You should never treat a training plan as gospel. It's impossible to always predict how your body will respond to training. When it doesn't respond quite as expected, adjust your training appropriately or your fitness will stagnate, or worse. Training well is about doing the right workouts at the right times, and the only way to do the right workout every time is to be responsive. On the other hand, don't get too creative. These training plans were designed with great care, such that, barring a major disruption such as injury, the amount of fine-tuning you need to do should be minimal, assuming you did indeed chose an appropriate plan. The occasional poor workout performance or stale patch is normal in triathlon training. Stay the course despite these annoyances, trust the plan, and see it through.

You'll notice that all of the workouts are prescribed in codes. The key to these codes is in the next chapter, which presents every format for every workout you'll ever need to do as a triathlete. In each of the subsequent chapters containing training plans you will find a "Quick Reference Guide" that provides only the details of the workouts used in the training plans presented in that chapter. This will allow you to decode the workouts in your plan without too much page flipping. The rationale for the code is economy. Without it this book would have to be about 1,000 pages long!

Finally, be sure to record the details of each workout in a training log. The Appendix at the end of the book is a 24-week blank training log that will get you started.

Chapter 2
WORKOUTS THAT WORK

*T*here's an amusing story about how Bruce Jenner trained to win the 1976 Olympic decathlon gold medal for the United States. As you probably know, the decathlon competition comprises 10 track-and-field events ranging from the shot put to the 1,500-meter run. By way of preparing to compete against the world's top decathletes in each of these events, Jenner would show up at the track every morning and look around to see who else was working out. Spying a group of hurdlers, he would approach them and say, "What are you guys doing today?" Then he would join them for their workout. After that he'd look around and spot some javelin throwers. "What are you guys doing today?" And so on.

The first triathletes did something similar. Instead of reinventing the proverbial wheel, they borrowed tried-and-true workout formats from swimmers, cyclists, and runners. If the workouts worked for these single-sport endurance athletes, they should work just as well for athletes dabbling in all three sports. And they did. The only workouts that triathletes had to invent for their special needs were so-called brick workouts (named after their putative creator, a triathlete named Matt Brick) and transition workouts, wherein a bike ride is followed immediately by a run.

In this chapter I will describe each type of swim, bike, and run workout that is used in the training plans to follow. I will tell you when to do each workout type, how to do it, and the benefits of doing it. While all of these workouts represent classic workout formats with proven effectiveness, each coach has his own preferences regarding exactly how to do them, and I am no exception; but the differences between my preferences and those of most other coaches are mostly minor.

Any given type of workout can be done at a variety of levels. For example, the duration of a long run may range from 1 hour and 5 minutes to 3 hours. The appropriate level at which to perform any given workout depends on the training plan you choose and where you are within the plan. Long runs are longer in an Ironman training plan than in a sprint plan; longer in, say, a Level 10 plan for any distance than in a Level 1 plan of the same distance; and longer toward the end of all plans than toward the beginning.

Each level of each workout type is assigned a unique code. It is these codes (to conserve space) that will appear in the week-by-week breakdown of the training plans. This chapter provides the information you will need to decode every level of every workout. But in each of the subsequent chapters containing training plans, you will find a Quick Reference Guide that provides only the details of the workouts used in the training plans presented in that chapter. This will allow you to decode the workouts in your plan without too much page flipping. Simply read the code for tomorrow's workout in the training plan you've chosen and use the Quick Reference Guide to learn the specifics. Alternatively, you can decode your workouts a week at a time and pencil the details into your training calendar (whether you use the one at the back of this book or another). Then record what you've actually done after completing each workout.

It's very important that you perform each workout or part thereof at the appropriate intensity (that is, the appropriate speed or pace). Intensity is the primary determinant of the training effect of any given workout. If you go too fast in a workout that is meant to be low to moderate intensity, you might not finish it. If you go too easy in a high-intensity workout, you won't get as much out of it as you should.

There are six workout intensity levels that apply to all three triathlon disciplines: recovery, moderate aerobic, high aerobic, threshold, VO_2 max, and speed. The simplest way to control the intensity of your training is by feel. The following table provides guidelines that will help you find each of the appropriate intensity levels in swimming, cycling, and running. The table uses a simple 1–10 Rating of Perceived Effort (RPE) scale, where a rating of 4 is the easiest effort that qualifies as exercise and a rating of 10 is maximal. Note that the difficulty of sustaining any given pace increases the longer you sustain it, so these ratings are specific to the initial perceived effort (i.e., how hard the effort feels after only 20–30 seconds). Also provided in the table are some pace/speed guidelines to help you "calibrate" your feel for intensity.

If you're an experienced triathlete, you probably can find these

INTENSITY	RATING OF PERCEIVED EFFORT (1–10)	FEELS LIKE	PACE/SPEED GUIDELINES
Recovery	4–5	Very easy, but still counts as "exercise"	10 percent slower than moderate aerobic pace
Moderate Aerobic	6–7	Comfortable but not easy	10 percent slower than high aerobic pace
High Aerobic	7–8	Still comfortable but requires effort	5 percent slower than threshold pace
Threshold	8–8.5	Fastest pace you can hold without straining	Beginners: fastest pace you can hold for 20:00 High fitness: fastest pace you can hold for 60:00
VO_2 max	9	Very hard but controlled	Fastest pace you can hold for 6–8:00
Speed	10	Relaxed sprint	Fastest pace you can hold for 1:00–1:30

intensity levels easily. If you're new to the sport, you may go too hard or too easy at first, but you'll get the hang of it quickly as you do the workouts repeatedly.

Before I present the workouts themselves, I need to say a few words about terminology and the notations used in the workout tables provided with each workout type.

"Intervals" are segments of hard work (i.e. relatively fast swimming, cycling, or running) separated by recovery periods.

RI = Rest. This is a short, passive recovery period in a swim set. This entails simply hanging on to the wall at the end of your lane (or standing at the end of your lane, if possible). For example, the notation "0:20 RI" means you are to rest for 20 seconds after each interval in the set.

AR = Active Recovery. This entails very easy cycling or running at recovery intensity between high-intensity intervals in a bike or run workout. For example, the notation "1:00 AR" indicates that you are to cycle or jog for one minute after each interval.

In notations such as "4 X 3:00" and "12 X 100," the number before the X equals the number of intervals prescribed in the workout and the number after the X indicates the duration or distance of each interval.

All swim intervals are prescribed by distance, while all bike and run intervals are prescribed by time.

Finally, for the sake of clarity, all durations of 1 hour or greater are presented in the following format: "1:00:00," "2:30:00," and so forth. If you see "1:00," you know it means 1 minute, not 1 hour. If you see "2:30," you know it means 2 minutes and 30 seconds, not 2 hours and 30 minutes.

Swim Workouts

Swim workouts are quite different from bike and run workouts. Whereas intervals are used rather sparingly in bike and run training, they are the bread and butter of swim training. Technique drills are likewise a small part of training for the bike and the run, but should be included in almost every swim workout.

Why are swim workouts so unique? The simple answer is that decades of collective experimentation have clearly demonstrated that emphasizing intervals and drills in swim training produces better results than any alternative.

Because they are so unlike bike and run workouts, I prescribe swim workouts differently. Specifically, whereas I prescribe complete bike and run workouts, I prescribe swim workouts in parts. The component parts of a swim workout are the warm-up, a drill set, one to three main sets, sometimes a kick set, and a cool-down set. In the training plans, you will see the codes representing the component parts of a given swim workout (SWU = swim warm-up, SDS = swim drill set, SKS = swim kick set, etc.) stacked in the proper order on the day that workout is to be performed (see example). Beneath this stack of codes you will see a number in parentheses that indicates the total distance of the workout.

Example of a Swim Workout
SWU2
SDS2
SBI10
SSI3
SKS2
SCD2
(2,050)

Warm-Up Sets

The purpose of the warm-up set is to gently prepare your body for the rest of the swim workout. Always perform your swim warm-up at recovery intensity (4–5 RPE). The various levels of warm-up are distinguished by distance. Some pools are measured in yards, others in meters. Because pools measured in yards are more common in the United States, all swim sets and workouts are prescribed in yards. (1 meter equals 1.1 yards, so the difference is minimal.)

LEVEL	CODE	FORMAT
1	SWU1	200
2	SWU2	250
3	SWU3	300
4	SWU4	350
5	SWU5	400
6	SWU6	450

Drill Sets

Technique drills are critical to improvement in swimming. Whether you're a beginner or a former college all-American, you need to do them. The number-one key to improvement in swimming is increasing your efficiency in the water: using less energy to make greater forward progress. Building swim-specific cardiovascular fitness, while also important, does very little to increase efficiency. Technique improvements are the best way to become more efficient, and drills are one of the most effective ways to improve technique. The majority of your swim workouts should include a drill set.

There is a large number of swim drills to choose from. Following are descriptions of those that I deem most helpful. Practice at least two and as many as six different drills in each drill set. The table of drill sets that follows prescribes only the number and length of drills, and does not prescribe specific drill types. That part is up to you. I recommend that you do each of these drills at least occasionally and focus on those that address the biggest problem areas in your swim stroke.

CHEST PRESS

Swim facedown with your arms at your sides and propel yourself by kicking only. Exhale into the water and turn your head to the side to inhale. Concentrate on keeping your chest deep and your hips and legs high toward the surface. This drill improves body position and kicking technique.

SIDE KICKING

Swim on one side with the lower arm extended straight forward and the upper arm resting on your upper side. Rest your head against your shoulder and look down so that your head is totally submerged. Propel yourself by kicking only. Exhale into the water and rotate your head slightly upward to inhale. Concentrate on keeping your hips and legs high. Swim one length and then switch sides. This drill promotes proper technique at maximum rotation.

LAYOUT FREESTYLE

Start by kicking on your side as in the Side Kicking drill. After 3 to 5 seconds, rotate onto your belly and catch up to your forward arm with the other arm, so that your two arms are now extended in front of you. Immediately perform a complete pull with the original leading arm and simultaneously rotate onto your other side. Kick for 3 to 5 seconds and then catch up and rotate once more. After swimming two to four lengths in this way, reduce the amount of time you spend on each side to just 2 seconds. This drill improves body position and rotation.

CATCH-UP FREESTYLE

Begin by kicking facedown with both arms extended in front of you. After 3 or 4 seconds, perform a complete pull with one arm and rotate fully to that side. Immediately rotate back onto your belly and catch up to the forward arm with the arm that just pulled. Kick for 3 or 4 seconds and then pull with the other arm and rotate. Swim one to two lengths in this manner and then reduce the amount of time you kick on your belly to just 1 second between pulls. Swim one to two lengths more and then pull twice with each arm before switching sides. This drill promotes better rotation and arm-stroke mechanics.

CHEATING CATCH-UP

Do the Catch-up Freestyle drill as prescribed above, but instead of waiting until your recovering hand is even with your forward hand before you begin to pull with the latter, start to pull when your recovery hand is about even with the elbow of your forward arm. Essentially, the Cheating Catch-up drill is a cross between the Catch-up drill and normal freestyle swimming. This drill helps you transfer the improvements you make with the Catch-up drill to your freestyle swim stroke.

COUNT-STROKE

Simply count the number of strokes you take while swimming one complete length of the pool with normal freestyle technique, and then try to lower the number of strokes taken in each of two or three subsequent lengths. You will achieve this by taking longer, more powerful pulls, rotating more, and allowing yourself to glide a little bit. Feel free to exaggerate these elements in order to decrease the stroke count. This drill helps to improve overall stroke efficiency.

FINGERTIP DRAG

Swim a normal freestyle stroke, except consciously drag your fingertips across the surface of the water during the recovery phase. This modification helps you relax and use as little energy as possible during the recovery phase of the arm cycle. The Fingertip Drag drill can be performed in conjunction with the **Thumb Scrape** drill, in which you purposely scrape your thumb against your thigh during the release phase of the arm cycle (as your hand exits the water). This modification promotes complete arm extension and proper hand position in the release.

FIST

Swim with your fists clenched. This drill teaches you to rotate your shoulder and bend your elbow in the catch portion of the arm cycle in order to create a powerful "paddle" for the pull. If you do this correctly, you will swim with only slightly less power than you do with open hands.

BILATERAL BREATHING

If, like most triathletes, you are only able to inhale with your head turned to one side (usually the right side for right-handed swimmers and the left side for left-handed swimmers), make this drill a regular part of your drill set repertoire until you are able to breathe as comfortably on your weak side as you are on your dominant side. Just swim your normal freestyle stroke while breathing on every third stroke (right-left-right) instead of every second or fourth stroke (right-only or left-only). You will be terribly clumsy on your weak side at first, but stick with it and you'll steadily improve.

SIGHTING

Sighting is an important skill when you swim in open water without lane lines to guide you. It consists in modifying your swim stroke to look ahead and spot a "landmark" to aim toward. In a normal freestyle stroke you turn your head directly to one side or the other to inhale and then turn your head back to a neutral position with your eyes looking toward the bottom. When you sight, you instead turn your head to look forward and spot a landmark, and inhale before submerging your face underwater to exhale, without interrupting your arm movements. When practicing your sighting, swim normally and sight every four to six strokes.

LEVEL	CODE	FORMAT
1	SDS1	4 x 25 (RI 0:10)
2	SDS2	6 x 25 (RI 0:10)
3	SDS3	8 x 25 (RI 0:10)
4	SDS4	10 x 25 (RI 0:10)
5	SDS5	12 x 25 (RI 0:10)
6	SDS6	4 x 50 (RI 0:10)
7	SDS7	6 x 50 (RI 0:10)
8	SDS8	8 x 50 (RI 0:10)

Main Sets

As mentioned above, main sets are the meat of the swim workout. There are six types of main set: base intervals, swim time trials, speed intervals, lactate intervals, threshold intervals, and fartlek intervals.

BASE INTERVALS

Base intervals are freestyle swim intervals performed at moderate aerobic intensity (6–7 RPE) and separated by short rests (5–15 seconds, except in the case of single base intervals SBI22–SBI35, where there is no rest). They build aerobic fitness, endurance, and efficiency.

LEVEL	CODE	FORMAT
1	SBI1	2 x 100 (RI 0:05)
2	SBI2	3 x 100 (RI 0:05)
3	SBI3	4 x 100 (RI 0:05)
4	SBI4	5 x 100 (RI 0:05)
5	SBI5	6 x 100 (RI 0:05)
6	SBI6	7 x 100 (RI 0:05)
7	SBI7	8 x 100 (RI 0:05)
8	SBI8	9 x 100 (RI 0:05)
9	SBI9	10 x 100 (RI 0:05)

cont.

Level	Code	Format
10	SBI10	11 x 100 (RI 0:05)
11	SBI11	12 x 100 (RI 0:05)
12	SBI12	2 x 200 (RI 0:10)
13	SBI13	3 x 200 (RI 0:10)
14	SBI14	4 x 200 (RI 0:10)
15	SBI15	5 x 200 (RI 0:10)
16	SBI16	6 x 200 (RI 0:10)
17	SBI17	7 x 200 (RI 0:10)
18	SBI18	8 x 200 (RI 0:10)
19	SBI19	2 x 400 (RI 0:15)
20	SBI20	3 x 400 (RI 0:15)
21	SBI21	4 x 400 (RI 0:15)
22	SBI22	1 x 600

Level	Code	Format
23	SBI23	1 x 800
24	SBI24	1 x 1,000
25	SBI25	1 x 1,200
26	SBI26	1 x 1,500
27	SBI27	1 x 1,800
28	SBI28	1 x 2,000
29	SBI29	1 x 2,400
30	SBI30	1 x 2,600
31	SBI31	1 x 2,800
32	SBI32	1 x 3,000
33	SBI33	1 x 3,200
34	SBI34	1 x 3,500
35	SBI35	1 x 3,800

Swim Time Trials

In a swim time trial you swim a given distance as fast as possible. Swim time trials help prepare you for the specific demands of racing and allow you to gauge your current swim performance level.

LEVEL	CODE	FORMAT
1	STT1	1 x 800
2	STT2	1 x 1,000
3	STT3	1 x 1,650 y (1,500 m)
4	STT4	1 x 1.2 miles (2,112 y, 1,930 m)
5	STT5	1 x 3,200
6	STT6	1 x 2.4 miles (4,225 y, 3,860 m)

Speed Intervals

Speed intervals are very short intervals swum at speed intensity (10 RPE). Doing them will increase your maximum swim speed, your efficiency, and your ability to quickly recover from hard swimming. The A and B variations involve shorter rest periods.

LEVEL	CODE	FORMAT	VARIATIONS
1	SSI1	4 x 25 (RI 0:20)	SSI1A (RI 0:10), SSI1B (RI 0:05)
2	SSI2	5 x 25 (RI 0:20)	SSI2A (RI 0:10), SSI2B (RI 0:05)
3	SSI3	6 x 25 (RI 0:20)	SSI3A (RI 0:10), SSI3B (RI 0:05)
4	SSI4	7 x 25 (RI 0:20)	SSI4A (RI 0:10), SSI4B (RI 0:05)
5	SSI5	8 x 25 (RI 0:20)	SSI5A (RI 0:10), SSI5B (RI 0:05)
6	SSI6	9 x 25 (RI 0:20)	SSI6A (RI 0:10), SSI6B (RI 0:05)
7	SSI7	10 x 25 (RI 0:20)	SSI7A (RI 0:10), SSI7B (RI 0:05)
8	SSI8	11 x 25 (RI 0:20)	SSI8A (RI 0:10), SSI8B (RI 0:05)
9	SSI9	12 x 25 (RI 0:20)	SSI9A (RI 0:10), SSI9B (RI 0:05)
10	SSI10	4 x 50 (RI 0:20)	SSI10A (RI 0:10), SSI10B (RI 0:05)
11	SSI11	5 x 50 (RI 0:20)	SSI11A (RI 0:10), SSI11B (RI 0:05)
12	SSI12	6 x 50 (RI 0:20)	SSI12A (RI 0:10), SSI12B (RI 0:05)
13	SSI13	7 x 50 (RI 0:20)	SSI13A (RI 0:10), SSI13B (RI 0:05)
14	SSI14	8 x 50 (RI 0:20)	SSI14A (RI 0:10), SSI14B (RI 0:05)
15	SSI15	9 x 50 (RI 0:20)	SSI15A (RI 0:10), SSI15B (RI 0:05)
16	SSI16	10 x 50 (RI 0:20)	SSI16A (RI 0:10), SSI16B (RI 0:05)
17	SSI17	11 x 50 (RI 0:20)	SSI17A (RI 0:10), SSI17B (RI 0:05)
18	SSI18	12 x 50 (RI 0:20)	SSI18A (RI 0:10), SSI18B (RI 0:05)

Lactate Intervals

Lactate intervals are middle-length intervals swum at VO_2 max intensity (9 RPE). They will maximize your swim-specific aerobic capacity and improve your ability to sustain faster swim speeds. The A and B variations involve shorter rest periods.

LEVEL	CODE	FORMAT	VARIATIONS
1	SLI1	4 x 75 (RI 0:45)	SLI1A (RI 0:30), SLI1B (RI 0:20)
2	SLI2	5 x 75 (RI 0:45)	SLI2A (RI 0:30), SLI2B (RI 0:20)
3	SLI3	6 x 75 (RI 0:45)	SLI3A (RI 0:30), SLI3B (RI 0:20)
4	SLI4	7 x 75 (RI 0:45)	SLI4A (RI 0:30), SLI4B (RI 0:20)
5	SLI5	8 x 75 (RI 0:45)	SLI5A (RI 0:30), SLI5B (RI 0:20)
6	SLI6	9 x 75 (RI 0:45)	SLI6A (RI 0:30), SLI6B (RI 0:20)
7	SLI7	10 x 75 (RI 0:45)	SLI7A (RI 0:30), SLI7B (RI 0:20)

cont.

Level	Code	Format	Variations
8	SLI8	3 x 100 (RI 1:00)	SLI8A (RI 0:45), SLI8B (RI 0:30)
9	SLI9	4 x 100 (RI 1:00)	SLI9A (RI 0:45), SLI9B (RI 0:30)
10	SLI10	5 x 100 (RI 1:00)	SLI10A (RI 0:45), SLI10B (RI 0:30)
11	SLI11	6 x 100 (RI 1:00)	SLI11A (RI 0:45), SLI11B (RI 0:30)
12	SLI12	7 x 100 (RI 1:00)	SLI12A (RI 0:45), SLI12B (RI 0:30)
13	SLI13	8 x 100 (RI 1:00)	SLI13A (RI 0:45), SLI13B (RI 0:30)
14	SLI14	4 x 150 (RI 1:15)	SLI14A (RI 1:00), SLI14B (RI 0:45)
15	SLI15	5 x 150 (RI 1:15)	SLI15A (RI 1:00), SLI15B (RI 0:45)
16	SLI16	6 x 150 (RI 1:15)	SLI16A (RI 1:00), SLI16B (RI 0:45)
17	SLI17	7 x 150 (RI 1:15)	SLI17A (RI 1:00), SLI17B (RI 0:45)
18	SLI18	8 x 150 (RI 1:15)	SLI18A (RI 1:00), SLI18B (RI 0:45)

Threshold Intervals

Threshold intervals are longer intervals swum at (you guessed it) threshold intensity (8–8.5 RPE). Threshold intervals substantially increase your intensive endurance, or the duration you're able to sustain a relatively fast swim speed. The A and B variations involve shorter rest periods.

LEVEL	CODE	FORMAT	VARIATIONS
1	STI1	2 x 200 (RI 0:45)	STI1A (RI 0:30), STI1B (RI 0:20)
2	STI2	3 x 200 (RI 0:45)	STI2A (RI 0:30), STI2B (RI 0:20)
3	STI3	4 x 200 (RI 0:45)	STI3A (RI 0:30), STI3B (RI 0:20)
4	STI4	5 x 200 (RI 0:45)	STI4A (RI 0:30), STI4B (RI 0:20)
5	STI5	6 x 200 (RI 0:45)	STI5A (RI 0:30), STI5B (RI 0:20)
6	STI6	7 x 200 (RI 0:45)	STI6A (RI 0:30), STI6B (RI 0:20)
7	STI7	8 x 200 (RI 0:45)	STI7A (RI 0:30), STI7B (RI 0:20)
8	STI8	2 x 300 (RI 1:00)	STI8A (RI 0:45), STI8B (RI 0:30)
9	STI9	3 x 300 (RI 1:00)	STI9A (RI 0:45), STI9B (RI 0:30)
10	STI10	4 x 300 (RI 1:00)	STI10A (RI 0:45), STI10B (RI 0:30)
11	STI11	5 x 300 (RI 1:00)	STI11A (RI 0:45), STI11B (RI 0:30)
12	STI12	2 x 400 (RI 1:15)	STI12A (RI 1:00), STI12B (RI 0:45)
13	STI13	3 x 400 (RI 1:15)	STI13A (RI 1:00), STI13B (RI 0:45)
14	STI14	4 x 400 (RI 1:15)	STI14A (RI 1:00), STI14B (RI 0:45)

Fartlek Intervals

Fartlek intervals comprise alternating segments of easy and hard swimming. Swim the easy segments at moderate aerobic intensity (6–7 RPE) and the hard segments at threshold intensity (8–8.5 RPE).

The A variation is a build/descend version of the fartlek intervals. The "easy" segments become build segments in which you start at moderate aerobic pace and gradually build to threshold pace. The "hard" segments become descending segments in which you start at threshold pace and gradually slow to moderate aerobic pace.

LEVEL	CODE	FORMAT	VARIATIONS
1	SFI1	4 x 100 (25 easy/25 hard/25 easy/25 hard) RI 0:10	SFI1A—Build/Descend
2	SFI2	6 x 100 (25 easy/25 hard/25 easy/25 hard) RI 0:10	SFI2A—Build/Descend
3	SFI3	8 x 100 (25 easy/25 hard/25 easy/25 hard) RI 0:10	SFI3A—Build/Descend
4	SFI4	4 x 150 (50 easy/25 hard/50 easy/25 hard) RI 0:15	SFI4A—Build/Descend
5	SFI5	5 x 150 (50 easy/25 hard/50 easy/25 hard) RI 0:15	SFI5A—Build/Descend
6	SFI6	6 x 150 (50 easy/25 hard/50 easy/25 hard) RI 0:15	SFI6A—Build/Descend
7	SFI7	3 x 200 (50 easy/50 hard/50 easy/50 hard) RI 0:20	SFI7A—Build/Descend
8	SFI8	4 x 200 (50 easy/50 hard/50 easy/50 hard) RI 0:20	SFI8A—Build/Descend
9	SFI9	5 x 200 (50 easy/50 hard/50 easy/50 hard) RI 0:20	SFI9A—Build/Descend
10	SFI10	6 x 200 (50 easy/50 hard/50 easy/50 hard) RI 0:20	SFI10A—Build/Descend

Kick Sets

Many of the swim workouts in my plans call for a kick set between the main set(s) and the cool-down. In a kick set you swim by flutter kicking only, either on your side, on your back, or belly-down using a kickboard. You also have the option of wearing fins during your kick sets. This increases the load on your legs, which in turn enhances the power-building effect. The main benefit of doing kick sets is to develop a more powerful and efficient kick.

LEVEL	CODE	FORMAT
1	SKS1	4 x 25 (RI 0:15)
2	SKS2	6 x 25 (RI 0:15)
3	SKS3	8 x 25 (RI 0:15)
4	SKS4	10 x 25 (RI 0:15)
5	SKS5	12 x 25 (RI 0:15)
6	SKS6	4 x 50 (RI 0:20)
7	SKS7	6 x 50 (RI 0:20)
8	SKS8	8 x 50 (RI 0:20)

Cool-Down Sets

It's helpful to swim a few easy laps at the end of each swim workout. A good cool-down clears metabolic wastes from your muscles and gently prepares your body to return from a stress state to a rest state. Swim your cool-down set at recovery intensity (4–5 RPE).

LEVEL	CODE	FORMAT
1	SCD1	200
2	SCD2	250
3	SCD3	300
4	SCD4	350
5	SCD5	400
6	SCD6	450

Cycling Workouts

There are 10 standard types of cycling workouts that have been proven effective through decades of collective practice:

1) recovery rides
2) foundation rides
3) long rides
4) power intervals
5) short hill climbs
6) long hill climbs
7) threshold rides
8) lactate intervals
9) speed intervals
10) steady-state rides

Recovery Ride

A recovery ride is a relatively short ride performed at recovery intensity (4–5 RPE). Recovery rides are appropriate cycling workouts to do between harder cycling workouts during the week. They are easy enough that they don't set back your recovery from the previous hard ride or sabotage your performance in the next hard ride, yet they still serve to increase your overall cycling training volume and cycling fitness.

LEVEL	CODE	FORMAT
1	CRR1	0:20:00
2	CRR2	0:30:00
3	CRR3	0:45:00
4	CRR4	1:00:00
5	CRR5	1:15:00
6	CRR6	1:30:00

Foundation Ride

A foundation ride is roughly the equivalent of base intervals in swimming. These workouts are performed at moderate aerobic intensity (6–7 RPE) to develop aerobic capacity, endurance, and cycling efficiency.

LEVEL	CODE	FORMAT
1	CFR1	0:30:00
2	CFR2	0:45:00
3	CFR3	1:00:00
4	CFR4	1:15:00
5	CFR5	1:30:00
6	CFR6	1:45:00
7	CFR7	2:00:00
8	CFR8	2:15:00
9	CFR9	2:30:00

Long Ride

Like foundation rides, long rides are steady rides at moderate aerobic intensity (6–7 RPE). The difference is that they are longer—although long is a relative term. An experienced long-distance triathlete will do some foundation rides that are longer than an inexperienced short-course triathlete's long rides. The main purpose of long rides is to build cycling endurance.

LEVEL	CODE	FORMAT
1	CLR1	2:00:00
2	CLR2	2:15:00
3	CLR3	2:30:00
4	CLR4	2:45:00
5	CLR5	3:00:00
6	CLR6	3:15:00
7	CLR7	3:30:00
8	CLR8	3:45:00
9	CLR9	4:00:00
10	CLR10	4:15:00
11	CLR11	4:30:00
12	CLR12	4:45:00
13	CLR13	5:00:00
14	CLR14	5:15:00
15	CLR15	5:30:00
16	CLR16	5:45:00
17	CLR17	6:00:00
18	CLR18	6:15:00
19	CLR19	6:30:00
20	CLR20	6:45:00
21	CLR21	7:00:00

Power Intervals

Power intervals are like lifting weights on the bike. To do a power interval, put your bike in a high gear and pedal at maximum intensity (10 RPE) on a flat stretch of road for 20 seconds. In a power intervals workout, a set of power intervals is performed in the middle of an otherwise recovery- to moderate aerobic-intensity ride (4–7 RPE). As the name suggests, power intervals develop pedaling power.

The numbers in the Format column provide guidelines for the intervals portion of the power intervals workout. Warm up thoroughly before doing a set of power intervals and cool down thoroughly afterward, so that the total ride time matches what is prescribed in the Total Time column of the table. *Warm-ups and cool-downs in all cycling and running workouts should always be performed at recovery intensity (4–5 RPE).*

LEVEL	CODE	FORMAT	TOTAL TIME
1	CPI1	4 x 0:20 (AR 2:00)	0:45:00
2	CPI2	5 x 0:20 (AR 2:00)	0:50:00
3	CPI3	6 x 0:20 (AR 2:00)	1:00:00
4	CPI4	7 x 0:20 (AR 2:00)	1:10:00
5	CPI5	8 x 0:20 (AR 2:00)	1:20:00
6	CPI6	9 x 0:20 (AR 2:00)	1:25:00
7	CPI7	10 x 0:20 (AR 2:00)	1:30:00
8	CPI8	11 x 0:20 (AR 2:00)	1:35:00
9	CPI9	12 x 0:20 (AR 2:00)	1:40:00
10	CPI10	13 x 0:20 (AR 2:00)	1:45:00
11	CPI11	14 x 0:20 (AR 2:00)	1:50:00
12	CPI12	15 x 0:20 (AR 2:00)	1:55:00
13	CPI13	16 x 0:20 (AR 2:00)	2:00:00

Short Hill Climbs

Hills are a fact of life in cycling. Since you will almost certainly have to race on them, it's a good idea to practice on them. Also, since hills vastly increase the effort required to move at any given speed, they are a great venue for high-intensity intervals. Short hill climbs are short climbing intervals performed at VO_2 max to speed intensity (9–10 RPE). They enhance your ability to climb hills fast and efficiently and to recover quickly afterward.

Choose a hill with a moderate grade (4–6 percent) and select the most efficient gear for climbing the hill quickly. Recover between intervals by coasting back down the hill and pedaling easily for 2 minutes. The numbers in the Format column provide guidelines for the intervals portion of the short hills intervals workout. Warm up thoroughly before doing a set of short hill intervals and cool down thoroughly afterward, so that the total ride time matches what is prescribed in the right column of the table.

LEVEL	CODE	FORMAT	TOTAL TIME
1	CSH1	4 x 1:00 (AR 2:00)	0:45:00
2	CSH2	5 x 1:00 (AR 2:00)	0:50:00
3	CSH3	6 x 1:00 (AR 2:00)	0:55:00
4	CSH4	7 x 1:00 (AR 2:00)	1:00:00
5	CSH5	8 x 1:00 (AR 2:00)	1:05:00
6	CSH6	9 x 1:00 (AR 2:00)	1:10:00
7	CSH7	10 x 1:00 (AR 2:00)	1:15:00
8	CSH8	11 x 1:00 (AR 2:00)	1:20:00
9	CSH9	12 x 1:00 (AR 2:00)	1:25:00
10	CSH10	4 x 1:30 (AR 3:00)	1:30:00
11	CSH11	5 x 1:30 (AR 3:00)	1:35:00
12	CSH12	6 x 1:30 (AR 3:00)	1:40:00
13	CSH13	7 x 1:30 (AR 3:00)	1:45:00
14	CSH14	8 x 1:30 (AR 3:00)	1:50:00
15	CSH15	9 x 1:30 (AR 3:00)	1:55:00
16	CSH16	10 x 1:30 (AR 3:00)	2:00:00
17	CSH17	11 x 1:30 (AR 3:00)	2:05:00
18	CSH18	12 x 1:30 (AR 3:00)	2:10:00

Long Hill Climbs

These workouts are performed like short hill climbs except that the climbs are of a longer duration and a slightly lower intensity—specifically, threshold to VO$_2$ max (8–9 RPE). Long hill climbs improve your ability to sustain a high effort level on any terrain, but on climbs especially. The numbers in the Format column provide guidelines for the intervals portion of the long hill intervals workout. Warm up thoroughly before doing a set of long hill intervals and cool down thoroughly afterward, so that the total ride time matches what is prescribed in the right column of the table.

LEVEL	CODE	FORMAT	TOTAL TIME
1	CLH1	2 x 5:00 (AR 3:00)	1:00:00
2	CLH2	3 x 5:00 (AR 3:00)	1:05:00
3	CLH3	4 x 5:00 (AR 3:00)	1:10:00
4	CLH4	5 x 5:00 (AR 3:00)	1:15:00

cont.

Level	Code	Format	Total Time
5	CLH5	6 x 5:00 (AR 3:00)	1:20:00
6	CLH6	7 x 5:00 (AR 3:00)	1:30:00
7	CLH7	8 x 5:00 (AR 3:00)	1:35:00
8	CLH8	2 x 8:00 (AR 3:00)	1:40:00
9	CLH9	3 x 8:00 (AR 3:00)	1:45:00
10	CLH10	4 x 8:00 (AR 3:00)	1:50:00
11	CLH11	5 x 8:00 (AR 3:00)	2:00:00

Threshold Ride

Threshold rides serve to increase the duration you can sustain a relatively high speed on the bike. They also increase the speed you can sustain for a relatively long duration. These workouts consist of one or two blocks of threshold-intensity riding (8–8.5 RPE) within a ride that is otherwise performed at moderate aerobic intensity (6–7 RPE). The numbers in the Format column provide guidelines for the threshold portion of the threshold ride workout. In threshold rides containing two blocks of threshold-intensity effort, ride for 10 minutes at moderate aerobic intensity between the blocks. Ride long enough before and after the threshold block(s) to reach the total prescribed time for the workout.

LEVEL	CODE	FORMAT	TOTAL TIME
1	CTR1	2 x 10:00 (AR 10:00)	0:45:00
2	CTR2	20:00	0:50:00
3	CTR3	22:00	0:55:00
4	CTR4	2 x 12:00 (AR 10:00)	1:00:00
5	CTR5	24:00	1:05:00
6	CTR6	26:00	1:10:00
7	CTR7	2 x 14:00 (AR 10:00)	1:15:00
8	CTR8	28:00	1:20:00
9	CTR9	30:00	1:25:00
10	CTR10	2 x 16:00 (AR 10:00)	1:30:00
11	CTR11	32:00	1:35:00
12	CTR12	34:00	1:40:00
13	CTR13	2 x 18:00 (AR 10:00)	1:45:00
14	CTR14	36:00	1:50:00
15	CTR15	38:00	1:55:00
16	CTR16	2 x 20:00 (AR 10:00)	2:00:00
17	CTR17	40:00	2:05:00

Lactate Intervals

Lactate intervals are 3- to 5-minute intervals performed at VO_2 max intensity (9 RPE) separated by 3-minute active recoveries. They boost aerobic capacity and resistance to neuromuscular fatigue. Do a set of lactate intervals as part of a longer ride in which the rest of the workout is performed at a low to moderate intensity (5–7 RPE). The numbers in the Format column provide guidelines for the intervals portion of the lactate intervals workout. Warm up thoroughly before doing a set of lactate intervals and cool down thoroughly afterward, so that the total ride time matches what is prescribed in the right column of the table.

LEVEL	CODE	FORMAT	TOTAL TIME
1	CLI1	2 x 3:00 (AR 3:00)	1:00:00
2	CLI2	3 x 3:00 (AR 3:00)	1:10:00
3	CLI3	4 x 3:00 (AR 3:00)	1:15:00
4	CLI4	5 x 3:00 (AR 3:00)	1:20:00
5	CLI5	6 x 3:00 (AR 3:00)	1:25:00
6	CLI6	7 x 3:00 (AR 3:00)	1:30:00
7	CLI7	8 x 3:00 (AR 3:00)	1:35:00
8	CLI8	2 x 5:00 (AR 3:00)	1:40:00
9	CLI9	3 x 5:00 (AR 3:00)	1:45:00
10	CLI10	4 x 5:00 (AR 3:00)	1:50:00
11	CLI11	5 x 5:00 (AR 3:00)	2:00:00

Speed Intervals

Speed intervals are short, fast intervals that develop efficiency at high speeds. Do them at the fastest pace you can sustain through the end of the last prescribed interval without slowing down (10 RPE). Always perform speed intervals on flat terrain or on an indoor trainer. The numbers in the Format column provide guidelines for the intervals portion of the speed intervals workout. The rest of the total workout time outside of the speed intervals themselves should consist of recovery to moderate aerobic-intensity riding (4–7 RPE).

LEVEL	CODE	FORMAT	TOTAL TIME
1	CSI1	4 x 1:00 (AR 2:00)	0:45:00
2	CSI2	5 x 1:00 (AR 2:00)	0:50:00
3	CSI3	6 x 1:00 (AR 2:00)	0:55:00
4	CSI4	7 x 1:00 (AR 2:00)	1:00:00
5	CSI5	8 x 1:00 (AR 2:00)	1:05:00

cont.

Level	Code	Format	Total Time
6	CSI6	9 x 1:00 (AR 2:00)	1:10:00
7	CSI7	10 x 1:00 (AR 2:00)	1:15:00
8	CSI8	11 x 1:00 (AR 2:00)	1:20:00
9	CSI9	12 x 1:00 (AR 2:00)	1:25:00
10	CSI10	4 x 1:30 (AR 3:00)	1:30:00
11	CSI11	5 x 1:30 (AR 3:00)	1:35:00
12	CSI12	6 x 1:30 (AR 3:00)	1:40:00
13	CSI13	7 x 1:30 (AR 3:00)	1:45:00
14	CSI14	8 x 1:30 (AR 3:00)	1:50:00
15	CSI15	9 x 1:30 (AR 3:00)	1:55:00
16	CSI16	10 x 1:30 (AR 3:00)	2:00:00
17	CSI17	11 x 1:30 (AR 3:00)	2:05:00
18	CSI18	12 x 1:30 (AR 3:00)	2:10:00

Steady-State Ride

A steady-state ride is a ride of moderately long duration performed at high aerobic intensity (7–8 RPE). There are two good uses for steady-state rides. When performed in the latter portion of the base phase, they build on the gains in aerobic capacity and endurance resulting from recent foundation rides and long rides. Steady-state rides are also useful in the latter part of the peak phase in half-Ironman and Ironman training plans, because steady-state intensity is close to race intensity at these longer distances.

LEVEL	CODE	FORMAT
1	CSS1	1:10:00
2	CSS2	1:15:00
3	CSS3	1:30:00
4	CSS4	1:45:00
5	CSS5	2:00:00
6	CSS6	2:15:00
7	CSS7	2:30:00
8	CSS8	2:45:00
9	CSS9	3:00:00

cont.

Level	Code	Format
10	CSS10	3:15:00
11	CSS11	3:30:00
12	CSS12	3:45:00
13	CSS13	4:00:00

Running Workouts

There are eight types of running workout that should be in your training repertoire:

1) recovery runs

2) foundation runs

3) long runs

4) fartlek runs

5) hill repeats

6) tempo runs

7) lactate intervals

8) speed intervals

In addition, drills called running strides are sometimes tacked onto the end of a recovery or foundation run.

Recovery Run

Recovery runs are short runs at recovery intensity (4–5 RPE). They provide a modest training stimulus without interrupting recovery from your most recent hard run or sabotaging your performance in the next hard run. By doing recovery runs, you can complete more total running than you could if you tried to go hard in every run, and perform at a higher level when you do mean to run hard.

LEVEL	CODE	FORMAT
1	RRR1	20:00
2	RRR2	25:00
3	RRR3	30:00
4	RRR4	35:00
5	RRR5	40:00
6	RRR6	45:00
7	RRR7	50:00
8	RRR8	55:00
9	RRR9	1:00:00

Foundation Run

Foundation runs are steady runs of short to moderate duration performed at moderate aerobic intensity (6–7 RPE). They serve to increase your aerobic capacity, endurance, and efficiency.

LEVEL	CODE	FORMAT
1	RFR1	20:00
2	RFR2	25:00
3	RFR3	30:00
4	RFR4	35:00
5	RFR5	40:00
6	RFR6	45:00
7	RFR7	50:00
8	RFR8	55:00
9	RFR9	1:00:00

Long Run

Like foundation runs, long runs are performed at moderate aerobic intensity (6–7 RPE). The only difference is that they last longer in order to challenge and increase your running endurance.

LEVEL	CODE	FORMAT
1	RLR1	1:05:00
2	RLR2	1:10:00
3	RLR3	1:20:00
4	RLR4	1:30:00
5	RLR5	1:40:00
6	RLR6	1:50:00
7	RLR7	2:00:00
8	RLR8	2:10:00
9	RLR9	2:20:00
10	RLR10	2:30:00
11	RLR11	2:40:00
12	RLR12	2:50:00
13	RLR13	3:00:00

Fartlek Run

A fartlek run is a foundation run with several high-intensity bursts at VO$_2$ max to speed intensity (9–10 RPE) scattered within it. Fartlek runs provide a good transition from the aerobic development of the base phase and the high-intensity work of the build phase. A fartlek run is less structured than other workout formats. Feel free to do the high-intensity bursts whenever you please, but give yourself at least a minute between them for adequate recovery. In the Format column, the numbers preceding the parentheses indicates the total run time; the numbers within parentheses provide guidelines for the fartlek intervals.

LEVEL	CODE	FORMAT
1	RFL1	30:00 (6 x 0:30)
2	RFL2	30:00 (8 x 0:30)
3	RFL3	35:00 (6 x 0:30)
4	RFL4	35:00 (8 x 0:30)
5	RFL5	40:00 (6 x 0:30)
6	RFL6	40:00 (8 x 0:30)
7	RFL7	45:00 (6 x 0:30)
8	RFL8	45:00 (8 x 0:30)
9	RFL9	50:00 (6 x 0:30)
10	RFL10	50:00 (8 x 0:30)

Hill Repeats

Hill repeats (a repeat is another name for an interval) are another workout that provides a useful bridge between base training and build training. The short, hard uphill intervals (10 RPE) in these workouts provide some of the same fitness benefits as speed intervals but are not as hard on the musculoskeletal system because there's less impact. Specifically, hill repeats increase stride power and efficiency and resistance to neuromuscular fatigue. Do them on a moderate gradient (4–6 percent) and recover after each repeat by jogging back down the hill at recovery intensity (4–5 RPE) for 1 minute.

The numbers in the Format column provide guidelines for the hill repeats portion of the hill repeats workout. Warm up thoroughly before doing a set of hill repeats and cool down thoroughly afterward, so that the total run time matches what is prescribed in the right column of the table.

LEVEL	CODE	FORMAT	TOTAL TIME
1	RHR1	4 x 0:30 (AR 1:00)	26:00
2	RHR2	6 x 0:30 (AR 1:00)	29:00
3	RHR3	8 x 0:30 (AR 1:00)	32:00
4	RHR4	10 x 0:30 (AR 1:00)	35:00
5	RHR5	12 x 0:30 (AR 1:00)	38:00
6	RHR6	4 x 1:00 (AR 2:00)	34:00
7	RHR7	6 x 1:00 (AR 2:00)	38:00
8	RHR8	8 x 1:00 (AR 2:00)	44:00
9	RHR9	10 x 1:00 (AR 2:00)	50:00
10	RHR10	12 x 1:00 (AR 2:00)	56:00

Tempo Run

A tempo run is a block of threshold-intensity running (8–8.5 RPE) sandwiched between a thorough warm-up and cool-down at recovery intensity (4–5 RPE). Tempo runs dramatically increase the duration you're able to sustain a relatively high running pace and increase the speed you're able to maintain for a relatively long duration.

LEVEL	CODE	FORMAT	TOTAL TIME
1	RTR1	10:00	30:00
2	RTR2	12:00	32:00
3	RTR3	14:00	34:00
4	RTR4	16:00	36:00
5	RTR5	18:00	38:00
6	RTR6	20:00	40:00
7	RTR7	22:00	42:00
8	RTR8	24:00	44:00
9	RTR9	26:00	46:00
10	RTR10	28:00	48:00
11	RTR11	30:00	50:00
12	RTR12	32:00	52:00
13	RTR13	34:00	54:00
14	RTR14	36:00	56:00
15	RTR15	38:00	58:00
16	RTR16	40:00	1:00:00

The numbers in the Format column represent the prescribed duration of threshold-intensity running. Warm up and cool down long enough that the total workout time matches what is prescribed in the right column of the table.

Lactate Intervals

Lactate intervals are 30-second to 4-minute segments of VO_2 max-intensity running (9 RPE) performed in a 1:1 ratio with active recoveries at a low intensity (5–6 RPE). Lactate intervals maximize aerobic capacity and increase resistance to neuromuscular fatigue while enhancing your ability to recover quickly from hard running. The numbers in the Format column provide guidelines for the intervals portion of the lactate intervals workout. Warm up thoroughly before doing a set of lactate intervals and cool down thoroughly afterward at recovery intensity (4–5 RPE), so that the total run time matches what is prescribed in the right column of the table.

LEVEL	CODE	FORMAT	TOTAL TIME
1	RLI1	12 x 0:30 (AR 0:30)	32:00
2	RLI2	14 x 0:30 (AR 0:30)	34:00
3	RLI3	16 x 0:30 (AR 0:30)	36:00
4	RLI4	18 x 0:30 (AR 0:30)	38:00
5	RLI5	20 x 0:30 (AR 0:30)	40:00
6	RLI6	8 x 1:00 (AR 1:00)	36:00
7	RLI7	10 x 1:00 (AR 1:00)	40:00
8	RLI8	12 x 1:00 (AR 1:00)	44:00
9	RLI9	3 x 3:00 (AR 3:00)	38:00
10	RLI10	4 x 3:00 (AR 3:00)	44:00
11	RLI11	5 x 3:00 (AR 3:00)	50:00
12	RLI12	6 x 3:00 (AR 3:00)	56:00
13	RLI13	5 x 4:00 (AR 4:00)	1:00:00

Speed Intervals

Speed intervals are short (30-second to 1-minute) bursts of speed-intensity running (10 RPE) separated by long active recoveries (4–5 RPE). They increase stride power and efficiency. Speed intervals are not full sprints; rather, they should be performed at the fastest pace you can maintain through the end of the last prescribed interval without slowing down. The numbers in the Format column provide guidelines for the intervals portion of the lactate intervals workout. Warm up thoroughly before doing a set of speed intervals and cool down thoroughly afterward at recovery intensity (4–5 RPE), so that the total run time matches what is prescribed in the right column of the table.

LEVEL	CODE	FORMAT	TOTAL TIME
1	RSI1	6 x 0:30 (AR 2:00)	34:00
2	RSI2	7 x 0:30 (AR 2:00)	37:00
3	RSI3	8 x 0:30 (AR 2:00)	39:00
4	RSI4	9 x 0:30 (AR 2:00)	42:00
5	RSI5	10 x 0:30 (AR 2:00)	45:00
6	RSI6	11 x 0:30 (AR 2:00)	47:00
7	RSI7	12 x 0:30 (AR 2:00)	50:00
8	RSI8	13 x 0:30 (AR 2:00)	52:00
9	RSI9	14 x 0:30 (AR 2:00)	55:00
10	RSI10	15 x 0:30 (AR 2:00)	57:00
11	RSI11	16 x 0:30 (AR 2:00)	1:00:00
12	RSI12	6 x 1:00 (AR 3:00)	47:00
13	RSI13	7 x 1:00 (AR 3:00)	54:00
14	RSI14	8 x 1:00 (AR 3:00)	57:00
15	RSI15	9 x 1:00 (AR 3:00)	1:01:00
16	RSI16	10 x 1:00 (AR 3:00)	1:05:00
17	RSI17	11 x 1:00 (AR 3:00)	1:09:00
18	RSI18	12 x 1:00 (AR 3:00)	1:12:00

Strides

Strides are 20-second relaxed sprints, usually performed after a recovery or foundation run to provide a small stride power-building stimulus. You can do strides on level ground, an uphill, or a downhill, and I recommend you do all three types. Uphill strides are better strength builders, while downhill strides do a better job of enhancing your body's ability to absorb impact forces.

LEVEL	CODE	FORMAT
1	RSS1	2 x 0:20 (AR 0:40)
2	RSS2	4 x 0:20 (AR 0:40)
3	RSS3	6 x 0:20 (AR 0:40)
4	RSS4	8 x 0:20 (AR 0:40)

Transition Runs

A transition run is a short, 10-minute run tacked onto the end of a bike ride. Its purpose is to train your body to make a smooth, efficient adjustment from cycling to running. The difference between transition workouts and brick workouts (described next) is that, in the latter, the run is longer—at least in proportion to the preceding ride. Whereas transition runs are really about the transition between cycling and running, brick workouts are intended to provide a proper run workout in addition to a cycling workout. Put another way, brick workouts teach your body to sustain a running effort in a "pre-fatigued" state.

There is only one level of transition run, because they're always 10 minutes. The code is "TR." If you see "+TR" following the code for a cycling workout, you know you are to do a 10-minute transition run after completing the ride.

Brick Workouts

A brick workout is a bike ride followed immediately by a run (with just enough time to change clothes, if you so choose). Running after a hard bike ride is one of the unique challenges of triathlon racing, and one you need to prepare for in training.

There are three types of brick workout. The basic type is a foundation/endurance type in which both the ride and run are performed at a moderate aerobic intensity (6–7 RPE). A second type calls for the bike and run to be done at a slightly more intense, high aerobic pace

LEVEL	CODE	FORMAT	VARIATIONS
1	BRW1	30:00/10:00	BRW1A (Run Tempo)
2	BRW2	30:00/15:00	BRW2A (Run Tempo)
3	BRW3	45:00/10:00	BRW3A (Run Tempo)
4	BRW4	45:00/15:00	BRW4A (Run Tempo)
5	BRW5	1:00:00/20:00	BRW5A (Run Tempo)
6	BRW6	1:00:00/30:00	BRW6A (Run Tempo)
7	BRW7	1:15:00/20:00	BRW7A (High Aerobic)
			BRW7B (Run Tempo)
8	BRW8	1:15:00/30:00	BRW8A (High Aerobic)
			BRW8B (Run Tempo)
9	BRW9	1:30:00/30:00	BRW9A (High Aerobic)
			BRW9B (Run Tempo)

	Level	Code	Format	Variations
cont.				
	10	BRW10	1:30:00/45:00	BRW10A (High Aerobic)
	11	BRW11	1:45:00/45:00	BRW11A (High Aerobic)
	12	BRW12	1:45:00/50:00	BRW12A (High Aerobic)
	13	BRW13	2:00:00/50:00	BRW13A (High Aerobic)
	14	BRW14	2:15:00/55:00	BRW14A (High Aerobic)
	15	BRW15	2:30:00/55:00	
	16	BRW16	3:00:00/1:00:00	
	17	BRW17	3:30:00/1:00:00	
	18	BRW18	4:00:00/1:00:00	

(7–8 RPE). A third type of brick workout entails a moderate aerobic-intensity ride followed by a tempo run (8–8.5 RPE).

The number preceding the slash in the Format column indicates the prescribed ride duration; the number following the slash indicates the run duration.

Chapter 3

SPRINT TRIATHLON TRAINING PLANS
Levels 1–4

*I*f you are new to the sport of triathlon, it makes sense to start with a sprint race—that is, a short one. The average beginner can complete a typical sprint race in 90 minutes or so. It doesn't take a long time to prepare for a sprint race, nor do you need to spend an inordinate amount of time working out each day.

The four training plans in this chapter are designed to prepare inexperienced triathletes to successfully complete a sprint triathlon in 12 weeks. All four plans in this chapter entail just one workout per day, six days per week: two swims, two rides, and two runs. (There's a third weekly run in Weeks 8 and 10, where Saturday's ride is replaced with a bike-run brick workout.) Monday is *always* an off (rest) day.

Like all of the training plans in this book, these are divided into three phases. Weeks 1–3 constitute the base phase; the next four weeks make up the build phase; and the last five are the peak phase. Weeks 4 and 8 are recovery weeks, with slightly reduced training to give your body a chance to absorb recent training and prepare for the harder workouts to come. Week 12—race week—is a taper week, meaning your training tapers off during the week to ensure you're rested and ready to perform on race day.

Level 1

Choose this plan if you are fit and healthy enough to train for a triathlon, but you have done little or no recent swimming, cycling, or running. The plan begins with a total of 1,000 yards of swimming, 40 minutes of cycling, and 40 minutes of running in Week 1. It peaks with 2,275 yards of swimming, 2 hours of cycling, and 1 hour and 14 minutes of running in Week 11.

Level 2

This is also a very low-volume plan for those beginning at square one, but the workouts are a little longer than those in Level 1. It begins with a total of 1,400 yards of swimming, 1 hour of cycling, and 45 minutes of running in Week 1. It peaks with 2,650 yards of swimming, 2 hours and 15 minutes of cycling, and 1 hour and 21 minutes of running in Week 11.

Level 3

Choose this plan if you have already started swimming and running, at least, but you still wish to train conservatively for your first sprint triathlon. This plan begins with a total of 1,700 yards of swimming, 1 hour of cycling, and 50 minutes of running in Week 1. It peaks with 3,125 yards of swimming, 2 hours and 45 minutes of cycling, and 1 hour and 28 minutes of running in Week 11.

Level 4

This plan takes a more aggressive approach to developing your fitness within the parameters of 12 weeks of training, 6 workouts per week, and a modest initial fitness level. It begins with a total of 2,100 yards of swimming, 1 hour and 30 minutes of cycling, and 50 minutes of running in Week 1. It peaks with 3,450 yards of swimming, 3 hours of cycling, and 1 hour and 37 minutes of running in Week 11.

Quick Reference Guide to Workout Codes for Sprint Triathlon Training Plans Levels 1–4

Code Prefix	Workout Type	Brief Description	Levels
BRW	Brick Workout	Bike ride followed by immediate run	BRW1: 30 min/10 min BRW2: 30 min/10 min BRW3: 45 min/10 min BRW4: 45 min/15 min
CFR	Foundation Bike	Steady ride @ moderate aerobic intensity	CFR1: 30 min CFR2: 45 min CFR3: 1 hr CFR4: 1 hr 15 min CFR5: 1 hr 30 min CFR6: 1 hr 45 min
CRR	Recovery Bike	Steady ride @ recovery intensity	CRR1: 20 min CRR2: 30 min
CSH	Bike Short Hills	1-minute hill climbs @ VO_2 max/speed intensity w/ 2-minute active recoveries; warm up and cool down long enough to reach total time	CSH1: 4 x 1 min (45 min total) CSH2: 5 x 1 min (50 min) CSH3: 6 x 1 min (55 min) CSH4: 7 x 1 min (1 hr) CSH5: 8 x 1 min (1 hr 5 min) CSH6: 9 x 1 min (1 hr 10 min)
CTR	Tempo Bike Ride	One or two blocks of riding @ threshold intensity (10-minute active recovery when threshold-intensity riding is divided into two blocks); warm up and cool down long enough to reach total time	CTR1: 2 x 10 min (45 min total) CTR2: 20 min (50 min) CTR3: 22 min (55 min) CTR4: 2 x 12 min (1 hr) CTR5: 24 min (1 hr 5 min) CTR6: 26 min (1 hr 10 min) CTR7: 2 x 14 min (1 hr 15 min)
RFL	Fartlek Run	Foundation run with 30-second bursts @ VO_2 max/speed intensity	RFL1: 6 x 30 sec (30 min total) RFL3: 6 x 30 sec (35 min) RFL4: 8 x 30 sec (35 min)
RFR	Foundation Run	Steady run @ moderate aerobic intensity	RFR1: 20 min RFR2: 25 min RFR3: 30 min

Code Prefix	Workout Type	Brief Description	Levels
RFR *(cont.)*			RFR4: 35 min RFR5: 40 min RFR6: 45 min RFR7: 50 min
RRR	Recovery Run	Short run @ recovery intensity	RRR1: 20 min
RTR	Tempo Run	Steady run @ threshold intensity; warm up and cool down long enough to reach total time	RTR1: 10 min (30 min total) RTR2: 12 min (32 min) RTR3: 14 min (34 min) RTR4: 16 min (36 min) RTR5: 18 min (38 min) RTR6: 20 min (40 min) RTR7: 22 min (42 min)
SBI	Swim Base Intervals	100-yard/meter intervals swum @ moderate aerobic intensity w/ 5-second rest periods	SBI1: 2 x 100 SBI2: 3 x 100 SBI3: 4 x 100 SBI4: 5 x 100 SBI5: 6 x 100 SBI6: 7 x 100 SBI7: 8 x 100 SBI8: 9 x 100 SBI9: 10 x 100 SBI10: 11 x 100
SCD	Swim Cool-Down	Easy swim @ recovery intensity	SCD1: 200 SCD2: 250
SDS	Swim Drill Set	25-yard intervals of mixed form drills w/ 10-second rest periods	SDS1: 4 x 25 SDS2: 6 x 25
SFI	Swim Fartlek Intervals	100–150-yard intervals with easy/hard or build/descend format (hard = threshold intensity, easy = moderate aerobic intensity) w/ 10-second rest periods	SFI1: 4 x 100 (25 easy/25 hard…) SFI1A: 4 x 100 (25 build/25 descend…) SFI2: 6 x 100 (25 easy/25 hard…)

Code Prefix	Workout Type	Brief Description	Levels
SKS	Swim Kick Set	25-yard intervals kicking only w/ 15-second rest periods	SKS1: 4 x 25 SKS2: 6 x 25
SLI	Swim Lactate Intervals	75-yard intervals swum @ VO_2 max intensity w/ rest periods of 20–45 seconds	SLI1: 4 x 75, 45-sec rest SLI2: 5 x 75, 45-sec rest SLI2A: 5 x 75, 30-sec rest SLI2B: 5 x 75, 20-sec rest SLI3: 6 x 75, 45-sec rest SLI3A: 6 x 75, 30-sec rest SLI3B: 6 x 75, 20-sec rest SLI4: 7 x 75, 45-sec rest SLI4A: 7 x 75, 30-sec rest SLI4B: 7 x 75, 20-sec rest SLI5: 8 x 75, 45-sec rest
SSI	Swim Sprint Intervals	25-yard intervals swim @ speed intensity w/ 30-second rest periods	SSI1: 4 x 25 SSI2: 5 x 25 SSI3: 6 x 25
STI	Swim Threshold Intervals	200-yard intervals swum @ threshold intensity w/ rest periods of 20–45 seconds	STI1: 2 x 200, 45-sec rest STI1A: 2 x 200, 30-sec rest STI1B: 2 x 200, 20-sec rest STI2: 3 x 200, 45-sec rest STI2A: 3 x 200, 30-sec rest STI2B: 3 x 200, 20-sec rest STI3: 4 x 200, 45-sec rest STI3A: 4 x 200, 30-sec rest STI3B: 4 x 200, 20-sec rest STI4: 5 x 200, 45-sec rest STI4A: 5 x 200, 30-sec rest STI4B: 5 x 200, 20-sec rest
SWU	Swim Warm-Up	Easy swim @ recovery intensity	SWU1: 200 SWU2: 250
TRR	Transition Run	10-minute run immediately following bike ride	TRR: 10 min

General Schedule

	Tuesday	Wednesday	Thursday	Friday	Saturday	Sunday
BASE PHASE						
Week 1	L1: Swim Drills L2–4: Swim Base Intervals	L1: Recovery Bike L2–4: Foundation Bike	Foundation Run	L1: Swim Drills L2–3: Swim Base Intervals L4: Swim Fartlek Intervals	L1: Recovery Bike L2–4: Foundation Bike	Foundation Run
Week 2	Swim Base Intervals	L1: Recovery Bike L2–4: Foundation Bike	Foundation Run	L1–2: Swim Base Intervals L3–4: Swim Fartlek Intervals	L1: Recovery Bike + Trans. Run L2–4: Foundation Bike + Trans. Run	Foundation Run
Week 3	Swim Base Intervals	Foundation Bike	Foundation Run	L1: Swim Base Intervals L2–4: Swim Fartlek Intervals	Foundation Bike	Foundation Run
BUILD PHASE						
Week 4 (Recovery)	Swim Base Intervals	L1: Foundation Bike L2–4: Bike Short Hills	L1: Recovery Run L2–4: Foundation Run	Swim Tempo Intervals	L1: Recovery Bike + Trans. Run L2–4: Foundation Bike + Trans. Run	L1: Recovery Run L2–4: Foundation Run
Week 5	Swim Base Intervals	Bike Short Hills	L1–3: Foundation Run L4: Fartlek Run	Swim Tempo Intervals	Foundation Bike	Foundation Run
Week 6	Swim Base Intervals	Bike Short Hills	L1–3: Foundation Run L4: Fartlek Run	Swim Tempo Intervals	Foundation Bike + Trans. Run	Foundation Run

	Tuesday	Wednesday	Thursday	Friday	Saturday	Sunday
Week 7	Swim Base Intervals	Bike Short Hills	L1–3: Foundation Run L4: Fartlek Run	Swim Tempo Intervals	Foundation Bike	Foundation Run
PEAK PHASE Week 8 (Recovery)	Swim Base Intervals	Tempo Bike	L1–3: Foundation Run L4: Tempo Run	Swim Lactate Intervals	Transition Workout	Foundation Run
Week 9	L1–3: Swim Base Intervals L4: Base + Sprint Intervals	Tempo Bike	Tempo Run	Swim Lactate Intervals	Foundation Bike	Foundation Run
Week 10	L1–3: Swim Base Intervals L4: Base + Sprint Intervals	Tempo Bike	Tempo Run	Swim Lactate Intervals	Transition Workout	Foundation Run
Week 11	L1–3: Swim Base Intervals L4: Base + Sprint Intervals	Tempo Bike	Tempo Run	Swim Lactate Intervals	Foundation Bike	Foundation Run
Week 12 (Taper)	L1–3: Swim Base Intervals L4: Base + Sprint Intervals	Tempo Bike	Tempo Run	Swim Lactate Intervals	Recovery Bike	Sprint Triathlon

Week-by-Week Schedule

Base Phase

Your goals in this three-week phase are to ease into a regular schedule of training, avoid injuries, and gradually build aerobic fitness and endurance.

WEEK 1

This week's goal: Get accustomed to your new workout schedule.

	Tuesday	Wednesday	Thursday	Friday	Saturday	Sunday
Level 1	SWU1 SDS1 SCD1 (500)	CRR1	RFR1	SWU1 SDS1 SCD1 (500)	CRR1	RFR1
Level 2	SWU1 SDS1 SBI1 SCD1 (700)	CFR1	RFR2	SWU1 SDS1 SBI1 SCD1 (700)	CFR1	RRR1
Level 3	SWU1 SDS2 SBI2 SCD1 (850)	CFR1	RFR2	SWU1 SDS2 SBI2 SCD1 (850)	CFR1	RFR2
Level 4	SWU1 SDS2 SBI3 SKS1 SCD1 (1,050)	CFR2	RFR2	SWU1 SDS2 SFI1 SKS1 SCD1 (1,050)	CFR2	RFR2

QUICK TIP:

Never train in pain. If you feel anything worse than normal workout soreness while swimming, cycling, or running, abandon the session and begin trying to figure out what caused the pain and how to keep it from coming back.

WEEK 2

This week's goal: Build momentum by completing all scheduled workouts.

	Tuesday	Wednesday	Thursday	Friday	Saturday	Sunday
Level 1	SWU1 SDS1 SBI1 SCD1 (700)	CRR2	RFR1	SWU1 SDS1 SBI1 SCD1 (700)	CFR1 + TRR	RFR1
Level 2	SWU1 SDS2 SBI2 SCD1 (850)	CFR1	RFR2	SWU1 SDS2 SBI2 SCD1 (850)	CFR1 + TRR	RFR2
Level 3	SWU1 SDS2 SBI3 SKS1 SCD1 (1,050)	CFR2	RFR2	SWU1 SDS2 SFI1A SKS1 SCD1 (1,050)	CFR2 + TRR	RFR2
Level 4	SWU2 SDS2 SBI4 SKS1 SCD1 (1,200)	CFR2	RFR3	SWU2 SDS2 SFI1A SKS1 SCD1 (1,100)	CFR3 + TRR	RFR3

WEEK 3

This week's goal: Hang in there—you have a recovery week coming up next week!

	Tuesday	Wednesday	Thursday	Friday	Saturday	Sunday
Level 1	SWU1 SDS2 SBI2 SCD1 (850)	CFR1	RFR2	SWU1 SDS2 SBI2 SCD1 (850)	CFR1	RFR2
Level 2	SWU1 SDS2 SBI3 SKS1 SCD1 (1,050)	CFR2	RFR2	SWU1 SDS2 SFI1 SKS1 SCD1 (1,050)	CFR2	RFR2

	Tuesday	Wednesday	Thursday	Friday	Saturday	Sunday
Level 3	SWU2￼SDS2￼SBI4￼SKS1￼SCD1￼(1,200)	CFR2	RFR3	SWU2￼SDS2￼SFI1￼SKS1￼SCD1￼(1,100)	CFR2	RFR3
Level 4	SWU2￼SDS2￼SBI5￼SKS1￼SCD1￼(1,300)	CFR3	RFR4	SWU2￼SDS2￼SFI2￼SKS1￼SCD1￼(1,300)	CFR4	RFR4

Build Phase

Your goal in this four-week phase is to continue developing your aerobic fitness and endurance while also improving your efficiency and speed with some high-intensity training.

WEEK 4
(Recovery)

This week's goal: Fully absorb your recent training and finish the week feeling rested and ready to return to harder training.

	Tuesday	Wednesday	Thursday	Friday	Saturday	Sunday
Level 1	SWU1￼SDS1￼SBI1￼SCD1￼(700)	CFR2	RRR1	SWU1￼SDS1￼STI1￼SCD1￼(900)	CRR2 + TRR	RRR1
Level 2	SWU1￼SDS2￼SBI2￼SCD1￼(850)	CSH1	RFR1	SWU1￼SDS2￼STI1￼SCD1￼(950)	CFR1 + TRR	RFR1
Level 3	SWU2￼SDS2￼SBI3￼SCD1￼(1,000)	CSH2	RFR2	SWU2￼SDS2￼STI2￼SCD1￼(1,200)	CFR2 + TRR	RFR2

	Tuesday	Wednesday	Thursday	Friday	Saturday	Sunday
Level 4	SWU2 SDS2 SBI4 SCD2 (1,150)	CSH3	RFR3	SWU2 SDS2 STI2 SCD2 (1,250)	CFR3 + TRR	RFR3

WEEK 5

This week's goal: Put in a good, solid effort in Wednesday's short hill climbs ride.

	Tuesday	Wednesday	Thursday	Friday	Saturday	Sunday
Level 1	SWU1 SDS1 SBI4 SCD1 (1,000)	CSH1	RFR2	SWU1 SDS1 STI1A SCD1 (900)	CFR1	RFR2
Level 2	SWU1 SDS2 SBI5 SCD1 (1,150)	CSH2	RFR2	SWU1 SDS2 STI2A SCD1 (1,150)	CFR2	RFR3
Level 3	SWU2 SDS2 SBI6 SKS1 SCD1 (1,400)	CSH3	RFR3	SWU2 SDS2 STI3 SKS1 SCD1 (1,500)	CFR2	RFR3
Level 4	SWU2 SDS2 SBI7 SKS2 SCD2 (1,600)	CSH4	RFL1	SWU2 SDS2 STI4 SKS2 SCD2 (1,800)	CFR4	RFR4

WEEK 6

This week's goal: Find a groove at your threshold swim pace in Friday's threshold swim intervals.

	Tuesday	Wednesday	Thursday	Friday	Saturday	Sunday
Level 1	SWU1 SDS1 SBI5 SCD1 (1,100)	CSH2	RFR2	SWU1 SDS1 STI1B SCD1 (900)	CFR2 + TRR	RFR3
Level 2	SWU1 SDS2 SBI6 SCD1 (1,250)	CSH3	RFR3	SWU1 SDS2 STI2B SCD1 (1,150)	CFR2 + TRR	RFR3
Level 3	SWU2 SDS2 SBI7 SKS1 SCD1 (1,500)	CSH4	RFR4	SWU2 SDS2 STI3A SKS1 SCD1 (1,500)	CFR3 + TRR	RFR4
Level 4	SWU2 SDS2 SBI8 SKS2 SCD2 (1,700)	CSH5	RFL3	SWU2 SDS2 STI4A SKS2 SCD2 (1,800)	CFR5 + TRR	RFR5

QUICK TIP:

Be sure to fuel your workouts properly. Sip regularly from a bottle of sports drink every 10–12 minutes throughout all high-intensity workouts (i.e., all workouts at 8 RPE and above) and all workouts lasting an hour or more. This will keep your heart working efficiently and supply your muscles with extra energy, so you perform better and get a bigger fitness benefit from the workout.

WEEK 7

This week's goal: Finish strong in this weekend's longer ride and run.

	Tuesday	Wednesday	Thursday	Friday	Saturday	Sunday
Level 1	SWU1 SDS1 SBI6 SCD1 (1,200)	CSH2	RFR3	SWU1 SDS1 STI2 SCD1 (1,100)	CFR2	RFR3
Level 2	SWU1 SDS2 SBI7 SCD1 (1,350)	CSH4	RFR4	SWU1 SDS2 STI3 SCD1 (1,350)	CFR3	RFR4
Level 3	SWU2 SDS2 SBI8 SKS1 SCD1 (1,600)	CSH5	RFR5	SWU2 SDS2 STI3B SKS1 SCD1 (1,500)	CFR4	RFR5
Level 4	SWU2 SDS2 SBI9 SKS2 SCD2 (1,800)	CSH6	RFL4	SWU2 SDS2 STI4B SKS2 SCD2 (1,800)	CFR5	RFR6

Peak Phase

In this five-week phase you will transform the general triathlon fitness you have developed into race-specific fitness with workouts including tempo rides, lactate swim intervals, and brick workouts.

WEEK 8
(Recovery)

This week's goal: Fully absorb your recent training and finish the week feeling rested and ready to return to harder training next week.

	Tuesday	Wednesday	Thursday	Friday	Saturday	Sunday
Level 1	SWU1 SDS1 SBI4 SCD1 (1,000)	CTR1	RFR2	SWU1 SDS1 SLI1 SCD1 (800)	BRW1	RFR2

47

	Tuesday	Wednesday	Thursday	Friday	Saturday	Sunday
Level 2	SWU1 SDS2 SBI5 SCD1 (1,150)	CTR1	RFR2	SWU1 SDS2 SLI2 SCD1 (925)	BRW1	RFR3
Level 3	SWU2 SDS2 SBI6 SKS1 SCD1 (1,400)	CTR3	RFR4	SWU2 SDS2 SLI3 SKS1 SCD1 (1,150)	BRW2	RFR4
Level 4	SWU2 SDS2 SBI7 SKS2 SCD2 (1,600)	CTR4	RTR4	SWU2 SDS2 SLI4 SKS2 SCD2 (1,325)	BRW3	RFR5

WEEK 9

This week's goal: Find a groove at threshold pace in Wednesday's tempo ride and in Thursday's tempo run.

	Tuesday	Wednesday	Thursday	Friday	Saturday	Sunday
Level 1	SWU1 SDS1 SBI6 SCD1 (1,200)	CTR2	RTR1	SWU1 SDS1 SLI2 SCD1 (875)	CFR3	RFR3
Level 2	SWU1 SDS2 SBI8 SCD1 (1,450)	CTR3	RTR2	SWU1 SDS2 SLI2A SCD1 (925)	CFR3	RFR4
Level 3	SWU2 SDS2 SBI9 SKS1 SCD1 (1,700)	CTR4	RTR3	SWU2 SDS2 SLI3A SKS1 SCD1 (1,150)	CFR4	RFR5

	Tuesday	Wednesday	Thursday	Friday	Saturday	Sunday
Level 4	SWU2 SDS2 SBI8 SSI1 SKS2 SCD2 (1,800)	CTR5	RTR5	SWU2 SDS2 SLI4A SKS2 SCD2 (1,325)	CFR5	RFR6

WEEK 10

This week's goal: Get accustomed to running off the bike in Saturday's brick workout.

	Tuesday	Wednesday	Thursday	Friday	Saturday	Sunday
Level 1	SWU1 SDS1 SBI7 SCD1 (1,300)	CTR3	RTR2	SWU1 SDS1 SLI2A SCD1 (875)	BRW2	RFR4
Level 2	SWU1 SDS2 SBI9 SCD1 (1,550)	CTR4	RTR3	SWU1 SDS2 SLI2B SCD1 (925)	BRW2	RFR5
Level 3	SWU2 SDS2 SBI10 SKS1 SCD1 (1,800)	CTR5	RTR4	SWU2 SDS2 SLI3B SKS1 SCD1 (1,150)	BRW3	RFR6
Level 4	SWU2 SDS2 SBI9 SSI2 SKS2 SCD2 (1,925)	CTR6	RTR6	SWU2 SDS2 SLI4B SKS2 SCD2 (1,325)	BRW4	RFR7

QUICK TIP:

A proper bike set-up is very important. Having the most expensive racing bike on the market is no better than having the cheapest one if it's not set up properly (correct saddle height, front stem length, and so forth). Poor set-up not only reduces efficiency and is less comfortable, but may also cause knee and low-back injuries. Take your bike to a good local shop for a proper fitting, which will run you $50 or so.

WEEK 11

This week's goal: Build confidence for next week's race as you feel your fitness begin to peak in this week's workouts.

	Tuesday	Wednesday	Thursday	Friday	Saturday	Sunday
Level 1	SWU1 SDS1 SBI8 SCD1 (1,400)	CTR4	RTR3	SWU1 SDS1 SLI2B SCD1 (875)	CFR3	RFR5
Level 2	SWU1 SDS2 SBI10 SCD1 (1,650)	CTR5	RTR4	SWU1 SDS2 SLI3 SCD1 (1,000)	CFR4	RFR6
Level 3	SWU2 SDS2 SBI11 SKS1 SCD1 (1,900)	CTR6	RTR5	SWU2 SDS2 SLI4 SKS1 SCD1 (1,225)	CFR5	RFR7
Level 4	SWU2 SDS2 SBI10 SSI3 SKS2 SCD2 (2,050)	CTR7	RTR7	SWU2 SDS2 SLI5 SKS2 SCD2 (1,400)	CFR6	RFR8

WEEK 12

This week's goal: Have a great race on Sunday!

	Tuesday	Wednesday	Thursday	Friday	Saturday	Sunday
Level 1	SWU1 SDS1 SBI7 SCD1 (1,300)	CTR1	RTR1	SWU1 SDS1 SLI1 SCD1 (800)	CRR1	Sprint Triathlon
Level 2	SWU1 SDS2 SBI9 SCD1 (1,550)	CTR2	RTR2	SWU1 SDS2 SLI1 SCD1 (850)	CRR1	Sprint Triathlon
Level 3	SWU2 SDS2 SBI10 SKS1 SCD1 (1,800)	CTR2	RTR3	SWU2 SDS2 SLI2 SCD1 (975)	CRR1	Sprint Triathlon
Level 4	SWU2 SDS2 SBI8 SSI1 SKS2 SCD2 (1,800)	CTR4	RTR4	SWU2 SDS2 SLI3 SCD2 (1,100)	CRR1	Sprint Triathlon

Chapter 4

SPRINT TRIATHLON TRAINING PLANS
Levels 5–7

Sprint triathlons aren't only for beginners. Some experienced triathletes like to do sprint triathlons because their athletic strengths are better suited to shorter races. Others like them because it's possible to achieve a peak performance in a sprint triathlon with less training than is needed to achieve a peak performance at longer distances.

The three 12-week sprint triathlon training plans in this chapter are appropriate for triathletes who already have a decent base of swim, bike, and run fitness and want not just to finish a sprint triathlon, but to finish well. All three of the plans include three swim workouts, three rides, and three runs in a typical week. There's a fourth run in the even-numbered weeks, which include either a 10-minute transition run following Saturday's foundation ride or a brick workout instead of Saturday's ride (Weeks 8 and 10).

In addition to more workouts per week, the Levels 5–7 sprint plans also feature longer workouts and more high-intensity training than the Levels 1–4 plans in the preceding chapter. Yet the overall training load is still moderate. The watchword for these plans is *efficiency*.

The base phase lasts from Week 1 through Week 4; the build phase from Week 5 through Week 8; and the peak phase from Week 9 through Week 12. Weeks 4 and 8 are recovery weeks. Week 12 is a taper week.

Level 5

Choose this plan if you're up to doing three workouts per week in each discipline, but wish to stay close to the minimum amount of training that such a schedule entails. The plan begins with a total of 4,100 yards of swimming, 2 hours and 30 minutes of cycling, and 1 hour and 43 minutes of running in Week 1. It peaks with a total of

5,500 yards of swimming, 4 hours and 20 minutes of cycling, and 2 hours and 32 minutes of running in Week 11.

Level 6

Most of the workouts in this plan are a notch or two more challenging than those in the Level 5 plan. It begins with a total of 4,650 yards of swimming, 3 hours of cycling, and 1 hour and 53 minutes of running in Week 1. It peaks with a total of 6,300 yards of swimming, 4 hours and 30 minutes of cycling, and 2 hours and 44 minutes of running in Week 11.

Level 7

Choose this plan if you want to achieve the highest fitness level possible within the parameters of a 12-week plan, 9 workouts per week, and a moderate level of initial fitness. The plan begins with a total of 5,000 yards of swimming, 3 hours and 15 minutes of cycling, and 2 hours and 8 minutes of running in Week 1. It peaks with a total of 6,800 yards of swimming, 4 hours and 40 minutes of cycling, and 2 hours and 51 minutes of running in Week 11.

Quick Reference Guide to Workout Codes for Sprint Triathlon Training Plans Levels 5–7

Code Prefix	Workout Type	Brief Description	Levels
BRW	Brick Workout	Bike ride followed by immediate run	BRW3: 45 min/10 min BRW4: 45 min/15 min BRW5: 1 hr/20 min BRW7: 1 hr 15 min/20 min
CFR	Foundation Bike	Steady ride @ moderate aerobic intensity	CFR2: 45 min CFR3: 1 hr CFR4: 1 hr 15 min CFR5: 1 hr 30 min CFR6: 1 hr 45 min CFR7: 2 hrs
CLI	Bike Lactate Intervals	3-minute intervals @ VO_2 max intensity w/ 3-minute active recoveries; warm up and cool down long enough to reach total time	CLI1: 2 x 3 min (1 hr total) CLI2: 3 x 3 min (1 hr 10 min) CLI3: 4 x 3 min (1 hr 15 min) CLI4: 5 x 3 min (1 hr 20 min) CLI5: 6 x 3 min (1 hr 25 min) CLI7: 8 x 3 min (1 hr 35 min)
CPI	Bike Power Intervals	20-second intervals done in a high gear @ speed intensity w/ 2-minute active recoveries; warm up and cool down long enough to reach total time	CPI1: 4 x 20 sec (45 min total) CPI2: 5 x 20 sec (50 min) CPI3: 6 x 20 sec (1 hr) CPI4: 7 x 20 sec (1 hr 10 min) CPI5: 8 x 20 sec (1 hr 20 min) CPI6: 9 x 20 sec (1 hr 25 min) CPI7: 10 x 20 sec (1 hr 30 min)
CRR	Recovery Bike	Steady ride @ recovery intensity	CRR1: 20 min
CSH	Bike Short Hills	1-minute hill climbs @ VO_2 max/speed intensity w/ 2-minute active recoveries; warm up and cool down long enough to reach total time	CSH3: 6 x 1 min (55 min total) CSH4: 7 x 1 min (1 hr) CSH5: 8 x 1 min (1 hr 5 min) CSH7: 10 x 1 min (1 hr 15 min) CSH12: 6 x 1 min 30 sec (1 hr 40 min)
CSI	Bike Speed Intervals	1-minute intervals @ speed intensity w/ 2-minute active recoveries; warm up and cool down long enough to reach total time	CSI1: 4 x 1 min (45 min total) CSI2: 5 x 1 min (50 min) CSI3: 6 x 1 min (55 min) CSI4: 7 x 1 min (1 hr) CSI5: 8 x 1 min (1 hr 5 min)

Code Prefix	Workout Type	Brief Description	Levels
CSI *(cont.)*			CSI6: 9 x 1 min (1 hr 10 min) CSI7: 10 x 1 min (1 hr 15 min)
CTR	Tempo Bike Ride	One or two blocks of riding @ threshold intensity (5-minute active recovery when threshold-intensity riding is divided into two blocks); warm up and cool down long enough to reach total time	CTR3: 22 min (55 min total) CTR4: 2 x 12 min (1 hr) CTR5: 24 min (1 hr 5 min) CTR6: 26 min (1 hr 10 min) CTR7: 2 x 14 min (1 hr 15 min) CTR8: 28 min (1 hr 20 min) CTR9: 30 min (1 hr 25 min)
RFL	Fartlek Run	Foundation run with 30-second bursts @ VO_2 max/speed intensity	RFL1: 6 x 30 sec (30 min total) RFL2: 8 x 30 sec (30 min) RFL3: 6 x 30 sec (35 min) RFL4: 8 x 30 sec (35 min) RFL5: 6 x 30 sec (40 min) RFL6: 8 x 30 sec (40 min) RFL7: 8 x 30 sec (45 min)
RFR	Foundation Run	Steady run @ moderate aerobic intensity	RFR3: 30 min RFR4: 35 min RFR5: 40 min RFR6: 45 min RFR7: 50 min RFR8: 55 min RFR9: 1 hr
RLI	Run Lactate Intervals	30-second to 1-minute intervals run @ VO_2 max intensity w/ active recoveries equal in duration to intervals; warm up and cool down long enough to reach total time	RLI1: 12 x 30 sec (32 min total) RLI2: 14 x 30 sec (34 min) RLI3: 16 x 30 sec (36 min) RLI4: 18 x 30 sec (38 min) RLI6: 8 x 1 min (36 min) RLI7: 10 x 1 min (40 min)
RLR	Long Run	Long, steady-pace run @ moderate aerobic intensity	RLR1: 1 hr 5 min RLR2: 1 hr 10 min
RRR	Recovery Run	Short run @ recovery intensity	RRR1: 20 min RRR2: 25 min RRR3: 30 min
RSS	Running Strides	20-second "relaxed sprints" @ speed intensity w/ 40-second active recoveries	RSS1: 2 x 20 sec RSS2: 4 x 20 sec RSS3: 6 x 20 sec

Code Prefix	Workout Type	Brief Description	Levels
RTR	Tempo Run	Steady run @ threshold intensity; warm up and cool down long enough to reach total time	RTR2: 12 min (32 min total) RTR3: 14 min (34 min) RTR4: 16 min (36 min) RTR5: 18 min (38 min) RTR6: 20 min (40 min) RTR7: 22 min (42 min)
SBI	Swim Base Intervals	100-yard intervals swum @ moderate aerobic intensity w/ 5-second rest periods, or single longer swims performed @ the same intensity	SBI3: 4 x 100 SBI4: 5 x 100 SBI5: 6 x 100 SBI6: 7 x 100 SBI7: 8 x 100 SBI23: 800 SBI24: 1,000 SBI25: 1,200 SBI26: 1,500 SBI27: 1,800
SCD	Swim Cool-Down	Easy swim @ recovery intensity	SCD1: 200 SCD2: 250 SCD3: 300
SDS	Swim Drill Set	25-yard intervals of mixed form drills w/ 10-second rest periods	SDS2: 6 x 25 SDS3: 8 x 25
SFI	Swim Fartlek Intervals	150–200-yard intervals with easy/hard or build/descend format (hard = threshold intensity, easy = moderate aerobic intensity) w/ 15–20-second rest periods	SFI4: 4 x 150 (50 easy/25 hard...), 15-sec rest SFI5: 5 x 150 (50 easy/25 hard...), 15-sec rest SFI5A: 5 x 150 (50 build/25 descend...), 15-sec rest SFI8: 4 x 200 (50 easy/50 hard...), 20-sec rest SFI8A: 4 x 200 (50 build/50 descend...), 20-sec rest SFI9: 5 x 200 (50 easy/50 hard...), 20-sec rest
SKS	Swim Kick Set	25-yard intervals kicking only w/ 15-second rest periods	SKS2: 6 x 25 SKS3: 8 x 25

Code Prefix	Workout Type	Brief Description	Levels
SLI	Swim Lactate Intervals	75–100-yard intervals swum @ VO$_2$ max intensity with rest periods of 20–45 seconds	SLI3: 6 x 75, 45-sec rest SLI4: 7 x 75, 45-sec rest SLI5: 8 x 75, 45-sec rest SLI5A: 8 x 75, 30-sec rest SLI5B: 8 x 75, 20-sec rest SLI6: 9 x 75, 45-sec rest SLI7: 10 x 75, 45-sec rest SLI7A: 10 x 75, 30-sec rest SLI7B: 1 x 75, 20-sec rest SLI11: 6 x 100, 1-min rest SLI12: 7 x 100, 1-min rest SLI12A: 7 x 100, 45-sec rest SLI12B: 7 x 100, 30-sec rest SLI13: 8 x 100, 1-min rest SLI13A: 8 x 100, 45-sec rest SLI13B: 8 x 100, 30-sec rest
SSI	Swim Sprint Intervals	25–50-yard intervals swum @ speed intensity w/ 5–20-second rest periods	SSI1: 4 x 25, 20-sec rest SSI2: 5 x 25, 20-sec rest SSI3: 6 x 25, 20-sec rest SSI3A: 6 x 25, 10-sec rest SSI3B: 6 x 25, 5-sec rest SSI5: 8 x 25, 20-sec rest SSI5A: 8 x 25, 10-sec rest SSI5B: 8 x 25, 5-sec rest SSI7: 10 x 25, 20-sec rest SSI9: 12 x 25, 20-sec rest SSI10: 4 x 50, 20-sec rest SSI11: 5 x 50, 20-sec rest SSI12: 6 x 50, 20-sec rest SSI13: 7 x 50, 20-sec rest SSI14: 8 x 50, 20-sec rest
STI	Swim Threshold Intervals	200-yard intervals swum @ threshold intensity w/ rest periods of 20–45 seconds	STI2: 3 x 200, 45-sec rest STI2A: 3 x 200, 30-sec rest STI2B: 3 x 200, 20-sec rest STI3: 4 x 200, 45-sec rest STI3A: 4 x 200, 30-sec rest STI3B: 4 x 200, 20-sec rest STI4: 5 x 200, 45-sec rest STI4A: 5 x 200, 30-sec rest STI4B: 5 x 200, 20-sec rest

Code Prefix	Workout Type	Brief Description	Levels
STT	Swim Time Trial	Designated distance swum @ maximum effort	STT1: 800 STT2: 1,000
SWU	Swim Warm-Up	Easy swim @ recovery intensity	SWU1: 200 SWU2: 250 SWU3: 300
TRR	Transition Run	10-minute run immediately following bike ride	TRR: 10 min

General Schedule						
	Tuesday	Wednesday	Thursday	Friday	Saturday	Sunday
BASE PHASE						
Week 1	Bike Short Hills	Swim Base Intervals Fartlek Run	Foundation Bike	Swim Fartlek Intervals Foundation Run + Strides	Foundation Bike	Foundation Run Swim Base Intervals
Week 2	Bike Short Hills	Swim Base Intervals Fartlek Run	Foundation Bike	Swim Fartlek Intervals Foundation Run + Strides	Foundation Bike + Trans. Run	Foundation Run Swim Base Intervals
Week 3	Bike Short Hills	Swim Base Intervals Fartlek Run	Foundation Bike	Swim Fartlek Intervals Foundation Run + Strides	Foundation Bike	Foundation Run Swim Base Intervals
BUILD PHASE						
Week 4 (Recovery)	Bike Lactate Intervals	Swim Lactate Intervals Run Lactate Intervals	Bike Power Intervals	Swim Threshold Intervals Foundation Run + Strides	Foundation Bike + Trans. Run	Foundation Run Swim Base Intervals
Week 5	Bike Lactate Intervals	Swim Lactate Intervals Run Lactate Intervals	Bike Power Intervals	Swim Threshold Intervals Foundation Run + Strides	Foundation Bike	Foundation Run Swim Base Intervals

	Tuesday	Wednesday	Thursday	Friday	Saturday	Sunday
Week 6	Bike Lactate Intervals	Swim Lactate Intervals	Bike Power Intervals	Swim Threshold Intervals	Foundation Bike + Trans. Run	Foundation Run
		Run Lactate Intervals		Foundation Run + Strides		Swim Base Intervals
Week 7	Bike Lactate Intervals	Swim Lactate Intervals	Bike Power Intervals	Swim Threshold Intervals	Foundation Bike	Foundation Run
		Run Lactate Intervals		Foundation Run + Strides		Swim Base Intervals
PEAK PHASE						
Week 8 (Recovery)	Tempo Bike	Swim Lactate Intervals	Bike Speed Intervals	Swim Threshold Intervals	Transition Workout	Foundation Run
				Foundation Run + Strides		Swim Base Intervals
Week 9	Tempo Bike	Swim Lactate Intervals	Bike Speed Intervals	Swim Threshold Intervals	Foundation Bike	Foundation Run
		Tempo Run		Foundation Run + Strides		Swim Base Intervals
Week 10	Tempo Bike	Swim Lactate Intervals	Bike Speed Intervals	Swim Threshold Intervals	Transition Workout	Foundation Run
		Run Lactate Intervals		Foundation Run + Strides		Swim Time Trial
Week 11	Tempo Bike	Swim Lactate Intervals	Bike Speed Intervals	Swim Threshold Intervals	Foundation Bike	Foundation Run
		Run Lactate Intervals		Foundation Run + Strides		Swim Base Intervals
Week 12 (Taper)	Tempo Bike	Swim Lactate Intervals	Bike Speed Intervals	Swim Threshold Intervals	Recovery Bike	Sprint Triathlon
		Run Lactate Intervals		Recovery Run + Strides		

Week-by-Week Schedule

Base Phase

Your objective in this four-week phase is to build your aerobic capacity and endurance with plenty of aerobic-intensity work supplemented by small amounts of high-intensity training to boost your power and efficiency.

WEEK 1

This week's goal: Get accustomed to your new workout schedule.

	Tuesday	Wednesday	Thursday	Friday	Saturday	Sunday
Level 5	CSH3	SWU2 SDS3 SBI3 SSI1 SKS2 SCD2 (1,350)	CFR2	SWU2 SDS3 SFI4 SSI1 SKS2 SCD2 (1,550)	CFR2	RFR3
		RFL1		RFR3 + RSS1		SWU1 SBI23 SCD1 (1,200)
Level 6	CSH3	SWU3 SDS3 SBI3 SSI5 SKS2 SCD3 (1,550)	CFR3	SWU3 SDS3 SFI5 SSI1 SKS2 SCD3 (1,800)	CFR3	RFR4
		RFL3		RFR4 + RSS1		SWU2 SBI23 SCD2 (1,300)
Level 7	CSH3	SWU3 SDS3 SBI4 SSI5 SKS3 SCD3 (1,700)	CFR3	SWU3 SDS3 SFI5 SSI3 SKS3 SCD3 (1,900)	CFR4	RFR5

	Tuesday	Wednesday	Thursday	Friday	Saturday	Sunday
Level 7 (cont.)		RFL5		RFR5 + RSS1		SWU3 SBI23 SCD3 (1,400)

WEEK 2

This week's goal: Build consistency and momentum by completing all scheduled workouts as prescribed.

	Tuesday	Wednesday	Thursday	Friday	Saturday	Sunday
Level 5	CSH4	SWU2 SDS3 SBI5 SSI3 SKS2 SCD2 (1,600)	CFR3	SWU2 SDS3 SFI5A SSI2 SKS2 SCD2 (1,725)	CFR3 + TRR	RFR4
		RFL2		RFR4 + RSS2		SWU2 SBI23 SCD2 (1,300)
Level 6	CSH5	SWU3 SDS3 SBI6 SSI7 SKS2 SCD3 (1,900)	CFR3	SWU3 SDS3 SFI8A SSI3 SKS2 SCD3 (1,900)	CFR4 + TRR	RFR5
		RFL4		RFR5 + RSS2		SWU1 SBI24 SCD1 (1,400)
Level 7	CSH7	SWU3 SDS3 SBI7 SSI7 SKS3 SCD3 (2,050)	CFR4	SWU3 SDS3 SFI8A SSI5 SKS3 SCD3 (2,000)	CFR5 + TRR	RFR6
		RFL6		RFR5 + RSS2		SWU3 SBI24 SCD3 (1,600)

QUICK TIP:

Wearing the right running shoes is crucial for avoiding injuries. Research has shown that the best way to choose the right shoes is by comfort. If a running shoe feels great while you test it in the store parking lot, it very likely has the right fit, cushioning, and stability characteristics to minimize the risk of injuries. If it feels less than great, something about the fit, cushioning, and/or stability characteristics is off.

WEEK 3

This week's goal: Hang tough through the cumulative fatigue you can expect to feel this week, as you have a recovery week to look forward to next week!

	Tuesday	Wednesday	Thursday	Friday	Saturday	Sunday
Level 5	CSH5	SWU2 SDS3 SBI5 SSI5 SKS2 SCD2 (1,650)	CFR3	SWU2 SDS3 SFI5 SSI3 SKS2 SCD2 (1,750)	CFR4	RFR5
		RFL4		RFR4 + RSS2		SWU1 SBI24 SCD1 (1,400)
Level 6	CSH7	SWU3 SDS3 SBI6 SSI9 SKS2 SCD3 (1,950)	CFR4	SWU3 SDS3 SFI8 SSI3 SKS2 SCD3 (1,900)	CFR5	RFR6
		RFL6		RFR6 + RSS3		SWU1 SBI25 SCD1 (1,600)
Level 7	CSH12	SWU3 SDS3 SBI7	CFR4	SWU3 SDS3 SFI9	CFR6	RFR7

	Tuesday	Wednesday	Thursday	Friday	Saturday	Sunday
Level 7 (cont.)		SSI9 SKS3 SCD3 (2,100)		SSI3 SKS3 SCD3 (2,150)		
		RFL7		RFR6 + RSS3		SWU3 SBI25 SCD3 (1,800)

WEEK 4
(Recovery)

This week's goal: Fully absorb your recent training and finish the week feeling rested and ready to return to harder training next week.

	Tuesday	Wednesday	Thursday	Friday	Saturday	Sunday
Level 5	CLI1	SWU2 SDS3 SLI3 SSI10 SCD2 (1,350)	CPI1	SWU2 SDS3 STI2 SSI1 SCD2 (1,400)	CFR3 + TRR	RFR4
		RLI1		RFR3 + RSS2		SWU1 SBI23 SCD1 (1,200)
Level 6	CLI2	SWU3 SDS3 SLI4 SSI11 SCD3 (1,575)	CPI2	SWU3 SDS3 STI2 SSI5 SCD3 (1,600)	CFR4 + TRR	RFR5
		RLI1		RFR5 + RSS2		SWU1 SBI24 SCD1 (1,400)
Level 7	CLI3	SWU3 SDS3 SLI11 SSI12 SCD3	CPI3	SWU3 SDS3 STI3 SSI5 SCD3	CFR5 + TRR	RFR6

	Tuesday	Wednesday	Thursday	Friday	Saturday	Sunday
Level 7 (cont.)		(1,700) RLI2		(1,800) RFR5 + RSS2		SWU3 SBI24 SCD3 (1,600)

Build Phase

The key workouts in this phase include lactate intervals in all three disciplines to increase your resistance to neuromuscular fatigue, as well as some maximal intensity work in all three disciplines (cycling power intervals, running strides, and swim sprint sets) to further boost your power, efficiency, and aerobic capacity.

WEEK 5

This week's goal: Dig deep in this week's challenging lactate intervals in swimming, cycling, and running.

	Tuesday	Wednesday	Thursday	Friday	Saturday	Sunday
Level 5	CLI2	SWU2 SDS3 SLI5 SSI10 SKS2 SCD2 (1,650)	CPI2	SWU2 SDS3 STI2 SSI5 SKS2 SCD2 (1,650)	CFR4	RFR5
		RLI2		RFR4 + RSS3		SWU1 SBI24 SCD1 (1,400)
Level 6	CLI3	SWU3 SDS3 SLI5 SSI12 SKS2 SCD3 (1,850)	CPI4	SWU3 SDS3 STI3 SSI1 SKS2 SCD3 (1,850)	CFR5	RFR6
		RLI3		RFR6 + RSS3		SWU1 SBI25 SCD1 (1,600)

	Tuesday	Wednesday	Thursday	Friday	Saturday	Sunday
Level 7	CLI4	SWU3 SDS3 SLI12 SSI12 SKS3 SCD3 (2,000)	CPI5	SWU3 SDS3 STI3 SSI5 SKS3 SCD3 (2,000)	CFR6	RFR7
		RLI4		RFR6 + RSS3		SWU3 SBI25 SCD3 (1,800)

WEEK 6

This week's goal: Finish strong in this weekend's longer ride and run.

	Tuesday	Wednesday	Thursday	Friday	Saturday	Sunday
Level 5	CLI3	SWU2 SDS3 SLI5A SSI10 SKS2 SCD2 (1,650)	CPI3	SWU2 SDS3 STI2A SSI5 SKS2 SCD2 (1,650)	CFR5 + TRR	RFR6
		RLI3		RFR5 + RSS3		SWU1 SBI25 SCD1 (1,600)
Level 6	CLI4	SWU3 SDS3 SLI5A SSI12 SKS2 SCD3 (1,850)	CPI5	SWU3 SDS3 STI3A SSI1 SKS2 SCD3 (1,850)	CFR6 + TRR	RFR7
		RLI6		RFR7 + RSS3		SWU1 SBI26 SCD1 (1,900)
Level 7	CLI5	SWU3 SDS3 SLI12A	CPI6	SWU3 SDS3 STI3A	CFR7 + TRR	RFR8

	Tuesday	Wednesday	Thursday	Friday	Saturday	Sunday
Level 7 (cont.)		SSI12 SKS3 SCD3 (2,000)		SSI5 SKS3 SCD3 (2,000)		
		RLI6		CFR7 + RSS3		SWU3 SBI26 SCD3 (2,100)

QUICK TIP:

When training with others, don't allow yourself to get pulled along at too fast a pace by the speediest person in the group. If you go too hard in workouts that are meant to be easier, you won't be able to perform at as high a level tomorrow, or whenever your next challenging workout is scheduled.

WEEK 7

This week's goal: Run hard but relaxed in Wednesday's tough lactate intervals run.

	Tuesday	Wednesday	Thursday	Friday	Saturday	Sunday
Level 5	CLI4	SWU2 SDS3 SLI5B SSI10 SKS2 SCD2 (1,650)	CPI4	SWU2 SDS3 STI2B SSI5 SKS2 SCD2 (1,650)	CFR6	RFR7
		RLI6		RFR5 + RSS3		SWU3 SBI25 SCD3 (1,800)
Level 6	CLI5	SWU3 SDS3 SLI5B SSI12 SKS2	CPI6	SWU3 SDS3 STI3B SSI1 SKS2	CFR6	RFR8

	Tuesday	Wednesday	Thursday	Friday	Saturday	Sunday
Level 6 (cont.)		SCD3 (1,850)		SCD3 (1,850)		
		RLI7		RFR7 + RSS3		SWU3 SBI26 SCD3 (2,100)
Level 7	CLI7	SWU3 SDS3 SLI12B SSI12 SKS3 SCD3 (2,000)	CPI7	SWU3 SDS3 STI3B SSI5 SKS3 SCD3 (2,000)	CFR7	RFR9
		RLI7		RFR8 + RSS3		SWU3 SBI27 SCD3 (2,400)

WEEK 8
(Recovery)

This week's goal: Fully absorb your recent training and finish the week feeling rested and ready to return to harder training next week.

	Tuesday	Wednesday	Thursday	Friday	Saturday	Sunday
Level 5	CTR3	SWU2 SDS3 SLI5 SSI10 SCD2 (1,500)	CSI1	SWU2 SDS3 STI2 SSI5 SCD2 (1,500)	BRW3	RFR4
		RTR2		RFR4 + RSS3		SWU1 SBI24 SCD1 (1,400)
Level 6	CTR4	SWU3 SDS3 SLI5 SSI11 SCD3 (1,650)	CSI2	SWU3 SDS3 STI3 SSI1 SCD3 (1,700)	BRW4	RFR5

	Tuesday	Wednesday	Thursday	Friday	Saturday	Sunday
Level 6 (cont.)		RTR3		RFR6 + RSS2		SWU1 SBI25 SCD1 (1,600)
Level 7	CTR5	SWU3 SDS3 SLI12 SSI12 SCD3 (1,800)	CSI3	SWU3 SDS3 STI3 SSI5 SCD3 (1,800)	BRW5	RFR6
		RTR4		RFR6 + RSS2		SWU3 SBI25 SCD3 (1,800)

Peak Phase

Your objective in this four-week phase is to hone your race-specific fitness with workouts including tempo rides and runs, a brick workout, and a swim time trial.

WEEK 9

This week's goal: Find a good groove at threshold pace (8–8.5 RPE) in Tuesday's tempo ride and in Wednesday's tempo run.

	Tuesday	Wednesday	Thursday	Friday	Saturday	Sunday
Level 5	CTR5	SWU2 SDS3 SLI12 SSI11 SKS2 SCD2 (1,800)	CSI3	SWU2 SDS3 STI3 SSI3 SKS2 SCD2 (1,800)	CFR6	RFR8
		RTR3		RFR5 + RSS3		SWU3 SBI25 SCD3 (1,800)
Level 6	CTR6	SWU3 SDS3 SLI12 SSI13 SKS2	CSI3	SWU3 SDS3 STI4 SSI3 SKS2	CFR7	RFR9

	Tuesday	Wednesday	Thursday	Friday	Saturday	Sunday
Level 6 (cont.)		SCD3 (2,000)		SCD3 (2,100)		
		RTR4		RFR7 + RSS3		SWU2 SBI26 SCD2 (2,000)
Level 7	CTR6	SWU3 SDS3 SLI13 SSI14 SKS3 SCD3 (2,200)	CSI4	SWU3 SDS3 STI4 SSI5 SKS3 SCD3 (2,200)	CFR7	RLR1
		RTR5		RFR8 + RSS3		SWU2 SBI27 SCD2 (2,300)

WEEK 10

This week's goal: Get accustomed to running off the bike in Saturday's brick workout, and then let it all hang out in Sunday's swim time trial.

	Tuesday	Wednesday	Thursday	Friday	Saturday	Sunday
Level 5	CTR6	SWU2 SDS3 SLI12A SSI11 SKS2 SCD2 (1,800)	CSI4	SWU2 SDS3 STI3A SSI3A SKS2 SCD2 (1,800)	BRW5	RFR6
		RTR4		RFR6 + RSS3		SWU1 STT1 SCD1 (1,200)
Level 6	CTR7	SWU3 SDS3 SLI12A SSI13 SKS2 SCD3 (2,000)	CSI4	SWU3 SDS3 STI4A SSI3A SKS2 SCD3 (2,100)	BRW5	RFR7

	Tuesday	Wednesday	Thursday	Friday	Saturday	Sunday
Level 6 (cont.)		RTR5		RFR8 + RSS3		SWU2 STT1 SCD2 (1,300)
Level 7	CTR7	SWU3 SDS3 SLI13A SSI14 SKS3 SCD3 (2,200)	CSI5	SWU3 SDS3 STI4A SSI5A SKS3 SCD3 (2,200)	BRW7	RFR8
		RTR6		RFR9 + RSS3		SWU3 STT2 SCD3 (1,600)

> **QUICK TIP:**
>
> The swim start is almost everyone's least favorite part of a triathlon. Avoiding contact with other swimmers is next to impossible. If you're a strong swimmer, the best way to minimize such contact is to get out very quickly—sprint the first 100 yards or so—and then ease back into a sustainable race pace. If you're not a fast swimmer, you can minimize contact by starting at the extreme left or right edge of your wave, or behind the others in it.

WEEK 11

This week's goal: Build confidence for next week's race by feeling your fitness begin to peak in this week's workouts.

	Tuesday	Wednesday	Thursday	Friday	Saturday	Sunday
Level 5	CTR7	SWU2 SDS3 SLI12B SSI11 SKS2 SCD2 (1,800)	CSI5	SWU2 SDS3 STI3B SSI3B SKS2 SCD2 (1,800)	CFR7	RFR9

	Tuesday	Wednesday	Thursday	Friday	Saturday	Sunday
Level 5 (cont.)		RTR5		RFR6 + RSS3		SWU1 SBI26 SCD1 (1,900)
Level 6	CTR8	SWU3 SDS3 SLI12B SSI13 SKS2 SCD3 (2,000)	CSI6	SWU3 SDS3 STI4B SSI3B SKS2 SCD3 (2,100)	CFR7	RLR1
		RTR6		RFR7 + RSS3		SWU1 SBI27 SCD1 (2,200)
Level 7	CTR9	SWU3 SDS3 SLI13B SSI14 SKS3 SCD3 (2,200)	CSI7	SWU3 SDS3 STI4B SSI5B SKS3 SCD3 (2,200)	CFR7	RLR2
		RTR7		CFR8 + RSS3		SWU3 SBI27 SCD3 (2,400)

WEEK 12
(Taper)

This week's goal: Have a great race on Sunday!

	Tuesday	Wednesday	Thursday	Friday	Saturday	Sunday
Level 5	CTR4	SWU2 SDS3 SLI12 SSI11 SCD2 (1,650)	CSI1	SWU2 STI2 SSI1 SCD2 (1,200)	CRR1	Sprint Triathlon
		RTR2		RRR1 + RSS3		

	Tuesday	Wednesday	Thursday	Friday	Saturday	Sunday
Level 6	CTR7	SWU3 SDS3 SLI12 SSI13 SCD3 (1,850)	CSI2	SWU2 STI2 SSI1 SCD2 (1,200)	CRR1	Sprint Triathlon
		RTR3		RRR2 + RSS3		
Level 7	CTR5	SWU3 SDS3 SLI13 SSI14 SCD3 (2,000)	CSI2	SWU2 STI2 SSI1 SCD2 (1,200)	CRR1	Sprint Triathlon
		RTR4		RRR3 + RSS3		

Chapter 5

SPRINT TRIATHLON TRAINING PLANS
Levels 8–10

*T*he sprint triathlon plans in this chapter are best thought of as crash training plans for triathletes with a sound base of swim, bike, and run fitness who, for whatever reason, decide they want to peak for a sprint triathlon soon—in 12 weeks. If you have a little more time available before your chosen sprint, you can actually use the higher-level Olympic distance training plans in Chapter 8 to prepare for a sprint race. But don't get me wrong—the plans in this chapter will make you plenty fit for a good performance.

The plans begin with a short three-week base phase. The following build phase is four weeks long and the final five weeks comprise the peak phase. All three plans include 12 workouts in a typical week—four swims, four rides, and four runs. Weeks 2, 4, and 6 include an extra 10-minute transition run after Friday's ride; in Weeks 8 and 10, the separate ride and run scheduled for Saturday are collapsed into a single bike-run brick workout. Monday is a rest day every week and Weeks 4 and 8 are recovery weeks. The final week is a taper week.

Level 8

This plan is a good fit for those who are prepared to handle 12 workouts per week but are not accustomed to such frequency of training. The plan begins with 8,200 yards of swimming, 4 hours and 15 minutes of cycling, and 2 hours and 48 minutes of running in Week 1. It peaks with 11,050 yards of swimming, 6 hours and 45 minutes of cycling, and 3 hours and 40 minutes of running in Week 11.

Level 9

This plan features slightly more high-intensity work and slightly longer long workouts than the Level 8 plan. It begins with 8,900 yards of swimming, 4 hours and 55 minutes of cycling, and 3 hours and 3 minutes of running in Week 1. It peaks with 11,750 yards of swimming, 7 hours and 35 minutes of cycling, and 3 hours and 55 minutes of running in Week 11.

Level 10

This plan packs as much sprint-focused training into 12 weeks as you will ever need to do. It's not so much the raw volume but the volume of high-intensity training that will whip you into fantastic shape—or wear you down, if you're not prepared to handle it. The plan begins with 9,700 yards of swimming, 5 hours and 20 minutes of cycling, and 3 hours and 3 minutes of running in Week 1. It peaks with 12,600 yards of swimming, 7 hours and 50 minutes of cycling, and 4 hours and 12 minutes of running in Week 11.

Quick Reference Guide to Workout Codes for Sprint Triathlon Training Plans Levels 8–10

Code Prefix	Workout Type	Brief Description	Levels
BRW	Brick Workout	Bike ride followed by immediate run	BRW5: 1 hr/20 min BRW6: 1 hr/30 min BRW7: 1 hr 15 min/20 min
CFR	Foundation Bike	Steady ride @ moderate aerobic intensity	CFR3: 1 hr CFR4: 1 hr 15 min CFR5: 1 hr 30 min CFR6: 1 hr 45 min CFR7: 2 hrs
CLI	Bike Lactate Intervals	3–5-minute intervals @ VO$_2$ max intensity w/ 3-minute active recoveries; warm up and cool down long enough to reach total time	CLI4: 5 x 3 min (1 hr 20 min total) CLI5: 6 x 3 min (1 hr 25 min) CLI6: 7 x 3 min (1 hr 30 min) CLI7: 8 x 3 min (1 hr 35 min) CLI10: 4 x 5 min (1 hr 50 min) CLI11: 5 x 5 min (2 hr)
CLR	Long Bike Ride	Steady ride @ moderate aerobic intensity	CLR1: 2 hr CLR2: 2 hr 15 min CLR3: 2 hr 30 min
CPI	Bike Power Intervals	20-second intervals done in a high gear @ speed intensity	CPI3: 6 x 20 sec (1 hr total) CPI4: 7 x 20 sec (1 hr 10 min)

Code Prefix	Workout Type	Brief Description	Levels
CPI *(cont.)*		w/ 2-minute active recoveries; warm up and cool down long enough to reach total time	CPI5: 8 x 20 sec (1 hr 20 min) CPI6: 9 x 20 sec (1 hr 25 min) CPI7: 10 x 20 sec (1 hr 30 min)
CRR	Recovery Bike	Steady ride @ recovery intensity	CRR1: 20 min CRR2: 30 min CRR3: 45 min CRR4: 1 hr CRR5: 1 hr 15 min
CSI	Bike Speed Intervals	1–1.5-minute intervals @ speed intensity w/ 2-minute active recoveries; warm up and cool down long enough to reach total time	CSI3: 6 x 1 min (55 min total) CSI4: 7 x 1 min (1 hr) CSI5: 8 x 1 min (1 hr 5 min) CSI6: 9 x 1 min (1 hr 10 min) CSI7: 10 x 1 min (1 hr 15 min) CSI8: 11 x 1 min (1 hr 20 min) CSI9: 12 x 1 min (1 hr 30 min) CSI12: 6 x 1 min 30 sec (1 hr 40 min) CSI13: 7 x 1 min 30 sec (1 hr 45 min) CSI14: 8 x 1 min 30 sec (1 hr 50 min)
CTR	Tempo Bike Ride	One or two blocks of riding @ threshold intensity (10-minute active recovery when threshold-intensity riding is divided into two blocks); warm up and cool down long enough to reach total time	CTR1: 2 x 10 min (45 min total) CTR5: 24 min (1 hr 5 min) CTR6: 26 min (1 hr 10 min) CTR7: 2 x 14 min (1 hr 15 min) CTR8: 28 min (1 hr 20 min) CTR9: 30 min (1 hr 25 min) CTR10: 2 x 16 min (1 hr 30 min) CTR11: 32 min (1 hr 35 min) CTR12: 34 min (1 hr 40 min) CTR13: 2 x 18 min (1 hr 45 min) CTR14: 36 min (1 hr 50 min) CTR15: 38 min (1 hr 55 min) CTR16: 2 x 20 min (2 hr) CTR17: 40 min (2 hr 5 min)
RFL	Fartlek Run	Foundation run with 30-second bursts @ VO_2 max/speed intensity	RFL5: 6 x 30 sec (40 min total) RFL6: 8 x 30 sec (40 min) RFL8: 8 x 30 sec (45 min)

Code Prefix	Workout Type	Brief Description	Levels
RFR	Foundation Run	Steady run @ moderate aerobic intensity	RFR5: 40 min RFR6: 45 min RFR7: 50 min RFR8: 55 min RFR9: 1 hr
RLI	Run Lactate Intervals	1–3-minute intervals run @ VO$_2$ max intensity w/ active recoveries equal to intervals in duration; warm up and cool down long enough to reach total time	RLI6: 8 x 1 min (36 min total) RLI7: 10 x 1 min (40 min) RLI8: 12 x 1 min (44 min) RLI9: 3 x 3 min (38 min) RLI10: 4 x 3 min (44 min) RLI11: 5 x 3 min (50 min) RLI12: 6 x 3 min (56 min)
RLR	Long Run	Long, steady-pace run @ moderate aerobic intensity	RLR1: 1 hr 5 min RLR2: 1 hr 10 min RLR3: 1 hr 20 min RLR4: 1 hr 30 min
RRR	Recovery Run	Short run @ recovery intensity	RRR3: 30 min RRR4: 35 min RRR5: 40 min RRR6: 45 min
RSI	Running Speed Intervals	30-second intervals run @ speed intensity w/ 2-minute active recoveries or 1-minute intervals run @ speed intensity w/ 3-minute active recoveries; warm up and cool down long enough to reach total time	RSI3: 8 x 30 sec (39 min total) RSI4: 9 x 30 sec (42 min) RSI5: 10 x 30 sec (47 min) RSI9: 14 x 30 sec (55 min) RSI10: 15 x 30 sec (57 min) RSI11: 16 x 30 sec (1 hr) RSI14: 8 x 1 min (57 min) RSI15: 9 x 1 min (1 hr 1 min) RSI16: 10 x 1 min (1 hr 5 min) RSI17: 11 x 1 min (1 hr 9 min) RSI18: 12 x 1 min (1 hr 12 min)
RSS	Running Strides	20-second "relaxed sprints" @ speed intensity w/ 40-second active recoveries	RSS1: 2 x 20 sec RSS2: 4 x 20 sec RSS3: 6 x 20 sec
RTR	Tempo Run	Steady run @ threshold intensity; warm up and cool down long enough to reach total time	RTR4: 16 min (36 min total) RTR5: 18 min (38 min) RTR6: 20 min (40 min)

Code Prefix	Workout Type	Brief Description	Levels
RTR (cont.)			RTR7: 22 min (42 min)
			RTR8: 24 min (44 min)
			RTR9: 26 min (46 min)
			RTR10: 28 min (48 min)
			RTR11: 30 min (50 min)
			RTR12: 32 min (52 min)
			RTR13: 34 min (54 min)
			RTR14: 36 min (56 min)
			RTR15: 38 min (58 min)
			RTR16: 40 min (1 hr)
SBI	Swim Base Intervals	100-yard intervals swum @ moderate aerobic intensity w/ 5-second rest periods or 200-yard intervals swum @ moderate aerobic intensity w/ 10-second rest periods, or single longer swims performed @ the same intensity	SBI3: 4 x 100
			SBI4: 5 x 100
			SBI5: 6 x 100
			SBI6: 7 x 100
			SBI7: 8 x 100
			SBI8: 9 x 100
			SBI13: 3 x 200
			SBI14: 4 x 200
			SBI15: 5 x 200
			SBI16: 6 x 200
			SBI17: 7 x 200
			SBI18: 8 x 200
			SBI25: 1,200
			SBI26: 1,500
			SBI27: 1,800
			SBI28: 2,000
			SBI29: 2,400
			SBI30: 2,600
SCD	Swim Cool-Down	Easy swim @ recovery intensity	SCD2: 250
			SCD3: 300
			SCD4: 350
			SCD5: 400
SDS	Swim Drill Set	25-yard intervals of mixed form drills w/ 10-second rest periods	SDS7: 6 x 50
			SDS8: 8 x 50
SFI	Swim Fartlek Intervals	150–200-yard intervals with easy/hard or build/descend format	SFI5: 5 x 150 (50 easy/25 hard…)
			SFI6: 6 x 150 (50 easy/25 hard…)
			SFI8: 4 x 200 (50 easy/50 hard…)

Code Prefix	Workout Type	Brief Description	Levels
SFI (cont.)		(hard = threshold intensity, easy = moderate aerobic intensity)	SFI8A: 4 x 200 (50 build/50 descend…) SFI9: 5 x 200 (50 easy/50 hard…) SFI9A: 4 x 200 (50 build/50 descend…) SFI10: 6 x 200 (50 easy/50 hard…)
SKS	Swim Kick Set	25-yard intervals kicking only w/ 15-second rests	SKS4: 10 x 25 SKS7: 6 x 50
SLI	Swim Lactate Intervals	100–150-yard intervals swum @ VO_2 max intensity with rest periods of 20 seconds to 1 minute 15 seconds	SLI11: 6 x 100, 1-min rest SLI12: 7 x 100, 1-min rest SLI12A: 7 x 100, 45-sec rest SLI12B: 7 x 100, 30-sec rest SLI13: 8 x 100, 1-min rest SLI13A: 8 x 100, 45-sec rest SLI13B: 8 x 100, 30-sec rest SLI14A: 4 x 150, 1-min rest SLI14B: 4 x 150, 45-sec rest SLI16: 6 x 150, 1-min 15-sec rest SLI16A: 6 x 150 1-min rest SLI16B: 6 x 150, 45-sec rest
SSI	Swim Sprint Intervals	25–50-yard intervals swum @ speed intensity w/ 5–20-second rest periods	SSI1: 4 x 25, 20-sec rest SSI3: 6 x 25, 20-sec rest SSI5: 8 x 25, 20-sec rest SSI5A: 8 x 25, 10-sec rest SSI5B: 8 x 25, 5-sec rest SSI7: 10 x 25, 5-sec rest SSI9: 12 x 25, 20-sec rest SSI12: 6 x 50, 20-sec rest SSI12A: 6 x 50, 10-sec rest SSI12B: 6 x 50, 5-sec rest SSI13: 7 x 50, 20-sec rest SSI13A: 7 x 50, 10-sec rest SSI13B: 7 x 50, 5-sec rest SSI14: 8 x 50, 20-sec rest SSI14A: 8 x 50, 10-sec rest SSI14B: 8 x 50, 5-sec rest SSI15: 9 x 50, 20-sec rest SSI15A: 9 x 50, 10-sec rest SSI15B: 9 x 50, 5-sec rest

Code Prefix	Workout Type	Brief Description	Levels
STI	Swim Threshold Intervals	200-yard intervals swum @ threshold intensity w/ rest periods of 20–45 seconds	STI3: 4 x 200, 45-sec rest STI3A: 4 x 200, 30-sec rest STI3B: 4 x 200, 20-sec rest STI4: 5 x 200, 45-sec rest STI4A: 5 x 200, 30-sec rest STI4B: 5 x 200, 20-sec rest STI5: 6 x 200, 45-sec rest STI5A: 6 x 200, 30-sec rest STI5B: 6 x 200, 20-sec rest
STT	Swim Time Trial	Designated distance swum @ maximum effort	STT1: 800 STT2: 1,000
SWU	Swim Warm-Up	Easy swim @ recovery intensity	SWU2: 200 SWU3: 300 SWU4: 350 SWU5: 400
TRR	Transition Run	10-minute run immediately following bike ride	TRR: 10 min

General Schedule						
	Tuesday	**Wednesday**	**Thursday**	**Friday**	**Saturday**	**Sunday**
BASE PHASE						
Week 1	Swim Base + Sprint Intervals	Swim Base Intervals	Foundation Bike	Foundation Bike	Foundation Bike	Swim Base Intervals
	Bike Power Intervals	Fartlek Run	Foundation Run + Drills	Swim Fartlek Intervals	Foundation Run	Foundation Run
Week 2	Swim Base + Sprint Intervals	Swim Base Intervals	Foundation Bike	Foundation Bike + Trans. Run	Foundation Bike	Swim Base Intervals
	Bike Power Intervals	Fartlek Run	Foundation Run + Drills	Swim Fartlek Intervals	Foundation Run	Foundation Run
Week 3	Swim Base + Sprint Intervals	Swim Base Intervals	Foundation Bike	Foundation Bike	Foundation Bike	Swim Base Intervals
	Bike Power Intervals	Fartlek Run	Foundation Run + Drills	Swim Fartlek Intervals	Foundation Run	Foundation Run

	Tuesday	Wednesday	Thursday	Friday	Saturday	Sunday
BUILD PHASE						
Week 4 (Recovery)	Swim Lactate + Speed Intervals	Swim Base Intervals	Recovery Bike	Tempo Bike + Trans. Run	Foundation Bike	Swim Base Intervals
	Bike Speed Intervals	Run Speed Intervals	Recovery Run	Swim Threshold + Speed Intervals	Tempo Run	Foundation Run
Week 5	Swim Lactate + Speed Intervals	Swim Base Intervals	Recovery Bike	Tempo Bike	L8: Foundation Bike L9–10: Long Bike	Swim Base Intervals
	Bike Speed Intervals	Run Speed Intervals	Recovery Run + Drills	Swim Threshold + Speed Intervals	Tempo Run	L8: Foundation Run L9–10: Long Run
Week 6	Swim Speed Lactate + Intervals	Swim Base Intervals	Recovery Bike	Tempo Bike + Trans. Run	Long Bike	Swim Base Intervals
	Bike Speed Intervals	Run Speed Intervals	Recovery Run + Drills	Swim Threshold + Speed Intervals	Tempo Run	Long Run
Week 7	Swim Lactate + Speed Intervals	Swim Base Intervals	Recovery Bike	Tempo Bike	Long Bike	Swim Time Trial
	Bike Speed Intervals	Run Speed Intervals	Recovery Run + Drills	Swim Threshold + Speed Intervals	Tempo Run	Long Run
PEAK PHASE						
Week 8 (Recovery)	Swim Lactate + Speed Intervals	Swim Base Intervals	Recovery Bike	Tempo Bike	Transition Workout	Swim Base Intervals
	Bike Lactate Intervals	Run Lactate Intervals	Recovery Run	Swim Threshold + Speed Intervals		Foundation Run

	Tuesday	Wednesday	Thursday	Friday	Saturday	Sunday
Week 9	Swim Lactate + Speed Intervals	Swim Base Intervals	Recovery Bike	Tempo Bike	Long Bike	Swim Base Intervals
	Bike Lactate Intervals	Run Lactate Intervals	Recovery Run + Drills	Swim Threshold + Speed Intervals	Tempo Run	Long Run
Week 10	Swim Lactate + Speed Intervals	Swim Base Intervals	Recovery Bike	Tempo Bike	Transition Workout	Swim Base Intervals
	Bike Lactate Intervals	Run Lactate Intervals	Recovery Run + Drills	Swim Threshold + Speed Intervals		L8–9: Foundation Run L10: Long Run
Week 11	Swim Lactate + Speed Intervals	Swim Base Intervals	Recovery Bike	Tempo Bike	Long Bike	Swim Base Intervals
	Bike Lactate Intervals	Run Lactate Intervals	Recovery Run + Drills	Swim Threshold + Speed Intervals	Tempo Run	Long Run
Week 12 (Taper)	Swim Lactate + Speed Intervals	Swim Base Intervals	Recovery Bike	Tempo Bike	Recovery Bike	Sprint Triathlon
	Bike Lactate Intervals	Run Lactate Intervals	Recovery Run	Swim Threshold + Speed Intervals	Run Drills	

Week-by-Week Schedule

Base Phase

Not your typical base phase, this one incorporates a fair amount of high-intensity training right away to boost your fitness level quickly. Still, plenty of attention is paid to developing your aerobic capacity and endurance.

WEEK 1

This week's goal: Get accustomed to your new workout schedule.

	Tuesday	Wednesday	Thursday	Friday	Saturday	Sunday
Level 8	SWU4 SDS7 SBI6 SSI5 SKS4 SCD4 (2,150)	SWU4 SDS7 SBI14 SBI3 SCD4 (2,200)	CFR3	CFR3	CFR4	SWU2 SBI25 SCD2 (1,700)
	CPI3	RFL5	RFR5 + RDR1	SWU4 SDS7 SFI5 SSI3 SKS4 SCD4 (2,150)	RFR5	RFR6
Level 9	SWU4 SDS7 SBI7 SSI7 SKS4 SCD4 (2,300)	SWU4 SDS7 SBI15 SBI3 SCD4 (2,400)	CFR4	CFR3	CFR5	SWU4 SBI25 SCD4 (1,900)
	CPI4	RFL5	RFR6 + RDR1	SWU4 SDS7 SFI6 SSI3 SKS4 SCD4 (2,300)	RFR6	RFR7
Level 10	SWU5 SDS8 SBI7 SSI7 SKS4 SCD5 (2,500)	SWU5 SDS8 SBI15 SBI4 SCD5 (2,700)	CFR5	CFR3	CFR5	SWU5 SBI25 SCD5 (2,000)
	CPI5	RFL5	RFR6 + RDR1	SWU5 SDS8 SFI8 SSI5 SKS7 SCD5 (2,500)	RFR6	RFR7

WEEK 2

This week's goal: Build momentum by completing all scheduled workouts as prescribed.

	Tuesday	Wednesday	Thursday	Friday	Saturday	Sunday
Level 8	SWU4 SDS7 SBI7 SSI5 SKS4 SCD4 (2,250)	SWU4 SDS7 SBI15 SBI4 SCD4 (2,500)	CFR3	CFR3 + TRR	CFR5	SWU4 SBI25 SCD4 (1,900)
	CPI4	RFL6	RFR5 + RDR2	SWU4	RFR6	RFR7 SDS7 SFI8A SSI3 SKS4 SCD4 (2,200)
Level 9	SWU4 SDS7 SBI8 SSI7 SKS4 SCD4 (2,400)	SWU4 SDS7 SBI16 SBI4 SCD4 (2,700)	CFR4	CFR4 + TRR	CFR6	SWU4 SBI25 SCD4 (1,900)
	CPI5	RFL6	RFR6 + RDR2	SWU4 SDS7 SFI9A SSI3 SKS4 SCD4 (2,400)	RFR7	RFR8
Level 10	SWU5 SDS8 SBI8 SSI7 SKS4 SCD5 (2,600)	SWU5 SDS8 SBI16 SBI5 SCD5 (3,000)	CFR5	CFR4 + TRR	CFR6	SWU5 SBI25 SCD5 (2,000)

	Tuesday	Wednesday	Thursday	Friday	Saturday	Sunday
Level 10 (cont.)	CPI6	RFL6	RFR6 + RDR2	SWU5 SDS8 SFI9A SSI3 SKS7 SCD5 (2,650)	RFR7	RFR8

QUICK TIP:

As you gain fitness, you will find your pace increasing at any given RPE. For example, over the course of this training program you may find your threshold swim intervals pace increase from 1:45 per 100 yards to 1:32 per 100 yards. The excitement of seeing your times drop can tempt you to push a little harder with each workout. It's important to resist this temptation, continue training at the appropriate RPE, and let the pace associated with this effort level increase naturally as you go.

WEEK 3

This week's goal: Hang in there—you have a recovery week coming up!

	Tuesday	Wednesday	Thursday	Friday	Saturday	Sunday
Level 8	SWU4 SDS7 SBI8 SSI5 SKS4 SCD4 (2,350)	SWU4 SDS7 SBI16 SBI3 SCD4 (2,600)	CFR3	CFR3	CFR6	SWU4 SBI26 SCD4 (2,200)
	CPI5	RFL8	RFR5 + RDR3	SWU4 SDS7 SFI9 SSI3 SKS4 SCD4 (2,400)	RFR6	RFR8

	Tuesday	Wednesday	Thursday	Friday	Saturday	Sunday
Level 9	SWU4￼SDS7￼SBI9￼SSI7￼SKS4￼SCD4￼(2,500)	SWU4￼SDS7￼SBI16￼SBI5￼SCD4￼(2,800)	CFR4	CFR4	CFR7	SWU4￼SBI27￼SCD4￼(2,500)
	CPI6	RFL8	RFR6 + RDR3	SWU4￼SDS7￼SFI10￼SSI3￼SKS4￼SCD4￼(2,600)	RFR7	RFR9
Level 10	SWU5￼SDS8￼SBI9￼SSI7￼SKS4￼SCD5￼(2,700)	SWU5￼SDS8￼SBI17￼SBI4￼SCD5￼(3,100)	CFR5	CFR5	CFR7	SWU5￼SBI27￼SCD5￼(2,600)
	CPI7	RFL8	RFR6 + RDR3	SWU5￼SDS8￼SFI10￼SSI3￼SKS7￼SCD5￼(2,850)	RFR7	RFR9

Build Phase

Things get serious in this phase with the introduction of lactate and threshold swim intervals, tempo rides and runs, and speed intervals in cycling and running. The overarching objective is to overreach—to do just a little more training than you could handle long-term—until Week 8, a recovery week that will allow you to fully absorb all the hard work and emerge much fitter.

WEEK 4
(Recovery)

This week's goal: Find the appropriate pace/intensity level in your lactate and threshold swim intervals, tempo rides and runs, and cycling and running speed intervals.

	Tuesday	Wednesday	Thursday	Friday	Saturday	Sunday
Level 8	SWU4 SDS7 SLI11 SSI12 SCD4 (1,900)	SWU4 SDS7 SBI6 SCD4 (1,700)	CRR2	CTR5 + TRR	CFR5	SWU4 SBI25 SCD4 (1,900)
	CSI3	RSI3	RRR3	SWU4 SDS7 STI3 SSI5 SCD4 (2,000)	RTR4	RFR6
Level 9	SWU4 SDS7 SLI12 SSI14 SCD4 (2,100)	SWU4 SDS7 SBI8 SCD4 (1,900)	CRR3	CTR6 + TRR	CFR6	SWU4 SBI26 SCD4 (2,200)
	CSI4	RSI4	RRR4	SWU4 SDS7 STI4 SSI5 SCD4 (2,200)	RTR5	RFR7
Level 10	SWU5 SDS8 SLI12 SSI14 SCD5 (2,300)	SWU5 SDS8 SBI8 SCD5 (2,100)	CFRR3	CTR7 + TRR	CFR6	SWU5 SBI26 SCD5 (2,300)
	CSI5	RSI5	RRR5	SWU5 SDS8 STI4 SSI5 SCD5 (2,400)	RTR6	RFR7

WEEK 5

This week's goal: Ride and run hard yet relaxed in Tuesday's cycling speed intervals and Wednesday's running speed intervals.

	Tuesday	Wednesday	Thursday	Friday	Saturday	Sunday
Level 8	SWU4 SDS7 SLI12 SSI12 SKS4 SCD4 (2,250)	SWU4 SDS7 SBI16 SBI3 SCD4 (2,600)	CRR4	CTR8	CFR6	SWU4 SBI26 SCD4 (2,200)
	CSI5	RSI9	RRR4 + RDR3	SWU4 SDS7 STI3A SSI5A SKS4 SCD4 (2,250)	RTR7	RFR8
Level 9	SWU4 SDS7 SLI13 SSI14 SKS4 SCD4 (2,450)	SWU4 SDS7 SBI17 SBI3 SCD4 (2,800)	CRR4	CTR9	CLR1	SWU4 SBI27 SCD4 (2,500)
	CSI6	RSI10	RRR5 + RDR3	SWU4 SDS7 STI4A SSI5A SKS4 SCD4 (2,450)	RTR8	RFR9
Level 10	SWU5 SDS8 SLI13 SSI14 SKS4 SCD5 (2,650)	SWU5 SDS8 SBI17 SBI3 SCD5 (3,000)	CRR5	CTR10	CLR2	SWU5 SBI27 SCD5 (2,600)
	CSI7	RSI11	RRR6 + RDR3	SWU5 SDS8 STI4A SSI5A SKS7 SCD5 (2,700)	RTR9	RLR1

WEEK 6

This week's goal: Finish strong in this weekend's long ride, run, and swim.

	Tuesday	Wednesday	Thursday	Friday	Saturday	Sunday
Level 8	SWU4 SDS7 SLI12A SSI12A SKS4 SCD4 (2,250)	SWU4 SDS7 SBI16 SBI4 SCD4 (2,700)	CRR4	CTR9 + TRR	CLR1	SWU4 SBI27 SCD4 (2,500)
	CSI7	RSI14	RRR4 + RDR3	SWU4 SDS7 STI3B SSI5B SKS4 SCD4 (2,250)	RTR9	RFR9
Level 9	SWU4 SDS7 SLI13A SSI14A SKS4 SCD4 (2,450)	SWU4 SDS7 SBI17 SBI4 SCD4 (2,900)	CRR4	CTR10 + TRR	CLR2	SWU4 SBI28 SCD4 (2,700)
	CSI8	RSI15	RRR5 + RDR3	SWU4 SDS7 STI4B SSI5B SKS4 SCD4 (2,450)	RTR10	RLR1
Level 10	SWU5 SDS8 SLI13A SSI14A SKS4 SCD5 (2,650)	SWU5 SDS8 SBI17 SBI4 SCD5 (3,100)	CRR5	CTR11 + TRR	CLR2	SWU5 SBI28 SCD5 (2,800)
	CSI9	RSI16	RRR6 + RDR3	SWU5 SDS8	RTR11	RLR2

	Tuesday	Wednesday	Thursday	Friday	Saturday	Sunday
Level 10 (cont.)				STI4B SSI5B SKS7 SCD5 (2,700)		

QUICK TIP:

Use a bike computer during all of your cycling workouts to measure the duration and distance of your ride and provide speed, and perhaps even cadence, heart rate, and power information in real time. These measurements help you keep track of your workload and track your progress. Entry-level bike computers (time, distance, and speed only) cost as little as $30.

WEEK 7

This week's goal: Don't worry if you feel flat in some of this week's workouts—that's to be expected. Just do the work and stay within yourself.

	Tuesday	Wednesday	Thursday	Friday	Saturday	Sunday
Level 8	SWU4 SDS7 SLI12B SSI12B SKS4 SCD4 (2,250)	SWU4 SDS7 SBI17 SBI4 SCD4 (2,900)	CRR4	CTR11	CLR2	SWU4 STT1 SCD4 (1,500)
	CSI12	RSI16	RRR4 + RDR3	SWU4 SDS7 STI4 SSI5 SKS4 SCD4 (2,450)	RTR10	RLR1
Level 9	SWU4 SDS7 SLI13B SSI14B	SWU4 SDS7 SBI17 SBI6	CRR4	CTR12	CLR2	SWU4 STT1 SCD4 (1,500)

	Tuesday	Wednesday	Thursday	Friday	Saturday	Sunday
Level 9 (cont.)	SKS4 SCD4 (2,450)	SCD4 (3,100)				
	CSI13	RSI17	RRR5 + RDR3	SWU4 SDS7 STI5 SSI5 SKS4 SCD4 (2,650)	RTR11	RLR2
Level 10	SWU5 SDS8 SLI13B SSI14B SKS4 SCD5 (2,650)	SWU5 SDS8 SBI17 SBI6 SCD5 (3,300)	CRR5	CTR13	CLR3	SWU5 STT1 SCD5 (1,600)
	CSI14	RSI18	RRR6 + RDR3	SWU5 SDS8 STI5 SSI5 SKS7 SCD5 (2,900)	RTR12	RLR2

Peak Phase

In this five-week peak phase, your workouts are focused on getting you race-ready with an emphasis on VO_2 max- and threshold-intensity training plus two bike-run brick workouts.

WEEK 8
(Recovery)

This week's goal: Fully absorb your recent training and finish the week feeling rested and ready to return to harder training next week.

	Tuesday	Wednesday	Thursday	Friday	Saturday	Sunday
Level 8	SWU4 SDS7 SLI11 SSI7 SCD4 (1,850)	SWU4 SDS7 SBI16 SBI3 SCD4 (2,600)	CRR4	CTR8	BRW5	SWU4 SBI26 SCD4 (2,300)

	Tuesday	Wednesday	Thursday	Friday	Saturday	Sunday
Level 8 (cont.)	CLI4	RLI6	RRR4	SWU4 SDS7 STI3 SSI1 SKS4 SCD4 (2,150)		RFR6
Level 9	SWU4 SDS7 SLI13 SSI7 SCD4 (2,050)	SWU4 SDS7 SBI16 SBI5 SCD4 (2,800)	CRR4	CTR9	BRW6	SWU3 SBI27 SCD3 (2,400)
	CLI5	RLI7	RRR5	SWU4 SDS7 STI4 SSI1 SKS4 SCD4 (2,350)		RFR7
Level 10	SWU5 SDS8 SLI13 SSI7 SCD5 (2,250)	SWU5 SDS8 SBI16 SBI5 SCD5 (3,000)	CRR5	CTR10	BRW7	SWU4 SBI27 SCD4 (2,500)
	CLI6	RLI8	RRR6	SWU5 SDS8 STI4 SSI1 SKS7 SCD5 (2,600)		RFR7

WEEK 9

This week's goal: Perform your lactate intervals in all three disciplines at the fastest pace you can maintain through the end of the last interval.

	Tuesday	Wednesday	Thursday	Friday	Saturday	Sunday
Level 8	SWU4 SDS7 SLI13 SSI13 SKS4 SCD4 (2,400)	SWU4 SDS7 SBI17 SBI4 SCD4 (2,900)	CRR4	CTR11	CLR2	SWU4 SBI28 SCD4 (2,700)
	CLI5	RLI9	RRR4 + RDR3	SWU4 SDS7 STI4 SSI5 SKS4 SCD4 (2,450)	RTR12	RLR1
Level 9	SWU4 SDS7 SLI16 SSI15 SKS4 SCD4 (2,600)	SWU4 SDS7 SBI18 SBI4 SCD4 (3,100)	CRR4	CTR12	CLR2	SWU4 SBI29 SCD4 (3,100)
	CLI6	RLI9	RRR5 + RDR3	SWU4 SDS7 STI5 SSI5 SKS4 SCD4 (2,650)	RTR13	RLR2
Level 10	SWU5 SDS8 SLI16 SSI15 SKS4 SCD5 (2,800)	SWU5 SDS8 SBI18 SBI4 SCD5 (3,300)	CRR5	CTR13	CLR3	SWU5 SBI29 SCD5 (3,200)
	CLI7	RLI10	RRR6 + RDR3	SWU5 SDS8 STI5 SSI5 SKS7 SCD5 (2,900)	RTR14	RLR3

WEEK 10

This week's goal: Quickly find your running legs in Sunday's brick workout.

	Tuesday	Wednesday	Thursday	Friday	Saturday	Sunday
Level 8	SWU4 SDS7 SLI13A SSI13A SKS4 SCD4 (2,400)	SWU4 SDS7 SBI17 SBI5 SCD4 (3,000)	CRR4	CTR13	BRW6	SWU4 STT2 SCD4 (1,700)
	CLI6	RLI10	RRR4 + RSS3	SWU4 SDS7 STI4A SSI5A SKS4 SCD4 (2,450)		RFR8
Level 9	SWU4 SDS7 SLI16A SSI15A SKS4 SCD4 (2,600)	SWU4 SDS7 SBI18 SBI5 SCD4 (3,200)	CRR4	CTR14	BRW7	SWU4 STT2 SCD4 (1,700)
	CLI7	RLI10	RRR5 + RSS3	SWU4 SDS7 STI5A SSI5A SKS4 SCD4 (2,650)		RFR9
Level 10	SWU5 SDS8 SLI16A SSI15A SKS4 SCD5 (2,800)	SWU5 SDS8 SBI18 SBI5 SCD5 (3,400)	CRR5	CTR15	BRW7	SWU5 STT2 SCD5 (1,800)

ESSENTIAL WEEK-BY-WEEK TRAINING GUIDE

	Tuesday	Wednesday	Thursday	Friday	Saturday	Sunday
Level 10 (cont.)	CLI10	RLI11	RRR6 + RSS3	SWU5 STI5A SSI5A SKS7 SCD5 (2,900)		RLR1

QUICK TIP:

To accelerate your improvement in swimming, get a one-on-one lesson from an experienced swim coach. By pointing out one or two key flaws in your stroke and showing you how to correct them, a good coach can help you improve more as a swimmer in one day than you can do through weeks of hard workouts.

WEEK 11

This week's goal: Gain confidence for next week's race by feeling your fitness begin to peak in this week's workouts.

	Tuesday	Wednesday	Thursday	Friday	Saturday	Sunday
Level 8	SWU4 SDS7 SLI13B SSI13B SKS4 SCD4 (2,400)	SWU4 SDS7 SBI18 SBI4 SCD4 (3,100)	CRR4	CTR15	CLR2	SWU4 SBI29 SCD4 (3,100)
	CLI7	RLI11	RRR4 + RSS3	SWU4 SDS7 STI4B SSI5B SKS4 SCD4 (2,450)	RTR14	RLR2
Level 9	SWU4 SDS7 SLI16B	SWU4 SDS7 SBI18	CRR4	CTR16	CLR3	SWU5 SBI29 SCD5

94

	Tuesday	Wednesday	Thursday	Friday	Saturday	Sunday
Level 9 *(cont.)*	SSI15B SKS4 SCD4 (2,600)	SBI6 SCD4 (3,300)				(3,200)
	CLI10	RLI12	RRR5 + RSS3	SWU4 SDS7 STI5B SSI5B SKS4 SCD4 (2,650)	RTR15	RLR3
Level 10	SWU5 SDS8 SLI16B SSI15B SKS4 SCD5 (2,800)	SWU5 SDS8 SBI18 SBI6 SCD5 (3,500)	CRR5	CTR17	CLR3	SWU5 SBI30 SCD5 (3,400)
	CLI11	RLI12	RRR6 + RSS3	SWU5 SDS8 STI5B SSI5B SKS7 SCD5 (2,900)	RTR16	RLR4

WEEK 12
(Taper)

This week's goal: Have a great race on Sunday!

	Tuesday	Wednesday	Thursday	Friday	Saturday	Sunday
Level 8	SWU4 SDS7 SLI12 SSI12 SKS4 SCD4 (2,250)	SWU4 SDS7 SBI14 SBI3 SCD4 (2,200)	CRR2	CTR1	CRR1	Sprint Triathlon
	CLI4		RRR3	SWU2 STI3 SSI5 SCD2 (1,500)	RSS3	

	Tuesday	Wednesday	Thursday	Friday	Saturday	Sunday
Level 9	SWU4 SDS7 SLI13 SSI14 SKS4 SCD4 (2,450)	SWU4 SDS7 SBI14 SBI5 SCD4 (2,400)	CRR3	CTR1	CRR1	Sprint Triathlon
	CLI5		RRR4	SWU2 STI3 SSI5 SCD2 (1,500)	RSS3	
Level 10	SWU5 SDS8 SLI13 SSI14 SKS4 SCD5 (2,650)	SWU5 SDS8 SBI14 SBI5 SCD5 (2,600)	CFRR3	CTR1	CRR1	Sprint Triathlon
	CLI5		RRR5	SWU2 STI3 SSI5 SCD2 (1,500)	RSS3	

Chapter 6

OLYMPIC-DISTANCE TRIATHLON TRAINING PLANS
Levels 1–3

My first triathlon was an Olympic-distance event: 1.5K swim, 40K bike, 10K run. I did not specifically train for the race and I suffered mightily as a result. I wish I had followed one of the training plans in this chapter instead of winging it. I also wish I had not used a borrowed 35-pound mountain bike that was stuck in one gear.

The three training plans in this chapter are well suited to beginning triathletes who want to start with an Olympic-distance race, and to any triathlete who wants or needs to prepare for such a race with a low-volume training plan. There are only six scheduled workouts in a typical week: two swims, two rides, and two runs. In Weeks 2, 4, 6, and 8, a 10-minute transition run is tacked onto the end of Saturday's bike ride. In Weeks 10 and 14 a bike-run brick workout takes the place of Sunday's run.

Each plan is 16 weeks in length and includes an optional sprint distance tune-up race at the end of Week 12. The base phase is six weeks long and the build and peak phases are five weeks apiece. Weeks 4, 8, and 12 are recovery weeks and the final one is a taper week. An optional tune-up sprint triathlon is scheduled for Week 12. If you don't have the opportunity to do one, do a brick workout instead.

Level 1

This is your bare-bones Olympic-distance training plan—the minimal training you need to do to complete such as race without suffering inordinately. It begins with 1,600 yards of swimming, 1 hour of cycling, and 50 minutes of running in Week 1. It peaks with 2,750 yards of swimming, 3 hours and 5 minutes of cycling, and 1 hour and 41 minutes of running in Week 15.

Level 2

If you want the comfort of building a little more than the minimum amount of fitness you'll need to complete an Olympic-distance triathlon successfully, use this plan. It begins with 1,900 yards of swimming, 1 hour and 30 minutes of cycling, and 1 hour of running in Week 1. It peaks with 3,225 yards of swimming, 3 hours and 10 minutes of cycling (with a tougher tempo workout than in the Level 1 plan), and 1 hour and 48 minutes of running in Week 15.

Level 3

This plan offers a good balance between time efficiency and results. There are still just two workouts per discipline each week, but they are challenging enough to get you quite fit. The plan begins with 2,300 yards of swimming, 1 hour and 30 minutes of cycling, and 1 hour and 10 minutes of running in Week 1. It peaks with 3,625 yards of swimming, 3 hours and 30 minutes of cycling, and 2 hours of running in Week 15.

Quick Reference Guide to Workout Codes for Olympic-Distance Triathlon Training Plans Levels 1–3			
Code Prefix	**Workout Type**	**Brief Description**	**Levels**
BRW	Brick Workout	Bike ride followed by immediate run	BRW5: 1 hr/20 min BRW7: 1 hr 15 min/20 min BRW8: 1 hr 15 min/30 min BRW9: 1 hr 30 min/30 min
CFR	Foundation Bike	Steady ride @ moderate aerobic intensity	CFR1: 30 min CFR2: 45 min CFR3: 1 hr CFR4: 1 hr 15 min CFR5: 1 hr 30 min CFR6: 1 hr 45 min
CLH	Bike Long Hill Climbs	5-minute climbing intervals @ threshold/VO$_2$ max intensity w/ 3-minute active recoveries; warm up and cool down long enough to reach total time	CLH1: 2 x 5 min (1 hr total) CLH2: 3 x 5 min (1 hr 5 min) CLH3: 4 x 5 min (1 hr 10 min) CLH4: 5 x 5 min (1 hr 15 min)

Code Prefix	Workout Type	Brief Description	Levels
CLI	Bike Lactate Intervals	3-minute intervals @ VO$_2$ max intensity w/ 3-minute active recoveries; warm up and cool down long enough to reach total time	CLI1: 2 x 3 min (1 hr total) CLI2: 3 x 3 min (1 hr 10 min) CLI3: 4 x 3 min (1 hr 15 min) CLI4: 5 x 3 min (1 hr 20 min)
CLR	Long Bike Ride	Long steady ride @ moderate aerobic intensity	CLR1: 2 hr CLR2: 2 hr 15 min
CRR	Recovery Bike	Steady ride @ recovery intensity	CRR1: 20 min
CSH	Bike Short Hill Climbs	1-minute hill climbs @ VO$_2$ max/speed intensity w/ 2-minute active recoveries; warm up and cool down long enough to reach total time	CSH1: 4 x 1 min (45 min total) CSH2: 5 x 1 min (50 min) CSH3: 6 x 1 min (55 min) CSH4: 7 x 1 min (1 hr) CSH5: 8 x 1 min (1 hr 5 min)
CTR	Tempo Bike Ride	One or two blocks of riding @ threshold intensity (10-minute active recovery when threshold-intensity riding is divided into two blocks); warm up and cool down long enough to reach total time	CTR1: 2 x 10 min (45 min total) CTR2: 20 min (50 min) CTR3: 22 min (55 min) CTR4: 2 x 12 min (1 hr) CTR5: 24 min (1 hr 5 min) CTR6: 26 min (1 hr 10 min) CTR7: 2 x 14 min (1 hr 15 min)
RFL	Fartlek Run	Foundation run with 30-second bursts @ VO$_2$ max/speed intensity	RFL1: 6 x 30 sec (30 min total) RFL2: 8 x 30 sec (35 min) RFL3: 6 x 30 sec (40 min) RFL4: 8 x 30 sec (35 min) RFL6: 8 x 30 sec (40 min)
RFR	Foundation Run	Steady run @ moderate aerobic intensity	RFR2: 25 min RFR3: 30 min RFR4: 35 min RFR5: 40 min RFR6: 45 min RFR7: 50 min RFR8: 55 min RFR9: 1 hr
RLI	Run Lactate Intervals	30-second–1-minute intervals run @ VO$_2$ max intensity w/ active recoveries equal to intervals in duration; warm up	RLI1: 12 x 30 sec (32 min total) RLI2: 14 x 30 sec (34 min) RLI3: 16 x 30 sec (36 min) RLI4: 18 x 30 sec (38 min)

Code Prefix	Workout Type	Brief Description	Levels
RLI (cont.)		and cool down long enough to reach total time	RLI6: 8 x 1 min (36 min) RLI7: 10 x 1 min (40 min) RLI8: 12 x 1 min (44 min)
RLR	Long Run	Long, steady-pace run @ moderate aerobic intensity	RLR1: 1 hr 5 min RLR2: 1 hr 10 min RLR3: 1 hr 20 min
RSI	Running Speed Intervals	30-second intervals run @ speed intensity w/ 2-minute active recoveries or 1-minute intervals run @ speed intensity w/ 3-minute active recoveries; warm up and cool down long enough to reach total time	RSI3: 8 x 30 sec (34 min total) RSI4: 9 x 30 sec (37 min) RSI5: 10 x 30 sec (39 min) RSI9: 14 x 30 sec (55 min) RSI10: 15 x 30 sec (57 min) RSI11: 16 x 30 sec (1 hr) RSI14: 8 x 1 min (57 min) RSI15: 9 x 1 min (1 hr 1 min) RSI16: 10 x 1 min (1 hr 5 min) RSI17: 11 x 1 min (1 hr 9 min) RSI18: 12 x 1 min (1 hr 12 min)
RTR	Tempo Run	Steady run @ threshold intensity; warm up and cool down long enough to reach total time	RTR1: 10 min (30 min total) RTR2: 12 min (32 min) RTR3: 14 min (34 min) RTR4: 16 min (36 min) RTR5: 18 min (38 min) RTR6: 20 min (40 min)
SBI	Swim Base Intervals	100-yard intervals swum @ moderate aerobic intensity w/ 5-second rest periods	SBI1: 2 x 100 SBI2: 3 x 100 SBI3: 4 x 100 SBI4: 5 x 100 SBI5: 6 x 100 SBI6: 7 x 100
SCD	Swim Cool-Down	Easy swim @ recovery intensity	SCD1: 200 SCD2: 250
SDS	Swim Drill Set	25-yard intervals of mixed form drills w/ 10-second rest periods	SDS1: 4 x 25 SDS2: 6 x 25
SFI	Swim Fartlek Intervals	100–200-yard intervals with easy/hard or build/descend	SFI1: 4 x 100 (25 easy/25 hard...), 10-sec rest

Code Prefix	Workout Type	Brief Description	Levels
SFI (cont.)		format (hard = threshold intensity, easy = moderate aerobic intensity) w/ 10–20-second rest periods	SFI1A: 4 x 100 (25 build/25 descend...), 10-sec rest SFI2: 6 x 100 (25 easy/25 hard...), 10-sec rest SFI2A: 6 x 100 (25 build/25 descend...), 10-sec rest SFI4: 4 x 150 (50 easy/25 hard...), 15-sec rest SFI4A: 4 x 150 (50 build/25 descend...), 15-sec rest SFI5: 5 x 150 (50 easy/25 hard...), 15-sec rest
SKS	Swim Kick Set	25-yard intervals kicking only w/ 15-second rest periods	SKS1: 4 x 25 SKS2: 6 x 25
SLI	Swim Lactate Intervals	75–100-yard intervals swum @ VO_2 max intensity w/ rest periods of 20 seconds to 1 minute	SLI1: 4 x 75, 45-sec rest SLI2: 5 x 75, 45-sec rest SLI3: 6 x 75, 45-sec rest SLI3A: 6 x 75, 30-sec rest SLI3B: 6 x 75, 20-sec rest SLI4: 7 x 75, 45-sec rest SLI4A: 7 x 75, 30-sec rest SLI4B: 7 x 75, 20-sec rest SLI10: 5 x 100, 1-min rest SLI10A: 5 x 100, 45-sec rest SLI10B: 5 x 100, 30-sec rest SLI11: 6 x 100, 1-min rest SLI11A: 6 x 100, 45-sec rest SLI11B: 6 x 100, 30-sec rest
SSI	Swim Sprint Intervals	25–50-yard intervals swum @ speed intensity w/ 20-second rest periods	SSI1: 4 x 25 SSI2: 5 x 25 SSI3: 6 x 25 SSI5: 8 x 25 SSI10: 4 x 50 SSI12: 6 x 50
STI	Swim Threshold Intervals	200–300-yard intervals swum @ threshold intensity w/ rest periods of 20 seconds to 1 minute	STI1: 2 x 200, 45-sec rest STI1B: 2 x 200, 20-sec rest STI2: 3 x 200, 45-sec rest STI3: 4 x 200, 45-sec rest STI3A: 4 x 200, 30-sec rest

Code Prefix	Workout Type	Brief Description	Levels
STI (cont.)			STI3B: 4 x 200, 20-sec rest
			STI4: 5 x 200, 45-sec rest
			STI4A: 5 x 200, 30-sec rest
			STI4B: 5 x 200, 20-sec rest
			STI8: 2 x 300, 1-min rest
			STI8A: 2 x 300, 45-sec rest
			STI8B: 2 x 300, 30-sec rest
			STI9: 3 x 300, 1-min rest
			STI9A: 3 x 300, 45-sec rest
			STI9B: 3 x 300, 30-sec rest
			STI10: 4x 300, 1-min rest
			STI10A: 4 x 300, 45-sec rest
			STI10B: 4 x 300, 30-sec rest
SWU	Swim Warm-Up	Easy swim @ recovery intensity	SWU1: 200 SWU2: 250
TRR	Transition Run	10-minute run immediately following bike ride	TRR: 10 min

General Schedule						
	Tuesday	Wednesday	Thursday	Friday	Saturday	Sunday
BASE PHASE						
Week 1	Swim Base Intervals	Foundation Bike	Foundation Run	L1–2: Swim Base Intervals L3: Swim Fartlek Intervals	Foundation Bike	Foundation Run
Week 2	Swim Base Intervals	Foundation Bike	Foundation Run	L1: Swim Base Intervals L2–3: Swim Fartlek Intervals	Foundation Bike + Trans. Run	Foundation Run
Week 3	Swim Base Intervals	Foundation Bike	Foundation Run	Swim Fartlek Intervals	Foundation Bike	Foundation Run

	Tuesday	Wednesday	Thursday	Friday	Saturday	Sunday
Week 4 (Recovery)	Swim Base + Sprint Intervals	Bike Short Hills	Fartlek Run	Swim Fartlek Intervals	Foundation Bike + Trans. Run	Foundation Run + Drills
Week 5	Swim Base + Sprint Intervals	Bike Short Hills	Fartlek Run	Swim Fartlek + Sprint Intervals	Foundation Bike	Foundation Run + Drills
Week 6	Swim Base + Sprint Intervals	Bike Short Hills	Fartlek Run	Swim Fartlek + Sprint Intervals	Foundation Bike + Trans. Run	Foundation Run + Drills
BUILD PHASE Week 7	Swim Lactate Intervals	Bike Long Hills	Run Lactate Intervals	Swim Threshold Intervals	Long Bike	Long Run
Week 8 (Recovery)	Swim Lactate Intervals	Bike Lactate Intervals	Run Lactate Intervals	Swim Threshold Intervals	Foundation Bike + Trans. Run	Long Run
Week 9	Swim Lactate Intervals	Bike Long Hills	Run Lactate Intervals	Swim Threshold Intervals	Long Bike	Long Run
Week 10	Swim Lactate Intervals	Bike Lactate Intervals	Run Lactate Intervals	Swim Threshold Intervals	Brick Workout	Foundation Run
Week 11	Swim Lactate Intervals	Bike Long Hills	Run Lactate Intervals	Swim Threshold Intervals	Long Bike	Long Run
PEAK PHASE Week 12 (Recovery)	Swim Lactate Intervals	Threshold Bike	Tempo Run	Swim Threshold Intervals	Recovery Bike or Foundation Bike	Sprint Triathlon or Brick Workout
Week 13	Swim Lactate Intervals	Threshold Bike	Tempo Run	Swim Threshold Intervals	Long Bike	Long Run

	Tuesday	Wednesday	Thursday	Friday	Saturday	Sunday
Week 14	Swim Lactate Intervals	Threshold Bike	Tempo Run	Swim Threshold Intervals	Brick Workout	Foundation Run
Week 15	Swim Lactate Intervals	Threshold Bike	Tempo Run	Swim Threshold Intervals	Long Bike	Long Run
Week 16 (Taper)	Swim Lactate Intervals	Threshold Bike	Tempo Run	Swim Threshold Intervals	Recovery Bike	Olympic-Distance Triathlon

Week-by-Week Schedule

Base Phase

The primary objectives of this phase are to build your aerobic capacity and endurance and prepare your body to handle the high-intensity training to come in the build phase.

WEEK 1

This week's goal: Get accustomed to your new workout schedule.

	Tuesday	Wednesday	Thursday	Friday	Saturday	Sunday
Level 1	SWU1 SDS1 SBI1 SKS1 SCD1 (800)	CFR1	RFR2	SWU1 SDS1 SBI1 SKS1 SCD1 (800)	CFR1	RFR2
Level 2	SWU1 SDS2 SBI2 SKS1 SCD1 (950)	CFR2	RFR3	SWU1 SDS2 SBI2 SKS1 SCD1 (950)	CFR2	RFR3
Level 3	SWU2 SDS2 SBI2 SKS2 SCD2 (1,100)	CFR2	RFR4	SWU2 SDS2 SFI1 SKS2 SCD2 (1,200)	CFR2	RFR4

WEEK 2

This week's goal: Build momentum by completing all scheduled workouts as prescribed.

	Tuesday	Wednesday	Thursday	Friday	Saturday	Sunday
Level 1	SWU1 SDS1 SBI2 SKS1 SCD1 (900)	CFR2	RFR3	SWU1 SDS1 SBI2 SKS1 SCD1 (900)	CFR2 + TRR	RFR3
Level 2	SWU1 SDS2 SBI3 SKS1 SCD1 (1,050)	CFR2	RFR4	SWU1 SDS2 SFI1A SKS1 SCD1 (1,050)	CFR2 + TRR	RFR4
Level 3	SWU2 SDS2 SBI3 SKS2 SCD2 (1,200)	CFR3	RFR4	SWU2 SDS2 SFI4A SKS2 SCD2 (1,400)	CFR3 + TRR	RFR5

QUICK TIP:

Getting ideas and feedback from other triathletes can be quite helpful for questions that arise as you train. Online triathlon chat forums are good places to get such information. Find *Triathlete* magazine's message boards at www.triathletemag.com. Also, Active.com has a lively triathlon message board (www.active.com) that I happen to moderate.

WEEK 3

This week's goal: Stay at the appropriate intensity levels throughout each workout. Resist the temptation to go harder—there will be plenty of that in the coming weeks!

	Tuesday	Wednesday	Thursday	Friday	Saturday	Sunday
Level 1	SWU1 SDS1 SBI3 SKS1 SCD1 (1,000)	CFR3	RFR4	SWU1 SDS1 SFI1 SKS1 SCD1 (1,000)	CFR3	RFR4
Level 2	SWU1 SDS2 SBI4 SKS1 SCD1 (1,150)	CFR3	RFR4	SWU1 SDS2 SFI4 SKS1 SCD1 (1,250)	CFR3	RFR5
Level 3	SWU2 SDS2 SBI4 SKS2 SCD2 (1,300)	CFR4	RFR5	SWU2 SDS2 SFI5 SKS2 SCD2 (1,550)	CFR4	RFR6

WEEK 4
(Recovery)

This week's goal: Fully absorb your recent training and finish the week feeling rested and ready for harder training next week.

	Tuesday	Wednesday	Thursday	Friday	Saturday	Sunday
Level 1	SWU1 SDS1 SBI2 SCD1 (800)	CSH1	RFL1	SWU1 SDS1 SFI1A SCD1 (900)	CFR1 + TRR	RFR3
Level 2	SWU1 SDS2 SBI3 SCD1 (950)	CSH2	RFL3	SWU1 SDS2 SFI1A SCD1 (950)	CFR2 + TRR	RFR4
Level 3	SWU2 SDS2 SBI3 SCD2 (1,050)	CSH2	RFL3	SWU2 SDS2 SFI4A SCD2 (1,250)	CFR3 + TRR	RFR5

WEEK 5

This week's goal: Ride and run hard but relaxed in Wednesday's short hill intervals and Thursday's fartlek running intervals.

	Tuesday	Wednesday	Thursday	Friday	Saturday	Sunday
Level 1	SWU1 SDS1 SBI4 SKS1 SCD1 (1,100)	CSH2	RFL2	SWU1 SDS1 SFI1 SSI1 SKS1 SCD1 (1,100)	CFR3	RFR5
Level 2	SWU1 SDS2 SBI5 SKS1 SCD1 (1,250)	CSH3	RFL4	SWU1 SDS2 SFI1 SSI5 SKS1 SCD1 (1,250)	CFR3	RFR6
Level 3	SWU2 SDS2 SBI5 SKS2 SCD2 (1,400)	CSH3	RFL4	SWU2 SDS2 SFI1 SSI5 SKS2 SCD2 (1,400)	CFR4	RFR7

WEEK 6

This week's goal: Do Wednesday's hill climbs at the fastest pace you can sustain through the end of the last interval without slowing down.

	Tuesday	Wednesday	Thursday	Friday	Saturday	Sunday
Level 1	SWU1 SDS1 SBI5 SKS1 SCD1 (1,200)	CSH3	RFL4	SWU1 SDS1 SFI1A SSI5 SKS1 SCD1 (1,200)	CFR3 + TRR	RFR6
Level 2	SWU1 SDS2	CSH4	RFL6	SWU1 SDS2	CFR4 + TRR	RFR7

	Tuesday	Wednesday	Thursday	Friday	Saturday	Sunday
Level 2 (cont.)	SBI6 SKS1 SCD1 (1,350)			SFI2A SSI3 SKS1 SCD1 (1,400)		
Level 3	SWU2 SDS2 SBI6 SKS2 SCD2 (1,500)	CSH5	RFL6	SWU2 SDS2 SFI2A SSI3 SKS2 SCD2 (1,550)	CFR4 + TRR	RFR8

QUICK TIP:

Runners often tense their arms and shoulders at higher speeds and as they become fatigued, which wastes energy. Learn to run with your upper body relaxed, even when you're working your tail off.

Build Phase

In this five-week phase you will continue to develop your endurance with longer weekend workouts while boosting your aerobic capacity and resistance to high-intensity fatigue with workouts at threshold intensity and above.

WEEK 7

This week's goal: Find the right effort level in this week's high-intensity workouts: lactate and threshold intervals in swimming, long hill intervals on the bike, and lactate intervals in running.

	Tuesday	Wednesday	Thursday	Friday	Saturday	Sunday
Level 1	SWU1 SDS1 SBI2 SLI2 SKS1 SCD1 (1,275)	CLH1	RLI1	SWU1 SDS1 STI2 SKS1 SCD1 (1,200)	CFR4	RFR7

	Tuesday	Wednesday	Thursday	Friday	Saturday	Sunday
Level 2	SWU1 SDS2 SBI3 SLI3 SKS1 SCD1 (1,500)	CLH2	RLI1	SWU1 SDS2 STI3 SKS1 SCD1 (1,450)	CFR4	RFR8
Level 3	SWU2 SDS2 SBI4 SLI3 SKS2 SCD2 (1,750)	CLH2	RLI2	SWU2 SDS2 STI3 SKS2 SCD2 (1,600)	CFR5	RFR9

WEEK 8
(Recovery)

This week's goal: Fully absorb your recent training and finish the week feeling rested and ready for harder training next week.

	Tuesday	Wednesday	Thursday	Friday	Saturday	Sunday
Level 1	SWU1 SDS1 SBI1 SLI1 SCD1 (1,000)	CLI1	RLI1	SWU1 SDS1 STI1 SCD1 (900)	CFR3 + TRR	RFR6
Level 2	SWU1 SDS2 SBI2 SLI2 SCD1 (1,225)	CLI1	RLI1	SWU1 SDS2 STI2 SCD1 (1,150)	CFR3 + TRR	RFR7
Level 3	SWU2 SDS2 SBI3 SLI2 SCD2 (1,425)	CLI2	RLI2	SWU2 SDS2 STI2 SCD2 (1,250)	CFR4 + TRR	RFR8

WEEK 9

This week's goal: finish strong in this weekend's longer ride and run.

	Tuesday	Wednesday	Thursday	Friday	Saturday	Sunday
Level 1	SWU1 SDS1 SBI2 SLI3 SKS1 SCD1 (1,350)	CLH2	RLI2	SWU1 SDS1 STI3 SKS1 SCD1 (1,400)	CFR4	RFR8
Level 2	SWU1 SDS2 SBI3 SLI4 SKS1 SCD1 (1,575)	CLH3	RLI3	SWU1 SDS2 STI4 SKS1 SCD1 (1,650)	CFR4	RFR9
Level 3	SWU2 SDS2 SBI4 SLI4 SKS2 SCD2 (1,825)	CLH3	RLI4	SWU2 SDS2 STI4 SKS2 SCD2 (1,800)	CFR5	RLR1

WEEK 10

This week's goal: Dig deep in this week's lactate intervals in all three disciplines.

	Tuesday	Wednesday	Thursday	Friday	Saturday	Sunday
Level 1	SWU1 SDS1 SBI2 SLI3A SKS1 SCD1 (1,350)	CLI3	RLI6	SWU1 SDS1 STI3A SKS1 SCD1 (1,400)	BRW5	RFR5
Level 2	SWU1 SDS2 SBI3	CLI3	RLI6	SWU1 SDS2 STI4A	BRW7	RFR6

	Tuesday	Wednesday	Thursday	Friday	Saturday	Sunday
Level 2 (cont.)	SLI4A SKS1 SCD1 (1,575)			SKS1 SCD1 (1,650)		
Level 3	SWU2 SDS2 SBI4 SLI4A SKS2 SCD2 (1,825)	CLI4	RLI7	SWU2 SDS2 STI4A SKS2 SCD2 (1,800)	BRW8	RFR7

QUICK TIP:

It's a good idea to do some of your workouts in the early morning, even if it's not your preferred time to work out. Due to the nature of our biorhythms, most of us are not able to perform optimally in the early morning, but this is precisely when most triathlons take place. By getting your body a little more accustomed to sunrise exertion you can race better.

WEEK 11

This week's goal: Don't be surprised to find yourself feeling a little flat as this week progresses; just stay within yourself, do the work, and look forward to the coming recovery week.

	Tuesday	Wednesday	Thursday	Friday	Saturday	Sunday
Level 1	SWU1 SDS1 SBI2 SLI3B SKS1 SCD1 (1,350)	CLH3	RLI7	SWU1 SDS1 STI3B SKS1 SCD1 (1,400)	CFR5	RLR1
Level 2	SWU1 SDS2 SBI3	CLH3	RLI7	SWU1 SDS2 STI4B	CFR6	RLR2

	Tuesday	Wednesday	Thursday	Friday	Saturday	Sunday
Level 2 (cont.)	SLI4B SKS1 SCD1 (1,575)			SKS1 SCD1 (1,650)		
Level 3	SWU2 SDS2 SBI4 SLI4B SKS2 SCD2 (1,825)	CLH4	RLI8	SWU2 SDS2 STI4B SKS2 SCD2 (1,800)	CLR1	RLR3

Peak Phase

In this five-week phase, your training gets more race-specific with tempo workouts in cycling and running, longer workouts generally, and bike-run brick workouts (and an optional sprint triathlon in Week 12).

WEEK 12
(Recovery)

This week's goal: Use Sunday's optional sprint triathlon or brick workout as a fitness test and an opportunity to gain experience in running off the bike.

	Tuesday	Wednesday	Thursday	Friday	Saturday	Sunday
Level 1	SWU1 SDS1 SBI1 SLI1 SKS1 SCD1 (1,100)	CTR1	RTR1	SWU1 SDS1 STI2 SKS1 SCD1 (1,200)	CRR1 or CFR2*	Sprint Triathlon or BRW7*
Level 2	SWU1 SDS2 SBI2 SLI2 SKS1 SCD1 (1,325)	CTR2	RTR2	SWU1 SDS2 STI3 SKS1 SCD1 (1,450)	CRR1 or CFR3*	Sprint Triathlon or BRW7*

*If not racing

	Tuesday	Wednesday	Thursday	Friday	Saturday	Sunday
Level 3	SWU2 SDS2 SBI3 SLI2 SKS2 SCD2 (1,575)	CTR3	RTR3	SWU2 SDS2 STI3 SKS2 SCD2 (1,600)	CRR1 or CFR3*	Sprint Triathlon or BRW7*

*If not racing

WEEK 13

This week's goal: Find a good groove at threshold intensity (8–8.5 RPE) in Wednesday's tempo ride and Thursday's tempo run.

	Tuesday	Wednesday	Thursday	Friday	Saturday	Sunday
Level 1	SWU1 SDS1 SBI3 SLI10 SKS1 SCD1 (1,500)	CTR3	RTR2	SWU1 SDS1 STI9 SKS1 SCD1 (1,500)	CFR6	RLR1
Level 2	SWU1 SDS2 SBI3 SLI11 SKS1 SCD1 (1,650)	CTR4	RTR3	SWU1 SDS2 STI8 STI1 SKS1 SCD1 (1,650)	CLR1	RLR2
Level 3	SWU2 SDS2 SBI4 SLI11 SKS2 SCD2 (1,900)	CTR5	RTR4	SWU2 SDS2 STI10 SKS2 SCD2 (2,000)	CLR1	RLR3

WEEK 14

This week's goal: Get accustomed to running off the bike in Sunday's brick workout.

	Tuesday	Wednesday	Thursday	Friday	Saturday	Sunday
Level 1	SWU1 SDS1 SBI3 SLI10A SKS1 SCD1 (1,500)	CTR4	RTR3	SWU1 SDS1 STI9A SKS1 SCD1 (1,500)	BRW7	RFR4
Level 2	SWU1 SDS2 SBI3 SLI11A SKS1 SCD1 (1,650)	CTR5	RTR4	SWU1 SDS2 STI8A STI1A SKS1 SCD1 (1,650)	BRW8	RFR5
Level 3	SWU2 SDS2 SBI4 SLI11A SKS2 SCD2 (1,900)	CTR6	RTR5	SWU2 SDS2 STI10A SKS2 SCD2 (2,000)	BRW9	RFR6

WEEK 15

This week's goal: Build confidence for next week's race as you feel your fitness begin to peak in this week's workouts.

	Tuesday	Wednesday	Thursday	Friday	Saturday	Sunday
Level 1	SWU1 SDS1 SBI3 SLI10B SKS1 SCD1 (1,500)	CTR5	RTR4	SWU1 SDS1 STI9B SKS1 SCD1 (1,500)	CLR1	RLR1
Level 2	SWU1 SDS2	CTR6	RTR5	SWU1 SDS2	CLR1	RLR2

	Tuesday	Wednesday	Thursday	Friday	Saturday	Sunday
Level 2 (cont.)	SBI3 SLI11B SKS1 SCD1 (1,650)			STI8B STI1B SKS1 SCD1 (1,650)		
Level 3	SWU2 SDS2 SBI4 SLI11B SKS2 SCD2 (1,900)	CTR7	RTR6	SWU2 SDS2 STI10B SKS2 SCD2 (2,000)	CLR2	RLR3

QUICK TIP:

Keep a list of everything you need to pack for a triathlon and refer to it before every race. Otherwise it's easy to forget something small but crucial such as sunscreen or your USA Triathlon membership card. You can find the packing list I use on page 164 of *Triathlete Magazine's Complete Triathlon Book*.

WEEK 16
(Taper)

This week's goal: Have a great race on Sunday!

	Tuesday	Wednesday	Thursday	Friday	Saturday	Sunday
Level 1	SWU1 SDS1 SBI1 SLI1 SKS1 SCD1 (1,100)	CTR1	RTR1	SWU1 SDS1 STI1 SCD1 (900)	CRR1	Olympic-Distance Triathlon
Level 2	SWU1 SDS2 SBI2 SLI2	CTR2	RTR2	SWU1 SDS2 STI2 SCD1	CRR1	Olympic-Distance Triathlon

	Tuesday	Wednesday	Thursday	Friday	Saturday	Sunday
Level 2 *(cont.)*	SKS1 SCD1 (1,325)			(1,150)		
Level 3	SWU2 SDS2 SBI3 SLI2 SKS2 SCD2 (1,575)	CTR3	RTR3	SWU2 SDS2 STI2 SCD2 (1,250)	CRR1	Olympic-Distance Triathlon

Chapter 7

OLYMPIC-DISTANCE TRIATHLON TRAINING PLANS
Levels 4–7

*I*f I were a betting man I would bet that the four training plans in this chapter will be among the most popular in this book. Due to their intermediate length—long enough to represent a worthy challenge, yet short enough to be doable on modest training—Olympic-distance triathlons are very popular. And the Olympic-distance triathlon training plans in this chapter are also intermediate: demanding enough to prepare you not just to finish but finish well, yet lean and time efficient.

All four plans are 16 weeks long. The base phase lasts six weeks and the build and peak phases last five weeks apiece. Weeks 4, 8, and 12 are recovery weeks and the final week is a taper week. An optional tune-up sprint triathlon is scheduled at the end of Week 12. If you can't find a sprint triathlon to do at that time, or if you prefer not to do one then, just do the alternative brick workout instead.

In a typical week there are nine scheduled workouts: three swims, three rides, and three runs. In Weeks 2, 4, and 6, a 10-minute transition run follows Saturday's bike ride. In Weeks 8, 10, and 14, a bike-run brick workout replaces Saturday's ride.

Level 4

Choose this plan if you are relatively new to doubling (doing two workouts in one day, as these plans require 3 times a week). It begins with 3,900 yards of swimming, 3 hours of cycling, and 1 hour and 53 minutes of running in Week 1. It peaks with 6,950 yards of swimming, 4 hours and 45 minutes of cycling, and 2 hours and 52 minutes of running in Week 15.

Level 5

In this plan the emphasis is still on time efficiency within the nine-workouts-per-week framework. But the average workout is a little more challenging than in the Level 4 plan, for those who are looking to improve on past performances. The plan begins with 4,400 yards of swimming, 3 hours and 15 minutes of cycling, and 1 hour and 53 minutes of running in Week 1. It peaks with 7,650 yards of swimming, 5 hours and 15 minutes of cycling, and 3 hours and 9 minutes of running in Week 15.

Level 6

If you're chasing age-group prizes but still want to keep a sensible ceiling on your training volume, this plan should be a good fit. It begins with 5,000 yards of swimming, 3 hours and 30 minutes of cycling, and 2 hours and 8 minutes of running in Week 1. It peaks with 8,100 yards of swimming, 5 hours and 30 minutes of cycling, and 3 hours and 16 minutes of running in Week 15.

Level 7

This plan packs a whole lot of specific Olympic-distance training into nine total workouts per week. The plan begins with 5,500 yards of swimming, 4 hours of cycling, and 2 hours and 11 minutes of running in Week 1. It peaks with 8,700 yards of swimming, 5 hours and 45 minutes of cycling, and 3 hours and 23 minutes of running in Week 15.

Quick Reference Guide to Workout Codes for Olympic-Distance Triathlon Training Plans Levels 4–7			
Code Prefix	**Workout Type**	**Brief Description**	**Levels**
BRW	Brick Workout	Bike ride followed by immediate run, both @ moderate aerobic intensity, except "A" suffix = run @ threshold intensity or bike and run @ high aerobic intensity, as indicated	BRW7: 1 hr 15 min/20 min BRW8: 1 hr 15 min/30 min BRW8A: 1 hr 15 min/30 min (run @ threshold) BRW9: 1 hr 30 min/30 min BRW9A: 1 hr 30 min/30 min (run @ threshold) BRW10: 1 hr 30 min/45 min BRW10A: 1 hr 30/45 min (bike and run @ high aerobic)
CFR	Foundation Bike	Steady ride @ moderate aerobic intensity	CFR3: 1 hr CFR4: 1 hr 15 min CFR5: 1 hr 30 min CFR6: 1 hr 45 min

Code Prefix	Workout Type	Brief Description	Levels
CLH	Bike Long Hill Climbs	5-minute climbing intervals @ threshold/VO$_2$ max intensity w/ 3-minute active recoveries; warm up and cool down long enough to reach total time	CLH3: 4 x 5 min (1 hr 10 min total) CLH4: 5 x 5 min (1 hr 15 min) CLH5: 6 x 5 min (1 hr 20 min) CLH6: 7 x 5 min (1 hr 30 min) CLH7: 8 x 5 min (1 hr 35 min)
CLI	Bike Lactate Intervals	3-minute intervals @ VO$_2$ max intensity w/ 3-minute active recoveries; warm up and cool down long enough to reach total time	CLI2: 3 x 3 min (1 hr 10 min total) CLI3: 4 x 3 min (1 hr 15 min) CLI4: 5 x 3 min (1 hr 20 min) CLI5: 6 x 3 min (1 hr 25 min) CLI6: 7 x 3 min (1 hr 30 min) CLI7: 8 x 3 min (1 hr 35 min)
CLR	Long Bike Ride	Steady ride @ moderate aerobic intensity	CLR1: 2 hr CLR2: 2 hr 15 min CLR3: 2 hr 30 min
CPI	Bike Power Intervals	20-second intervals done in a high gear @ speed intensity w/ 2-minute active recoveries; warm up and cool down long enough to reach total time	CPI2: 5 x 20 sec (50 min total) CPI3: 6 x 20 sec (1 hr) CPI4: 7 x 20 sec (1 hr 10 min) CPI5: 8 x 20 sec (1 hr 20 min) CPI6: 9 x 20 sec (1 hr 25 min) CPI7: 10 x 20 sec (1 hr 30 min)
CRR	Recovery Bike	Steady ride @ recovery intensity	CRR1: 20 min CRR4: 1 hr CRR5: 1 hr 15 min
CSH	Bike Short Hill Climbs	1-minute hill climbs @ VO$_2$ max/speed intensity w/ 2-minute active recoveries; warm up and cool down long enough to reach total time	CSH3: 6 x 1 min (55 min total) CSH4: 7 x 1 min (1 hr) CSH5: 8 x 1 min (1 hr 5 min) CSH6: 9 x 1 min (1 hr 10 min CSH7: 10 x 1 min (1 hr 15 min)
CSI	Bike Speed Intervals	1-minute intervals @ speed intensity w/ 2-minute active recoveries; warm up and cool down long enough to reach total time	CSI2: 5 x 1 min (50 min total) CSI3: 6 x 1 min (55 min) CSI4: 7 x 1 min (1 hr) CSI5: 8 x 1 min (1 hr 5 min) CSI6: 9 x 1 min (1 hr 10 min) CSI7: 10 x 1 min (1 hr 15 min) CSI8: 11 x 1 min (1 hr 20 min)

Code Prefix	Workout Type	Brief Description	Levels
CSS	Steady-State Ride	Steady ride @ high aerobic intensity	CSS1: 1 hr 10 min CSS2: 1 hr 15 min CSS3: 1 hr 30 min CSS4: 1 hr 45 min
CTR	Tempo Bike Ride	One or two blocks of riding @ threshold intensity (10-minute active recovery when threshold-intensity riding is divided into two blocks); warm up and cool down long enough to reach total time	CTR3: 22 min (55 min total) CTR4: 2 x 12 min (1 hr) CTR5: 24 min (1 hr 5 min) CTR6: 26 min (1 hr 10 min) CTR7: 2 x 14 min (1 hr 15 min) CTR8: 28 min (1 hr 20 min) CTR9: 30 min (1 hr 25 min) CTR10: 2 x 16 min (1 hr 30 min) CTR11: 32 min (1 hr 35 min)
RFL	Fartlek Run	Foundation run with 30-second bursts @ VO_2 max/speed intensity	RFL2: 8 x 30 sec (35 min total) RFL3: 6 x 30 sec (40 min) RFL4: 8 x 30 sec (35 min) RFL6: 8 x 30 sec (40 min) RFL7: 6 x 30 sec (45 min) RFL8: 8 x 30 sec (45 min) RFL10: 8 x 30 sec (50 min)
RFR	Foundation Run	Steady run @ moderate aerobic intensity	RFR3: 30 min RFR4: 35 min RFR5: 40 min RFR6: 45 min RFR7: 50 min RFR8: 55 min RFR9: 1 hr
RLI	Run Lactate Intervals	30-second–3-minute intervals run @ VO_2 max intensity w/ active recoveries equal in duration to intervals; warm up and cool down long enough to reach total time	RLI2: 14 x 30 sec (34 min total) RLI3: 16 x 30 sec (36 min) RLI4: 18 x 30 sec (38 min) RLI5: 20 x 30 sec (40 min) RLI7: 10 x 1 min (40 min) RLI8: 12 x 1 min (44 min) RLI9: 3 x 3 min (38 min) RLI10: 4 x 3 min (44 min)
RLR	Long Run	Long, steady-pace run @ moderate aerobic intensity	RLR1: 1 hr 5 min RLR2: 1 hr 10 min RLR3: 1 hr 20 min

Code Prefix	Workout Type	Brief Description	Levels
RLR (cont.)			RLR4: 1 hr 30 min RLR5: 1 hr 40 min
RRR	Recovery Run	Short run @ recovery intensity	RRR3: 30 min RRR4: 35 min
RSS	Running Strides	20-second "relaxed sprints" @ speed intensity w/ 40-second active recoveries	RSS1: 2 x 20 sec RSS2: 4 x 20 sec RSS3: 6 x 20 sec RSS4: 8 x 20 sec
RTR	Tempo Run	Steady run @ threshold intensity; warm up and cool down long enough to reach total time	RTR4: 16 min (36 min total) RTR5: 18 min (38 min) RTR6: 20 min (40 min) RTR7: 22 min (42 min) RTR8: 24 min (44 min) RTR9: 26 min (46 min) RTR10: 28 min (48 min)
SBI	Swim Base Intervals	100-yard intervals swum @ moderate aerobic intensity w/ 5-second rest periods or single longer swims @ moderate aerobic intensity	SBI3: 4 x 100 SBI4: 5 x 100 SBI5: 6 x 100 SBI6: 7 x 100 SBI7: 8 x 100 SBI8: 9 x 100 SBI9: 10 x 100 SBI11: 12 x 100 SBI23: 800 SBI24: 1,000 SBI25: 1,200 SBI26: 1,500 SBI27: 1,800 SBI28: 2,000 SBI29: 2,400
SCD	Swim Cool-Down	Easy swim @ recovery intensity	SCD1: 200 SCD2: 250 SCD3: 300 SCD4: 350 SCD5: 400
SDS	Swim Drill Set	25-yard intervals of mixed form drills w/ 10-second rest periods	SDS2: 6 x 25 SDS3: 8 x 25

Code Prefix	Workout Type	Brief Description	Levels
SFI	Swim Fartlek Intervals	100–200-yard intervals with easy/hard or build/descend format (hard = threshold intensity, easy = moderate aerobic intensity) w/ rest periods of 10–20 seconds	SFI1: 4 x 100 (25 easy/25 hard…), 10-sec rest SFI1A: 4 x 100 (25 build/25 descend…), 10-sec rest SFI2: 6 x 100 (25 easy/25 hard…), 10-sec rest SFI2A: 6 x 100 (25 build/25 descend…), 10-sec rest SFI3: 8 x 100 (25 easy/25 hard…), 10-sec rest SFI4: 4 x 150 (50 easy/25 hard…), 15-sec rest SFI4A: 4 x 150 (50 build/25 descend…), 15-sec rest SFI5: 5 x 150 (50 easy/25 hard…), 15-sec rest SFI5A: 5 x 150 (50 build/25 descend…), 15-sec rest SFI6: 6 x 150 (50 easy/25 hard…), 15-sec rest SFI8: 4 x 200 (50 easy/50 hard…), 20-sec rest SFI8A: 4 x 200 (50 build/50 descend…), 20-sec rest
SKS	Swim Kick Set	25-yard intervals kicking only w/ 15-second rest periods	SKS2: 6 x 25 SKS3: 8 x 25
SLI	Swim Lactate Intervals	75–150-yard intervals swum @ VO_2 max intensity with rest periods of 20 seconds to 1 min 15 seconds	SLI3: 6 x 75, 45-sec rest SLI4: 7 x 75, 45-sec rest SLI5: 8 x 75, 45-sec rest SLI5A: 8 x 75, 30-sec rest SLI5B: 8 x 75, 20-sec rest SLI12: 7 x 100, 1-min rest SLI12A: 7 x 100, 45-sec rest SLI12B: 7 x 100, 30-sec rest SLI13: 8 x 100, 1-min rest SLI13A: 8 x 100, 45-sec rest SLI13B: 8 x 100, 30-sec rest SLI16: 6 x 150, 1-min 15-sec rest SLI16A: 6 x 150, 1-min rest SLI16B: 6 x 150, 45-sec rest

Code Prefix	Workout Type	Brief Description	Levels
SSI	Swim Sprint Intervals	25–50-yard intervals swum @ speed intensity w/ 20-second rest periods	SSI1: 4 x 25 SSI2: 5 x 25 SSI3: 6 x 25 SSI5: 8 x 25 SSI10: 4 x 50 SSI12: 6 x 50 SSI14: 8 x 50
STI	Swim Threshold Intervals	200–400-yard intervals swum @ threshold intensity w/ rest periods of 20–45 seconds	STI1: 2 x 200, 45-sec rest STI2: 3 x 200, 45-sec rest STI2A: 3 x 200, 30-sec rest STI2B: 3 x 200, 20-sec rest STI3: 4 x 200, 45-sec rest STI4: 5 x 200, 45-sec rest STI5: 6 x 200, 45-sec rest STI5A: 6 x 200, 30-sec rest STI5B: 6 x 200, 20-sec rest STI6: 7 x 200, 45-sec rest STI6A: 7 x 200, 30-sec rest STI6B: 7 x 200, 20-sec rest STI10: 4 x 300, 1-min rest STI10A: 4 x 300, 45-sec rest STI10B: 4 x 300, 30-sec rest STI11: 5 x 300, 1-min rest STI11A: 5 x 300, 45-sec rest STI11B: 5 x 300, 30-sec rest STI14: 4 x 400, 1-min 15-sec rest STI14A: 4 x 400, 1-min rest STI14B: 4 x 400, 45-sec rest
STT	Swim Time Trial	Designated distance swum @ maximum effort	STT1: 800 STT2: 1,000 STT3: 1,650
SWU	Swim Warm-Up	Easy swim @ recovery intensity	SWU1: 200 SWU2: 250 SWU3: 300 SWU4: 350 SWU5: 400
TRR	Transition Run	10-minute run immediately following bike ride	TRR: 10 min

General Schedule

	Tuesday	Wednesday	Thursday	Friday	Saturday	Sunday
BASE PHASE						
Week 1	Foundation Bike	Swim Base Intervals	Bike Power Intervals	Swim Fartlek + Sprint Intervals	Foundation Bike	Swim Base Intervals
		Foundation Run		Foundation Run + Strides		Foundation Run
Week 2	Foundation Bike	Swim Base Intervals	Bike Power Intervals	Swim Fartlek + Sprint Intervals	Foundation Bike + Trans. Run	Swim Base Intervals
		Foundation Run		Foundation Run + Strides		Foundation Run
Week 3	Foundation Bike	Swim Base Intervals	Bike Power Intervals	Swim Fartlek + Sprint Intervals	L4–6: Foundation Bike	Swim Base Intervals
		Foundation Run		Foundation Run + Strides	L7: Long Bike	Foundation Run
Week 4 (Recovery)	Foundation Bike	Swim Base Intervals	Bike Power Intervals	Swim Fartlek + Sprint Intervals	Foundation Bike + Trans. Run	Swim Base Intervals
		Fartlek Run		Foundation Run + Strides		Foundation Run
Week 5	Foundation Bike	Swim Base Intervals	Bike Power Intervals	Swim Fartlek + Sprint Intervals	L4–6: Foundation Bike	Swim Base Intervals
		Fartlek Run		Foundation Run + Strides	L7: Long Bike	L4–6: Foundation Run L7: Long Run
Week 6	Foundation Bike	Swim Base Intervals	Bike Power Intervals	Swim Fartlek + Speed Intervals	L4–6: Foundation Bike + Trans. Run	Swim Time Trial
		Foundation Run		Foundation Run + Strides	L7: Long Bike + Trans. Run	L4–5: Foundation Run L6–7: Long Run

	Tuesday	Wednesday	Thursday	Friday	Saturday	Sunday
BUILD PHASE Week 7	Bike Long Hills	Swim Lactate Intervals	Bike Speed Intervals	Swim Threshold + Speed Intervals	L4: Foundation Bike L5–7:	Swim Base Intervals
		Run Lactate Intervals		Fartlek Run	Long Bike	Long Run
Week 8 (Recovery)	Bike Lactate Intervals	Swim Lactate Intervals	Bike Speed Intervals	Swim Threshold + Speed Intervals	Brick Workout	Swim Base Intervals
		Run Lactate Intervals		Fartlek Run		Foundation Run
Week 9	Bike Long Hills	Swim Lactate Intervals	Bike Speed Intervals	Swim Threshold + Speed Intervals	L4: Foundation Bike L5–7:	Swim Base Intervals
		Run Lactate Intervals		Fartlek Run	Long Bike	Long Run
Week 10	Bike Lactate Intervals	Swim Lactate Intervals	Bike Speed Intervals	Swim Threshold + Speed Intervals	Brick Workout	Swim Base Intervals
		Run Lactate Intervals		Fartlek Run		Foundation Run
Week 11	Bike Long Hills	Swim Lactate Intervals	Bike Speed Intervals	Swim Threshold + Speed Intervals	Long Bike	Swim Base Intervals
		Run Lactate Intervals		Fartlek Run		Long Run
PEAK PHASE Week 12 (Recovery)	Tempo Bike	Swim Lactate Intervals	Recovery Bike	Swim Threshold + Speed Intervals	Recovery Bike or Foundation Bike	Sprint Triathlon or Brick Workout
		Tempo Run		High Aerobic Run		Sprint Triathlon or Swim Time Trial

	Tuesday	Wednesday	Thursday	Friday	Saturday	Sunday
Week 13	Tempo Bike	Swim Lactate Intervals	Steady-State Bike	Swim Threshold + Speed Intervals	Long Bike	Swim Base Intervals
		Tempo Run		Foundation Run		Long Run
Week 14	Tempo Bike	Swim Lactate Intervals	Steady-State Bike	Swim Threshold + Speed Intervals	Brick Workout	Swim Time Trial
		Tempo Run		Foundation Run		Foundation Run
Week 15	Tempo Bike	Swim Lactate Intervals	Steady-State Bike	Swim Threshold + Speed Intervals	Long Bike	Swim Base Intervals
		Tempo Run		Foundation Run		Long Run
Week 16	Tempo Bike	Swim Lactate Intervals	Foundation Bike	L4–5: Swim Threshold Intervals L6–7: Swim Threshold + Speed Intervals	Recovery Bike	Olympic-Distance Triathlon
		Tempo Run		Recovery Run		

Week-by-Week Schedule

Base Phase

In this six-week phase you will gradually build aerobic capacity and endurance with plenty of moderate aerobic-intensity swimming, cycling, and running. You also begin to work on power and efficiency with cycling power intervals, running strides, and swimming sprint sets.

WEEK 1

This week's goal: Get accustomed to your new workout schedule.

	Tuesday	Wednesday	Thursday	Friday	Saturday	Sunday
Level 4	CFR3	SWU2 SDS2 SBI3 SKS2 SCD2 (1,200)	CPI3	SWU2 SDS2 SFI1 SSI10 SKS2 SCD2 (1,400)	CFR3	SWU2 SBI23 SCD2 (1,300)
		RFR4		RFR4 + RSS1		RFR5
Level 5	CFR3	SWU3 SDS3 SBI3 SKS3 SCD3 (1,400)	CPI3	SWU3 SDS3 SFI1 SSI10 SKS3 SCD3 (1,600)	CFR4	SWU3 SBI23 SCD3 (1,400)
		RFR4		RFR4 + RSS1		RFR5
Level 6	CFR3	SWU3 SDS3 SBI5 SKS3 SCD3 (1,600)	CPI4	SWU3 SDS3 SFI2 SSI10 SKS3 SCD3 (1,800)	CFR4	SWU3 SBI24 SCD3 (1,600)
		RFR5		RFR5 + RSS1		RFR6
Level 7	CFR4	SWU3 SDS3 SBI7 SKS3 SCD3 (1,800)	CPI4	SWU3 SDS3 SFI3 SSI10 SKS3 SCD3 (2,000)	CFR5	SWU4 SBI24 SCD4 (1,700)
		RFR5		RFR5 + RSS2		RFR6

WEEK 2

This week's goal: Gather momentum by completing all scheduled workouts as prescribed.

	Tuesday	Wednesday	Thursday	Friday	Saturday	Sunday
Level 4	CFR4	SWU2 SDS2 SBI4 SKS2 SCD2 (1,300)	CPI3	SWU2 SDS2 SFI1A SSI12 SKS2 SCD2 (1,500)	CFR4 + TRR	SWU2 SBI24 SCD2 (1,500)
		RFR5		RFR5 + RSS2		RFR6
Level 5	CFR4	SWU3 SDS3 SBI4 SKS3 SCD3 (1,500)	CPI4	SWU3 SDS3 SFI1A SSI12 SKS3 SCD3 (1,700)	CFR5 + TRR	SWU3 SBI24 SCD3 (1,600)
		RFR5		RFR5 + RSS2		RFR7
Level 6	CFR4	SWU3 SDS3 SBI6 SKS3 SCD3 (1,700)	CPI4	SWU3 SDS3 SFI2A SSI12 SKS3 SCD3 (1,900)	CFR5 + TRR	SWU3 SBI25 SCD3 (1,800)
		RFR5		RFR5 + RSS2		RFR7
Level 7	CFR5	SWU3 SDS3 SBI8 SKS3 SCD3 (1,900)	CPI4	SWU3 SDS3 SFI5A SSI12 SKS3 SCD3 (2,050)	CFR6 + TRR	SWU2 SBI26 SCD2 (2,000)
		RFR6		RFR6 + RSS2		RFR8

QUICK TIP:

If you're not able to fix a flat tire on your bike in less than two minutes, practice this important skill outside the context of your cycling workouts. Time yourself while changing and inflating your inner tube several times, aiming to get faster with each repetition. You'll be glad you made the effort if you ever suffer a flat in a race.

WEEK 3

This week's goal: Pace yourself evenly through the longer swim, bike, and run workouts on the weekend.

	Tuesday	Wednesday	Thursday	Friday	Saturday	Sunday
Level 4	CFR5	SWU2 SDS2 SBI5 SKS2 SCD2 (1,400)	CPI4	SWU2 SDS2 SFI5 SSI10 SKS2 SCD2 (1,750)	CFR5	SWU3 SBI24 SCD3 (1,600)
		RFR5		RFR5 + RSS3		RFR7
Level 5	CFR5	SWU3 SDS3 SBI5 SKS3 SCD3 (1,600)	CPI4	SWU3 SDS3 SFI5 SSI10 SKS3 SCD3 (1,950)	CFR5	SWU3 SBI25 SCD3 (1,800)
		RFR5		RFR5 + RSS3		RFR8
Level 6	CFR5	SWU3 SDS3 SBI7 SKS3 SCD3 (1,800)	CPI4	SWU3 SDS3 SFI6 SSI10 SKS3 SCD3 (2,100)	CFR6	SWU4 SBI25 SCD4 (1,900)
		RFR6		RFR6 + RSS3		RFR9

	Tuesday	Wednesday	Thursday	Friday	Saturday	Sunday
Level 7	CFR5	SWU3 SDS3 SBI9 SKS3 SCD3 (2,000)	CPI5	SWU3 SDS3 SFI6 SSI12 SKS3 SCD3 (2,200)	CLR1	SWU3 SBI26 SCD3 (2,100)
		RFR7		RFR7 + RSS3		RFR9

WEEK 4
(Recovery)

This week's goal: Fully absorb your recent training and finish the week feeling rested and ready to return to harder training next week.

	Tuesday	Wednesday	Thursday	Friday	Saturday	Sunday
Level 4	CSH3	SWU2 SDS2 SBI4 SCD2 (1,150)	CPI2	SWU2 SDS2 SFI1A SSI2 SCD2 (1,175)	CFR4 + TRR	SWU2 SBI23 SCD2 (1,300)
		RFR5		RFR4 + RSS1		RFR6
Level 5	CSH3	SWU3 SDS3 SBI4 SCD3 (1,300)	CPI2	SWU3 SDS3 SFI1A SSI2 SCD3 (1,325)	CFR5 + TRR	SWU3 SBI23 SCD3 (1,400)
		RFR5		RFR4 + RSS2		RFR7
Level 6	CSH4	SWU3 SDS3 SBI6 SCD3 (1,500)	CPI3	SWU3 SDS3 SFI2A SSI2 SCD3 (1,525)	CFR5 + TRR	SWU3 SBI24 SCD3 (1,600)
		RFR6		RFR5 + RSS2		RFR7

	Tuesday	Wednesday	Thursday	Friday	Saturday	Sunday
Level 7	CSH4	SWU3 SDS3 SBI8 SCD3 (1,700)	CPI3	SWU3 SDS3 SFI5A SSI5 SCD3 (1,750)	CFR6 + TRR	SWU4 SBI24 SCD4 (1,700)
		RFR6		RFR5 + RSS3		RFR8

WEEK 5

This week's goal: Do Tuesday's short hill climbs at the fastest pace you can maintain through the end of the last one without slowing down.

	Tuesday	Wednesday	Thursday	Friday	Saturday	Sunday
Level 4	CSH4	SWU2 SDS2 SBI6 SKS2 SCD2 (1,500)	CPI4	SWU2 SDS2 SFI4 SSI10 SKS2 SCD2 (1,600)	CFR5	SWU3 SBI24 SCD3 (1,600)
		RFR6		RFR5 + RSS3		RFR8
Level 5	CSH4	SWU3 SDS3 SBI6 SKS3 SCD3 (1,700)	CPI5	SWU3 SDS3 SFI4 SSI10 SKS3 SCD3 (1,800)	CFR5	SWU3 SBI25 SCD3 (1,800)
		RFR6		RFR5 + RSS4		RFR9
Level 6	CSH5	SWU3 SDS3 SBI8 SKS3 SCD3 (1,900)	CPI5	SWU3 SDS3 SFI8 SSI10 SKS3 SCD3 (2,000)	CFR6	SWU4 SBI25 SCD4 (1,900)
		RFR7		RFR6 + RSS4		RFR9

131

	Tuesday	Wednesday	Thursday	Friday	Saturday	Sunday
Level 7	CSH6	SWU3 SDS3 SBI9 SKS3 SCD3 (2,000)	CPI6	SWU3 SDS3 SFI8 SSI12 SKS3 SCD3 (2,100)	CLR1	SWU3 SBI26 SCD3 (2,100)
		RFR8		RFR7 + RSS4		RLR1

WEEK 6

This week's goal: Go all out in Sunday's swim time trial for a good assessment of your current swimming performance level.

	Tuesday	Wednesday	Thursday	Friday	Saturday	Sunday
Level 4	CSH6	SWU2 SDS2 SBI7 SKS2 SCD2 (1,600)	CPI5	SWU2 SDS2 SFI4A SSI12 SKS2 SCD2 (1,700)	CFR5 + TRR	SWU5 STT1 SCD5 (1,600)
		RFR8		RFR5 + RSS4		RFR9
Level 5	CSH6	SWU3 SDS3 SBI7 SKS3 SCD3 (1,800)	CPI6	SWU3 SDS3 SFI4A SSI12 SKS3 SCD3 (1,900)	CFR6 + TRR	SWU5 STT1 SCD5 (1,600)
		RFR8		RFR6 + RSS4		RFR9
Level 6	CSH7	SWU3 SDS3 SBI9 SKS3 SCD3 (2,000)	CPI6	SWU3 SDS3 SFI8A SSI12 SKS3 SCD3 (2,100)	CFR6 + TRR	SWU5 STT1 SCD5 (1,600)
		RFR8		RFR6 + RSS4		RLR1

	Tuesday	Wednesday	Thursday	Friday	Saturday	Sunday
Level 7	CSH7	SWU3 SDS3 SBI11 SKS3 SCD3 (2,200)	CPI7	SWU3 SDS3 SFI8A SSI14 SKS3 SCD3 (2,200)	CLR1 + TRR	SWU5 STT1 SCD5 (1,600)
		RFR10		RFR7 + RSS4		RLR2

QUICK TIP:

Overstriding (i.e., landing heel first) is one of the most common technique flaws in running. To correct this flaw, tilt your entire body slightly forward as you run. This will naturally encourage you to shorten your stride so your foot lands flat underneath your chin.

Build Phase

In this five-week phase your training focus turns toward workouts and sets at threshold intensity and above. Key workouts include long hill climbs and speed intervals in cycling, fartlek runs, and threshold intervals in swimming. At this same time, your weekend endurance workouts continue to get longer to push your endurance continually upward.

WEEK 7

This week's goal: Get a feel for the appropriate pace in this week's new workouts: long hill climbs and speed intervals on the bike and Friday's swim threshold intervals and fartlek run.

	Tuesday	Wednesday	Thursday	Friday	Saturday	Sunday
Level 4	CLH3	SWU2 SDS2 SBI5 SLI4 SKS2 SCD2 (1,925)	CSI3	SWU2 SDS2 STI4 SSI1 SKS2 SCD2 (1,900)	CFR6	SWU3 SBI25 SCD3 (1,800)
		RLI2		RFL3		RLR1

ESSENTIAL WEEK-BY-WEEK TRAINING GUIDE

	Tuesday	Wednesday	Thursday	Friday	Saturday	Sunday
Level 5	CLH4	SWU3 SDS3 SBI5 SLI4 SKS3 SCD3 (2,125)	CSI4	SWU3 SDS3 STI4 SSI1 SKS3 SCD3 (2,100)	CLR1	SWU3 SBI26 SCD3 (2,100)
		RLI3		RFL5		RLR1
Level 6	CLH4	SWU3 SDS3 SBI7 SLI4 SKS3 SCD3 (2,325)	CSI5	SWU3 SDS3 STI5 SSI1 SKS3 SCD3 (2,300)	CLR1	SWU4 SBI26 SCD4 (2,200)
		RLI3		RFL6		RLR2
Level 7	CLH5	SWU3 SDS3 SBI8 SLI5 SKS3 SCD3 (2,500)	CSI6	SWU3 SDS3 STI6 SSI1 SKS3 SCD3 (2,500)	CLR2	SWU4 SBI27 SCD4 (2,500)
		RLI4		RFL8		RLR2

WEEK 8
(Recovery)

This week's goal: Fully absorb your recent training and finish the week feeling rested and ready to return to harder training next week.

	Tuesday	Wednesday	Thursday	Friday	Saturday	Sunday
Level 4	CLI2	SWU2 SDS2 SBI4 SLI3 SCD2 (1,600)	CSI2	SWU2 SDS2 STI3 SSI1 SCD2 (1,550)	BRW7	SWU3 SBI23 SCD3 (1,400)
		RLI2		RFL2		RFR3

	Tuesday	Wednesday	Thursday	Friday	Saturday	Sunday
Level 5	CLI3	SWU3 SDS3 SBI4 SLI3 SCD3 (1,750)	CSI2	SWU3 SDS3 STI3 SSI1 SCD3 (1,700)	BRW8	SWU3 SBI24 SCD3 (1,600)
		RLI3		RFL4		RFR4
Level 6	CLI3	SWU3 SDS3 SBI6 SLI3 SCD3 (1,950)	CSI3	SWU3 SDS3 STI4 SSI1 SCD3 (1,900)	BRW8	SWU3 SBI25 SCD3 (1,800)
		RLI3		RFL4		RFR5
Level 7	CLI4	SWU3 SDS3 SBI7 SLI5 SCD3 (2,200)	CSI4	SWU3 SDS3 STI5 SSI1 SCD3 (2,100)	BRW9	SWU2 SBI26 SCD2 (2,000)
		RLI4		RFL7		RFR6

WEEK 9

This week's goal: Push yourself a little harder in your high-intensity workouts this week.

	Tuesday	Wednesday	Thursday	Friday	Saturday	Sunday
Level 4	CLH4	SWU2 SDS2 SBI5 SLI5 SKS2 SCD2 (2,000)	CSI3	SWU2 SDS2 STI5 SSI1 SKS2 SCD2 (2,100)	CFR6	SWU3 SBI26 SCD3 (2,100)
		RLI3		RFL3		RLR2
Level 5	CLH4	SWU3 SDS3 SBI5 SLI5	CSI4	SWU3 SDS3 STI5 SSI1	CLR1	SWU4 SBI26 SCD4 (2,200)

	Tuesday	Wednesday	Thursday	Friday	Saturday	Sunday
Level 5 (cont.)		SKS3 SCD3 (2,200)		SKS3 SCD3 (2,300)		
		RLI4		RFL5		RLR2
Level 6	CLH5	SWU3 SDS3 SBI6 SLI12 SKS3 SCD3 (2,400)	CSI5	SWU3 SDS3 STI6 SSI1 SKS3 SCD3 (2,500)	CLR1	SWU3 SBI27 SCD3 (2,400)
		RLI4		RFL5		RLR3
Level 7	CLH6	SWU3 SDS3 SBI7 SLI13 SKS3 SCD3 (2,600)	CSI6	SWU3 SDS3 STI6 SSI5 SKS3 SCD3 (2,600)	CLR2	SWU3 SBI28 SCD3 (2,600)
		RLI5		RFL8		RLR3

WEEK 10

This week's goal: Aim for a better result in this Sunday's swim time trial than you achieved in the previous one.

	Tuesday	Wednesday	Thursday	Friday	Saturday	Sunday
Level 4	CLI5	SWU2 SDS2 SBI5 SLI5A SKS2 SCD2 (2,000)	CSI4	SWU2 SDS2 STI5A SSI1 SKS2 SCD2 (2,100)	BRW8	SWU3 STT2 SCD3 (1,600)
		RLI7		RFL6		RFR4
Level 5	CLI5	SWU3 SDS3 SBI5 SLI5A SKS3 SCD3 (2,200)	CSI5	SWU3 SDS3 STI5A SSI1 SKS3 SCD3 (2,300)	BRW9	SWU4 STT2 SCD4 (1,700)
		RLI7		RFL6		RFR5

	Tuesday	Wednesday	Thursday	Friday	Saturday	Sunday
Level 6	CLI6	SWU3 SDS3 SBI6 SLI12A SKS3 SCD3 (2,400)	CSI6	SWU3 SDS3 STI6A SSI1 SKS3 SCD3 (2,500)	BRW9	SWU5 STT2 SCD5 (1,800)
		RLI8		RFL8		RFR6
Level 7	CLI7	SWU3 SDS3 SBI7 SLI13A SKS3 SCD3 (2,600)	CSI7	SWU3 SDS3 STI6A SSI5 SKS3 SCD3 (2,600)	BRW10	SWU5 STT2 SCD5 (1,800)
		RLI8		RFL8		RFR7

QUICK TIP:

Try to consume some carbohydrates, protein, and fluids within an hour of completing each workout. Research has shown that muscle recovery is much faster and subsequent workout performance is much better in athletes who do. If you can't eat a full meal within an hour of working out, use a performance recovery drink such as Endurox R4.

Week 11

This week's goal: Finish strong in Sunday's long endurance workouts (swim and run).

	Tuesday	Wednesday	Thursday	Friday	Saturday	Sunday
Level 4	CLH4	SWU2 SDS2 SBI5 SLI5B SKS2 SCD2 (2,000)	CSI5	SWU2 SDS2 STI5B SSI1 SKS2 SCD2 (2,100)	CLR1	SWU2 SBI27 SCD2 (2,300)
		RLI8		RFL8		RLR3

	Tuesday	Wednesday	Thursday	Friday	Saturday	Sunday
Level 5	CLH5	SWU3 SDS3 SBI5 SLI5B SKS3 SCD3 (2,200)	CSI6	SWU3 SDS3 STI5B SSI1 SKS3 SCD3 (2,300)	CLR2	SWU2 SBI28 SCD2 (2,500)
		RLI9		RFL8		RLR3
Level 6	CLH6	SWU3 SDS3 SBI6 SLI12B SKS3 SCD3 (2,400)	CSI7	SWU3 SDS3 STI6B SSI1 SKS3 SCD3 (2,500)	CLR2	SWU4 SBI28 SCD4 (2,700)
		RLI9		RFL10		RLR4
Level 7	CLH7	SWU3 SDS3 SBI7 SLI13B SKS3 SCD3 (2,600)	CSI8	SWU3 SDS3 STI6B SSI5 SKS3 SCD3 (2,600)	CLR3	SWU2 SBI29 SCD2 (2,900)
		RLI10		RFL10		RLR4

Peak Phase

You're in the final stretch. The first week of this five-week phase is a recovery week ending with either an optional sprint triathlon tune-up race or a brick workout. It is followed by three weeks of very challenging training that emphasizes threshold intensity work and longer endurance workouts on the weekends. The final week is a taper week.

WEEK 12
(Recovery)

This week's goal: Fully absorb your recent training and have a solid sprint triathlon performance on Sunday, if you have the opportunity.

	Tuesday	Wednesday	Thursday	Friday	Saturday	Sunday
Level 4	CTR3	SWU2 SDS2 SBI4 SLI3 SCD2 (1,600)	CRR4	SWU2 SDS2 STI4 SSI1 SCD2 (1,750)	CRR1 or CFR4*	Race or SWU3 SBI26 SCD3 (2,100)*
		RTR4		RFR5		BRW9*
Level 5	CTR4	SWU3 SDS3 SBI4 SLI3 SCD3 (1,750)	CRR4	SWU3 SDS3 STI4 SSI1 SCD3 (1,900)	CRR1 or CFR4*	Sprint Triathlon or SWU4 SBI26 SCD4 (2,200)*
		RTR4		RFR5		BRW9*
Level 6	CTR5	SWU3 SDS3 SBI5 SLI4 SCD3 (1,925)	CRR5	SWU3 SDS3 STI5 SSI1 SCD3 (2,100)	CRR1 or CFR4*	Sprint Triathlon or SWU3 SBI27 SCD3 (2,400)*
		RTR5		RFR6		BRW9*
Level 7	CTR6	SWU3 SDS3 SBI6 SLI5 SCD3 (2,100)	CRR5	SWU3 SDS3 STI5 SSI5 SCD3 (2,200)	CRR1 or CFR5*	Sprint Triathlon or SWU3 SBI28 SCD3 (2,600)*
		RTR6		RFR6		BRW9*

*If not racing

WEEK 13

This week's goal: Find a groove at threshold intensity in Tuesday's tempo ride and Wednesday's tempo run.

	Tuesday	Wednesday	Thursday	Friday	Saturday	Sunday
Level 4	CTR6	SWU2 SDS2 SBI5 SLI12 SKS2 SCD2 (2,100)	CSS1	SWU2 SDS2 STI10 SSI5 SKS2 SCD2 (2,200)	CLR2	SWU3 SBI27 SCD3 (2,400)
		RTR5		RFR7		RLR3
Level 5	CTR7	SWU3 SDS3 SBI5 SLI12 SKS3 SCD3 (2,300)	CSS2	SWU3 SDS3 STI10 SSI5 SKS3 SCD3 (2,400)	CLR2	SWU3 SBI28 SCD3 (2,600)
		RTR6		RFR7		RLR4
Level 6	CTR8	SWU3 SDS3 SBI6 SLI13 SKS3 SCD3 (2,500)	CSS2	SWU3 SDS3 STI11 SSI5 SKS3 SCD3 (2,700)	CLR3	SWU1 SBI29 SCD1 (2,800)
		RTR7		RFR7		RLR4
Level 7	CTR9	SWU3 SDS3 SBI7 SLI16 SKS3 SCD3 (2,700)	CSS3	SWU3 SDS3 STI14 SSI5 SKS3 SCD3 (2,800)	CLR3	SWU3 SBI29 SCD3 (3,000)
		RTR8		RFR7		RLR5

WEEK 14

This week's goal: Try to match your swim split times from last week's lactate and threshold swim sets in this week's sets, despite the shorter rest intervals.

	Tuesday	Wednesday	Thursday	Friday	Saturday	Sunday
Level 4	CTR7	SWU2 SDS2 SBI5 SLI12A SKS2 SCD2 (2,100)	CSS2	SWU2 SDS2 STI10A SSI5A SKS2 SCD2 (2,200)	BRW8A	SWU2 STT3 SCD2 (2,150)
		RTR6		RFR7		RFR5
Level 5	CTR8	SWU3 SDS3 SBI5 SLI12A SKS3 SCD3 (2,300)	CSS2	SWU3 SDS3 STI10A SSI5A SKS3 SCD3 (2,400)	BRW9A	SWU2 STT3 SCD2 (2,150)
		RTR7		RFR7		RFR6
Level 6	CTR9	SWU3 SDS3 SBI6 SLI13A SKS3 SCD3 (2,500)	CSS3	SWU3 SDS3 STI11A SSI5A SKS3 SCD3 (2,700)	BRW9A	SWU3 STT3 SCD3 (2,250)
		RTR8		RFR8		RFR7
Level 7	CTR10	SWU3 SDS3 SBI7 SLI16A SKS3 SCD3 (2,700)	CSS3	SWU3 SDS3 STI14A SSI5A SKS3 SCD3 (2,800)	BRW10A	SWU4 STT3 SCD4 (2,350)
		RTR9		RFR8		RFR8

WEEK 15

This week's goal: Gain confidence for next week's race by feeling your fitness begin to peak in this week's workouts.

	Tuesday	Wednesday	Thursday	Friday	Saturday	Sunday
Level 4	CTR8	SWU2 SDS2 SBI5 SLI12B SKS2 SCD2 (2,100)	CSS2	SWU2 SDS2 STI10B SSI5B SKS2 SCD2 (2,200)	CLR2	SWU2 SBI28 SCD2 (2,500)
		RTR7		RFR7		RLR3
Level 5	CTR9	SWU3 SDS3 SBI5 SLI12B SKS3 SCD3 (2,300)	CSS3	SWU3 SDS3 STI10B SSI5B SKS3 SCD3 (2,400)	CLR2	SWU4 SBI28 SCD4 (2,700)
		RTR8		RFR8		RLR4
Level 6	CTR10	SWU3 SDS3 SBI6 SLI13B SKS3 SCD3 (2,500)	CSS3	SWU3 SDS3 STI11B SSI5B SKS3 SCD3 (2,700)	CLR3	SWU2 SBI29 SCD2 (2,900)
		RTR9		RFR8		RLR5
Level 7	CTR11	SWU3 SDS3 SBI7 SLI16B SKS3 SCD3 (2,700)	CSS4	SWU3 SDS3 STI14B SSI5B SKS3 SCD3 (2,800)	CLR3	SWU4 SBI29 SCD4 (3,100)
		RTR10		RFR9		RLR5

WEEK 16

(Taper)

This week's goal: Have a great race on Sunday!

	Tuesday	Wednesday	Thursday	Friday	Saturday	Sunday
Level 4	CTR4	SWU2 SDS2 SBI4 SLI3 SCD2 (1,600) RTR4	CFR3	SWU2 SDS2 STI1 SCD2 (1,050) RRR3	CRR1	Olympic-Distance Triathlon
Level 5	CTR5	SWU3 SDS3 SBI4 SLI3 SCD3 (1,750) RTR5	CFR3	SWU2 SDS2 STI2 SCD2 (1,250) RRR3	CRR1	Olympic-Distance Triathlon
Level 6	CTR6	SWU3 SDS3 SBI4 SLI4 SCD3 (1,825) RTR6	CFR4	SWU2 SDS2 STI2 SCD2 (1,250) RRR4	CRR1	Olympic-Distance Triathlon
Level 7	CTR7	SWU3 SDS3 SBI5 SLI5 SCD3 (2,000) RTR7	CFR4	SWU2 SDS2 STI2 SCD2 (1,250) RRR4	CRR1	Olympic-Distance Triathlon

QUICK TIP:

If you're feeling a little burned out by training, try shopping therapy—that is, buy yourself a new swimsuit, bike jersey, or something else to use in your next workout. It works for me!

Chapter 8

OLYMPIC-DISTANCE TRIATHLON TRAINING PLANS
Levels 8–10

*T*he Olympic-distance triathlon format is, of course, the official triathlon format of the Olympic games. If you would like to compete in the Olympic Triathlon, I recommend that you follow one of the training plans in this chapter.

I'm pulling your chain, but only a little. The typical Olympic triathlete's training regimen is perhaps slightly tougher than my Level 10 plan for the distance. In other words, the plans in this chapter are very challenging and will suffice to prepare you for the Olympic distance triathlon race performance of your life.

Each of the three plans is 16 weeks long. The base phase lasts six weeks and the build and peak phases last five weeks apiece. Weeks 4, 8, and 12 are recovery weeks and the final week is a taper week. An optional tune-up sprint triathlon is scheduled at the end of Week 12. If you can't find a sprint triathlon to do at that time, or if you prefer not to do one then, just do the alternative brick workout instead.

In a typical week there are 12 scheduled workouts: four swims, four rides, and four runs. An extra 10-minute transition run follows Friday's bike ride in Weeks 2, 4, and 6. In Weeks 8, 10, and 14, Saturday's bike and run workouts are combined into a single bike-run brick workout.

Level 8

This plan will probably be a good fit if you are not accustomed to doing two workouts per day, six days a week, but you feel prepared to do so now. The plan begins with 7,750 yards of swimming, 4 hours and 25 minutes of cycling, and 2 hours and 38 minutes of running in

Week 1. It peaks with 11,900 yards of swimming, 6 hours and 50 minutes of cycling, and 3 hours and 53 minutes of running in Week 15.

Level 9

Choose this plan if you have serious competitive ambitions at the Olympic distance but you still need a little more development time before you reach your personal limit. (In other words, Level 10 can wait a year or two.) The plan begins with 8,550 yards of swimming, 5 hours and 5 minutes of cycling, and 2 hours and 48 minutes of running in Week 1. It peaks with 12,400 yards of swimming, 7 hours and 30 minutes of cycling, and 4 hours and 10 minutes of running in Week 15.

Level 10

This training plan is no joke. Tackle it only if you can look at yourself in a mirror and say, "I'm ready for elite-level triathlon training," without blinking or laughing. The plan begins with 9,100 yards of swimming, 5 hours and 40 minutes of cycling, and 2 hours and 58 minutes of running in Week 1. It peaks with 13,050 yards of swimming, 8 hours and 30 minutes of cycling, and 4 hours and 25 minutes of running in Week 15.

Quick Reference Guide to Workout Codes for Olympic-Distance Triathlon Training Plans Levels 8–10

Code Prefix	Workout Type	Brief Description	Levels
BRW	Brick Workout	Bike ride followed by immediate run, both @ moderate aerobic intensity, except "A" suffix = run @ threshold intensity or bike and run @ high aerobic intensity, as indicated	BRW7: 1 hr 15 min/20 min BRW8: 1 hr 15 min/30 min BRW8A: 1 hr 15 min/30 min (run @ threshold) BRW9: 1 hr 30 min/30 min BRW9A: 1 hr 30 min/30 min (run @ threshold) BRW10: 1 hr 30 min/45 min BRW10A: 1 hr 30/45 min (bike and run @ high aerobic) BRW11: 1 hr 45 min/45 min BRW11A: 1 hr 45 min/45 min (bike and run @ high aerobic)

Code Prefix	Workout Type	Brief Description	Levels
CFR	Foundation Bike	Steady ride @ moderate aerobic intensity	CFR3: 1 hr CFR4: 1 hr 15 min CFR5: 1 hr 30 min CFR6: 1 hr 45 min
CLH	Bike Long Hill Climbs	5–8-minute climbing intervals @ threshold/VO$_2$ max intensity w/ 3-minute active recoveries; warm up and cool down long enough to reach total time	CLH4: 5 x 5 min (1 hr 15 min total) CLH5: 6 x 5 min (1 hr 20 min) CLH6: 7 x 5 min (1 hr 30 min) CLH7: 8 x 5 min (1 hr 35 min) CLH11: 5 x 8 min (2 hr)
CLI	Bike Lactate Intervals	3–5-minute intervals @ VO$_2$ max intensity w/ 3-minute active recoveries; warm up and cool down long enough to reach total time	CLI1: 2 x 3 min (1 hr total) CLI4: 5 x 3 min (1 hr 20 min) CLI5: 6 x 3 min (1 hr 25 min) CLI6: 7 x 3 min (1 hr 30 min) CLI7: 8 x 3 min (1 hr 35 min) CLI11: 5 x 5 min (2 hr)
CLR	Long Bike Ride	Long steady ride @ moderate aerobic intensity	CLR1: 2 hr CLR2: 2 hr 15 min CLR3: 2 hr 30 min CLR4: 2 hr 45 min CLR5: 3 hr CLR6: 3 hr 15 min
CPI	Bike Power Intervals	20-second intervals done in a high gear @ speed intensity w/ 2-minute active recoveries; warm up and cool down long enough to reach total time	CPI4: 7 x 20 sec (1 hr 10 min total) CPI5: 8 x 20 sec (1 hr 20 min) CPI6: 9 x 20 sec (1 hr 25 min) CPI7: 10 x 20 sec (1 hr 30 min) CPI8: 11 x 20 sec (1 hr 35 min)
CRR	Recovery Bike	Steady ride @ recovery intensity	CRR1: 20 min CRR3: 45 min CRR4: 1 hr CRR5: 1 hr 15 min CRR6: 1 hr 30 min
CSH	Bike Short Hill Climbs	1.5-minute hill climbs @ VO$_2$ max/speed intensity w/ 3-minute active recoveries; warm up and cool down long enough to reach total time	CSH10: 4 x 1 min 30 sec (1 hr 30 min total) CSH11: 5 x 1 min 30 sec (1 hr 35 min) CSH12: 6 x 1 min 30 sec (1 hr 40 min) CSH13: 7 x 1 min 30 sec (1 hr 45 min) CSH14: 8 x 1 min 30 sec (1 hr 50 min)

Code Prefix	Workout Type	Brief Description	Levels
CSI	Bike Speed Intervals	1-minute intervals @ speed intensity w/ 2-minute active recoveries or 1.5-minute intervals @ speed intensity w/ 3-minute active recoveries; warm up and cool down long enough to reach total time	CSI9: 12 x 1 min (1 hr 25 min total) CSI10: 4 x 1 min 30 sec (1 hr 30 min) CSI11: 5 x 1 min 30 sec (1 hr 35 min) CSI12: 6 x 1 min 30 sec (1 hr 40 min) CSI13: 7 x 1 min 30 sec (1 hr 45 min) CSI14: 8 x 1 min 30 sec (1 hr 50 min)
CTR	Tempo Bike Ride	One or two blocks of riding @ threshold intensity (10-minute active recovery when threshold-intensity riding is divided into two blocks); warm up and cool down long enough to reach total time	CTR10: 2 x 16 min (1 hr 30 min total) CTR11: 32 min (1 hr 35 min) CTR12: 34 min (1 hr 40 min) CTR13: 2 x 18 min (1 hr 45 min) CTR14: 36 (1 hr 50 min) CTR15: 38 min (1 hr 55 min) CTR16: 2 x 20 min (2 hr)
RFL	Fartlek Run	Foundation run with 30-second bursts @ VO_2 max/speed intensity	RFL5: 6 x 30 sec (40 min total) RFL6: 8 x 30 sec (40 min) RFL7: 6 x 30 sec (45 min) RFL8: 8 x 30 sec (45 min) RFL10: 8 x 30 sec (50 min)
RFR	Foundation Run	Steady run @ moderate aerobic intensity	RFR3: 30 min RFR4: 35 min RFR5: 40 min RFR6: 45 min RFR7: 50 min RFR8: 55 min RFR9: 1 hr
RHR	Run Hill Repeats	30-second uphill running intervals @ speed intensity w/ 1-minute active recoveries or 1-minute uphill running intervals @ speed intensity w/ 2-minute active recoveries; warm up and cool down long enough to reach total time	RHR3: 8 x 30 sec (32 min total) RHR4: 10 x 30 sec (35 min) RHR5: 12 x 30 sec (38 min) RHR7: 6 x 1 min (38 min) RHR8: 8 x 1 min (44 min)
RLI	Run Lactate Intervals	30-second–3-minute intervals run @ VO_2 max intensity w/ active recoveries equal to intervals in duration; warm up	RLI2: 14 x 30 sec (34 min total) RLI3: 16 x 30 sec (36 min) RLI4: 18 x 30 sec (38 min) RLI5: 20 x 30 sec (40 min)

Code Prefix	Workout Type	Brief Description	Levels
RLI (cont.)		and cool down long enough to reach total time	RLI7: 10 x 1 min (40 min) RLI8: 12 x 1 min (44 min) RLI9: 3 x 3 min (38 min) RLI10: 4 x 3 min (44 min) RLI11: 5 x 3 min (50 min) RLI12: 6 x 3 min (56 min)
RLR	Long Run	Long, steady-pace run @ moderate aerobic intensity	RLR1: 1 hr 5 min RLR2: 1 hr 10 min RLR3: 1 hr 20 min RLR4: 1 hr 30 min RLR5: 1 hr 40 min RLR6: 1 hr 50 min RLR7: 2 hr
RRR	Recovery Run	Short run @ recovery intensity	RRR3: 30 min RRR4: 35 min RRR5: 40 min
RSS	Running Strides	20-second "relaxed sprints" @ speed intensity w/ 40-second active recoveries	RSS1: 2 x 20 sec RSS2: 4 x 20 sec RSS3: 6 x 20 sec RSS4: 8 x 20 sec
RTR	Tempo Run	Steady run @ threshold intensity; warm up and cool down long enough to reach total time	RTR7: 22 min (42 min total) RTR8: 24 min (44 min) RTR9: 26 min (46 min) RTR10: 28 min (48 min) RTR11: 30 min (50 min) RTR12: 32 min (52 min) RTR13: 34 min (54 min) RTR14: 36 min (56 min)
SBI	Swim Base Intervals	100-yard intervals swum @ moderate aerobic intensity w/ 5-second rest periods or 200-yard intervals swum @ moderate aerobic intensity w/ 10-second rest periods or 400-yard intervals swum @ moderate aerobic intensity w/ 15-second rest periods or single longer swims @ moderate aerobic intensity	SBI3: 4 x 100 SBI4: 5 x 100 SBI5: 6 x 100 SBI6: 7 x 100 SBI7: 8 x 100 SBI8: 9 x 100 SBI9: 10 x 100 SBI11: 12 x 100 SBI12: 2 x 200 SBI15: 5 x 200 SBI16: 6 x 200

Code Prefix	Workout Type	Brief Description	Levels
SBI (cont.)			SBI17: 7 x 200
			SBI21: 4 x 400
			SBI24: 1,000
			SBI25: 1,200
			SBI26: 1,500
			SBI27: 1,800
			SBI28: 2,000
			SBI29: 2,400
			SBI30: 2,600
			SBI31: 2,800
SCD	Swim Cool-Down	Easy swim @ recovery intensity	SCD3: 300
			SCD4: 350
			SCD5: 400
SDS	Swim Drill Set	25-yard intervals of mixed form drills w/ 10-second rest periods	SDS3: 8 x 25
			SDS4: 10 x 25
			SDS7: 6 x 50
SFI	Swim Fartlek Intervals	150–200-yard intervals with easy/hard or build/descend format (hard = threshold intensity, easy = moderate aerobic intensity) w/ rest periods of 10–20 seconds	SFI3A: 8 x 100 (25 build/25 descend...), 10-sec rest
			SFI5: 5 x 150 (50 easy/25 hard...), 15-sec rest
			SFI5A: 5 x 150 (50 build/25 descend...), 15-sec rest
			SFI6: 6 x 150 (50 easy/25 hard...), 15-sec rest
			SFI6A: 6 x 150 (50 build/25 descend...), 15-sec rest
			SFI8: 4 x 200 (50 easy/50 hard...), 20-sec rest
			SFI8A: 4 x 200 (50 build/50 descend...), 20-sec rest
			SFI9: 5 x 200 (50 easy/50 hard...), 20-sec rest
			SFI9A: 5 x 200 (50 build/50 descend...), 20-sec rest
			SFI10A: 6 x 200 (50 build/50 descend...), 20-sec rest
SKS	Swim Kick Set	25-yard intervals kicking only w/ 15-second rest periods	SKS3: 8 x 25
			SKS4: 10 x 25

Code Prefix	Workout Type	Brief Description	Levels
SLI	Swim Lactate Intervals	75–150-yard intervals swum @ VO$_2$ max intensity with rest periods of 30 seconds to 1 minute 15 seconds	SLI5: 8 x 75, 45-sec rest SLI6: 9 x 75, 45-sec rest SLI7: 10 x 75, 45-sec rest SLI13: 8 x 100, 1-min rest SLI13A: 8 x 100, 45-sec rest SLI13B: 8 x 100, 30-sec rest SLI16: 6 x 150, 1-min 15-sec rest SLI16A: 6 x 150, 1-min rest SLI16B: 6 x 150, 45-sec rest SLI17: 7 x 150, 1-min 15-sec rest SLI17A: 7 x 150, 1-min rest SLI17B: 7 x 150, 45-sec rest
SSI	Swim Sprint Intervals	25–50-yard intervals swum @ speed intensity w/ 20-second rest periods	SSI1: 4 x 25 SSI3: 6 x 25 SSI5: 8 x 25 SSI10: 4 x 50 SSI11: 5 x 50 SSI12: 6 x 50 SSI14: 8 x 50
STI	Swim Threshold Intervals	200–400-yard intervals swum @ threshold intensity w/ rest periods of 20 seconds to 1 minute 15 seconds	STI1: 2 x 200, 45-sec rest STI1A: 2 x 200, 30-sec rest STI1B: 2 x 200, 20-sec rest STI2: 3 x 200, 45-sec rest STI2A: 3 x 200, 30-sec rest STI2B: 3 x 200, 20-sec rest STI3: 4 x 200, 45-sec rest STI3A: 4 x 200, 30-sec rest STI3B: 4 x 200, 20-sec rest STI5: 6 x 200, 45-sec rest STI6: 7 x 200, 45-sec rest STI7: 8 x 200, 1-min rest STI7A: 8 x 200, 45-sec rest STI7B: 8 x 200, 30-sec rest STI13: 3 x 400, 1-min 15-sec rest STI13A: 3 x 400, 1-min rest STI13B: 3 x 400, 45-sec rest
STT	Swim Time Trial	Designated distance swum @ maximum effort	STT1: 800 STT2: 1,000 STT3: 1,650

Code Prefix	Workout Type	Brief Description	Levels
SWU	Swim Warm-Up	Easy swim @ recovery intensity	SWU3: 300 SWU4: 350 SWU5: 400

General Schedule

	Tuesday	Wednesday	Thursday	Friday	Saturday	Sunday
BASE PHASE Week 1	Swim Base + Sprint Intervals	Swim Base Intervals	Foundation Bike	Foundation Bike	Foundation Bike	Swim Base Intervals
	Bike Power Intervals	Foundation Run	Foundation Run	Swim Fartlek + Sprint Intervals	Foundation Run + Drills	Foundation Run
Week 2	Swim Base + Sprint Intervals	Swim Base Intervals	Foundation Bike	Foundation Bike + Trans. Run	L8–9: Foundation Bike L10: Long Bike	Swim Base Intervals
	Bike Power Intervals	Foundation Run	Foundation Run	Swim Fartlek + Sprint Intervals	Foundation Run + Drills	Foundation Run
Week 3	Swim Base + Sprint Intervals	Swim Base Intervals	Foundation Bike	Foundation Bike	L8: Foundation Bike L9–10: Long Bike	Swim Base Intervals
	Bike Power Intervals	Foundation Run	Foundation Run	Swim Fartlek + Sprint Intervals	Foundation Run + Drills	Foundation Run
Week 4	Swim Base + Sprint Intervals	Swim Base Intervals	Foundation Bike	Foundation Bike + Trans. Run	Foundation Bike	Swim Base Intervals
	Bike Power Intervals	Foundation Run	Foundation Run	Swim Fartlek + Sprint Intervals	Recovery Run + Drills	Foundation Run

	Tuesday	Wednesday	Thursday	Friday	Saturday	Sunday
Week 5	Swim Base + Sprint Intervals	Swim Base Intervals	Bike Short Hills	Recovery Bike	L8: Foundation Bike L9–10: Long Bike	Swim Base Intervals
	Bike Speed Intervals	Run Hill Repeats	Fartlek Run	Swim Fartlek + Sprint Intervals	Foundation Run + Strides	Long Run
Week 6	Swim Base + Sprint Intervals	Swim Base Intervals	Bike Short Hills	Recovery Bike + Trans. Run	Long Bike	Swim Time Trial
	Bike Speed Intervals	Run Hill Repeats	Fartlek Run	Swim Fartlek + Sprint Intervals	Foundation Run + Strides	Long Run
Build Phase						
Week 7	Swim Base + Lactate Intervals	Swim Base Intervals	Short Hills Bike	Recovery Bike	Long Bike	Swim Base Intervals
	Bike Speed Intervals	Run Hill Repeats	Fartlek Run	Swim Threshold + Sprint Intervals	Recovery Run + Drills	Long Run
Week 8	Swim Base + Lactate Intervals Bike Speed Intervals	Swim Base Intervals Run Hill Repeats	Recovery Bike Recovery Run	Foundation Bike Swim Threshold + Sprint Intervals	Brick Workout	Swim Base Intervals Foundation Run
Week 9	Swim Base + Lactate Intervals	Swim Base Intervals	Bike Long Hills	Recovery Bike	Long Bike	Swim Base Intervals
	Tempo Bike	Tempo Run	Run Lactate Intervals	Swim Threshold + Sprint Intervals	Recovery Run + Strides	Long Run
Week 10	Swim Base + Lactate Intervals	Swim Base Intervals	Bike Long Hills	Recovery Bike	Brick Workout	Swim Time Trial

	Tuesday	Wednesday	Thursday	Friday	Saturday	Sunday
Week 10 (cont.)	Tempo Bike	Tempo Run	Run Lactate Intervals	Swim Threshold + Sprint Intervals		Foundation Run
Week 11	Swim Base + Lactate Intervals	Swim Base Intervals	Bike Long Hills	Recovery Bike	Long Bike	Swim Base Intervals
	Tempo Bike	Tempo Run	Run Lactate Intervals	Swim Threshold + Sprint Intervals	Recovery Run + Strides	Long Run
Peak Phase						
Week 12	Swim Base + Lactate Intervals	Swim Base Intervals	Recovery Bike	Recovery Bike	Recovery Bike or Foundation Bike	Sprint Triathlon or Brick Workout + Swim Base Intervals
	Tempo Bike	Tempo Run	Recovery Run	Swim Threshold + Sprint Intervals	Recovery Run	
Week 13	Swim Base + Lactate Intervals	Swim Base Intervals	Bike Lactate Intervals	Recovery Bike	Long Bike	Swim Base Intervals
	Tempo Bike	Tempo Run	Run Lactate Intervals	Swim Threshold + Sprint Intervals	Recovery Run + Strides	Long Run
Week 14	Swim Base + Lactate Intervals	Swim Base Intervals	Bike Lactate Intervals	Recovery Bike	Brick Workout	Swim Time Trial
	Tempo Bike	Tempo Run	Run Lactate Intervals	Swim Threshold + Sprint Intervals		Foundation Run
Week 15	Swim Base + Lactate Intervals	Swim Base Intervals	Bike Lactate Intervals	Recovery Bike	Long Bike	Swim Base Intervals

	Tuesday	Wednesday	Thursday	Friday	Saturday	Sunday
Week 15 (cont.)	Tempo Bike	Tempo Run	Run Lactate Intervals	Swim Threshold + Sprint Intervals	Recovery Run + Strides	Long Run
Week 16	Swim Base + Lactate Intervals	Swim Base Intervals	Bike Lactate Intervals	Swim Threshold + Sprint Intervals	Recovery Bike	Olympic-Distance Triathlon
	Tempo Bike	Tempo Run	Recovery Run + Drills		Run Strides	

Week-by-Week Schedule

Base Phase

In this six-week phase the primary training emphasis is on building aerobic capacity and endurance with swim base intervals and foundation and long runs and rides. You will also build sport-specific strength and power through high-intensity stimuli including cycling power intervals, running strides, and swim sprint intervals.

WEEK 1

This week's goal: Get accustomed to your new workout schedule.

	Tuesday	Wednesday	Thursday	Friday	Saturday	Sunday
Level 8	SWU4 SDS3 SBI7 SSI1 SKS3 SCD4 (2,000)	SWU4 SDS3 SBI9 SCD4 (1,900)	CFR3	CFR3	CFR4	SWU3 SBI25 SCD3 (1,800)
	CPI4	RFR5	RFR5	SWU4 SDS3 SFI5 SSI10 SKS3 SCD4 (2,050)	RFR3 + RSS1	RFR6

	Tuesday	Wednesday	Thursday	Friday	Saturday	Sunday
Level 9	SWU4 SDS4 SBI8 SSI1 SKS4 SCD4 (2,200)	SWU4 SDS4 SBI10 SCD4 (2,050)	CFR3	CFR4	CFR5	SWU2 SBI26 SCD2 (2,000)
	CPI5	RFR5	RFR5	SWU4 SDS4 SFI6 SSI10 SKS4 SCD4 (2,300)	RFR4 + RSS1	RFR7
Level 10	SWU4 SDS4 SBI9 SSI3 SKS4 SCD4 (2,350)	SWU4 SDS4 SBI11 SCD4 (2,150)	CFR4	CFR4	CFR6	SWU4 SBI26 SCD4 (2,200)
	CPI6	RFR5	RFR5	SWU4 SDS4 SFI9 SSI10 SKS4 SCD4 (2,400)	RFR5 + RSS1	RFR8

WEEK 2

This week's goal: Gather momentum by completing all scheduled workouts as prescribed.

	Tuesday	Wednesday	Thursday	Friday	Saturday	Sunday
Level 8	SWU4 SDS3 SBI8 SSI1 SKS3 SCD4 (2,100)	SWU4 SDS3 SBI10 SCD4 (2,000)	CFR4	CFR3 + TRR	CFR5	SWU3 SBI26 SCD3 (2,100)

	Tuesday	Wednesday	Thursday	Friday	Saturday	Sunday
Level 8 (cont.)	CPI5	RFR5	RFR5	SWU4 SDS3 SFI3A SSI12 SKS3 SCD4 (2,200)	RFR3 + RSS2	RFR7
Level 9	SWU4 SDS4 SBI9 SSI1 SKS4 SCD4 (2,300)	SWU4 SDS4 SBI11 SCD4 (2,150)	CFR4 TRR	CFR3 +	CFR6	SWU4 SBI26 SCD4 (2,200)
	CPI6	RFR5	RFR5	SWU4 SDS4 SFI9A SSI10 SKS4 SCD4 (2,400)	RFR4 + RSS2	RFR8
Level 10	SWU4 SDS4 SBI10 SSI3 SKS4 SCD4 (2,450)	SWU4 SDS4 SBI17 SCD4 (2,350)	CFR5	CFR4 + TRR	CLR1	SWU4 SBI27 SCD4 (2,500)
	CPI7	RFR6	RFR6	SWU4 SDS4 SFI10A SSI10 SKS4 SCD4 (2,600)	RFR5 + RSS2	RFR9

WEEK 3

This week's goal: Finish strong in Saturday's long ride.

	Tuesday	Wednesday	Thursday	Friday	Saturday	Sunday
Level 8	SWU4 SSI1 SKS3 SCD4 (2,200)	SWU4 SDS3 SBI11 SCD4 (2,100)	CFR4	CFR4	CFR6	SWU4 SBI26 SCD4 (2,200)
	CPI6	RFR6	RFR6	SWU4 SDS3 SFI6 SSI12 SKS3 SCD4 (2,300)	RFR3 + RSS3	RFR8
Level 9	SWU4 SDS4 SBI10 SSI1 SKS4 SCD4 (2,400)	SWU4 SDS4 SBI17 SCD4 (2,350)	CFR5	CFR4	CLR1	SWU5 SBI26 SCD5 (2,300)
	CPI7	RFR6	RFR6	SWU4 SDS4 SFI6 SSI14 SKS4 SCD4 (2,500)	RFR4 + RSS3	RFR9
Level 10	SWU4 SDS4 SBI10 SSI3 SKS4 SCD4 (2,450)	SWU4 SDS4 SBI21 SCD4 (2,550)	CFR5	CFR5	CLR2	SWU5 SBI27 SCD5 (2,600)
	CPI8	RFR6	RFR6	SWU4 SDS4 SFI9 SSI14 SKS4 SCD4 (2,600)	RFR5 + RSS3	RLR1

> **QUICK TIP:**
>
> Don't automatically push to better your split times from week to week. Focus on doing each workout at the same perceived effort level from week to week and your split times will naturally improve as you gain fitness.

WEEK 4
(Recovery)

This week's goal: Fully absorb your recent training and finish the week feeling rested and ready to return to harder training next week.

	Tuesday	Wednesday	Thursday	Friday	Saturday	Sunday
Level 8	SWU4 SDS3 SBI8 SSI1 SCD4 (1,900)	SWU4 SDS3 SBI9 SCD4 (1,900)	CFR3	CFR3	CFR4	SWU5 SBI24 SCD5 (1,800)
	CPI4	RFR4	RFR4	SWU4 SDS3 SFI5A SSI5 SCD4 (1,850)	RRR2 + RSS1	RFR5
Level 9	SWU4 SDS4 SBI8 SSI1 SCD4 (1,950)	SWU4 SDS4 SBI10 SCD4 (2,050)	CFR3	CFR3	CFR5	SWU5 SBI25 SCD5 (2,000)
	CPI5	RFR4	RFR4	SWU4 SDS4 SFI6A SSI10 SCD4 (2,050)	RRR3 + RSS1	RFR6
Level 10	SWU4 SDS4 SBI9	SWU4 SDS4 SBI11	CFR4	CFR4	CFR6	SWU4 SBI26 SCD4

	Tuesday	Wednesday	Thursday	Friday	Saturday	Sunday
Level 10 (cont.)	SSI3 SCD4 (2,100)	SCD4 (2,150)				(2,200)
	CPI6	RFR4	RFR4	SWU4 SDS4 SFI6A SSI12 SCD4 (2,150)	RRR4 + RSS1	RFR7

WEEK 5

This week's goal: Find the appropriate pace for the high-intensity segments in this week's new workouts—cycling speed intervals (speed intensity) and a fartlek run (VO$_2$ max intensity).

	Tuesday	Wednesday	Thursday	Friday	Saturday	Sunday
Level 8	SWU4 SDS3 SBI8 SSI5 SKS3 SCD4 (2,200)	SWU4 SDS3 SBI11 SCD4 (2,100)	CSH10	CRR4	CFR6	SWU4 SBI26 SCD4 (2,200)
	CSI10	RHR3	RFL5	SWU4 SDS3 SFI8 SSI12 SKS3 SCD4 (2,200)	RFR3 + RSS3	RFR9
Level 9	SWU4 SDS4 SBI10 SSI5 SKS4 SCD4 (2,400)	SWU4 SDS4 SBI17 SCD4 (2,350)	CSH11	CRR5	CLR1	SWU5 SBI26 SCD5 (2,300)
	CSI11	RHR4	RFL5	SWU4 SDS4 SFI6 SSI14	RFR4 + RSS3	RLR1

	Tuesday	Wednesday	Thursday	Friday	Saturday	Sunday
Level 9 (cont.)				SKS4 SCD4 (2,500)		
Level 10	SWU4 SDS4 SBI10 SSI5 SKS4 SCD4 (2,500)	SWU4 SDS4 SBI21 SCD4 (2,550)	CSH12	CRR6	CLR2	SWU5 SBI27 SCD5 (2,600)
	CSI12	RHR5	RFL7	SWU4 SDS4 SFI9 SSI14 SKS4 SCD4 (2,600)	RFR5 + RSS3	RLR2

WEEK 6

This week's goal: Go all out and get a good assessment of your current swimming level in Sunday's swim time trial.

	Tuesday	Wednesday	Thursday	Friday	Saturday	Sunday
Level 8	SWU4 SDS3 SBI11 SSI1 SKS3 SCD4 (2,400)	SWU4 SDS3 SBI6 SBI5 SCD4 (2,200)	CSH11	CRR4	CLR1	SWU5 STT1 SCD5 (1,600)
	CSI11	RHR4	RFL6	SWU4 SDS3 SFI8A SSI14 SKS3 SCD4 (2,300)	RFR3 + RSS3	RLR1
Level 9	SWU4 SDS4 SBI11 SSI3	SWU4 SDS4 SBI21 SCD4	CSH12	CRR5	CLR2	SWU5 STT1 SCD5 (1,600)

		Tuesday	Wednesday	Thursday	Friday	Saturday	Sunday
Level 9 (cont.)		SKS4 SCD4 (2,550)	(2,550)				
		CSI12	RHR5	RFL6	SWU4 SDS4 SFI9A SSI12 SKS4 SCD4 (2,500)	RFR4 + RSS3	RLR2
Level 10		SWU4 SDS4 SBI17 SSI3 SKS4 SCD4 (2,750)	SWU4 SDS4 SBI17 SBI3 SCD4 (2,750)	CSH13	CRR6	CLR3	SWU5 STT1 SCD5 (1,600)
		CSI13	RHR7	RFL8	SWU4 SDS4 SFI10A SSI12 SKS4 SCD4 (2,700)	RFR5 + RSS3	RLR3

QUICK TIP:

When doing a brick workout, take as little time as possible transitioning from the bike segment to the run segment. The whole idea, after all, is to simulate the demands of bike-run transitions in races.

Build Phase

The build phase is five weeks in length. You will continue to build endurance in your long weekend workouts, but the primary training emphasis is the high-intensity workouts during the week, including swim lactate intervals, short hill climbs on the bike, and running hill repetitions.

WEEK 7

This week's goal: Finish strong in Sunday's long run.

	Tuesday	Wednesday	Thursday	Friday	Saturday	Sunday
Level 8	SWU4 SDS3 SBI8 SLI5 SKS3 SCD4 (2,600)	SWU4 SDS7 SBI16 SBI3 SCD4 (2,600)	CSH12	CRR4	CLR2	SWU5 SBI27 SCD5 (2,600)
	CSI12	RHR5	RFL8	SWU4 SDS3 STI6 SSI1 SKS3 SCD4 (2,600)	RRR4 + RSS3	RLR2
Level 9	SWU4 SDS4 SBI8 SLI7 SKS4 SCD4 (2,850)	SWU4 SDS7 SBI16 SBI4 SCD4 (2,700)	CSH13	CRR5	CLR3	SWU4 SBI28 SCD4 (2,800)
	CSI13	RHR7	RFL8	SWU4 SDS4 STI6 SSI3 SKS4 SCD4 (2,750)	RRR5 + RSS3	RLR3
Level 10	SWU4 SDS4 SBI9 SLI7 SKS4 SCD4 (2,950)	SWU4 SDS7 SBI16 SBI6 SCD4 (2,900)	CSH14	CRR6	CLR4	SWU2 SBI29 SCD2 (2,900)

	Tuesday	Wednesday	Thursday	Friday	Saturday	Sunday
Level 10 (cont.)	CSI14	RHR8	RFL10	SWU4 SDS4 STI7 SSI3 SKS4 SCD4 (2,950)	RRR6 + RSS3	RLR4

WEEK 8
(Recovery)

This week's goal: Fully absorb your recent training and finish the week feeling rested and ready to return to harder training next week.

	Tuesday	Wednesday	Thursday	Friday	Saturday	Sunday
Level 8	SWU4 SDS3 SBI7 SLI5 SCD4 (2,300)	SWU4 SDS7 SBI15 SBI3 SCD4 (2,400)	CRR4	CFR3	BRW7	SWU4 SBI26 SCD4 (2,200)
	CSI9	RHR3	RRR4	SWU4 SDS3 STI5 SSI1 SCD4 (2,200)		RFR5
Level 9	SWU4 SDS4 SBI7 SLI6 SCD4 (2,425)	SWU4 SDS7 SBI15 SBI5 SCD4 (2,600)	CRR5	CFR4	BRW8	SWU5 SBI26 SCD5 (2,300)
	CSI10	RHR4	RRR5	SWU4 SDS4 STI5 SSI3 SCD4 (2,300)		RFR6

	Tuesday	Wednesday	Thursday	Friday	Saturday	Sunday
Level 10	SWU4 SDS4 SBI7 SLI7 SCD4 (2,500)	SWU4 SDS7 SBI15 SBI6 SCD4 (2,700)	CRR6	CFR4	BRW9	SWU4 SBI27 SCD4 (2,500)
	CSI11	RHR5	RRR5	SWU4 SDS4 STI6 SSI3 SCD4 (2,500)		RFR7

WEEK 9

This week's goal: Find a groove at threshold intensity in Tuesday's tempo ride and Wednesday's tempo run.

	Tuesday	Wednesday	Thursday	Friday	Saturday	Sunday
Level 8	SWU4 SDS3 SBI7 SLI13 SKS3 SCD4 (2,700)	SWU4 SDS7 SBI16 SBI3 SCD4 (2,600)	CLH4	CRR4	CLR2	SWU4 SBI28 SCD4 (2,700)
	CTR10	RTR8	RLI2	SWU4 SDS3 STI6 SSI5 SKS3 SCD4 (2,700)	RRR4 + RSS3	RLR3
Level 9	SWU4 SDS4 SBI8 SLI13 SKS4 SCD4 (2,900)	SWU4 SDS7 SBI16 SBI5 SCD4 (2,800)	CLH5	CRR5	CLR3	SWU5 SBI28 SCD5 (2,800)

	Tuesday	Wednesday	Thursday	Friday	Saturday	Sunday
Level 9 (cont.)	CTR11	RTR9	RLI3	SWU4 SDS4 STI6 SSI12 SKS4 SCD4 (2,900)	RRR5 + RSS3	RLR4
Level 10	SWU4 SDS4 SBI9 SLI16 SKS4 SCD4 (3,100)	SWU4 SDS7 SBI16 SBI7 SCD4 (3,000)	CLH6	CRR6	CLR4	SWU2 SBI29 SCD2 (2,900)
	CTR12	RTR10	RLI4	SWU4 SDS4 STI7 SSI12 SKS4 SCD4 (3,100)	RRR6 + RSS3	RLR5

WEEK 10

This week's goal: Aim for a better performance in this Sunday's swim time trial than you achieved in the last one.

	Tuesday	Wednesday	Thursday	Friday	Saturday	Sunday
Level 8	SWU4 SDS3 SBI7 SLI13A SKS3 SCD4 (2,700)	SWU4 SDS7 SBI16 SBI4 SCD4 (2,700)	CLH5	CRR4	BRW8	SWU5 STT2 SCD5 (1,800)
	CTR11	RTR9	RLI3	SWU4 SDS3 STI6A SSI5 SKS3 SCD4 (2,700)	RRR4 + RSS3	RFR6

	Tuesday	Wednesday	Thursday	Friday	Saturday	Sunday
Level 9	SWU4 SDS4 SBI8 SLI13A SKS4 SCD4 (2,900)	SWU4 SDS7 SBI16 SBI6 SCD4 (2,900)	CLH6	CRR5	BRW9	SWU5 STT2 SCD5 (1,800)
	CTR12	RTR10	RLI4	SWU4 SDS4 STI6A SSI12 SKS4 SCD4 (2,900)	RRR5 + RSS3	RFR7
Level 10	SWU4 SDS4 SBI9 SLI16A SKS4 SCD4 (3,100)	SWU4 SDS7 SBI16 SBI7 SCD4 (3,000)	CLH7	CRR6	BRW10	SWU5 STT2 SCD5 (1,800)
	CTR13	RTR11	RLI5	SWU4 SDS4 STI7A SSI12 SKS4 SCD4 (3,100)	RRR6 + RSS3	RFR8

QUICK TIP:

Use positive self-talk and verbal cues to get through the tougher portions of workouts. For example, during a tempo run, tell yourself, "Stay relaxed," and repeat the phrase like a mantra over and over. Research by sports psychologists shows that most top athletes use positive self-talk and verbal cues, and that they are effective.

WEEK 11

This week's goal: Expect to experience accumulating fatigue as this week wears on; just stay within yourself, push through, and look forward to next week—a recovery week!

	Tuesday	Wednesday	Thursday	Friday	Saturday	Sunday
Level 8	SWU4 SDS3 SBI7 SLI13B SKS3 SCD4 (2,700)	SWU4 SDS7 SBI16 SBI4 SCD4 (2,800)	CLH6	CRR4	CLR3	SWU3 SBI29 SCD3 (3,000)
	CTR12	RTR10	RLI6	SWU4 SDS3 STI6B SSI5 SKS3 SCD4 (2,700)	RRR4 + RSS4	RLR4
Level 9	SWU4 SDS4 SBI8 SLI13B SKS4 SCD4 (2,900)	SWU4 SDS7 SBI16 SBI6 SCD4 (2,900)	CLH7	CRR5	CLR4	SWU4 SBI29 SCD4 (3,100)
	CTR13	RTR11	RLI7	SWU4 SDS4 STI6B SSI12 SKS4 SCD4 (2,900)	RRR5 + RSS4	RLR5
Level 10	SWU4 SDS4 SBI9 SLI16B SKS4 SCD4 (3,100)	SWU4 SDS7 SBI16 SBI7 SCD4 (3,000)	CLH11	CRR6	CLR5	SWU4 SBI30 SCD4 (3,300)

	Tuesday	Wednesday	Thursday	Friday	Saturday	Sunday
Level 10 *(cont.)*	CTR14	RTR12	RLI8	SWU4 SDS4 STI7B SSI12 SKS4 SCD4 (3,100)	RRR5 + RSS	RLR6

Peak Phase

In this five-week phase, three weeks of very challenging training are sandwiched between an initial recovery week and a concluding taper week. Top workout priorities are threshold intensity swimming, cycling, and running, brick workouts, and long endurance swims, rides, and runs.

WEEK 12
(Recovery)

This week's goal: Fully absorb your recent training and have a solid sprint triathlon performance on Sunday, if you have the opportunity.

	Tuesday	Wednesday	Thursday	Friday	Saturday	Sunday
Level 8	SWU4 SDS3 SBI6 SLI5 SCD4 (2,200)	SWU4 SDS7 SBI15 SBI3 SCD4 (2,400)	CRR4	CRR3	CRR1 or CFR4*	Sprint Triathlon or SWU4 SBI28 SCD4 (2,700)*
	CTR10	RTR7	RRR4	SWU4 SDS3 STI5 SSI5 SCD4 (2,300)	RRR3*	BRW8A*
Level 9	SWU4 SDS4 SBI6 SLI6 SCD4 (2,325)	SWU4 SDS7 SBI15 SBI5 SCD4 (2,600)	CRR5	CRR3	CRR1 or CFR4*	Sprint Triathlon or SWU5 SBI28 SCD5 (2,800)*

*If not racing

	Tuesday	Wednesday	Thursday	Friday	Saturday	Sunday
Level 9 (cont.)	CTR11	RTR8	RRR5	SWU4 SDS4 STI5 SSI5 SCD4 (2,350)	RRR4*	BRW9A*
Level 10	SWU4 SDS4 SBI6 SLI7 SCD4 (2,400)	SWU4 SDS7 SBI15 SBI6 SCD4 (2,700)	CRR6	CRR3	CRR1 or CFR4*	Sprint Triathlon or SWU2 SBI29 SCD2 (2,900)*
	CTR12	RTR9	RRR6	SWU4 SDS4 STI6 SSI5 SCD4 (2,550)	RRR4*	BRW10A*

*If not racing

WEEK 13

This week's goal: Finish strong in this weekend's long endurance workouts.

	Tuesday	Wednesday	Thursday	Friday	Saturday	Sunday
Level 8	SWU4 SDS3 SBI8 SLI16 SKS3 SCD4 (2,900)	SWU4 SDS7 SBI17 SBI4 SCD4 (2,900)	CLI4	CRR4	CLR4	SWU2 SBI30 SCD2 (3,100)
	CTR12	RTR10	RLI9	SWU4 SDS3 STI13 STI1 SSI5 SKS3 SCD4 (2,900)	RRR4 + RSS3	RLR5

	Tuesday	Wednesday	Thursday	Friday	Saturday	Sunday
Level 9	SWU4 SDS4 SBI9 SLI16 SKS4 SCD4 (3,100)	SWU4 SDS7 SBI17 SBI5 SCD4 (3,000)	CLI5	CRR5	CLR5	SWU3 SBI30 SCD3 (3,200)
	CTR13	RTR11	RLI10	SWU4 SDS3 STI13 STI2 SSI5 SKS3 SCD4 (3,100)	RRR5 + RSS3	RLR6
Level 10	SWU4 SDS4 SBI9 SLI17 SKS4 SCD4 (3,250)	SWU4 SDS7 SBI17 SBI6 SCD4 (3,100)	CLI6	CRR6	CLR6	SWU4 SBI30 SCD4 (3,300)
	CTR14	RTR12	RLI10	SWU4 SDS3 STI13 STI3 SSI5 SKS3 SCD4 (3,300)	RRR6 + RSS3	RLR7

WEEK 14

This week's goal: Build race-specific fitness in Saturday's brick work-out and Sunday's swim time trial.

	Tuesday	Wednesday	Thursday	Friday	Saturday	Sunday
Level 8	SWU4 SDS3 SBI8 SLI16A SKS3 SCD4	SWU4 SDS7 SBI17 SBI5 SCD4 (3,000)	CLI5	CRR4	BRW9A	SWU2 STT3 SCD2 (2,150)

	Tuesday	Wednesday	Thursday	Friday	Saturday	Sunday
Level 8 *(cont.)*	(2,900)					
	CTR13	RTR11	RLI10	SWU4 SDS3 STI13A STI1A SSI5 SKS3 SCD4 (2,900)		RFR6
Level 9	SWU4 SDS4 SBI9 SLI16A SKS4 SCD4 (3,100)	SWU4 SDS7 SBI17 SBI5 SCD4 (3,000)	CLI6	CRR5	BRW10A	SWU3 STT3 SCD3 (2,250)
	CTR14	RTR12	RLI10	SWU4 SDS3 STI13A STI2A SSI5 SKS3 SCD4 (3,100)		RFR7
Level 10	SWU4 SDS4 SBI9 SLI17A SKS4 SCD4 (3,250)	SWU4 SDS7 SBI17 SBI6 SCD4 (3,100)	CLI7	CRR6	BRW11A	SWU4 STT3 SCD4 (2,350)
	CTR15	RTR13	RLI11	SWU4 SDS3 STI13A STI4A SSI5 SKS3 SCD4 (3,300)		RFR8

QUICK TIP:

If you finish a workout feeling particularly sore in a certain area, give yourself a 10-minute ice massage in that area once every hour for the next few hours. This will reduce inflammation and with it the so-called secondary tissue damage that can occur in sore spots between workouts.

WEEK 15

This week's goal: Gain confidence for next weekend's race by feeling your fitness begin to peak in this week's workouts.

	Tuesday	Wednesday	Thursday	Friday	Saturday	Sunday
Level 8	SWU4 SDS3 SBI8 SLI16B SKS3 SCD4 (2,900)	SWU4 SDS7 SBI17 SBI4 SCD4 (2,900)	CLI6	CRR4	CLR3	SWU3 SBI30 SCD3 (3,200)
	CTR14	RTR12	RLI10	SWU4 SDS3 STI13B STI1B SSI5 SKS3 SCD4 (2,900)	RRR4 + RSS2	RLR5
Level 9	SWU4 SDS4 SBI9 SLI16B SKS4 SCD4 (3,100)	SWU4 SDS7 SBI17 SBI5 SCD4 (3,000)	CLI7	CRR5	CLR4	SWU4 SBI30 SCD4 (3,300)
	CTR15	RTR13	RLI11	SWU4 SDS3 STI13B STI2B SSI5 SKS3 SCD4 (3,100)	RRR5 + RSS2	RLR6

	Tuesday	Wednesday	Thursday	Friday	Saturday	Sunday
Level 10	SWU4 SDS4 SBI9 SLI17B SKS4 SCD4 (3,250)	SWU4 SDS7 SBI17 SBI6 SCD4 (3,100)	CLI11	CRR6	CLR5	SWU3 SBI31 SCD3 (3,400)
	CTR16	RTR14	RLI12	SWU4 SDS3 STI13B STI4B SSI5 SKS3 SCD4 (3,300)	RRR6 + RSS2	RLR7

WEEK 16
(Taper)

This week's goal: Have a great race on Sunday!

	Tuesday	Wednesday	Thursday	Friday	Saturday	Sunday
Level 8	SWU4 SDS3 SBI5 SLI5 SKS3 SCD4 (2,300)	SWU4 SDS7 SBI15 SCD4 (2,000)	CLI1	SWU4 STI2 SSI3 SCD4 (1,450)	CRR1 + RSS2	Olympic-Distance Triathlon
	CTR10	RTR8	RRR3 + RSS3			
Level 9	SWU4 SDS4 SBI5 SLI6 SKS4 SCD4 (2,475)	SWU4 SDS7 SBI15 SCD4 (2,000)	CLI1	SWU4 STI2 SSI3 SCD4 (1,450)	CRR1 + RSS2	Olympic-Distance Triathlon
	CTR11	RTR9	RRR3 + RSS3			

ESSENTIAL WEEK-BY-WEEK TRAINING GUIDE

	Tuesday	Wednesday	Thursday	Friday	Saturday	Sunday
Level 10	SWU4 SDS4 SBI6 SLI6 SKS4 SCD4 (2,575)	SWU4 SDS7 SBI15 SCD4 (2,000)	CLI1	SWU4 STI2 SSI3 SCD4 (1,450)	CRR1 + RSS2	Olympic- Distance Triathlon
	CR12	RTR10	RRR3 + RSS3			

Chapter 9
HALF-IRONMAN TRIATHLON TRAINING PLANS
Levels 1–4

Anyone who has completed at least one half-Ironman and at least one Ironman knows that the latter is much more than twice the challenge of the former. That's what makes the half-Ironman distance so great. Although it is long enough to present a worthy challenge, a half-Ironman does not take nearly as much out of you as an Ironman. The preparation is less demanding, the post-race recuperation period swifter, and consequently you can do half-Ironmans more often than you can do Ironmans.

The four half-Ironman training plans in this chapter are suited to first-time half-Ironman participants and to any triathlete who wishes to prepare for a half-Ironman with a schedule of nine workouts per week. Each plan is 20 weeks long. Odd-numbered training weeks include three swims, three rides, and three runs. Weeks 2, 6, and so forth include three swims, two rides, three runs, and a bike-run brick workout. Weeks 4, 8, and so forth include three swims, three rides, two runs, and a bike-run brick workout.

Every fourth week is a recovery week. Optional tune-up triathlons are scheduled in Week 12 (sprint) and Week 16 (Olympic distance). The final 10 days of each plan constitute a tapering period.

Level 1

This plan is for first-time half-Ironman participants who want to do just enough training for a successful finish. It begins with 3,900 yards of swimming, 2 hours and 45 minutes of cycling, and 1 hour and 45 minutes of running in Week 1. It peaks with 6,700 yards of swimming, 5 hours and 20 minutes of cycling, and 3 hours and 7 minutes of running in Week 17.

Level 2

If you can handle the Level 1 plan you can probably handle this plan, which offers a little more than the minimum training needed for a successful half-Ironman finish. It begins with 4,300 yards of swimming, 3 hours and 5 minutes of cycling, and 1 hour and 55 minutes of running in Week 1. It peaks with 7,050 yards of swimming, 5 hours and 55 minutes of cycling, and 3 hours and 19 minutes of running in Week 17.

Level 3

Choose this plan if you are starting with a decent level of triathlon fitness but you still want a training plan with nine workouts per week. It begins with 4,500 yards of swimming, 3 hours and 30 minutes of cycling, and 2 hours of running in Week 1. It peaks with 7,550 yards of swimming, 6 hours and 30 minutes of cycling, and 3 hours and 36 minutes of running in Week 17.

Level 4

This plan will be a good fit for you if your half-Ironman goal is more ambitious than just finishing, yet time efficiency is very important to you in your training. It begins with 4,900 yards of swimming, 3 hours and 55 minutes of cycling, and 2 hours and 15 minutes of running in Week 1. It peaks with 8,000 yards of swimming, 7 hours and 5 minutes of cycling, and 3 hours and 53 minutes of running in Week 17.

Quick Reference Guide to Workout Codes for Half-Ironman Triathlon Training Plans Levels 1–4

Code Prefix	Workout Type	Brief Description	Levels
BRW	Brick Workout	Bike ride followed by immediate run, both @ moderate aerobic intensity	BRW3: 45 min/10 min BRW4: 45 min/15 min BRW5: 1 hr/20 min BRW7: 1 hr 15 min/20 min BRW8: 1 hr 15 min/30 min BRW9: 1 hr 30 min/30 min BRW10: 1 hr 30 min/45 min BRW11: 1 hr 45 min/45 min BRW12: 1 hr 45 min/50 min BRW13: 2 hr/50 min BRW14: 2 hr 15 min/55 min
CFR	Foundation Bike	Steady ride @ moderate aerobic intensity	CFR1: 30 min CFR2: 45 min CFR3: 1 hr CFR4: 1 hr 15 min CFR5: 1 hr 30 min CFR6: 1 hr 45 min CFR7: 2 hr
CLH	Bike Long Hill Climbs	5-minute climbing intervals @ threshold/VO_2 max intensity w/ 3-minute active recoveries; warm up and cool down long enough to reach total time	CLH1: 2 x 5 min (1 hr total) CLH2: 3 x 5 min (1 hr 5 min) CLH3: 4 x 5 min (1 hr 10 min) CLH4: 5 x 5 min (1 hr 15 min) CLH5: 6 x 5 min (1 hr 20 min) CLH6: 7 x 5 min (1 hr 30 min)
CLI	Bike Lactate Intervals	3-minute intervals @ VO_2 max intensity w/ 3-minute active recoveries; warm up and cool down long enough to reach total time	CLI1: 2 x 3 min (1 hr total) CLI2: 3 x 3 min (1 hr 10 min) CLI3: 4 x 3 min (1 hr 15 min) CLI4: 5 x 3 min (1 hr 20 min) CLI5: 6 x 3 min (1 hr 25 min) CLI6: 7 x 3 min (1 hr 30 min)
CLR	Long Bike Ride	Long steady ride @ moderate aerobic intensity	CLR1: 2 hr CLR2: 2 hr 15 min CLR3: 2 hr 30 min CLR4: 2 hr 45 min CLR5: 3 hr CLR6: 3 hr 15 min CLR7: 3 hr 30 min CLR8: 3 hr 45 min

Code Prefix	Workout Type	Brief Description	Levels
CPI	Bike Power Intervals	20-second intervals done in a high gear @ speed intensity w/ 2-minute active recoveries; warm up and cool down long enough to reach total time	CPI1: 4 x 20 sec (45 min total) CPI2: 5 x 20 sec (50 min) CPI3: 6 x 20 sec (1 hr) CPI4: 7 x 20 sec (1 hr 10 min)
CRR	Recovery Bike	Steady ride @ recovery intensity	CRR1: 20 min
CSH	Bike Short Hill Climbs	1-minute hill climbs @ VO_2 max/speed intensity w/ 2-minute active recoveries; warm up and cool down long enough to reach total time	CSH3: 6 x 1 min (55 min total) CSH4: 7 x 1 min (1 hr) CSH5: 8 x 1 min (1 hr 5 min) CSH6: 9 x 1 min (1 hr 10 min) CSH7: 10 x 1 min (1 hr 15 min) CSH8: 11 x 1 min (1 hr 20 min)
CTR	Tempo Bike Ride	One or two blocks of riding @ threshold intensity (10-minute active recovery when threshold-intensity riding is divided into two blocks); warm up and cool down long enough to reach total time	CTR3: 22 min (55 min total) CTR4: 2 x 12 min (1 hr) CTR5: 24 min (1 hr 5 min) CTR6: 26 min (1 hr 10 min) CTR7: 2 x 14 min (1 hr 15 min) CTR8: 28 min (1 hr 20 min) CTR9: 30 min (1 hr 25 min) CTR10: 2 x 16 min (1 hr 30 min)
RFL	Fartlek Run	Foundation run with 30-second bursts @ VO_2 max/speed intensity	RFL1: 6 x 30 sec (30 min total) RFL2: 8 x 30 sec (30 min) RFL3: 6 x 30 sec (35 min) RFL4: 8 x 30 sec (35 min) RFL5: 6 x 30 sec (40 min) RFL6: 8 x 30 sec (40 min) RFL8: 8 x 30 sec (45 min)
RFR	Foundation Run	Steady run @ moderate aerobic intensity	RFR2: 25 min RFR3: 30 min RFR4: 35 min RFR5: 40 min RFR6: 45 min RFR7: 50 min RFR8: 55 min RFR9: 1 hr
RLI	Run Lactate Intervals	30-second–3-minute intervals run @ VO_2 max intensity w/ active recoveries equal to	RLI1: 12 x 30 sec (32 min total) RLI2: 14 x 30 sec (34 min) RLI3: 16 x 30 sec (36 min)

Code Prefix	Workout Type	Brief Description	Levels
RLI (cont.)		intervals in duration; warm up and cool down long enough to reach total time	RLI4: 18 x 30 sec (38 min) RLI5: 20 x 30 sec (40 min) RLI7: 10 x 1 min (40 min) RLI8: 12 x 1 min (44 min) RLI10: 4 x 3 min (44 min)
RLR	Long Run	Long, steady-pace run @ moderate aerobic intensity	RLR1: 1 hr 5 min RLR2: 1 hr 10 min RLR3: 1 hr 20 min RLR4: 1 hr 30 min RLR5: 1 hr 40 min RLR6: 1 hr 50 min RLR7: 2 hr
RSI	Running Speed Intervals	30-second intervals run @ speed intensity w/ 2-minute active recoveries; warm up and cool down long enough to reach total time	RSI3: 8 x 30 sec (39 min total) RSI4: 9 x 30 sec (42 min) RSI5: 10 x 30 sec (45 min) RSI6: 11 x 30 sec (47 min) RSI7: 12 x 30 sec (50 min) RSI8: 13 x 30 sec (52 min)
RSS	Running Strides	20-second "relaxed sprints" @ speed intensity w/ 40-second active recoveries	RSS1: 2 x 20 sec RSS2: 4 x 20 sec RSS3: 6 x 20 sec
RTR	Tempo Run	Steady run @ threshold intensity; warm up and cool down long enough to reach total time	RTR4: 16 min (36 min total) RTR5: 18 min (38 min) RTR6: 20 min (40 min) RTR7: 22 min (42 min) RTR8: 24 min (44 min) RTR9: 26 min (46 min)
SBI	Swim Base Intervals	100-yard intervals swum @ moderate aerobic intensity w/ 5-second rest periods or single longer swims @ moderate aerobic intensity	SBI1: 2 x 100 SBI2: 3 x 100 SBI3: 4 x 100 SBI4: 5 x 100 SBI5: 6 x 100 SBI6: 7 x 100 SBI7: 8 x 100 SBI24: 1,000 SBI25: 1,200 SBI26: 1,500 SBI27: 1,800 SBI28: 2,000 SBI29: 2,400

Code Prefix	Workout Type	Brief Description	Levels
SCD	Swim Cool-Down	Easy swim @ recovery intensity	SCD1: 200 SCD2: 250 SCD3: 300 SCD4: 350
SDS	Swim Drill Set	25–50-yard intervals of mixed form drills w/ 10-second rest periods	SDS3: 8 x 25 SDS7: 6 x 50
SFI	Swim Fartlek Intervals	100–200-yard intervals with easy/hard or build/descend format (hard = threshold intensity, easy = moderate aerobic intensity) w/ rest periods of 10–20 seconds	SFI1: 4 x 100 (25 easy/25 hard...), 10-sec rest SFI1A: 4 x 100 (25 build/25 descend...), 10-sec rest SFI2: 6 x 100 (25 easy/25 hard...), 10-sec rest SFI2A: 6 x 100 (25 build/25 descend...), 10-sec rest SFI3: 8 x 100 (25 easy/25 hard...), 10-sec rest SFI3A: 8 x 100 (25 build/25 descend...), 10-sec rest SFI4: 4 x 150 (50 easy/25 hard...), 15-sec rest SFI4A: 4 x 150 (50 build/25 descend...), 15-sec rest SFI5: 5 x 150 (50 easy/25 hard...), 15-sec rest SFI5A: 5 x 150 (50 build/25 descend...), 15-sec rest SFI6A: 6 x 150 (50 build/25 descend...), 15-sec rest SFI7: 3 x 200 (50 easy/50 hard...), 15-sec rest SFI9: 5 x 200 (50 easy/50 hard...), 20-sec rest
SKS	Swim Kick Set	25-yard intervals kicking only w/ 15-second rest periods	SKS3: 8 x 25 SKS4: 10 x 25
SLI	Swim Lactate Intervals	75–150-yard intervals swum @ VO_2 max intensity with rest periods of 45 seconds to 1 minute 15 seconds	SLI1: 4 x 75, 45-sec rest SLI2: 5 x 75, 45-sec rest SLI3: 6 x 75, 45-sec rest SLI4: 7 x 75, 45-sec rest SLI5: 8 x 75, 45-sec rest

Code Prefix	Workout Type	Brief Description	Levels
SLI (cont.)			SLI6: 9 x 75, 45-sec rest
			SLI9: 4 x 100, 1-min rest
			SLI10: 5 x 100, 1-min rest
			SLI11: 6 x 100, 1-min rest
			SLI12: 7 x 100, 1-min rest
			SLI14: 4 x 150, 1-min 15-sec rest
			SLI14A: 4 x 150, 1-min rest
			SLI14B: 4 x 150, 45-sec rest
			SLI15: 5 x 150, 1-min 15-sec rest
			SLI15A: 5 x 150, 1-min rest
			SLI15B: 5 x 150, 45-sec rest
			SLI16: 6 x 150, 1-min 15-sec rest
			SLI16A: 6 x 150, 1-min rest
			SLI16B: 6 x 150, 45-sec rest
SSI	Swim Sprint Intervals	25–50-yard intervals swum @ speed intensity w/ 20-second rest periods	SSI1: 4 x 25
			SSI2: 5 x 25
			SSI3: 6 x 25
			SSI4: 7 x 25
			SSI5: 8 x 25
			SSI6: 9 x 25
			SSI7: 10 x 25
			SSI8: 11 x 25
			SSI10: 4 x 50
			SSI12: 6 x 50
			SSI14: 8 x 50
STI	Swim Threshold Intervals	200–400-yard intervals swum @ threshold intensity w/ rest periods of 30 seconds–1 minute 15 seconds	STI1: 2 x 200, 45-sec rest
			STI2: 3 x 200, 45-sec rest
			STI3: 4 x 200, 45-sec rest
			STI4: 5 x 200, 45-sec rest
			STI5: 6 x 200, 45-sec rest
			STI9: 3 x 300, 1-min rest
			STI9A: 3 x 300, 45-sec rest
			STI9B: 3 x 300, 30-sec rest
			STI10: 4 x 300, 1-min rest
			STI10A: 4 x 300, 45-sec rest
			STI10B: 4 x 300, 30-sec rest
			STI12: 2 x 400, 1-min 15-sec rest
			STI12A: 2 x 400, 1-min rest
			STI12B: 2 x 400, 45-sec rest
			STI13: 3 x 400, 1-min 15-sec rest
			STI13A: 3 x 400, 1-min rest

Code Prefix	Workout Type	Brief Description	Levels
STT	Swim Time Trial	Designated distance swum @ maximum effort	STT2: 1,000 STT3: 1,650 STT4: 1.2 miles (2,112)
SWU	Swim Warm-Up	Easy swim @ recovery intensity	SWU1: 200 SWU2: 250 SWU3: 300 SWU4: 350

General Schedule

	Tuesday	Wednesday	Thursday	Friday	Saturday	Sunday
BASE PHASE						
Week 1	Bike Power Intervals	Swim Base Intervals Fartlek Run	Foundation Bike	Swim Fartlek Intervals Foundation Run	L1–2: Foundation Bike L3–4: Long Bike	Swim Base Intervals Foundation Run
Week 2	Bike Power Intervals	Swim Base Intervals Fartlek Run	Foundation Bike	Swim Fartlek Intervals Foundation Run	Brick Workout	Swim Base Intervals Foundation Run
Week 3	Bike Power Intervals	Swim Base Intervals Fartlek Run	Foundation Bike	Swim Fartlek Intervals Foundation Run	L1–2: Foundation Bike L3–4: Long Bike	Swim Base Intervals L1: Foundation Run L2–4: Long Run
Week 4	Bike Power Intervals	Swim Base Intervals Fartlek Run	Foundation Bike	Swim Fartlek Intervals Foundation Run	Foundation Bike	Swim Base Intervals Brick Workout
Week 5	Bike Short Hills	Swim Base + Speed Intervals	Foundation Bike	Swim Fartlek Intervals	Long Bike	Swim Base Intervals

	Tuesday	Wednesday	Thursday	Friday	Saturday	Sunday
Week 5 (cont.)		Run Speed Intervals		Foundation Run + Strides		L1–3: Foundation Run L4: Long Run
Week 6	Bike Short Hills	Swim Base + Speed Intervals	Foundation Bike	Swim Fartlek Intervals	Brick Workout	Swim Time Trial
		Run Speed Intervals		Foundation Run + Strides		Foundation Run
Week 7	Bike Short Hills	Swim Base + Speed Intervals	Foundation Bike	Swim Fartlek Intervals	Long Bike	Swim Base Intervals
		Run Speed Intervals		Foundation Run + Strides		L1–2: Foundation Run L3–4: Long Run
Week 8	Bike Short Hills	Swim Base + Speed Intervals	Foundation Bike	Swim Fartlek Intervals	Foundation Bike	Swim Base Intervals
		Run Speed Intervals		Foundation Run + Strides		Brick Workout
BUILD PHASE Week 9	Bike Long Hills	Swim Base + Speed + Lactate Intervals	Foundation Bike	Swim Threshold + Speed Intervals	Long Bike	Swim Base Intervals
		Run Lactate Intervals		Foundation Run + Strides		L1: Foundation Run L2–4: Long Run
Week 10	Bike Lactate Intervals	Swim Base + Speed + Lactate Intervals	Foundation Bike	Swim Threshold + Speed Intervals	Brick Workout	Swim Base Intervals
		Run Lactate Intervals		Foundation Run + Strides		Foundation Run

		Tuesday	Wednesday	Thursday	Friday	Saturday	Sunday
Week 11		Bike Long Hills	Swim Base + Speed + Lactate Intervals	Foundation Bike	Swim Threshold + Speed Intervals	Long Bike	Swim Time Trial
			Run Lactate Intervals		Foundation Run + Strides		Long Run
Week 12		Bike Lactate Intervals	Swim Base + Lactate Intervals	Foundation Bike	Swim Threshold Intervals	Recovery Bike or Foundation Bike	Sprint Triathlon or Swim Base Intervals + Brick Workout
			Run Lactate Intervals		Foundation Run + Strides		
Week 13		Bike Long Hills	Swim Base + Lactate Intervals	Foundation Bike	Swim Threshold + Speed Intervals	Long Bike	Swim Base Intervals
			Run Lactate Intervals		Foundation Run + Strides		Long Run
Week 14		Bike Lactate Intervals	Swim Base + Lactate Intervals	Foundation Bike	Swim Threshold + Speed Intervals	Long Bike	Swim Base Intervals
			Run Lactate Intervals		Foundation Run + Strides		Brick Workout
PEAK PHASE							
Week 15		Tempo Bike	Swim Base + Lactate Intervals	Foundation Bike	Swim Threshold + Speed Intervals	Long Bike	Swim Base Intervals
			Tempo Run		Foundation Run + Strides		Long Run
Week 16		Tempo Bike	Swim Base + Lactate Intervals	Foundation Bike	Swim Threshold + Speed Intervals	Recovery Bike or Long Bike	Olympic-Distance Triathlon or Swim Base Intervals
			Tempo Run		Foundation Run + Strides		Olympic-Distance Triathlon or Transition Workout

	Tuesday	Wednesday	Thursday	Friday	Saturday	Sunday
Week 17	Tempo Bike	Swim Base + Lactate Intervals	Foundation Bike	Swim Threshold + Speed Intervals	Long Bike	Swim Base Intervals
		Tempo Run		Foundation Run + Strides		Long Run
Week 18	Tempo Bike	Swim Base + Lactate Intervals	Foundation Bike	Swim Threshold + Speed Intervals	Brick Workout	Swim Time Trial
		Tempo Run		Foundation Run + Strides		Foundation Run
Week 19	Tempo Bike	Swim Base + Lactate Intervals	Foundation Bike	Swim Threshold + Speed Intervals	Long Bike	Swim Base Intervals
		Tempo Run		Foundation Run + Strides		Long Run
Week 20	Tempo Bike	Swim Base + Lactate Intervals	Foundation Bike	Swim Threshold + Speed Intervals	Recovery Bike + Run Strides	Half-Ironman Triathlon
		Tempo Run				

Week-by-Week Schedule

Base Phase

This phase is eight weeks long to allow a gradual, steady buildup of training volume. The primary objectives are developing aerobic capacity, endurance, and resistance to injury. The small amount of high-intensity training you do in this phase will prepare you to handle the more challenging high-intensity workouts of the build phase.

WEEK 1

This week's goal: Get accustomed to your new workout schedule.

	Tuesday	Wednesday	Thursday	Friday	Saturday	Sunday
Level 1	CPI1	SWU3 SDS3 SBI1 SKS3 SCD3 (1,200)	CFR3	SWU3 SDS3 SFI1 SCD3 (1,200)	CFR3	SWU2 SBI24 SCD2 (1,500)
		RFL1		RFR4		RFR5
Level 2	CPI2	SWU3 SDS3 SBI2 SKS3 SCD3 (1,300)	CFR3	SWU3 SDS3 SFI2 SCD3 (1,400)	CFR4	SWU3 SBI24 SCD3 (1,600)
		RFL3		RFR4		RFR6
Level 3	CPI3	SWU3 SDS3 SBI3 SKS3 SCD3 (1,400)	CFR3	SWU3 SDS3 SFI2 SCD3 (1,400)	CFR5	SWU2 SBI25 SCD2 (1,700)
		RFL3		RFR4		RFR7
Level 4	CPI4	SWU3 SDS3 SBI4 SKS3 SCD3 (1,500)	CFR3	SWU3 SDS3 SFI3 SCD3 (1,600)	CFR6	SWU3 SBI25 SCD3 (1,800)
		RFL5		RFR5		RFR8

WEEK 2

This week's goal: Gather momentum by completing all scheduled workouts as prescribed.

	Tuesday	Wednesday	Thursday	Friday	Saturday	Sunday
Level 1	CPI2	SWU3 SDS3 SBI2 SKS3 SCD3 (1,300)	CFR3	SWU3 SDS3 SFI1A SKS1 SCD3 (1,300)	BRW3	SWU3 SBI24 SCD3 (1,600)
		RFL2		RFR4		RFR5

	Tuesday	Wednesday	Thursday	Friday	Saturday	Sunday
Level 2	CPI2	SWU3 SDS3 SBI3 SKS3 SCD3 (1,400)	CFR3	SWU3 SDS3 SFI2A SKS1 SCD3 (1,500)	BRW4	SWU2 SBI25 SCD2 (1,700)
		RFL4		RFR4		RFR6
Level 3	CPI3	SWU3 SDS3 SBI4 SKS3 SCD3 (1,500)	CFR4	SWU3 SDS3 SFI2A SKS3 SCD3 (1,600)	BRW4	SWU3 SBI25 SCD3 (1,800)
		RFL4		RFR5		RFR7
Level 4	CPI4	SWU3 SDS3 SBI5 SKS3 SCD3 (1,600)	CFR4	SWU3 SDS3 SFI3A SKS3 SCD3 (1,800)	BRW5	SWU2 SBI26 SCD2 (2,000)
		RFL6		RFR5		RFR7

WEEK 3

This week's goal: Hang in there—you have a recovery week coming up next week.

	Tuesday	Wednesday	Thursday	Friday	Saturday	Sunday
Level 1	CPI2	SWU3 SDS3 SBI3 SKS3 SCD3 (1,400)	CFR3	SWU3 SDS3 SFI1 SKS3 SCD3 (1,400)	CFR4	SWU2 SBI25 SCD2 (1,700)
		RFL4		RFR5		RFR6
Level 2	CPI3	SWU3 SDS3 SBI4 SKS3 SCD3 (1,500)	CFR3	SWU3 SDS3 SFI2 SKS3 SCD3 (1,600)	CFR5	SWU3 SBI25 SCD3 (1,800)
		RFL6		RFR5		RFR7

	Tuesday	Wednesday	Thursday	Friday	Saturday	Sunday
Level 3	CPI4	SWU3 SDS3 SBI5 SKS3 SCD3 (1,600)	CFR4	SWU3 SDS3 SFI2 SKS3 SCD3 (1,600)	CFR6	SWU2 SBI26 SCD2 (2,000)
		RFL6		RFR5		RFR8
Level 4	CPI4	SWU3 SDS3 SBI6 SKS3 SCD3 (1,700)	CFR4	SWU3 SDS3 SFI3 SKS3 SCD3 (1,800)	CLR1	SWU3 SBI26 SCD3 (2,100)
		RFL8		RFR6		RFR9

QUICK TIP:

Creatine is a popular muscle-building supplement for strength athletes and bodybuilders, but new research shows it may also reduce muscle damage during endurance exercise and accelerate post-workout recovery. Few studies of the long-term health effects have been conducted, but so far there is no evidence of any risks associated with prolonged creatine supplementation.

WEEK 4
(Recovery)

This week's goal: Fully absorb your recent training and finish the week feeling rested and ready to return to harder training next week.

	Tuesday	Wednesday	Thursday	Friday	Saturday	Sunday
Level 1	CPI1	SWU3 SDS3 SBI1 SCD3 (1,000)	CFR1	SWU3 SDS3 SFI1A SCD3 (1,200)	CFR2	SWU1 SBI24 SCD1 (1,400)
		RFL1		RFR4		BRW3

	Tuesday	Wednesday	Thursday	Friday	Saturday	Sunday
Level 2	CPI2	SWU3 SDS3 SBI2 SCD3 (1,100)	CFR2	SWU3 SDS3 SFI2A SCD3 (1,400)	CFR3	SWU2 SBI24 SCD2 (1,500)
		RFL3		RFR4		BRW4
Level 3	CPI2	SWU3 SDS3 SBI3 SCD3 (1,200)	CFR2	SWU3 SDS3 SFI2A SCD3 (1,400)	CFR4	SWU1 SBI25 SCD1 (1,600)
		RFL3		RFR4		BRW4
Level 4	CPI3	SWU3 SDS3 SBI4 SCD3 (1,300)	CFR3	SWU3 SDS3 SFI3A SCD3 (1,600)	CFR5	SWU2 SBI25 SCD2 (1,700)
		RFL5		RFR5		BRW5

WEEK 5

This week's goal: Finish strong in this weekend's long endurance workouts.

	Tuesday	Wednesday	Thursday	Friday	Saturday	Sunday
Level 1	CSH3	SWU3 SDS3 SBI2 SSI3 SKS3 SCD3 (1,450)	CFR3	SWU3 SDS3 SFI4 SKS3 SCD3 (1,600)	CFR5	SWU3 SBI25 SCD3 (1,800)
		RSI3		RFR5 + RSS1		RFR7
Level 2	CSH4	SWU3 SDS3 SBI3 SSI4 SKS3 SCD3 (1,575)	CFR4	SWU3 SDS7 SFI4 SKS3 SCD3 (1,700)	CFR6	SWU2 SBI26 SCD2 (2,000)
		RSI4		RFR5 + RSS1		RFR8

	Tuesday	Wednesday	Thursday	Friday	Saturday	Sunday
Level 3	CSH5	SWU3 SDS3 SBI4 SSI5 SKS3 SCD3 (1,700)	CFR4	SWU3 SDS7 SFI5 SKS3 SCD3 (1,850)	CLR1	SWU3 SBI26 SCD3 (2,100)
		RSI5		RFR5 + RSS1		RFR9
Level 4	CSH6	SWU3 SDS3 SBI5 SSI6 SKS3 SCD3 (1,825)	CFR4	SWU3 SDS7 SFI3 SKS3 SCD3 (1,900)	CLR2	SWU2 SBI27 SCD2 (2,300)
		RSI6		RFR6 + RSS1		RLR1

WEEK 6

This week's goal: Go all out in Sunday's swim time trial.

	Tuesday	Wednesday	Thursday	Friday	Saturday	Sunday
Level 1	CSH4	SWU3 SDS3 SBI3 SSI4 SKS3 SCD3 (1,575)	CFR4	SWU3 SDS7 SFI4A SKS3 SCD3 (1,700)	BRW4	SWU1 STT2 SCD1 (1,400)
		RSI4		RFR5 + RSS2		RFR2
Level 2	CSH5	SWU3 SDS3 SBI4 SSI5 SKS3 SCD3 (1,700)	CFR4	SWU3 SDS7 SFI5A SKS3 SCD3 (1,850)	BRW4	SWU2 STT2 SCD2 (1,500)
		RSI5		RFR6 + RSS2		RFR3
Level 3	CSH6	SWU3 SDS3 SBI5	CFR4	SWU3 SDS7 SFI3A	BRW5	SWU3 STT2 SCD3

	Tuesday	Wednesday	Thursday	Friday	Saturday	Sunday
Level 3 *(cont.)*		SSI6 SKS3 SCD3 (1,825)		SKS3 SCD3 (1,900)		(1,600)
		RSI6		RFR6 + RSS2		RFR4
Level 4	CSH7	SWU3 SDS3 SBI6 SSI7 SKS3 SCD3 (1,950)	CFR5	SWU3 SDS7 SFI6A SKS3 SCD3 (2,000)	BRW6	SWU4 STT2 SCD4 (1,700)
		RSI7		RFR7 + RSS2		RFR5

WEEK 7

This week's goal: Pace yourself through this week's workouts—this is your third consecutive week of hard training.

	Tuesday	Wednesday	Thursday	Friday	Saturday	Sunday
Level 1	CSH5	SWU3 SDS3 SBI4 SSI5 SKS3 SCD3 (1,700)	CFR4	SWU3 SDS3 SFI5 SKS3 SCD3 (1,750)	CFR6	SWU2 SBI26 SCD2 (2,000)
		RSI5		RFR5 + RSS3		RFR8
Level 2	CSH6	SWU3 SDS3 SBI5 SSI6 SKS3 SCD3 (1,825)	CFR4	SWU3 SDS3 SFI3 SKS3 SCD3 (1,800)	CLR1	SWU3 SBI26 SCD3 (2,100)
		RSI6		RFR6 + RSS3		RFR9
Level 3	CSH7	SWU3 SDS3 SBI6 SSI7	CFR5	SWU3 SDS3 SFI6 SKS3	CLR2	SWU2 SBI27 SCD2 (2,300)

HALF-IRONMAN TRIATHLON TRAINING PLANS • LEVELS 1–4

191

	Tuesday	Wednesday	Thursday	Friday	Saturday	Sunday
Level 3 *(cont.)*		SKS3 SCD3 (1,950)		SCD3 (1,900)		
		RSI7		RFR6 + RSS3		RLR1
Level 4	CSH8	SWU3 SDS3 SBI7 SSI8 SKS3 SCD3 (2,075)	CFR5	SWU3 SDS3 SFI9 SKS3 SCD3 (2,000)	CLR3	SWU3 SBI27 SCD3 (2,400)
		RSI8		RFR6 + RSS3		RLR2

QUICK TIP:

Many triathletes put a Vulcan death grip on their handlebars while climbing tough hills. This wastes a lot of energy. Concentrate on keeping your hands, arms, and shoulders relaxed while climbing.

WEEK 8
(Recovery)

This week's goal: Fully absorb your recent training and finish the week feeling rested and ready to return to harder training next week.

	Tuesday	Wednesday	Thursday	Friday	Saturday	Sunday
Level 1	CSH3	SWU3 SDS3 SBI2 SSI3 SCD3 (1,250)	CFR2	SWU3 SDS3 SFI4A SKS3 SCD3 (1,600)	CFR3	SWU3 SBI24 SCD3 (1,600)
		RSI3		RFR4 + RSS2		BRW4
Level 2	CSH4	SWU3 SDS3 SBI3 SSI4 SCD3 (1,375)	CFR2	SWU3 SDS3 SFI5A SKS3 SCD3 (1,750)	CFR4	SWU2 SBI25 SCD2 (1,700)
		RSI4		RFR4 + RSS2		BRW4

	Tuesday	Wednesday	Thursday	Friday	Saturday	Sunday
Level 3	CSH5	SWU3 SDS3 SBI4 SSI5 SCD3 (1,500)	CFR3	SWU3 SDS3 SFI6A SKS3 SCD3 (1,800)	CFR5	SWU3 SBI25 SCD3 (1,800)
		RSI5		RFR4 + RSS2		BRW5
Level 4	CSH6	SWU3 SDS3 SBI5 SSI6 SCD3 (1,625)	CFR4	SWU3 SDS3 SFI6A SKS3 SCD3 (1,900)	CFR6	SWU2 SBI26 SCD2 (2,000)
		RSI6		RFR4 + RSS2		BRW6

Build Phase

This six-week phase will add some challenging high-intensity workouts—including lactate intervals in all three disciplines—to maximize your aerobic capacity and enhance your ability to sustain faster speeds. At the same time you will continue building endurance with long swims, rides, runs, and brick workouts.

WEEK 9

This week's goal: Climb hard but stay relaxed and in the saddle in Tuesday's long cycling hill climbs (8–9 RPE).

	Tuesday	Wednesday	Thursday	Friday	Saturday	Sunday
Level 1	CLH1	SWU3 SDS3 SBI2 SLI1 SSI3 SKS3 SCD3 (1,750)	CFR4	SWU3 SDS3 STI2 SSI10 SKS3 SCD3 (1,800)	CLR1	SWU3 SBI26 SCD3 (2,100)
		RLI1		RFR6 + RSS3		RFR9
Level 2	CLH2	SWU3 SDS3 SBI3 SLI2	CFR5	SWU3 SDS3 STI2 SSI12	CLR2	SWU2 SBI27 SCD2 (2,300)

	Tuesday	Wednesday	Thursday	Friday	Saturday	Sunday
Level 2 (cont.)		SSI3 SKS3 SCD3 (1,925)		SKS3 SCD3 (1,900)		
		RLI2		RFR6 + RSS3		RLR1
Level 3	CLH3	SWU3 SDS3 SBI4 SLI3 SSI3 SKS3 SCD3 (2,100)	CFR5	SWU3 SDS3 STI3 SSI10 SKS3 SCD3 (2,000)	CLR3	SWU3 SBI27 SCD3 (2,400)
		RLI3		RFR7 + RSS3		RLR2
Level 4	CLH4	SWU3 SDS3 SBI5 SLI4 SSI3 SKS3 SCD3 (2,275)	CFR5	SWU3 SDS3 STI3 SSI12 SKS3 SCD3 (2,100)	CLR4	SWU2 SBI28 SCD2 (2,500)
		RLI4		RFR7 + RSS3		RLR3

WEEK 10

This week's goal: Find your running groove quickly during Saturday's bike-run brick workout.

	Tuesday	Wednesday	Thursday	Friday	Saturday	Sunday
Level 1	CLI1	SWU3 SDS3 SBI2 SLI2 SSI3 SKS3 SCD3 (1,825)	CFR5	SWU3 SDS3 STI2 SSI12 SKS3 SCD3 (1,900)	BRW5	SWU2 SBI27 SCD2 (2,300)
		RLI2		RFR6 + RSS3		RFR3

	Tuesday	Wednesday	Thursday	Friday	Saturday	Sunday
Level 2	CLI2	SWU3 SDS3 SBI3 SLI3 SSI3 SKS3 SCD3 (2,000)	CFR5	SWU3 SDS3 STI3 SSI10 SKS3 SCD3 (2,000)	BRW6	SWU3 SBI27 SCD3 (2,400)
		RLI3		RFR7 + RSS3		RFR4
Level 3	CLI3	SWU3 SDS3 SBI4 SLI4 SSI3 SKS3 SCD3 (2,175)	CFR5	SWU3 SDS3 STI3 SSI12 SKS3 SCD3 (2,100)	BRW7	SWU2 SBI28 SCD2 (2,500)
		RLI4		RFR7 + RSS3		RFR5
Level 4	CLI4	SWU3 SDS3 SBI5 SLI5 SSI3 SKS3 SCD3 (2,350)	CFR6	SWU3 SDS3 STI4 SSI10 SKS3 SCD3 (2,200)	BRW8	SWU3 SBI28 SCD3 (2,600)
		RLI5		RFR8 + RSS3		RFR6

WEEK 11

This week's goal: Aim for a better performance in this week's 1,650-yard swim time trial than you achieved in Week 6's 1,000-yard time trial (i.e., equal pace over longer distance).

	Tuesday	Wednesday	Thursday	Friday	Saturday	Sunday
Level 1	CLH2	SWU3 SDS3 SBI2 SLI3 SSI3 SKS3 SCD3 (1,900)	CFR5	SWU3 SDS3 STI3 SSI10 SKS3 SCD3 (2,000)	CLR2	SWU2 STT3 SCD2 (2,150)
		RLI3		RFR6 + RSS3		RLR1

	Tuesday	Wednesday	Thursday	Friday	Saturday	Sunday
Level 2	CLH3	SWU3 SDS3 SBI3 SLI4 SSI3 SKS3 SCD3 (2,075)	CFR5	SWU3 SDS3 STI3 SSI12 SKS3 SCD3 (2,100)	CLR3	SWU3 STT3 SCD3 (2,250)
		RLI4		RFR7 + RSS3		RLR2
Level 3	CLH4	SWU3 SDS3 SBI4 SLI5 SSI3 SKS3 SCD3 (2,250)	CFR5	SWU3 SDS3 STI4 SSI10 SKS3 SCD3 (2,200)	CLR4	SWU4 STT3 SCD4 (2,350)
		RLI5		RFR7 + RSS3		RLR3
Level 4	CLH5	SWU3 SDS3 SBI5 SLI6 SSI3 SKS3 SCD3 (2,425)	CFR6	SWU3 SDS3 STI5 SSI10 SKS3 SCD3 (2,400)	CLR5	SWU4 STT3 SCD4 (2,350)
		RLI7		RFR8 + RSS3		RLR4

WEEK 12
(Recovery)

This week's goal: Fully absorb your recent training. Have a solid tune-up sprint triathlon on Sunday if you're able to do one.

	Tuesday	Wednesday	Thursday	Friday	Saturday	Sunday
Level 1	CLI1	SWU3 SDS3 SBI2 SLI1 SCD3 (1,400)	CFR4	SWU3 SDS3 STI2 SKS3 SCD3 (1,600)	CRR1 or CFR3*	Sprint Triathlon or SWU3 SBI24 SCD3 (1,600)*
		RLI1		RFR4 + RSS3		BRW4*

	Tuesday	Wednesday	Thursday	Friday	Saturday	Sunday
Level 2	CLI1	SWU3 SDS3 SBI3 SLI2 SCD3 (1,575)	CFR4	SWU3 SDS3 STI2 SKS3 SCD3 (1,600)	CRR1 or CFR4*	Sprint Triathlon or SWU2 SBI25 SCD2 (1,700)*
		RLI2		RFR5 + RSS2		BRW5*
Level 3	CLI2	SWU3 SDS3 SBI4 SLI3 SCD3 (1,750)	CFR4	SWU3 SDS3 STI3 SKS3 SCD3 (1,800)	CRR1 or CFR5*	Sprint Triathlon or SWU3 SBI25 SCD3 (1,800)*
		RLI3		RFR5 + RSS2		BRW6*
Level 4	CLI3	SWU3 SDS3 SBI5 SLI4 SCD3 (1,925)	CFR5	SWU3 SDS3 STI4 SKS3 SCD3 (2,000)	CRR1 or CFR6*	Sprint Triathlon or SWU2 SBI26 SCD2 (2,000)*
		RLI4		RFR6 + RSS2		BRW7*

*If not racing

WEEK 13

This week's goal: Finish strong in this weekend's long swim, ride, and run.

	Tuesday	Wednesday	Thursday	Friday	Saturday	Sunday
Level 1	CLH3	SWU3 SDS3 SBI4 SLI9 SKS3 SCD3 (1,900)	CFR5	SWU3 SDS3 STI9 SSI10 SKS3 SCD3 (2,100)	CLR3	SWU2 SBI27 SCD2 (2,300)
		RLI4		RFR6 + RSS3		RLR2
Level 2	CLH4	SWU3 SDS3 SBI5 SLI9 SKS3	CFR5	SWU3 SDS3 STI9 SSI12 SKS3	CLR4	SWU3 SBI27 SCD3 (2,400)

	Tuesday	Wednesday	Thursday	Friday	Saturday	Sunday
Level 2 (cont.)		SCD3 (2,000)		SCD3 (2,200)		
		RLI5		RFR7 + RSS3		RLR3
Level 3	CLH5	SWU3 SDS3 SBI5 SLI10 SKS3 SCD3 (2,100)	CFR6	SWU3 SDS3 STI10 SSI10 SKS3 SCD3 (2,400)	CLR5	SWU2 SBI28 SCD2 (2,500)
		RLI7		RFR7 + RSS3		RLR4
Level 4	CLH6	SWU3 SDS3 SBI6 SLI10 SKS3 SCD3 (2,200)	CFR6	SWU3 SDS3 STI10 SSI12 SKS3 SCD3 (2,500)	CLR6	SWU3 SBI28 SCD3 (2,600)
		RLI8		RFR8 + RSS3		RLR5

QUICK TIP:

Knee pain on the bike is often an indicator of improper saddle height. If the pain is in the front of your knee, there's a good chance your seat is set a little too low. Pain in the back of the knee usually means the seat is too high.

WEEK 14

This week's goal: Dig deep in this week's tough lactate interval session in cycling (Tuesday) and in swimming and running (Wednesday).

	Tuesday	Wednesday	Thursday	Friday	Saturday	Sunday
Level 1	CLI3	SWU3 SDS3 SBI5 SLI9 SKS3 SCD3 (2,000)	CFR5	SWU3 SDS3 STI9A SSI10 SKS3 SCD3 (2,100)	CFR6	SWU3 SBI27 SCD3 (2,400)
		RLI5		RFR7 + RSS3		BRW8

	Tuesday	Wednesday	Thursday	Friday	Saturday	Sunday
Level 2	CLI4	SWU3 SDS3 SBI5 SLI10 SKS3 SCD3 (2,100)	CFR5	SWU3 SDS3 STI9A SSI12 SKS3 SCD3 (2,200)	CLR1	SWU2 SBI28 SCD2 (2,500)
		RLI7		RFR8 + RSS3		BRW9
Level 3	CLI5	SWU3 SDS3 SBI6 SLI10 SKS3 SCD3 (2,200)	CFR6	SWU3 SDS3 STI10A SSI10 SKS3 SCD3 (2,400)	CLR2	SWU3 SBI28 SCD3 (2,600)
		RLI8		RFR8 + RSS3		BRW10
Level 4	CLI6	SWU3 SDS3 SBI7 SLI11 SKS3 SCD3 (2,400)	CFR7	SWU3 SDS3 STI10A SSI12 SKS3 SCD3 (2,500)	CLR3	SWU1 SBI29 SCD1 (2,800)
		RLI10		RFR9 + RSS3		BRW11

Peak Phase

Your long endurance workouts on the weekends become really long in this six-week phase to ensure you're able to go the distance on race day. The second training priority is threshold-intensity training in all three disciplines. Long brick workouts, a swim time trial, and an optional Olympic-distance tune-up triathlon also help build race-specific fitness.

WEEK 15

This week's goal: Try to complete Friday's threshold swim intervals at the same pace you did last week with longer rest periods.

	Tuesday	Wednesday	Thursday	Friday	Saturday	Sunday
Level 1	CTR4	SWU3 SDS3 SBI5 SLI10 SKS3 SCD3 (2,100) RTR4	CFR5	SWU3 SDS3 STI9B SSI10 SKS3 SCD3 (2,100) RFR7 + RSS3	CLR4	SWU2 SBI28 SCD2 (2,500) RLR3
Level 2	CTR5	SWU3 SDS3 SBI6 SLI10 SKS3 SCD3 (2,200) RTR5	CFR6	SWU3 SDS3 STI9B SSI12 SKS3 SCD3 (2,200) RFR8 + RSS3	CLR5	SWU3 SBI28 SCD3 (2,600) RLR4
Level 3	CTR6	SWU3 SDS3 SBI6 SLI11 SKS3 SCD3 (2,300) RTR6	CFR6	SWU3 SDS3 STI10B SSI10 SKS3 SCD3 (2,400) RFR9 + RSS3	CLR6	SWU1 SBI29 SCD1 (2,800) RLR5
Level 4	CTR7	SWU3 SDS3 SBI7 SLI12 SKS3 SCD3 (2,500) RTR7	CFR7	SWU3 SDS3 STI10B SSI12 SKS3 SCD3 (2,500) RLR1 + RSS3	CLR7	SWU2 SBI29 SCD2 (2,900) RLR6

WEEK 16
(Recovery)

This week's goal: Fully absorb your recent training and have a solid Olympic-distance triathlon performance if you have the opportunity.

	Tuesday	Wednesday	Thursday	Friday	Saturday	Sunday
Level 1	CTR3	SWU3 SDS3 SBI3 SLI9 SCD3 (1,600)	CFR3	SWU3 SDS3 STI2 SCD3 (1,400)	CRR1 or CLR1*	Olympic- Distance Triathlon or SWU3 SBI24 SCD3 (1,600)*
		RTR3		RFR5 + RSS2		BRW5*
Level 2	CTR4	SWU3 SDS3 SBI3 SLI10 SCD3 (1,700)	CFR3	SWU3 SDS3 STI2 SCD3 (1,400)	CRR1 or CLR2*	Olympic- Distance Triathlon or SWU2 SBI25 SCD2 (1,700)*
		RTR4		RFR6 + RSS2		BRW6*
Level 3	CTR5	SWU3 SDS3 SBI4 SLI10 SCD3 (1,800)	CFR4	SWU3 SDS3 STI3 SCD3 (1,600)	CRR1 or CLR3*	Olympic- Distance Triathlon or SWU3 SBI25 SCD3 (1,800)*
		RTR5		RFR6 + RSS2		BRW7*
Level 4	CTR6	SWU3 SDS3 SBI4 SLI11 SCD3 (1,900)	CFR4	SWU3 SDS3 STI4 SCD3 (1,800)	CRR1 or CLR4*	Olympic- Distance Triathlon or SWU2 SBI26 SCD2 (2,000)*
		RTR6		RFR7 + RSS2		BRW8*

*If not racing

WEEK 17

This week's goal: Finish strong in this weekend's very long swim, ride, and run.

	Tuesday	Wednesday	Thursday	Friday	Saturday	Sunday
Level 1	CTR5	SWU3 SDS3 SBI4 SLI14 SKS3 SCD3 (2,100) RTR4	CFR5	SWU3 SDS3 STI12 SSI12 SKS3 SCD3 (2,100) RFR8 + RSS2	CLR5	SWU2 SBI28 SCD2 (2,500) RLR4
Level 2	CTR6	SWU3 SDS3 SBI4 SLI15 SKS3 SCD3 (2,250) RTR5	CFR5	SWU3 SDS3 STI12 SSI14 SKS3 SCD3 (2,200) RFR8 + RSS2	CLR6	SWU3 SBI28 SCD3 (2,600) RLR5
Level 3	CTR7	SWU3 SDS3 SBI5 SLI15 SKS3 SCD3 (2,350) RTR6	CFR6	SWU3 SDS3 STI13 SSI10 SKS3 SCD3 (2,400) RFR9 + RSS2	CLR7	SWU1 SBI29 SCD1 (2,800) RLR6
Level 4	CTR8	SWU3 SDS3 SBI5 SLI16 SKS3 SCD3 (2,500) RTR7	CFR7	SWU3 SDS3 STI13 SSI12 SKS3 SCD3 (2,500) RLR1 + RSS2	CLR8	SWU3 SBI29 SCD3 (3,000) RLR7

WEEK 18

This week's goal: Build race-specific fitness in Saturday's long brick workout and Sunday's long time trial.

	Tuesday	Wednesday	Thursday	Friday	Saturday	Sunday
Level 1	CTR6	SWU3 SDS3 SBI4 SLI14A SKS3 SCD3 (2,100) RTR5	CFR6	SWU3 SDS3 STI12A SSI12 SKS3 SCD3 (2,100) RFR9 + RSS2	BRW11	SWU1 STT4 SCD1 (2,512) RFR3
Level 2	CTR7	SWU3 SDS3 SBI4 SLI15A SKS3 SCD3 (2,250) RTR6	CFR6	SWU3 SDS3 STI12A SSI14 SKS3 SCD3 (2,200) RFR9 + RSS2	BRW12	SWU2 STT4 SCD2 (2,612) RFR4
Level 3	CTR8	SWU3 SDS3 SBI5 SLI15A SKS3 SCD3 (2,350) RTR7	CFR7	SWU3 SDS3 STI13A SSI10 SKS3 SCD3 (2,400) RLR1 + RSS2	BRW13	SWU3 STT4 SCD3 (2,712) RFR5
Level 4	CTR9	SWU3 SDS3 SBI5 SLI16A SKS3 SCD3 (2,500) RTR8	CFR7	SWU3 SDS3 STI13A SSI12 SKS3 SCD3 (2,500) RLR2 + RSS2	BRW14	SWU4 STT4 SCD4 (2,812) RFR6

HALF-IRONMAN TRIATHLON TRAINING PLANS • LEVELS 1–4

203

QUICK TIP:

Get to know each racecourse as well as possible before you compete on it. Familiarity with such things as the direction of currents in the swim course, where the hills lie on the bike course, and where you're supposed to enter and exit the transition area could save you precious seconds—even minutes—during the race.

WEEK 19
(Half Taper)

This week's goal: Gain confidence for next weekend's race by feeling your fitness begin to peak during this week's workouts.

	Tuesday	Wednesday	Thursday	Friday	Saturday	Sunday
Level 1	CTR7	SWU3 SDS3 SBI4 SLI14B SKS3 SCD3 (2,100)	CFR5	SWU3 SDS3 STI12B SSI12 SKS3 SCD3 (2,100)	CLR2	SWU2 SBI26 SCD2 (2,000)
		RTR6		RFR8 + RSS2		RLR1
Level 2	CTR8	SWU3 SDS3 SBI4 SLI15B SKS3 SCD3 (2,250)	CFR5	SWU3 SDS3 STI12B SSI14 SKS3 SCD3 (2,200)	CLR3	SWU3 SBI26 SCD3 (2,100)
		RTR7		RFR8 + RSS2		RLR2
Level 3	CTR9	SWU3 SDS3 SBI5 SLI15B SKS3 SCD3 (2,350)	CFR5	SWU3 SDS3 STI13B SSI10 SKS3 SCD3 (2,400)	CLR4	SWU1 SBI27 SCD1 (2,200)
		RTR8		RFR9 + RSS2		RLR3

	Tuesday	Wednesday	Thursday	Friday	Saturday	Sunday
Level 4	CTR10	SWU3 SDS3 SBI5 SLI16B SKS3 SCD3 (2,500)	CFR6	SWU3 SDS3 STI13B SSI12 SKS3 SCD3 (2,500)	CLR5	SWU3 SBI27 SCD3 (2,400)
		RTR9		RFR9 + RSS2		RLR4

WEEK 20
(Taper)

This week's goal: Have a great half-Ironman on Sunday!

	Tuesday	Wednesday	Thursday	Friday	Saturday	Sunday
Level 1	CTR4	SWU3 SDS3 SBI2 SLI14 SCD3 (1,700) RTR2	CFR2	SWU3 STI1 SSI1 SCD3 (1,100)	CRR1 + RSS2	Half- Ironman Triathlon
Level 2	CTR5	SWU3 SDS3 SBI3 SLI14 SCD3 (1,800) RTR3	CFR2	SWU3 STI1 SSI1 SCD3 (1,100)	CRR1 + RSS2	Half- Ironman Triathlon
Level 3	CTR6	SWU3 SDS3 SBI3 SLI15 SCD3 (1,850) RTR4	CFR2	SWU3 STI1 SSI10 SCD3 (1,200)	CRR1 + RSS2	Half- Ironman Triathlon
Level 4	CTR7	SWU3 SDS3 SBI3 SLI15 SCD3 (1,950) RTR4	CFR3	SWU3 STI1 SSI10 SCD3 (1,200)	CRR1 + RSS2	Half- Ironman Triathlon

Chapter 10
HALF-IRONMAN TRIATHLON TRAINING PLANS
Levels 5–7

*I*n order to prepare for a competitive half-Ironman, you need to do some long endurance workouts: swims that are longer than the half-Ironman's 1.2 miles; rides that are longer than the half-IM's 56 miles; and runs that are longer than its 13.1-mile concluding leg. But outside of these necessary long sessions your workout schedule can be fairly lean without holding back your fitness development whatsoever. As long as the shorter workouts you do during the week (the long workouts of course being scheduled for the weekends) are focused, specific, varied, and progressive, you can rip off a great half-Ironman with this training approach, which is the approach taken by the three training plans in this chapter.

Each plan is 20 weeks long and comprises an eight-week base phase and six-week build and peak phases. A typical training week includes three swims, three rides, three runs, and a bike-run brick workout. The brick workouts fall on Wednesday in odd-numbered weeks and on Saturday in even-numbered weeks. As in all of the other training plans in this book, every fourth week is a recovery week. The final 10 days of the plan constitute a taper period.

Two tune-up races are scheduled. A sprint race is scheduled in Week 12 and an Olympic-distance race in Week 16. If you are unable to find opportunities for tune-up races you will do additional brick workouts instead.

Level 5

This plan is best suited to triathletes aiming to better their performance in previous half-Ironmans using a highly time-efficient training plan. It begins with 4,500 yards of swimming, 4 hours and 15 minutes of cycling, and 2 hours and 10 minutes of running in Week 1. It peaks with 7,800 yards of swimming, 7 hours and 50 minutes of cycling, and 3 hours and 38 minutes of running in Week 17.

Level 6

Choose this plan if you are willing and ready to work very hard to achieve a great half-Ironman performance, but you don't want even an ounce of waste in your training schedule. The plan begins with 5,200 yards of swimming, 4 hours and 40 minutes of cycling, and 2 hours and 23 minutes of running in Week 1. It peaks with 8,400 yards of swimming, 8 hours and 25 minutes of cycling, and 4 hours and 3 minutes of running in Week 17.

Level 7

Choose this plan if you wish you could quit your job and train full-time, but you can't. The best you can do is pack as much high-quality training in your limited free time as possible, which is what this plan offers. It begins with 5,900 yards of swimming, 4 hours and 55 minutes of cycling, and 2 hours and 31 minutes of running in Week 1. It peaks with 9,050 yards of swimming, 9 hours of cycling, and 4 hours and 18 minutes of running in Week 17.

Quick Reference Guide to Workout Codes for Half-Ironman Triathlon Training Plans Levels 5–7

Code Prefix	Workout Type	Brief Description	Levels
BRW	Brick Workout	Bike ride followed by immediate run, both @ moderate aerobic intensity, except "A" suffix = run @ threshold intensity or bike and run @ high aerobic intensity, as indicated; "B" suffix = run @ threshold intensity	BRW3A: 45 min/10 min (run @ threshold) BRW4: 45 min/15 min BRW4A: 45 min/15 min (run @ threshold) BRW5: 1 hr/20 min BRW5A: 1 hr/20 min (run @ threshold) BRW6: 1 hr/30 min BRW6A: 1 hr/30 min (run @ tempo) BRW7: 1 hr 15 min/20 min BRW7A: 1 hr 15 min/20 min (bike and run @ high aerobic) BRW7B: 1 hr 15 min/20 min (run @ tempo) BRW8: 1 hr 15 min/30 min BRW8A: 1 hr 15 min/30 min (bike and run @ high aerobic) BRW8B: 1 hr 15 min/30 min (run @ threshold) BRW9: 1 hr 30 min/30 min BRW9A: 1 hr 30 min/30 min (bike and run @ high aerobic) BRW10: 1 hr 30 min/45 min BRW11: 1 hr 45 min/45 min BRW12: 1 hr 45 min/50 min BRW13: 2 hr/50 min BRW14: 2 hr 15 min/55 min
CFR	Foundation Bike	Steady ride @ moderate aerobic intensity	CFR2: 45 min CFR3: 1 hr CFR4: 1 hr 15 min CFR5: 1 hr 30 min CFR6: 1 hr 45 min CFR7: 2 hr
CLH	Bike Long Hill Climbs	5-minute climbing intervals @ threshold/VO$_2$ max intensity w/ 3-minute active recoveries; warm up and cool down long enough to reach total time	CLH3: 4 x 5 min (1 hr 10 min total) CLH4: 5 x 5 min (1 hr 15 min) CLH5: 6 x 5 min (1 hr 20 min) CLH6: 7 x 5 min (1 hr 30 min) CLH7: 8 x 5 min (1 hr 30 min)

Code Prefix	Workout Type	Brief Description	Levels
CLI	Bike Lactate Intervals	3–5-minute intervals @ VO_2 max intensity w/ 3-minute active recoveries; warm up and cool down long enough to reach total time	CLI3: 4 x 3 min (1 hr 15 min total) CLI4: 5 x 3 min (1 hr 20 min) CLI5: 6 x 3 min (1 hr 25 min) CLI6: 7 x 3 min (1 hr 30 min) CLI7: 8 x 3 min (1 hr 35 min) CLI11: 5 x 5 min (2 hr)
CLR	Long Bike Ride	Long steady ride @ moderate aerobic intensity	CLR1: 2 hr CLR2: 2 hr 15 min CLR3: 2 hr 30 min CLR4: 2 hr 45 min CLR5: 3 hr CLR6: 3 hr 15 min CLR7: 3 hr 30 min CLR8: 3 hr 45 min CLR9: 4 hr
CPI	Bike Power Intervals	20-second intervals done in a high gear @ speed intensity w/ 2-minute active recoveries; warm up and cool down long enough to reach total time	CPI3: 6 x 20 sec (1 hr total) CPI4: 7 x 20 sec (1 hr 10 min) CPI5: 8 x 20 sec (1 hr 20 min)
CRR	Recovery Bike	Steady ride @ recovery intensity	CRR1: 20 min CRR4: 1 hr CRR5: 1 hr 15 min
CSH	Bike Short Hill Climbs	1-minute hill climbs @ VO_2 max/speed intensity w/ 2-minute active recoveries or 1.5-minute hill climbs @ VO_2 max/speed intensity w/ 3-minute active recoveries; warm up and cool down long enough to reach total time	CSH5: 8 x 1 min (1 hr 5 min total) CSH6: 9 x 1 min (1 hr 10 min) CSH7: 10 x 1 min (1 hr 15 min) CSH8: 11 x 1 min (1 hr 20 min) CSH9: 12 x 1 min (1 hr 25 min) CSH14: 8 x 1 min 30 sec (1 hr 50 min)
CSS	Steady-State Ride	Steady ride @ high aerobic intensity	CSS1: 1 hr 10 min CSS2: 1 hr 15 min
CTR	Tempo Bike Ride	One or two blocks of riding @ threshold intensity (10-minute active recovery when threshold-intensity riding is divided into two blocks); warm up and cool down long enough to reach total time	CTR7: 2 x 14 min (1 hr 15 min total) CTR8: 28 min (1 hr 20 min) CTR9: 30 min (1 hr 25 min) CTR10: 2 x 16 min (1 hr 30 min) CTR11: 32 min (1 hr 35 min) CTR12: 34 min (1 hr 40 min)

Code Prefix	Workout Type	Brief Description	Levels
RFL	Fartlek Run	Foundation run with 30-second bursts @ VO$_2$ max/speed intensity	RFL3: 6 x 30 sec (35 min total) RFL4: 8 x 30 sec (35 min) RFL5: 6 x 30 sec (40 min) RFL6: 8 x 30 sec (40 min) RFL8: 8 x 30 sec (45 min)
RFR	Foundation Run	Steady run @ moderate aerobic intensity	RFR3: 30 min RFR4: 35 min RFR5: 40 min RFR6: 45 min RFR7: 50 min RFR8: 55 min RFR9: 1 hr
RLI	Run Lactate Intervals	30-second–3-minute intervals run @ VO$_2$ max intensity w/ active recoveries equal to intervals in duration; warm up and cool down long enough to reach total time	RLI3: 16 x 30 sec (36 min total) RLI4: 18 x 30 sec (38 min) RLI5: 20 x 30 sec (40 min) RLI7: 10 x 1 min (40 min) RLI11: 5 x 3 min (50 min)
RLR	Long Run	Long, steady-pace run @ moderate aerobic intensity	RLR1: 1 hr 5 min RLR2: 1 hr 10 min RLR3: 1 hr 20 min RLR4: 1 hr 30 min RLR5: 1 hr 40 min RLR6: 1 hr 50 min RLR7: 2 hr RLR8: 2 hr 10 min
RSI	Running Speed Intervals	30-second intervals run @ speed intensity w/ 2-minute active recoveries or 1-minute intervals run @ speed intensity w/ 3-minute active recoveries; warm up and cool down long enough to reach total time	RSI6: 11 x 30 sec (47 min total) RSI7: 12 x 30 sec (50 min) RSI8: 13 x 30 sec (52 min) RSI12: 6 x 1 min (47 min) RSI13: 7 x 1 min (54 min) RSI14: 8 x 1 min (1 hr 1 min) RSI15: 9 x 1 min (1 hr 5 min)
RSS	Running Strides	20-second "relaxed sprints" @ speed intensity w/ 40-second active recoveries	RSS1: 2 x 20 sec RSS2: 4 x 20 sec RSS3: 6 x 20 sec RSS4: 8 x 20 sec

Code Prefix	Workout Type	Brief Description	Levels
RTR	Tempo Run	Steady run @ threshold intensity; warm up and cool down long enough to reach total time	RTR4: 16 min (36 min total) RTR5: 18 min (38 min) RTR6: 20 min (40 min) RTR7: 22 min (42 min) RTR8: 24 min (44 min) RTR9: 26 min (46 min) RTR10: 28 min (48 min) RTR11: 30 min (50 min)
SBI	Swim Base Intervals	100-yard intervals swum @ moderate aerobic intensity w/ 5-second rest periods or single longer swims @ moderate aerobic intensity	SBI3: 4 x 100 SBI4: 5 x 100 SBI5: 6 x 100 SBI6: 7 x 100 SBI7: 8 x 100 SBI8: 9 x 100 SBI24: 1,000 SBI25: 1,200 SBI26: 1,500 SBI27: 1,800 SBI28: 2,000 SBI29: 2,400 SBI30: 2,600
SCD	Swim Cool-Down	Easy swim @ recovery intensity	SCD1: 200 SCD2: 250 SCD3: 300 SCD4: 350
SDS	Swim Drill Set	25-yard intervals of mixed form drills w/ 10-second rest periods	SDS3: 8 x 25 SDS4: 10 x 25
SFI	Swim Fartlek Intervals	100–200-yard intervals with easy/hard or build/descend format (hard = threshold intensity, easy = moderate aerobic intensity) w/ rest periods of 10–20 seconds	SFI1A: 4 x 100 (25 build/25 descend...), 10-sec rest SFI2: 6 x 100 (25 easy/25 hard...), 10-sec rest SFI2A: 6 x 100 (25 build/25 descend...), 10-sec rest SFI3A: 8 x 100 (25 build/25 descend...), 10-sec rest SFI4: 4 x 150 (50 easy/25 hard...), 15-sec rest

Code Prefix	Workout Type	Brief Description	Levels
SFI *(cont.)*			SFI4A: 4 x 150 (50 build/25 descend...), 15-sec rest
			SFI5: 5 x 150 (50 easy/25 hard...), 15-sec rest
			SFI6: 6 x 150 (50 easy/25 hard...), 15-sec rest
			SFI6A: 6 x 150 (50 build/25 descend...), 15-sec rest
			SFI8: 4 x 200 (50 easy/50 hard...), 20-sec rest
			SFI8A: 4 x 200 (50 build/50 descend...), 20-sec rest
			SFI9: 5 x 200 (50 easy/50 hard...), 20-sec rest
			SFI9A: 5 x 200 (50 build/50 descend...), 20-sec rest
			SFI10: 6 x 200 (50 easy/50 hard...), 20-sec rest
			SFI10A: 6 x 200 (50 build/50 descend...), 20-sec rest
SKS	Swim Kick Set	25-yard intervals kicking only w/ 15-second rest periods	SKS3: 8 x 25
			SKS4: 10 x 25
SLI	Swim Lactate Intervals	75–150-yard intervals swum @ VO_2 max intensity with rest periods of 45 seconds to 1 minute 15 seconds	SLI4: 7 x 75, 45-sec rest
			SLI5: 8 x 75, 45-sec rest
			SLI6: 9 x 75, 45-sec rest
			SLI10: 5 x 100, 1-min rest
			SLI11: 6 x 100, 1-min rest
			SLI12: 7 x 100, 1-min rest
			SLI15: 5 x 150, 1-min 15-sec rest
			SLI16: 6 x 150, 1-min 15-sec rest
			SLI16A: 6 x 150, 1-min rest
			SLI16B: 6 x 150, 45-sec rest
			SLI17: 7 x 150, 1-min 15-sec rest
			SLI17A: 7 x 150, 1-min rest
			SLI17B: 7 x 150, 45-sec rest
SSI	Swim Sprint Intervals	25–50-yard intervals swum @ speed intensity w/ 20-second rest periods	SSI1: 4 x 25
			SSI3: 6 x 25
			SSI6: 9 x 25
			SSI7: 10 x 25

Code Prefix	Workout Type	Brief Description	Levels
SSI (cont.)			SSI8: 11 x 25 SSI10: 4 x 50 SSI12: 6 x 50 SSI14: 8 x 50
STI	Swim Threshold Intervals	200–400-yard intervals swum @ threshold intensity w/ rest periods of 20 seconds to 1 minute 15 seconds	STI3: 4 x 200, 45-sec rest STI3A: 4 x 200, 30-sec rest STI3B: 4 x 200, 20-sec rest STI4: 5 x 200, 45-sec rest STI4A: 5 x 200, 30-sec rest STI4B: 5 x 200, 20-sec rest STI5: 6 x 200, 45-sec rest STI5A: 6 x 200, 30-sec rest STI5B: 6 x 200, 20-sec rest STI10: 4 x 300, 1-min rest STI10A: 4 x 300, 45-sec rest STI10B: 4 x 300, 30-sec rest STI11: 5 x 300, 1-min rest STI11A: 5 x 300, 45-sec rest STI11B: 5 x 300, 30-sec rest STI13: 3 x 400, 1-min 15-sec rest STI13A: 3 x 400, 1-min rest STI13B: 3 x 400, 45-sec rest
STT	Swim Time Trial	Designated distance swum @ maximum effort	STT3: 1,650 STT4: 1.2 miles (2,112)
SWU	Swim Warm-Up	Easy swim @ recovery intensity	SWU1: 200 SWU2: 250 SWU3: 300 SWU4: 350

General Schedule

	Tuesday	Wednesday	Thursday	Friday	Saturday	Sunday
BASE PHASE						
Week 1	Swim Base Intervals	Fartlek Run	Brick Workout	Foundation Bike	L5–6: Foundation Bike L7: Long Bike	Swim Base Intervals
	Bike Power Intervals			Swim Fartlek Intervals	L5: Foundation Run L6–7: Foundation Run + Strides	Foundation Run
Week 2	Swim Base Intervals	Fartlek Run	Foundation Bike	Foundation Bike	Brick Workout	Swim Base Intervals
	Bike Power Intervals		L5: Foundation Run L6–7: Foundation Run + Strides	Swim Fartlek Intervals		Foundation Run
Week 3	Swim Base Intervals	Fartlek Run	Brick Workout	Foundation Bike	L5: Foundation Bike L6–7: Long Bike	Swim Base Intervals
	Bike Power Intervals			Swim Fartlek Intervals	Foundation Run + Strides	L5–6: Foundation Run L7: Long Run
Week 4 (Recovery)	Swim Base Intervals	Fartlek Run	Foundation Bike	Recovery Bike	Brick Workout	Swim Base Intervals
	Bike Power Intervals		Foundation Run + Strides	Swim Fartlek Intervals		Foundation Run
Week 5	Swim Base + Sprint Intervals	Run Speed Intervals	Brick Workout	Foundation Bike	Long Bike	Swim Base Intervals

	Tuesday	Wednesday	Thursday	Friday	Saturday	Sunday
Week 5 (cont.)	Bike Short Hills			Swim Fartlek Intervals	Foundation Run + Strides	L5: Foundation Run L6–7: Long Run
Week 6	Swim Base + Sprint Intervals	Run Speed Intervals	Foundation Bike	Foundation Bike	Brick Workout	Swim Time Trial
	Bike Short Hills		Foundation Run + Strides	Swim Fartlek Intervals		Foundation Run
Week 7	Swim Base + Sprint Intervals	Run Speed Intervals	Brick Workout	Foundation Bike	Long Bike	Swim Base Intervals
	Bike Short Hills			Swim Fartlek Intervals	Foundation Run + Strides	Long Run
Week 8 (Recovery)	Swim Base + Sprint Intervals	Run Speed Intervals	Foundation Bike	Recovery Bike	Brick Workout	Swim Base Intervals
	Bike Short Hills		Foundation Run + Strides	Swim Fartlek Intervals		Long Run
BUILD PHASE						
Week 9	Swim Base + Lactate + Sprint Intervals	Run Lactate Intervals	Brick Workout	Foundation Bike	Long Bike	Swim Base Intervals
	Bike Long Hills			Swim Threshold + Sprint Intervals	Foundation Run + Strides	Long Run
Week 10	Swim Base + Lactate + Sprint Intervals	Run Lactate Intervals	Foundation Bike	Foundation Bike	Brick Workout	Swim Base Intervals
	Bike Lactate Intervals		Foundation Run + Strides	Swim Threshold + Sprint Intervals		Foundation Run

	Tuesday	Wednesday	Thursday	Friday	Saturday	Sunday
Week 11	Swim Base + Lactate + Sprint Intervals	Run Lactate Intervals	Brick Workout	Foundation Bike	Long Bike	Swim Time Trial
	Bike Long Hills			Swim Threshold + Sprint Intervals	Foundation Run + Strides	Long Run
Week 12 (Recovery)	Swim Base + Lactate + Sprint Intervals	Run Lactate Intervals	Foundation Bike	Recovery Bike	Recovery Bike (if racing) or Brick Workout	Sprint Triathlon or Swim Base Intervals + Foundation Run
	Bike Lactate Intervals		Foundation Run + Strides	Swim Threshold Intervals		
Week 13	Swim Base + Lactate + Sprint Intervals	Run Lactate Intervals	Brick Workout	Foundation Bike	Long Bike	Swim Time Trial
	Bike Long Hills			Swim Threshold + Sprint Intervals	Foundation Run + Strides	Long Run
Week 14	Swim Base + Lactate + Sprint Intervals	Run Lactate Intervals	Foundation Bike	Foundation Bike	Brick Workout	Swim Base Intervals
	Bike Lactate Intervals		Foundation Run + Strides	Swim Threshold + Sprint Intervals		L5-6: Foundation Run L7: Long Run
PEAK PHASE Week 15	Swim Base + Lactate Intervals	Tempo Run	Brick Workout	Foundation Bike	Long Bike	Swim Time Trial
	Tempo Bike			Swim Threshold + Sprint Intervals	Foundation Run + Strides	Long Run

	Tuesday	**Wednesday**	**Thursday**	**Friday**	**Saturday**	**Sunday**
Week 16 (Recovery)	Swim Base + Lactate Intervals	Tempo Run	Foundation Bike	Recovery Bike	Recovery Bike or Brick Workout	Olympic-Distance Triathlon or Swim Base Intervals
	Tempo Bike		Foundation Run + Strides	Swim Threshold + Sprint Intervals		Olympic-Distance Triathlon or Foundation Run (L5–6) or Long Run (L7)
Week 17	Swim Base + Lactate Intervals	Tempo Run	Brick Workout	Foundation Bike	Long Bike	Swim Base Intervals
	Tempo Bike			Swim Threshold + Sprint Intervals	Foundation Run + Strides	Long Run
Week 18	Swim Base + Lactate Intervals	Tempo Run	Foundation Bike	Recovery Bike	Brick Workout	Swim Time Trial
	Tempo Bike		Foundation Run + Strides	Swim Threshold + Sprint Intervals		Long Run
Week 19 (Half Taper)	Swim Base + Lactate Intervals	Tempo Run	Brick Workout	Foundation Bike	Long Bike	Swim Base Intervals
	Tempo Bike			Swim Threshold + Sprint Intervals	Foundation Run + Strides	Long Run
Week 20 (Taper)	Swim Base + Lactate Intervals	Tempo Run	Foundation Bike	Swim Threshold Intervals	Recovery Bike	Half-Ironman Triathlon
	Tempo Bike		Foundation Run + Strides			

Week-by-Week Schedule

Base Phase

This phase is eight weeks long to allow a gradual, steady buildup of training volume. The primary objectives are developing aerobic capacity, endurance, and injury-resistance. The small amount of high-intensity training you do in this phase will prepare you to handle the more challenging high-intensity workouts of the build phase.

WEEK 1

This week's goal: Get accustomed to your new workout schedule.

	Tuesday	Wednesday	Thursday	Friday	Saturday	Sunday
Level 5	SWU3 SDS3 SBI4 SKS3 SCD3 (1,500)	RFL3	BRW4	CFR3	CFR5	SWU3 SBI24 SCD3 (1,600)
	CPI3			SWU3 SDS3 SFI1A SKS3 SCD3 (1,400)	RFR3	RFR7
Level 6	SWU4 SDS3 SBI5 SKS3 SCD4 (1,700)	RFL5	BRW4	CFR3	CFR6	SWU3 SBI25 SCD3 (1,800)
	CPI4			SWU4 SDS3 SFI2A SKS3 SCD4 (1,700)	RFR3 + RSS1	RFR8
Level 7	SWU4 SDS4 SBI6 SKS4	RFL5	BRW4	CFR3	CLR1	SWU2 SBI26 SCD2 (2,000)

	Tuesday	Wednesday	Thursday	Friday	Saturday	Sunday
Level 7 (cont.)	SCD4 (1,900)					
	CPI4			SWU4 SDS4 SFI3A SKS4 SCD4 (2,000)	RFR3 + RSS2	RFR9

QUICK TIP:

If while running you experience pain just above and outside your knee, the problem is probably iliotibial band friction syndrome. Usually this problem can be solved with deep tissue sports massage. You can also do an at-home self-massage of your IT band using a "foam roller." These $15–$30 products are available through many functional exercise and physical therapy equipment retailers.

WEEK 2

This week's goal: Gather momentum by completing all scheduled workouts as prescribed.

	Tuesday	Wednesday	Thursday	Friday	Saturday	Sunday
Level 5	SWU3 SDS3 SBI5 SKS3 SCD3 (1,600)	RFL4	CFR4	CFR3	BRW5	SWU2 SBI25 SCD2 (1,700)
	CPI4		RFR5	SWU3 SDS3 SFI2 SKS3 SCD3 (1,600)		RFR6

	Tuesday	Wednesday	Thursday	Friday	Saturday	Sunday
Level 6	SWU4 SDS3 SBI5 SKS3 SCD4 (1,700)	RFL6	CFR4	CFR3	BRW6	SWU4 SBI25 SCD4 (1,900)
	CPI4		RFR5 + RSS1	SWU4 SDS3 SFI4 SKS3 SCD4 (1,700)		RFR7
Level 7	SWU4 SDS4 SBI6 SKS4 SCD4 (1,900)	RFL6	CFR4	CFR4	BRW7	SWU3 SBI26 SCD3 (2,100)
	CPI5		RFR5 + RSS2	SWU4 SDS4 SFI6 SKS4 SCD4 (2,100)		RFR8

WEEK 3

This week's goal: Find your "running legs" quickly in Thursday's brick workout.

	Tuesday	Wednesday	Thursday	Friday	Saturday	Sunday
Level 5	SWU3 SDS3 SBI5 SKS3 SCD3 (1,700)	RFL6	BRW5	CFR3	CFR6	SWU3 SBI25 SCD3 (1,800)
	CPI4			SWU3 SDS3 SFI4A SKS3 SCD3 (1,600)	RFR3 + RSS1	RFR8

	Tuesday	Wednesday	Thursday	Friday	Saturday	Sunday
Level 6	SWU4 SDS3 SBI6 SKS3 SCD4 (1,800)	RFL6	BRW5	CFR4	CLR1	SWU2 SBI26 SCD2 (2,000)
	CPI5			SWU4 SDS3 SFI6A SKS3 SCD4 (2,000)	RFR3 + RSS2	RFR9
Level 7	SWU4 SDS4 SBI7 SKS4 SCD4 (2,000)	RFL8	BRW5	CFR4	CLR2	SWU1 SBI27 SCD1 (2,200)
	CPI5			SWU4 SDS4 SFI8A SKS4 SCD4 (2,000)	RFR4 + RSS3	RLR1

WEEK 4
(Recovery)

This week's goal: Fully absorb your recent training and finish the week feeling rested and ready to return to harder training next week.

	Tuesday	Wednesday	Thursday	Friday	Saturday	Sunday
Level 5	SWU3 SDS3 SBI4 SCD3 (1,300)	RFL4	CFR3	CRR4	BRW4	SWU3 SBI24 SCD3 (1,600)
	CPI3		RFR5 + RSS1	SWU3 SDS3 SFI4 SCD3 (1,400)		RFR5

	Tuesday	Wednesday	Thursday	Friday	Saturday	Sunday
Level 6	SWU4 SDS3 SBI5 SCD4 (1,500)	RFL6	CFR3	CRR4	BRW5	SWU3 SBI25 SCD3 (1,800)
	CPI3		RFR5 + RSS2	SWU4 SDS3 SFI5 SCD4 (1,650)		RFR6
Level 7	SWU4 SDS4 SBI6 SCD4 (1,650)	RFL6	CFR3	CRR4	BRW6	SWU4 SBI25 SCD4 (1,900)
	CPI4		RFR5 + RSS3	SWU4 SDS4 SFI8 SCD4 (1,750)		RFR7

WEEK 5

This week's goal: Do Tuesday's short cycling hill climbs at the fastest pace you can maintain through the end of the last climb without slowing down.

	Tuesday	Wednesday	Thursday	Friday	Saturday	Sunday
Level 6	SWU3 SDS3 SBI5 SSI6 SKS3 SCD3 (1,825)	RSI6	BRW5	CFR4	CLR1	SWU4 SBI25 SCD4 (1,900)
	CSH5			SWU3 SDS3 SFI3A SKS3 SCD3 (1,800)	RFR4 + RSS2	RFR9

	Tuesday	Wednesday	Thursday	Friday	Saturday	Sunday
Level 6	SWU4 SDS3 SBI5 SSI6 SKS3 SCD4 (1,925)	RSI12	BRW6	CFR4	CLR2	SWU3 SBI26 SCD3 (2,100)
	CSH6			SWU4 SDS3 SFI9A SKS3 SCD4 (2,100)	RFR4 + RSS3	RLR1
Level 7	SWU4 SDS4 SBI5 SSI6 SKS4 SCD4 (2,025)	RSI13	BRW6	CFR5	CLR3	SWU2 SBI27 SCD2 (2,300)
	CSH7			SWU4 SDS4 SFI9A SKS4 SCD4 (2,200)	RFR4 + RSS3	RLR2

WEEK 6

This week's goal: Go all out to get a good sense of your current swimming performance level in Sunday's swim time trial.

	Tuesday	Wednesday	Thursday	Friday	Saturday	Sunday
Level 5	SWU3 SDS3 SBI4 SSI7 SKS3 SCD3 (1,750)	RSI7	CFR5	CFR4	BRW7	SWU4 STT3 SCD4 (2,350)

	Tuesday	Wednesday	Thursday	Friday	Saturday	Sunday
Level 5 (cont.)	CSH6		RFR7 + RSS3	SWU3 SDS3 SFI3 SKS3 SCD3 (1,800)		RFR6
Level 6	SWU4 SDS3 SBI5 SSI7 SKS3 SCD4 (1,950)	RSI13	CFR5	CFR5	BRW8	SWU4 STT3 SCD4 (2,350)
	CSH7		RFR7 + RSS3	SWU4 SDS3 SFI9 SKS3 SCD4 (2,100)		RFR7
Level 7	SWU4 SDS4 SBI6 SSI7 SKS4 SCD4 (2,150)	RSI14	CFR5	CFR5	BRW9	SWU4 STT3 SCD4 (2,350)
	CSH8		RFR5 + RSS4	SWU4 SDS4 SFI10 SKS4 SCD4 (2,400)		RFR8

QUICK TIP:

Being a triathlete doesn't require that you maintain a special diet. It does, however, increase your need for all three macronutrients: carbohydrate for energy, fat for energy and cellular repair, and protein for muscle rebuilding.

WEEK 7

This week's goal: Finish strong in Sunday's long run.

	Tuesday	Wednesday	Thursday	Friday	Saturday	Sunday
Level 5	SWU3 SDS3 SBI5 SSI8 SKS3 SCD3 (1,875)	RSI8	BRW6	CFR5	CLR2	SWU2 SBI26 SCD2 (2,000)
	CSH8			SWU3 SDS3 SFI6A SKS3 SCD3 (1,900)	RFR4 + RSS3	RLR1
Level 6	SWU4 SDS3 SBI6 SSI8 SKS3 SCD4 (2,075)	RSI14	BRW6	CFR5	CLR3	SWU1 SBI27 SCD1 (2,200)
	CSH9			SWU4 SDS3 SFI10A SKS3 SCD4 (2,300)	RFR4 + RSS4	RLR2
Level 7	SWU4 SDS4 SBI7 SSI8 SKS4 SCD4 (2,275)	RSI15	BRW7	CFR5	CLR4	SWU3 SBI27 SCD3 (2,400)
	CSH14			SWU4 SDS4 SFI10A SKS4 SCD4 (2,400)	RFR5 + RSS4	RLR3

WEEK 8
(Recovery)

This week's goal: Fully absorb your recent training and finish the week feeling rested and ready to return to harder training next week.

	Tuesday	Wednesday	Thursday	Friday	Saturday	Sunday
Level 5	SWU3 SDS3 SBI5 SSI6 SCD3 (1,625)	RSI6	CFR6	CRR4	BRW5	SWU1 SBI25 SCD1 (1,600)
	CSH6		RFR4 + RSS1	SWU3 SDS3 SFI3 SCD3 (1,600)		RFR6
Level 6	SWU4 SDS3 SBI5 SSI6 SCD4 (1,725)	RSI12	CFR6	CRR4	BRW6	SWU3 SBI25 SCD3 (1,800)
	CSH7		RFR4 + RSS2	SWU4 SDS3 SFI6 SCD4 (1,800)		RFR7
Level 7	SWU4 SDS4 SBI5 SSI6 SCD4 (1,875)	RSI13	CFR6	CRR4	BRW7	SWU2 SBI26 SCD2 (2,000)
	CSH8		RFR4 + RSS3	SWU4 SDS4 SFI9 SCD4 (1,950)		RFR8

Build Phase

The primary training emphasis in this six-week phase is high-intensity workouts—including lactate intervals in all three disciplines—to maximize your aerobic capacity and enhance your ability to sustain faster speeds. At the same time you will continue building endurance with long swims, rides, runs, and brick workouts.

WEEK 9

This week's goal: Find a groove at threshold pace in both the cycling and running segments of Thursday's brick workout.

	Tuesday	Wednesday	Thursday	Friday	Saturday	Sunday
Level 5	SWU3 SDS3 SBI4 SLI4 SSI3 SKS3 SCD3 (2,175)	RLI3	BRW3A	CFR5	CLR3	SWU3 SBI26 SCD3 (2,100)
	CLH3			SWU3 SDS3 STI3 SSI10 SKS3 SCD3 (2,000)	RFR4 + RSS3	RLR2
Level 6	SWU4 SDS3 SBI5 SLI4 SSI3 SKS3 SCD4 (2,375)	RLI3	BRW4A	CFR5	CLR4	SWU2 SBI27 SCD2 (2,300)
	CLH4			SWU4 SDS3 STI4 SSI10 SKS3 SCD4 (2,300)	RFR5 + RSS3	RLR3

	Tuesday	Wednesday	Thursday	Friday	Saturday	Sunday
Level 7	SWU4 SDS4 SBI5 SLI5 SSI3 SKS4 SCD4 (2,550)	RLI4	BRW5A	CFR6	CLR5	SWU2 SBI28 SCD2 (2,500)
	CLH5			SWU4 SDS4 STI5 SSI10 SKS4 SCD4 (2,600)	RFR5 + RSS4	RLR4

WEEK 10

This week's goal: Swim hard but relaxed in Tuesday's lactate intervals set.

	Tuesday	Wednesday	Thursday	Friday	Saturday	Sunday
Level 5	SWU3 SDS3 SBI4 SLI5 SSI3 SKS3 SCD3 (2,250)	RLI4	CFR6	CFR5	BRW8	SWU1 SBI27 SCD1 (2,200)
	CLI4		RFR8 + RSS3	SWU3 SDS3 STI3A SSI10 SKS3 SCD3 (2,000)		RFR7
Level 6	SWU4 SDS3 SBI5 SLI5 SSI3 SKS3	RLI4	CFR6	CFR6	BRW9	SWU3 SBI27 SCD3 (2,400)

		Tuesday	Wednesday	Thursday	Friday	Saturday	Sunday
Level 6 (cont.)		SCD4 (2,450)					
		CLI5		RFR8 + RSS4	SWU4 SDS3 STI4A SSI10 SKS3 SCD4 (2,300)		RFR8
Level 7		SWU4 SDS4 SBI5 SLI5 SSI6 SKS4 SCD4 (2,625)	RLI5	CFR7	CFR6	BRW10	SWU3 SBI28 SCD3 (2,600)
		CLI6		RFR8 + RSS4	SWU4 SDS4 STI5A SSI10 SKS4 SCD4 (2,600)		RFR9

WEEK 11

This week's goal: Try to swim at a faster pace in this Sunday's swim time trial than you did in Week 6's.

		Tuesday	Wednesday	Thursday	Friday	Saturday	Sunday
Level 5		SWU3 SDS3 SBI4 SLI6 SSI3 SKS3 SCD3 (2,325)	RLI7	BRW4A	CFR6	CLR4	SWU4 STT3 SCD4 (2,350)
		CLH5			SWU3 SDS3 STI3B	RFR5 + RSS3	RLR3

	Tuesday	Wednesday	Thursday	Friday	Saturday	Sunday
Level 5 (cont.)				SSI10 SKS3 SCD3 (2,000)		
Level 6	SWU4 SDS3 SBI5 SLI6 SSI3 SKS3 SCD4 (2,525)	RLI8	BRW5A	CFR6	CLR5	SWU4 STT3 SCD4 (2,350)
	CLH6			SWU4 SDS3 STI4B SSI10 SKS3 SCD4 (2,300)	RFR5 + RSS4	RLR4
Level 7	SWU4 SDS4 SBI5 SLI6 SSI6 SKS4 SCD4 (2,700)	RLI8	BRW6A	CFR6	CLR6	SWU4 STT3 SCD4 (2,350)
	CLH7			SWU4 SDS4 STI5B SSI10 SKS4 SCD4 (2,600)	RFR5 + RSS4	RLR5

WEEK 12
(Recovery)

This week's goal: Fully absorb your recent training and have a good sprint triathlon performance on Sunday, if you have the opportunity.

	Tuesday	Wednesday	Thursday	Friday	Saturday	Sunday
Level 5	SWU3 SDS3 SBI4 SLI4 SCD3 (1,825)	RLI3	CFR5	CRR4	CRR1 or BRW6*	Sprint Triathlon or SWU2 SBI26 SCD2 (2,000)*
	CLI3		RFR6 + RSS1	SWU3 SDS3 STI4 SCD3 (1,800)		RFR7*
Level 6	SWU4 SDS3 SBI5 SLI4 SCD4 (2,025)	RLI4	CFR5	CRR5	CRR1 or BRW7*	Sprint Triathlon or SWU3 SBI26 SCD3 (2,100)*
	CLI4		RFR6 + RSS2	SWU4 SDS3 STI4 SCD4 (1,900)		RFR8*
Level 7	SWU4 SDS4 SBI6 SLI4 SCD4 (2,175)	RLI4	CFR5	CRR5	CRR1 or BRW8*	Sprint Triathlon or SWU4 SBI26 SCD4 (2,200)*
	CLI5		RFR6 + RSS3	SWU4 SDS4 STI5 SCD4 (2,150)		RFR9*

*If not racing

QUICK TIP:

In races, you'll save some time in your swim-bike triathlon transition if you preclip your cycling shoes to the pedals and run out of the transition area in bare feet (or with socks on). Likewise, you can save some time in the bike-run transition by pulling your feet out of the shoes during the last 200 meters and performing a running dismount. These skills require practice to perfect, so don't try them for the first time in a race!

WEEK 13

This week's goal: Pace yourself through Thursday's longer threshold-pace brick workout.

	Tuesday	Wednesday	Thursday	Friday	Saturday	Sunday
Level 5	SWU3 SDS3 SBI5 SLI10 SKS3 SCD3 (2,100)	RLI9	BRW5A	CFR6	CLR5	SWU2 SBI27 SCD2 (2,300)
	CLH5			SWU3 SDS3 STI10 SSI1 SKS3 SCD3 (2,300)	RFR5 + RSS3	RLR4
Level 6	SWU4 SDS3 SBI6 SLI10 SKS3 SCD4 (2,300)	RLI9	BRW6A	CFR6	CLR6	SWU2 SBI28 SCD2 (2,500)
	CLH6			SWU4 SDS3 STI10 SSI10 SKS3 SCD4 (2,500)	RFR5 + RSS4	RLR5

	Tuesday	Wednesday	Thursday	Friday	Saturday	Sunday
Level 7	SWU4 SDS4 SBI6 SLI11 SKS4 SCD4 (2,500)	RLI10	BRW7B	CFR7	CLR7	SWU4 SBI28 SCD4 (2,700)
	CLH7			SWU4 SDS4 STI11 SSI1 SKS4 SCD4 (2,800)	RFR5 + RSS4	RLR6

WEEK 14

This week's goal: Finish strong in Sunday's long endurance swim.

	Tuesday	Wednesday	Thursday	Friday	Saturday	Sunday
Level 5	SWU3 SDS3 SBI6 SLI11 SKS3 SCD3 (2,300)	RLI10	CFR7	CFR6	BRW10	SWU1 SBI28 SCD1 (2,400)
	CLI6		RFR9 + RSS3	SWU3 SDS3 STI10A SSI1 SKS3 SCD3 (2,300)		RFR8
Level 6	SWU4 SDS3 SBI7 SLI11 SKS3 SCD4 (2,500)	RLI10	CSS1	CFR7	BRW11	SWU3 SBI28 SCD3 (2,600)

	Tuesday	Wednesday	Thursday	Friday	Saturday	Sunday
Level 6 (cont.)	CLI7		RFR9 + RSS4	SWU4 SDS3 STI10A SSI10 SKS3 SCD4 (2,500)		RFR9
Level 7	SWU4 SDS4 SBI8 SLI11 SKS4 SCD4 (2,700)	RLI11	CSS1	CFR7	BRW12	SWU2 SBI29 SCD2 (2,900)
	CLI11		RLR1 + RSS4	SWU4 SDS4 STI11A SSI1 SKS4 SCD4 (2,800)		RLR1

Peak Phase

To ensure you're able to go the distance on race day, your long endurance workouts on the weekends become especially long in this six-week phase. The second training priority is threshold-intensity training in swimming, cycling, and running. Long brick workouts, a swim time trial, and an optional Olympic-distance tune-up triathlon also help build race-specific fitness.

WEEK 15

This week's goal: Find a smooth groove at threshold intensity (8–8.5 RPE) in Wednesday's tempo run.

	Tuesday	Wednesday	Thursday	Friday	Saturday	Sunday
Level 5	SWU3 SDS3 SBI6 SLI12 SKS3 SCD3 (2,400)	RTR7	BRW6A	CFR7	CLR6	SWU2 SBI28 SCD2 (2,500)

	Tuesday	Wednesday	Thursday	Friday	Saturday	Sunday
Level 5 (cont.)	CTR7			SWU3 SDS3 STI10B SSI1 SKS3 SCD3 (2,300)	RFR5	RLR5
Level 6	SWU4 SDS3 SBI7 SLI12 SKS3 SCD4 (2,600)	RTR8	BRW7B	CFR7	CLR7	SWU4 SBI28 SCD4 (2,700)
	CTR8			SWU4 SWU4 SDS3 STI10B SSI10 SKS3 SCD4 (2,500)	RFR5	RLR6
Level 7	SWU4 SDS4 SBI8 SLI12 SKS4 SCD4 (2,800)	RTR9	BRW8B	CFR7	CLR8	SWU3 SBI29 SCD3 (3,000)
	CTR9			SWU4 SDS4 STI11B SSI1 SKS4 SCD4 (2,800)	RFR5	RLR7

WEEK 16
(Recovery)

This week's goal: Fully absorb your recent training and have a solid Olympic-distance triathlon performance on Sunday, if you have the opportunity.

	Tuesday	Wednesday	Thursday	Friday	Saturday	Sunday
Level 5	SWU3 SDS3 SBI3 SLI11 SCD3 (1,800)	RTR6	CFR4	CRR4	CRR1 or BRW7*	Olympic-Distance Triathlon or SWU2 SBI26 SCD2 (2,000)*
	CTR6		RFR7 + RSS1	SWU3 SDS3 STI4 SCD3 (1,800)		RFR8*
Level 6	SWU4 SDS3 SBI4 SLI11 SCD4 (2,000)	RTR7	CFR5	CRR5	CRR1 or BRW8*	Olympic-Distance Triathlon or SWU3 SBI26 SCD3 (2,100)*
	CTR7		RFR7 + RSS2	SWU4 SDS3 STI4 SCD4 (1,900)		RFR9*
Level 7	SWU4 SDS4 SBI5 SLI11 SCD4 (2,150)	RTR8	CFR5	CRR5	CRR1 or BRW9*	Olympic-Distance Triathlon or SWU2 SBI27 SCD2 (2,300)*
	CTR8		RFR7 + RSS3	SWU4 SDS4 STI5 SCD4 (2,150)		RLR1*

*If not racing

WEEK 17

This week's goal: Put your head down and grind through Saturday's very long ride and Sunday's peak endurance run.

	Tuesday	Wednesday	Thursday	Friday	Saturday	Sunday
Level 5	SWU3 SDS3 SBI6 SLI16 SKS3 SCD3 (2,600)	RTR7	BRW7A	CFR6	CLR7	SWU1 SBI29 SCD1 (2,800)
	CTR8			SWU3 SDS3 STI13 SSI10 SKS3 SCD3 (2,400)	RFR5 + RSS2	RLR6
Level 6	SWU4 SDS3 SBI7 SLI16 SKS3 SCD4 (2,800)	RTR8	BRW8A	CFR7	CLR8	SWU3 SBI29 SCD3 (3,000)
	CTR9			SWU4 SDS3 STI13 SSI12 SKS3 SCD4 (2,600)	RFR5 + RSS3	RLR7
Level 7	SWU4 SDS4 SBI7 SLI17 SKS4 SCD4 (3,050)	RTR9	BRW9A	CFR7	CLR9	SWU3 SBI30 SCD3 (3,200)

	Tuesday	Wednesday	Thursday	Friday	Saturday	Sunday
Level 7 (cont.)	CTR10			SWU4 SDS4 STI13 SSI14 SKS4 SCD4 (2,800)	RFR5 + RSS4	RLR8

WEEK 18

This week's goal: Build race-specific fitness with Saturday's brick workout and Sunday's swim time trial.

	Tuesday	Wednesday	Thursday	Friday	Saturday	Sunday
Level 5	SWU3 SDS3 SBI6 SLI16A SKS3 SCD3 (2,600)	RTR8	CFR7	CFR6	BRW12	SWU3 STT4 SCD3 (2,712)
	CTR9		RLR1 + RSS3	SWU3 SDS3 STI13A SSI10 SKS3 SCD3 (2,400)		RFR5
Level 6	SWU4 SDS3 SBI7 SLI16A SKS3 SCD4 (2,800)	RTR9	CSS1	CFR6	BRW13	SWU3 STT4 SCD3 (2,712)
	CTR10		RLR2 + RSS4	SWU4 SDS3 STI13A SSI12 SKS3 SCD4 (2,600)		RFR6

	Tuesday	Wednesday	Thursday	Friday	Saturday	Sunday
Level 7	SWU4 SDS4 SBI7 SLI17A SKS4 SCD4 (3,050)	RTR10	CSS2	CFR7	BRW14	SWU3 STT4 SCD3 (2,712)
	CTR11		RLR2 + RSS4	SWU4 SDS4 STI13A SSI14 SKS4 SCD4 (2,800)		RFR7

QUICK TIP:

Use music to calm your prerace nerves and get yourself psyched to race. Warm up, set up your brick area, and so forth while wearing a portable digital music player such as a Rio Fuse playing just the right music to make you feel relaxed, confident, and ready for action.

WEEK 19
(Half Taper)

This week's goal: Gain confidence for next week's race by feeling your fitness begin to peak in this week's workouts.

	Tuesday	Wednesday	Thursday	Friday	Saturday	Sunday
Level 5	SWU3 SDS3 SBI6 SLI16B SKS3 SCD3 (2,600)	RTR9	BRW6A	CFR5	CLR4	SWU3 SBI27 SCD3 (2,400)
	CTR10			SWU3 SDS3 STI13B	RFR3 + RSS2	RLR2

	Tuesday	Wednesday	Thursday	Friday	Saturday	Sunday
Level 5 (cont.)				SSI10 SKS3 SCD3 (2,400)		
Level 6	SWU4 SDS3 SBI7 SLI16B SKS3 SCD4 (2,800)	RTR10	BRW7A	CFR5	CLR5	SWU3 SBI28 SCD3 (2,600)
	CTR11			SWU4 SDS3 STI13B SSI12 SKS3 SCD4 (2,600)	RFR3 + RSS3	RLR3
Level 7	SWU4 SDS4 SBI7 SLI17B SKS4 SCD4 (3,050)	RTR11	BRW8A	CFR6	CLR6	SWU1 SBI29 SCD1 (2,800)
	CTR12			SWU4 SDS4 STI13B SSI14 SKS4 SCD4 (2,800)	RFR4 + RSS3	RLR4

WEEK 20

This week's goal: Have a great half-Ironman on Sunday!

	Tuesday	Wednesday	Thursday	Friday	Saturday	Sunday
Level 5	SWU4 SDS3 SBI2 SLI11 SCD4 (1,800)	RTR4	CFR2	SWU3 STI2 SSI10 SCD3 (1,400)	CRR1	Half-Ironman Triathlon
	CTR7		RFR3 + RSS3			
Level 6	SWU4 SDS4 SBI2 SLI12 SCD4 (1,950)	RTR5	CFR2	SWU3 STI2 SSI10 SCD3 (1,400)	CRR1	Half-Ironman Triathlon
	CTR8		RFR3 + RSS3			
Level 7	SWU4 SDS4 SBI3 SLI15 SCD4 (2,100)	RTR6	CFR2	SWU3 STI2 SSI10 SCD3 (1,400)	CRR1	Half-Ironman Triathlon
	CTR9		RFR3 + RSS3			

Chapter 11
HALF-IRONMAN TRIATHLON TRAINING PLANS
Levels 8–10

*I*n most cases, triathletes who are willing and able to do as much training for a half-Ironman as the three plans in this chapter call for would prefer to complete the half-Ironman as a tune-up race preceding a full Ironman. But there are exceptions. The legendary Australian triathlete Michellie Jones, for example, competed in short-course triathlons for many years before transforming herself into a long-course racer. During a couple of transitional seasons she raced half-Ironman triathlons but not full Ironmans. And while uncommon, there are serious age-group triathletes who set their limit at the half distance: they do sprints, Olympic-distance races, and half-IMs, and that's it.

If you are looking to achieve a lifetime peak performance at the half-Ironman distance, these are the plans for you. Like the lower-level half-Ironman training plans they are 20 weeks long and comprise an eight-week base phase, a six-week build phase, and a six-week peak phase. The three plans in this chapter also include two optional tune-up races: a sprint at the end of Week 12 and an Olympic-distance race at the end of Week 16. Every fourth week is a recovery week and the last 10 days constitute a tapering period.

You will train four times per week in each discipline. This includes a weekly bike-run brick workout. The brick falls on Thursday in odd-numbered weeks and on Saturday in even-numbered weeks.

Level 8

Choose this plan if you are ready for a very heavy training schedule, but not the heaviest. There's a little restraint in the workouts that comprise this plan to suit those who don't want to risk overdoing it, yet are very competitive. The plan begins with 7,550 yards of swimming,

5 hours and 15 minutes of cycling, and 2 hours and 31 minutes of running in Week 1. It peaks with 11,850 yards of swimming, 9 hours and 5 minutes of cycling, and 4 hours and 21 minutes of running in Week 17.

Level 9

If you are almost willing and able to train as hard as any triathlete, but not quite, here's your half-Ironman training plan. It begins with 8,050 yards of swimming, 5 hours and 45 minutes of cycling, and 2 hours and 46 minutes of running in Week 1. It peaks with 12,300 yards of swimming, 9 hours and 30 minutes of cycling, and 4 hours and 48 minutes of running in Week 17.

Level 10

If time is no object and you have trained as much as 18 to 20 hours a week in the past, then this is your half-Ironman training plan. It begins with 8,600 yards of swimming, 6 hours and 15 minutes of cycling, and 2 hours and 56 minutes of running in Week 1. It peaks with 12,950 yards of swimming, 10 hours and 10 minutes of cycling, and 4 hours and 55 minutes of running in Week 17.

Code Prefix	Workout Type	Brief Description	Levels
BRW	Brick Workout	Bike ride followed by immediate run, both @ moderate aerobic intensity, except "A" suffix = bike and run @ high aerobic intensity, as indicated	BRW4: 45 min/15 min BRW5: 1 hr/20 min BRW6: 1 hr/30 min BRW7: 1 hr 15 min/20 min BRW7A: 1 hr 15 min/20 min (bike and run @ high aerobic) BRW8: 1 hr 15 min/30 min BRW8A: 1 hr 15 min/30 min (bike and run @ high aerobic) BRW9: 1 hr 30 min/30 min BRW9A: 1 hr 30 min/30 min (bike and run @ high aerobic) BRW10: 1 hr 30 min/45 min BRW11: 1 hr 45 min/45 min BRW11A: 1 hr 45 min/45 min (bike and run @ high aerobic) BRW12: 1 hr 45 min/50 min BRW13: 2 hr/50 min BRW14: 2 hr 15 min/55 min BRW15: 2 hr 30 min/55 min
CFR	Foundation Bike	Steady ride @ moderate aerobic intensity	CFR2: 45 min CFR3: 1 hr CFR4: 1 hr 15 min CFR5: 1 hr 30 min CFR6: 1 hr 45 min CFR7: 2 hr
CLH	Bike Long Hill Climbs	5–8-minute climbing intervals @ threshold/VO$_2$ max intensity w/ 3-minute active recoveries; warm up and cool down long enough to reach total time	CLH3: 4 x 5 min (1 hr 10 min total) CLH4: 5 x 5 min (1 hr 15 min) CLH5: 6 x 5 min (1 hr 20 min) CLH6: 7 x 5 min (1 hr 30 min) CLH7: 8 x 5 min (1 hr 30 min) CLH8: 2 x 8 min (1 hr 40 min)
CLI	Bike Lactate Intervals	3-minute intervals @ VO$_2$ max intensity w/ 3-minute active recoveries; warm up and cool down long enough to reach total time	CLI2: 3 x 3 min (1 hr 10 min total) CLI5: 6 x 3 min (1 hr 25 min) CLI6: 7 x 3 min (1 hr 30 min) CLI7: 8 x 3 min (1 hr 35 min)

Code Prefix	Workout Type	Brief Description	Levels
CLR	Long Bike Ride	Long steady ride @ moderate aerobic intensity	CLR2: 2 hr 15 min CLR3: 2 hr 30 min CLR4: 2 hr 45 min CLR5: 3 hr CLR6: 3 hr 15 min CLR7: 3 hr 30 min CLR8: 3 hr 45 min CLR9: 4 hr CLR10: 4 hr 15 min CLR11: 4 hr 30 min CLR12: 4 hr 45 min
CPI	Bike Power Intervals	20-second intervals done in a high gear @ speed intensity w/ 2-minute active recoveries; warm up and cool down long enough to reach total time	CPI3: 6 x 20 sec (1 hr total) CPI4: 7 x 20 sec (1 hr 10 min) CPI5: 8 x 20 sec (1 hr 20 min) CPI6: 9 x 20 sec (1 hr 25 min) CPI7: 10 x 20 sec (1 hr 30 min) CPI8: 11 x 20 sec (1 hr 35 min)
CRR	Recovery Bike	Steady ride @ recovery intensity	CRR1: 20 min
CSI	Bike Speed Intervals	1-minute intervals @ speed intensity w/ 2-minute active recoveries or 1.5-minute intervals @ speed intensity w/ 3-minute active recoveries; warm up and cool down long enough to reach total time	CSI3: 6 x 1 min (55 min total) CSI4: 7 x 1 min (1 hr) CSI5: 8 x 1 min (1 hr 5 min) CSI10: 4 x 1 min 30 sec (1 hr 30 min) CSI11: 5 x 1 min 30 sec (1 hr 35 min) CSI12: 6 x 1 min 30 sec (1 hr 40 min) CSI13: 7 x 1 min 30 sec (1 hr 45 min) CSI14: 8 x 1 min 30 sec (1 hr 50 min) CSI15: 9 x 1 min 30 sec (1 hr 55 min)
CSH	Bike Short Hill Climbs	1-minute hill climbs @ VO_2 max/speed intensity w/ 2-minute active recoveries or 1.5-minute hill climbs @ VO_2 max/speed intensity w/ 3-minute active recoveries; warm up and cool down long enough to reach total time	CSH10: 4 x 1 min 30 sec (1 hr 30 min total) CSH11: 5 x 1 min 30 sec (1 hr 35 min) CSH12: 6 x 1 min 30 sec (1 hr 40 min) CSH13: 7 x 1 min 30 sec (1 hr 45 min)

Code Prefix	Workout Type	Brief Description	Levels
CSH (cont.)			CSH14: 8 x 1 min 30 sec (1 hr 50 min)
CSS	Steady-State Ride	Steady ride @ high aerobic intensity	CSS1: 1 hr 10 min CSS2: 1 hr 15 min CSS3: 1 hr 30 min
CTR	Tempo Bike Ride	One or two blocks of riding @ threshold intensity (10-minute active recovery when threshold-intensity riding is divided into two blocks); warm up and cool down long enough to reach total time	CTR7: 2 x 14 min (1 hr 15 min total) CTR8: 28 min (1 hr 20 min) CTR9: 30 min (1 hr 25 min) CTR10: 2 x 16 min (1 hr 30 min) CTR11: 32 min (1 hr 35 min) CTR12: 34 min (1 hr 40 min) CTR13: 2 x 18 min (1 hr 45 min) CTR14: 36 min (1 hr 50 min) CTR15: 38 min (1 hr 55 min) CTR16: 2 x 20 min (2 hr) CTR17: 40 min (2 hr 5 min)
RFL	Fartlek Run	Foundation run with 30-second bursts @ VO_2 max/speed intensity	RFL4: 8 x 30 sec (35 min total) RFL6: 8 x 30 sec (40 min) RFL7: 6 x 30 sec (45 min) RFL8: 8 x 30 sec (45 min)
RFR	Foundation Run	Steady run @ moderate aerobic intensity	RFR3: 30 min RFR4: 35 min RFR5: 40 min RFR6: 45 min RFR7: 50 min RFR8: 55 min RFR9: 1 hr
RLI	Run Lactate Intervals	1–3-minute intervals run @ VO_2 max intensity w/ active recoveries equal to intervals in duration; warm up and cool down long enough to reach total time	RLI6: 8 x 1 min (36 min total) RLI7: 10 x 1 min (40 min) RLI8: 12 x 1 min (44 min) RLI9: 3 x 3 min (38 min) RLI10: 4 x 3 min (44 min) RLI11: 5 x 3 min (50 min) RLI12: 6 x 3 min (56 min) RLI12: 5 x 4 min (56 min)
RLR	Long Run	Long, steady-pace run @ moderate aerobic intensity	RLR1: 1 hr 5 min RLR2: 1 hr 10 min

Code Prefix	Workout Type	Brief Description	Levels
RLR (cont.)			RLR3: 1 hr 20 min RLR4: 1 hr 30 min RLR5: 1 hr 40 min RLR6: 1 hr 50 min RLR7: 2 hr RLR8: 2 hr 10 min RLR9: 2 hr 20 min RLR10: 2 hr 30 min
RSI	Running Speed Intervals	1-minute intervals run @ speed intensity w/ 3-minute active recoveries; warm up and cool down long enough to reach total time	RSI12: 6 x 1 min (47 min total) RSI13: 7 x 1 min (54 min) RSI14: 8 x 1 min (1 hr 1 min) RSI15: 9 x 1 min (1 hr 5 min) RSI16: 10 x 1 min (1 hr 5 min) RSI17: 11 x 1 min (1 hr 9 min) RSI18: 12 x 1 min (1 hr 12 min)
RSS	Running Strides	20-second "relaxed sprints" @ speed intensity w/ 40-second active recoveries	RSS1: 2 x 20 sec RSS2: 4 x 20 sec RSS3: 6 x 20 sec
RTR	Tempo Run	Steady run @ threshold intensity; warm up and cool down long enough to reach total time	RTR7: 22 min (42 min total) RTR8: 24 min (44 min) RTR9: 26 min (46 min) RTR10: 28 min (48 min) RTR11: 30 min (50 min) RTR12: 32 min (52 min) RTR13: 34 min (54 min) RTR14: 36 min (56 min) RTR15: 38 min (58 min) RTR17: 40 min (1 hr)
SBI	Swim Base Intervals	100-yard intervals swum @ moderate aerobic intensity w/ 5-second rest periods or 200-yard intervals swum @ moderate aerobic intensity w/ 10-second rest periods or single longer swims @ moderate aerobic intensity	SBI3: 4 x 100 SBI4: 5 x 100 SBI5: 6 x 100 SBI6: 7 x 100 SBI7: 8 x 100 SBI8: 9 x 100 SBI9: 10 x 100 SBI10: 11 x 100 SBI11: 12 x 100 SBI15: 5 x 200 SBI16: 6 x 200

Code Prefix	Workout Type	Brief Description	Levels
SBI (cont.)			SBI17: 7 x 200 SBI21: 4 x 400 SBI24: 1,000 SBI25: 1,200 SBI26: 1,500 SBI27: 1,800 SBI28: 2,000 SBI29: 2,400 SBI30: 2,600 SBI31: 2,800
SCD	Swim Cool-Down	Easy swim @ recovery intensity	SCD1: 200 SCD2: 250 SCD3: 300 SCD4: 350 SCD5: 400
SDS	Swim Drill Set	25–50-yard intervals of mixed form drills w/ 10-second rest periods	SDS4: 10 x 25 SDS5: 12 x 25 SDS7: 6 x 50
SFI	Swim Fartlek Intervals	100–200-yard intervals with easy/hard or build/descend format (hard = threshold intensity, easy = moderate aerobic intensity) w/ rest periods of 10–20 seconds	SFI1: 4 x 100 (25 easy/25 hard...), 10-sec rest SFI1A: 4 x 100 (25 build/25 descend...), 10-sec rest SFI4: 4 x 150 (50 easy/25 hard...), 15-sec rest SFI4A: 4 x 150 (50 build/25 descend...), 15-sec rest SFI5: 5 x 150 (50 easy/25 hard...), 15-sec rest SFI5A: 5 x 150 (50 build/25 descend...), 15-sec rest SFI6: 6 x 150 (50 easy/25 hard...), 15-sec rest SFI6A: 6 x 150 (50 build/25 descend...), 15-sec rest SFI8: 4 x 200 (50 easy/50 hard...), 20-sec rest SFI9: 5 x 200 (50 easy/50 hard...), 20-sec rest SFI9A: 5 x 200 (50 build/50 descend...), 20-sec rest

Code Prefix	Workout Type	Brief Description	Levels
SFI (cont.)			SFI10: 6 x 200 (50 easy/50 hard...), 20-sec rest SFI10A: 6 x 200 (50 build/50 descend...), 20-sec rest
SKS	Swim Kick Set	25-yard intervals kicking only w/ 15-second rest periods	SKS5: 12 x 25
SLI	Swim Lactate Intervals	75–150-yard intervals swum @ VO_2 max intensity with rest periods of 30 seconds to 1 min 15 seconds	SLI4: 7 x 75, 45-sec rest SLI5: 8 x 75, 45-sec rest SLI6: 9 x 75, 45-sec rest SLI10: 5 x 100, 1-min rest SLI11: 6 x 100, 1-min rest SLI11A: 6 x 100, 45-sec rest SLI11B: 6 x 100, 30-sec rest SLI12: 7 x 100, 1-min rest SLI12A: 7 x 100, 45-sec rest SLI12B: 7 x 100, 30-sec rest SLI13: 8 x 100, 1-min rest SLI13A: 8 x 100, 45-sec rest SLI13B: 8 x 100, 30-sec rest SLI15: 5 x 150, 1-min 15-sec rest SLI15A: 5 x 150, 1-min rest SLI15B: 5 x 150, 30-sec rest SLI16: 6 x 150, 1-min 15-sec rest SLI16A: 6 x 150, 1-min rest SLI16B: 6 x 150, 45-sec rest SLI17: 7 x 150, 1-min 15-sec rest SLI17A: 7 x 150, 1-min rest SLI17B: 7 x 150, 45-sec rest
SSI	Swim Sprint Intervals	25–50-yard intervals swum @ speed intensity w/ 20-second rest periods	SSI1: 4 x 25 SSI3: 6 x 25 SSI5: 8 x 25 SSI6: 9 x 25 SSI7: 10 x 25 SSI8: 11 x 25 SSI9: 12 x 25 SSI10: 4 x 50 SSI12: 6 x 50 SSI14: 8 x 50

Code Prefix	Workout Type	Brief Description	Levels
STI	Swim Threshold Intervals	200–400-yard intervals swum @ threshold intensity w/ rest periods of 30 seconds to 1 minute 15 seconds	STI3: 4 x 200, 45-sec rest STI4: 5 x 200, 45-sec rest STI5: 6 x 200, 45-sec rest STI6: 7 x 200, 45-sec rest STI10: 4 x 300, 1-min rest STI10A: 4 x 300, 45-sec rest STI10B: 4 x 300, 30-sec rest STI11: 5 x 300, 1-min rest STI11A: 5 x 300, 45-sec rest STI11B: 5 x 300, 30-sec rest STI13: 3 x 400, 1-min 15-sec rest STI13A: 3 x 400, 1-min rest STI13B: 3 x 400, 45-sec rest STI14: 4 x 400, 1-min 15-sec rest STI14A: 4 x 400, 1-min rest STI14B: 4 x 400, 45-sec rest
STT	Swim Time Trial	Designated distance swum @ maximum effort	STT3: 1,650 STT4: 1.2 miles (2,112)
SWU	Swim Warm-Up	Easy swim @ recovery intensity	SWU1: 200 SWU2: 250 SWU3: 300 SWU4: 350 SWU5: 400

General Schedule						
	Tuesday	**Wednesday**	**Thursday**	**Friday**	**Saturday**	**Sunday**
BASE PHASE						
Week 1	Swim Base Intervals	Swim Base Intervals	Brick Workout	Foundation Bike	Long Bike	Swim Base Intervals
	Foundation Bike	Foundation Run		Swim Fartlek Intervals	Foundation Run + Strides	L8: Foundation Run L9–10: Long Run
Week 2	Swim Base Intervals	Swim Base Intervals	Foundation Bike	Foundation Bike	Brick Workout	Swim Base Intervals
	Foundation Bike	Foundation Run	Foundation Run + Strides	Swim Fartlek Intervals		L8: Foundation L9–10: Long Run
Week 3	Swim Base Intervals	Swim Base Intervals	Brick Workout	Foundation Bike	Long Bike	Swim Base Intervals
	Foundation Bike	Foundation Run		Swim Fartlek Intervals	Foundation Run + Strides	Long Run
Week 4 (Recovery)	Swim Base Intervals	Swim Base Intervals	Foundation Bike	Foundation Bike	Brick Workout	Swim Base Intervals
	Foundation Bike	Foundation Run	Foundation Run + Strides	Swim Fartlek Intervals		L8–9: Foundation Run L10: Long Run
Week 5	Swim Base + Sprint Intervals	Swim Base Intervals	Brick Workout	Bike Power Intervals	Long Bike	Swim Base Intervals
	Steady-State Bike	Foundation Run		Swim Fartlek Intervals	Fartlek Run	Long Run
Week 6	Swim Base + Sprint Intervals	Swim Base Intervals	Foundation Bike	Bike Power Intervals	Brick Workout	Swim Time Trial
	Steady-State Bike	Foundation Run	Fartlek Run	Swim Fartlek Intervals		Long Run

	Tuesday	Wednesday	Thursday	Friday	Saturday	Sunday
Week 7	Swim Base + Sprint Intervals	Swim Base Intervals	Brick Workout	Bike Power Intervals	Long Bike	Swim Base Intervals
	Steady-State Bike	Foundation Run		Fartlek Intervals	Fartlek Run	Long Run
Week 8 (Recovery)	Swim Base + Sprint Intervals	Swim Base Intervals	Foundation Bike	Bike Power Intervals	Brick Workout	Swim Base Intervals
	Steady-State Bike	Foundation Run	Fartlek Run	Swim Fartlek Intervals		Long Run
BUILD PHASE						
Week 9	Swim Base + Lactate + Sprint Intervals	Swim Base Intervals	Brick Workout	Bike Short Hills	Long Bike	Swim Base Intervals
	Tempo Bike	Tempo Run		Swim Threshold + Sprint Intervals	Run Speed Intervals	Long Run
Week 10	Swim Base + Lactate + Sprint Intervals	Swim Base Intervals	Foundation Bike	Bike Speed Intervals	Brick Workout	Swim Base Intervals
	Tempo Bike	Tempo Run	Run Speed Intervals	Swim Threshold + Sprint Intervals		Long Run
Week 11	Swim Base + Lactate + Sprint Intervals	Swim Base Intervals	Brick Workout	Bike Short Hills	Long Bike	Swim Time Trial
	Tempo Bike	Tempo Run		Swim Threshold + Sprint Intervals	Run Speed Intervals	Long Run
Week 12 (Recovery)	Swim Base + Lactate + Sprint Intervals	Swim Base Intervals	Foundation Bike	Bike Speed Intervals	Recovery Bike or Brick Workout	Sprint Triathlon or Swim Base Intervals

	Tuesday	Wednesday	Thursday	Friday	Saturday	Sunday
Week 12 (cont.)	Tempo Bike	Tempo Run	Run Speed Intervals	Swim Threshold + Sprint Intervals		Sprint Triathlon or Long Run
Week 13	Swim Base + Lactate + Sprint Intervals	Swim Base Intervals	Brick Workout	Bike Short Hills	Long Bike	Swim Base Intervals
	Tempo Bike	Tempo Run		Swim Threshold + Sprint Intervals	Run Speed Intervals	Long Run
Week 14	Swim Base + Lactate + Sprint Intervals	Swim Base Intervals	Foundation Bike	Bike Speed Intervals	Brick Workout	Swim Base Intervals
	Tempo Bike	Tempo Run	Run Speed Intervals	Swim Threshold + Sprint Intervals		Long Run
PEAK PHASE Week 15	Swim Base + Lactate Intervals	Swim Base Intervals	Brick Workout	Bike Long Hills	Long Bike	Swim Base Intervals
	Tempo Bike	Tempo Run		Swim Threshold + Sprint Intervals	Run Lactate Intervals	Long Run
Week 16 (Recovery)	Swim Base + Lactate Intervals	Swim Base Intervals	Foundation Bike	Bike Lactate Intervals	Recovery Bike or Brick Workout	Olympic-Distance Triathlon or Swim Base Intervals
	Tempo Bike	Tempo Run	Run Lactate Intervals	Swim Threshold + Sprint Intervals		Olympic-Distance Triathlon or Foundation Run (L8) or Long Run (L9–10)

	Tuesday	Wednesday	Thursday	Friday	Saturday	Sunday
Week 17	Swim Base + Lactate Intervals	Swim Base Intervals	Brick Workout	Bike Long Hills	Long Bike	Swim Base Intervals
	Tempo Bike	Tempo Run		Swim Threshold + Sprint Intervals	Run Lactate Intervals	Long Run
Week 18	Swim Base + Lactate Intervals	Swim Base Intervals	Foundation Bike	Bike Lactate Intervals	Brick Workout	Swim Time Trial
	Tempo Bike	Tempo Run	Run Lactate Intervals	Swim Threshold + Sprint Intervals		Long Run
Week 19	Swim Base + Lactate Intervals	Swim Base Intervals	Brick Workout	Bike Long Hills	Long Bike	Swim Base Intervals
	Tempo Bike	Tempo Run		Swim Threshold + Sprint Intervals	Run Lactate Intervals	Long Run
Week 20	Swim Base + Lactate Intervals	Swim Base Intervals	Foundation Bike	Swim Threshold + Sprint Intervals	Recovery Bike	Half-Ironman Triathlon
	Tempo Bike	Tempo Run	Foundation Run + Strides			

Week-by-Week Schedule

Base Phase

This is an eight-week phase focused on building aerobic capacity with lots of moderate aerobic-intensity training throughout the week and on boosting endurance with long workouts on the weekends.

WEEK 1

This week's goal: Get accustomed to your new training schedule.

	Tuesday	Wednesday	Thursday	Friday	Saturday	Sunday
Level 8	SWU4 SDS5 SBI5 SKS5 SCD4 (1,900)	SWU4 SDS4 SBI9 SCD4 (1,950)	BRW4	CFR3	CLR2	SWU3 SBI25 SCD3 (1,800)
	CFR4	RFR5		SWU4 SDS5 SFI4 SKS5 SCD4 (1,900)	RFR3 + RSS2	RFR9
Level 9	SWU5 SDS5 SBI5 SKS5 SCD5 (2,000)	SWU4 SDS4 SBI10 SCD4 (2,050)	BRW5	CFR3	CLR3	SWU2 SBI26 SCD2 (2,000)
	CFR4	RFR6		SWU5 SDS5 SFI4 SKS5 SCD5 (2,000)	RFR3 + RSS2	RLR1
Level 10	SWU5 SDS5 SBI6 SKS5 SCD5 (2,100)	SWU4 SDS4 SBI11 SCD4 (2,150)	BRW5	CFR3	CLR4	SWU4 SBI26 SCD4 (2,200)
	CFR5	RFR6		SWU5 SDS5 SFI5 SKS5 SCD5 (2,150)	RFR4 + RSS2	RLR2

QUICK TIP:

Don't try too hard to maintain a low-fat diet. In a study of runners, those who ate the most fat had the lowest injury rate. Eating fat appears to help in the muscle repair processes that prevent minor damage from become major. Try to get most of your fats from seafood, nuts and seeds, and extra virgin olive oil, as these sources have a good balance of saturated and unsaturated fats. Limit your intake of whole-milk dairy foods, fatty cuts of meat, processed oils (e.g., partially hydrogenated vegetable oil), and especially fried foods, which are higher in saturated fats (which are not inherently bad, but are consumed excessively by most Americans) and trans fats, which are unhealthy in any amount.

WEEK 2

This week's goal: Gather momentum by completing all scheduled workouts as prescribed.

	Tuesday	Wednesday	Thursday	Friday	Saturday	Sunday
Level 8	SWU4 SDS5 SBI6 SKS5 SCD4 (2,000)	SWU4 SDS4 SBI10 SCD4 (2,050)	CFR4	CFR3	BRW6	SWU4 SBI25 SCD4 (1,900)
	CFR5	RFR6	RFR5 + RSS2	SWU4 SDS5 SFI6A SKS5 SCD4 (2,200)		RFR9
Level 9	SWU5 SDS5 SBI6 SKS5 SCD5 (2,100)	SWU4 SDS4 SBI11 SCD4 (2,150)	CFR4	CFR3	BRW7	SWU3 SBI26 SCD3 (2,100)

	Tuesday	Wednesday	Thursday	Friday	Saturday	Sunday
Level 9 (cont.)	CFR5	RFR6	RFR5 + RSS2	SWU5 SDS5 SFI6A SKS5 SCD5 (2,300)		RLR1
Level 10	SWU5 SDS5 SBI7 SKS5 SCD5 (2,200)	SWU4 SDS4 SBI17 SCD4 (2,350)	CFR5	CFR4	BRW8	SWU2 SBI27 SCD2 (2,300)
	CFR5	RFR7	RFR5 + RSS2	SWU5 SDS5 SFI9A SKS5 SCD5 (2,400)		RLR2

WEEK 3

This week's goal: Find your running legs quickly in Thursday's brick workout.

	Tuesday	Wednesday	Thursday	Friday	Saturday	Sunday
Level 8	SWU4 SDS5 SBI6 SKS5 SCD4 (2,000)	SWU4 SDS4 SBI11 SCD4 (2,150)	BRW5	CFR3	CLR3	SWU2 SBI26 SCD2 (2,000)
	CFR5	RFR6		SWU4 SDS5 SFI6 SKS5 SCD4 (2,200)	RFR4 + RSS3	RLR1
Level 9	SWU5 SDS5 SBI7 SKS5 SCD5 (2,200)	SWU4 SDS4 SBI17 SCD4 (2,350)	BRW5	CFR4	CLR4	SWU1 SBI27 SCD1 (2,200)

	Tuesday	Wednesday	Thursday	Friday	Saturday	Sunday
Level 9 (cont.)	CFR6	RFR7		SWU5 SDS5 SFI6 SKS5 SCD5 (2,300)	RFR4 + RSS3	RLR2
Level 10	SWU5 SDS5 SBI8 SKS5 SCD5 (2,300)	SWU4 SDS4 SBI21 SCD4 (2,550)	BRW6	CFR4	CLR5	SWU3 SBI27 SCD3 (2,400)
	CFR6	RFR8		SWU5 SDS5 SFI9 SKS5 SCD5 (2,400)	RFR4 + RSS3	RLR3

WEEK 4
(Recovery)

This week's goal: Fully absorb your recent training and finish the week feeling rested and ready to return to harder training next week.

	Tuesday	Wednesday	Thursday	Friday	Saturday	Sunday
Level 8	SWU4 SDS5 SBI5 SCD4 (1,600)	SWU4 SDS4 SBI9 SCD4 (1,950)	CFR3	CFR2	BRW5	SWU3 SBI24 SCD3 (1,600)
	CFR3	RFR3	RFR4 + RSS2	SWU4 SDS5 SFI4A SCD4 (1,600)		RFR8
Level 9	SWU5 SDS5 SBI5 SCD5 (1,700)	SWU4 SDS4 SBI10 SCD4 (2,050)	CFR3	CFR2	BRW6	SWU3 SBI25 SCD3 (1,800)

	Tuesday	Wednesday	Thursday	Friday	Saturday	Sunday
Level 9 *(cont.)*	CFR3	RFR4	RFR5 + RSS2	SWU5 SDS5 SFI4A SCD5 (1,700)		RFR9
Level 10	SWU5 SDS5 SBI6 SCD5 (1,800)	SWU4 SDS4 SBI11 SCD4 (2,150)	CFR4	CFR3	BRW7	SWU2 SBI26 SCD2 (2,000)
	CFR4	RFR4	RFR5 + RSS2	SWU5 SDS5 SFI5A SCD5 (1,850)		RLR1

WEEK 5

This week's goal: Do Friday's cycling power intervals at maximum intensity (10 RPE).

	Tuesday	Wednesday	Thursday	Friday	Saturday	Sunday
Level 8	SWU4 SDS5 SBI5 SSI6 SKS5 SCD4 (2,125)	SWU4 SDS4 SBI11 SCD4 (2,150)	BRW5	CPI4	CLR4	SWU3 SBI26 SCD3 (2,100)
	CSS2	RFR6		SWU4 SDS5 SFI6 SKS5 SCD4 (2,200)	RFL5	RLR2

259

	Tuesday	Wednesday	Thursday	Friday	Saturday	Sunday
Level 9 (cont.)	CSS2	RFR7		SWU5 SDS5 SFI9 SKS5 SCD5 (2,400)	RFL7	RLR3
Level 10	SWU5 SDS5 SBI7 SSI6 SKS5 SCD5 (2,425)	SWU4 SDS4 SBI21 SCD4 (2,550)	BRW6	CPI6	CLR6	SWU2 SBI28 SCD2 (2,500)
	CSS3	RFR8		SWU5 SDS5 SFI10 SKS5 SCD5 (2,600)	RFL7	RLR4

WEEK 6

This week's goal: Run hard but stay relaxed at VO$_2$ max intensity in Thursday's fartlek running intervals.

	Tuesday	Wednesday	Thursday	Friday	Saturday	Sunday
Level 8	SWU4 SDS5 SBI6 SSI7 SKS5 SCD4 (2,250)	SWU4 SDS4 SBI7 SCD4 (2,350)	CFR5	CPI5	BRW7	SWU2 STT3 SCD2 (2,150)
	CSS3	RFR7	RFL6	SWU4 SDS5 SFI10A SKS5 SCD4 (2,500)		RLR2
Level 9	SWU5 SDS5 SBI7	SWU4 SDS4 SBI21	CFR5	CPI6	BRW8	SWU3 STT3 SCD3

	Tuesday	Wednesday	Thursday	Friday	Saturday	Sunday
Level 9 (cont.)	SSI7 SKS5 SCD5 (2,450)	SCD4 (2,550)				(2,250)
	CSS3	RFR8	RFL8	SWU5 SDS5 SFI10A SKS5 SCD5 (2,600)		RLR3
Level 10	SWU5 SDS5 SBI8 SSI7 SKS5 SCD5 (2,550)	SWU4 SDS4 SBI17 SBI3 SCD4 (2,750)	CFR6	CPI7	BRW9	SWU4 STT3 SCD4 (2,350)
	CSS4	RFR9	RFL8	SWU5 SDS5 SFI9A SFI1A SKS5 SCD5 (2,800)		RLR4

WEEK 7

This week's goal: Pace yourself evenly through Sunday's long swim.

	Tuesday	Wednesday	Thursday	Friday	Saturday	Sunday
Level 8	SWU4 SDS5 SBI7 SSI8 SKS5 SCD4 (2,375)	SWU4 SDS7 SBI16 SBI3 SCD4 (2,600)	BRW6	CPI6	CLR5	SWU4 SBI26 SCD4 (2,200)
	CSS3	RFR8		SWU4 SDS5 SFI10 SKS5 SCD4 (2,500)	RFL8	RLR3

	Tuesday	Wednesday	Thursday	Friday	Saturday	Sunday
Level 9	SWU5 SDS5 SBI7 SSI9 SKS5 SCD5 (2,500)	SWU4 SDS7 SBI16 SBI4 SCD4 (2,700)	BRW6	CPI7	CLR6	SWU3 SBI27 SCD3 (2,400)
	CSS3	RFR9		SWU5 SDS5 SFI10 SKS5 SCD5 (2,600)	RFL8	RLR4
Level 10	SWU5 SDS5 SBI8 SSI9 SKS5 SCD5 (2,600)	SWU4 SDS7 SBI16 SBI6 SCD4 (2,900)	BRW7	CPI8	CLR7	SWU3 SBI28 SCD3 (2,600)
	CSS4	RFR9		SWU5 SDS5 SFI9 SFI1 SKS5 SCD5 (2,800)	RFL8	RLR5

QUICK TIP:

Don't limit yourself to the suggested weekly goals. Feel free to set as many weekly training goals as you like. Sports psychologists believe an athlete can't set too many goals, as long as each is sensible.

WEEK 8
(Recovery)

This week's goal: Fully absorb your recent training and finish the week feeling rested and ready to return to harder training next week.

	Tuesday	Wednesday	Thursday	Friday	Saturday	Sunday
Level 8	SWU4 SDS5 SBI5 SSI6 SCD4 (1,825)	SWU4 SDS7 SBI15 SCD4 (2,000)	CFR6	CPI3	BRW6	SWU3 SBI25 SCD3 (1,800)
	CFR4	RFR4	RFL4	SWU4 SDS5 SFI8 SCD4 (1,800)		RLR3
Level 9	SWU5 SDS5 SBI6 SSI6 SCD5 (2,025)	SWU4 SDS7 SBI16 SCD4 (2,200)	CFR6	CPI4	BRW7	SWU2 SBI26 SCD2 (2,000)
	CFR4	RFR4	RFL6	SWU5 SDS5 SFI6 SCD5 (2,000)		RLR2
Level 10	SWU5 SDS5 SBI7 SSI7 SCD5 (2,150)	SWU4 SDS7 SBI7 SCD4 (2,400)	CFR6	CPI5	BRW8	SWU4 SBI26 SCD4 (2,200)
	CFR4	RFR4	RFL6	SWU5 SDS5 SFI9 SCD5 (2,100)		RLR3

Build Phase

This challenging six-week phase combines a lot of training at threshold intensity and above with continued increases in the duration of your endurance-boosting weekend workout.

WEEK 9

This week's goal: Find a good groove at threshold pace (8–8.5 RPE) in Tuesday's tempo ride and in Wednesday's tempo run.

	Tuesday	Wednesday	Thursday	Friday	Saturday	Sunday
Level 8	SWU4 SDS5 SBI5 SLI5 SSI3 SKS5 SCD4 (2,650)	SWU4 SDS7 SBI16 SBI3 SCD4 (2,600)	BRW7	CSH10	CLR6	SWU2 SBI27 SCD2 (2,300)
	CTR7	RTR9		SWU4 SDS5 STI4 SSI12 SKS5 SCD4 (2,600)	RSI12	RLR4
Level 9	SWU5 SDS5 SBI5 SLI5 SSI3 SKS5 SCD5 (2,750)	SWU4 SDS7 SBI16 SBI5 SCD4 (2,800)	BRW7	CSH11	CLR7	SWU2 SBI28 SCD2 (2,500)
	CTR8	RTR10		SWU5 SDS5 STI4 SSI12 SKS5 SCD5 (2,700)	RSI13	RLR5
Level 10	SWU5 SDS5 SBI6 SLI5 SSI3 SKS5 SCD5 (2,850)	SWU4 SDS7 SBI16 SBI7 SCD4 (3,000)	BRW8	CSH12	CLR8	SWU4 SBI28 SCD4 (2,700)

	Tuesday	Wednesday	Thursday	Friday	Saturday	Sunday
Level 10 (cont.)	CTR9	RTR11		SWU5 SDS5 STI5 SSI12 SKS5 SCD5 (2,900)	RSI14	RLR6

WEEK 10

This week's goal: Finish strong in Saturday's long brick workout.

	Tuesday	Wednesday	Thursday	Friday	Saturday	Sunday
Level 8	SWU4 SDS5 SBI5 SLI5 SSI6 SKS5 SCD4 (2,725)	SWU4 SDS7 SBI16 SBI4 SCD4 (2,700)	CFR7	CSI10	BRW9	SWU3 SBI27 SCD3 (2,400)
	CTR8	RTR10	RSI13	SWU4 SDS5 STI4 SSI12 SKS5 SCD4 (2,600)		RLR3
Level 9	SWU5 SDS5 SBI5 SLI5 SSI7 SKS5 SCD5 (2,850)	SWU4 SDS7 SBI16 SBI6 SCD4 (2,900)	CFR7	CSI11	BRW10	SWU3 SBI28 SCD3 (2,600)
	CTR9	RTR11	RSI14	SWU5 SDS5 STI5 SSI10 SKS5 SCD5 (2,800)		RLR3

	Tuesday	Wednesday	Thursday	Friday	Saturday	Sunday
Level 10	SWU5 SDS5 SBI6 SLI5 SSI7 SKS5 SCD5 (2,950)	SWU4 SDS7 SBI16 SBI7 SCD4 (3,000)	CFR8	CSI12	BRW11	SWU1 SBI29 SCD1 (2,800)
	CTR10	RTR12	RSI15	SWU5 SDS5 STI5 SSI12 SKS5 SCD5 (2,900)		RLR4

WEEK 11

This week's goal: Go all out to test your current swim performance level in Sunday's swim time trial.

	Tuesday	Wednesday	Thursday	Friday	Saturday	Sunday
Level 8	SWU4 SDS5 SBI5 SLI6 SSI6 SKS5 SCD4 (2,800)	SWU4 SDS7 SBI17 SBI3 SCD4 (2,800)	BRW7A	CSH11	CLR7	SWU4 STT3 SCD4 (2,350)
	CTR9	RTR11		SWU4 SDS5 STI5 SSI12 SKS5 SCD4 (2,800)	RSI14	RLR5
Level 9	SWU5 SDS5 SBI5 SLI6 SSI6 SKS5	SWU4 SDS7 SBI16 SBI6 SCD4 (2,900)	BRW7A	CSH12	CLR8	SWU4 STT3 SCD4 (2,350)

	Tuesday	Wednesday	Thursday	Friday	Saturday	Sunday
Level 9 (cont.)	SCD5 (2,900)					
	CTR10	RTR12		SWU5 SDS5 STI5 SSI12 SKS5 SCD5 (2,900)	RSI15	RLR6
Level 10	SWU5 SDS5 SBI6 SLI6 SSI6 SKS5 SCD5 (3,000)	SWU4 SDS7 SBI16 SBI7 SCD4 (3,000)	BRW8A	CSH13	CLR9	SWU4 STT3 SCD4 (2,350)
	CTR11	RTR13		SWU5 SDS5 STI6 SSI10 SKS5 SCD5 (3,000)	RSI16	RLR7

WEEK 12
(Recovery)

This week's goal: Fully absorb your recent training and have a good sprint triathlon performance on Sunday if you have the opportunity.

	Tuesday	Wednesday	Thursday	Friday	Saturday	Sunday
Level 8	SWU4 SDS5 SBI5 SLI4 SCD4 (2,175)	SWU4 SDS7 SBI16 SCD4 (2,200)	CFR5	CSI3	CRR1 or BRW8*	Sprint Triathlon or SWU3 SBI25 SCD3 (1,800)*
	CTR7	RTR8	RSI12	SWU4 SDS5		RLR1*

*If not racing

	Tuesday	Wednesday	Thursday	Friday	Saturday	Sunday
Level 8 (cont.)				STI4 SSI1 SCD4 (2,100)		
Level 9	SWU5 SDS5 SBI5 SLI4 SCD5 (2,275)	SWU4 SDS7 SBI17 SCD4 (2,600)	CFR5	CSI4	CRR1 or BRW9*	Sprint Triathlon or SWU2 SBI26 SCD2 (2,000)*
	CTR8	RTR9	RSI12	SWU5 SDS5 STI4 SSI1 SCD5 (2,200)		RLR2*
Level 10	SWU5 SDS5 SBI6 SLI4 SCD5 (2,375)	SWU4 SDS7 SBI21 SBI6 SCD4 (2,600)	CFR5	CSI5	CRR1 or BRW10 *	Sprint Triathlon or SWU4 SBI26 SCD4 (2,200)*
	CTR9	RTR10	RSI12	SWU5 SDS5 STI4 SSI5 SCD5 (2,300)		RLR3*

*If not racing

WEEK 13

This week's goal: Run Saturday's speed intervals at the fastest pace you can sustain through the end of the final interval without slowing.

	Tuesday	Wednesday	Thursday	Friday	Saturday	Sunday
Level 8	SWU4 SDS5 SBI7 SLI11 SKS5 SCD4 (2,700)	SWU4 SDS7 SBI17 SBI4 SCD4 (2,900)	BRW7A	CSH12	CLR8	SWU3 SBI28 SCD3 (2,600)
	CTR10	RTR11		SWU4 SDS5 STI10 SSI12 SKS5 SCD4 (2,800)	RSI15	RLR6
Level 9	SWU5 SDS5 SBI7 SLI12 SKS5 SCD5 (2,900)	SWU4 SDS7 SBI17 SBI5 SCD4 (3,000)	BRW8A	CSH13	CLR9	SWU4 SBI28 SCD4 (2,700)
	CTR11	RTR12		SWU5 SDS5 STI10 SSI12 SKS5 SCD5 (2,900)	RSI16	RLR7
Level 10	SWU5 SDS5 SBI7 SLI13 SKS5 SCD5 (3,000)	SWU4 SDS7 SBI17 SBI6 SCD4 (3,100)	BRW8A	CSH14	CLR10	SWU2 SBI29 SCD2 (2,900)
	CTR12	RTR13		SWU5 SDS5 STI11 SSI10 SKS5 SCD5 (3,100)	RSI17	RLR8

QUICK TIP:

A study of various prerace warm-up strategies found that athletes performed best following a warm-up that began with low-intensity activity and ended with a few high-intensity bursts within a few minutes of the race start. This approach seems to do the best job of priming the muscles for a maximum-intensity effort.

WEEK 14

This week's goal: Finish strong in Saturday's long brick workout.

	Tuesday	Wednesday	Thursday	Friday	Saturday	Sunday
Level 8	SWU4 SDS5 SBI8 SLI11A SKS5 SCD4 (2,800)	SWU4 SDS7 SBI17 SBI5 SCD4 (3,000)	CSS1	CSI13	BRW12	SWU4 SBI28 SCD4 (2,700)
	CTR11	RTR12	RSI16	SWU4 SDS5 STI10A SSI12 SKS5 SCD4 (2,800)		RLR1
Level 9	SWU5 SDS5 SBI8 SLI12A SKS5 SCD5 (3,000)	SWU4 SDS7 SBI17 SBI5 SCD4 (3,000)	CSS1	CSI14	BRW13	SWU1 SBI29 SCD1 (2,800)
	CTR12	RTR13	RSI17	SWU5 SDS5 STI10A SSI12 SKS5 SCD5 (2,900)		RLR2

	Tuesday	Wednesday	Thursday	Friday	Saturday	Sunday
Level 10	SWU5 SDS5 SBI8 SLI13A SKS5 SCD5 (3,100)	SWU4 SDS7 SBI17 SBI6 SCD4 (3,100)	CSS2	CSI15	BRW14	SWU3 SBI29 SCD3 (3,000)
	CTR13	RTR14	RSI18	SWU5 SDS5 STI11A SSI10 SKS5 SCD5 (3,100)		RLR3

Peak Phase

This six-week phase prioritizes very long endurance workouts in all three disciplines and contains challenging threshold-intensity sessions, to give a race-ready edge to your fitness.

WEEK 15

This week's goal: Finish strong in Sunday's long swim.

	Tuesday	Wednesday	Thursday	Friday	Saturday	Sunday
Level 8	SWU4 SDS5 SBI8 SLI11B SKS5 SCD4 (2,800)	SWU4 SDS7 SBI17 SBI5 SCD4 (3,000)	BRW8A	CLH4	CLR9	SWU2 SBI29 SCD2 (2,900)
	CTR12	RTR13		SWU4 SDS5 STI10B SSI12 SKS5 SCD4 (2,800)	RLI7	RLR7
Level 9	SWU5 SDS5 SBI8	SWU4 SDS7 SBI17	BRW8A	CLH5	CLR10	SWU3 SBI29 SCD3

	Tuesday	Wednesday	Thursday	Friday	Saturday	Sunday
Level 9 (cont.)	SLI12B SKS5 SCD5 (3,000)	SBI5 SCD4 (3,000)				(3,000)
	CTR13	RTR14		SWU5 SDS5 STI10B SSI12 SKS5 SCD5 (2,900)	RLI7	RLR9
Level 10	SWU5 SDS5 SBI8 SLI13B SKS5 SCD5 (3,100)	SWU4 SDS7 SBI17 SBI6 SCD4 (3,100)	BRW9A	CLH6	CLR11	SWU3 SBI30 SCD3 (3,200)
	CTR14	RTR15		SWU5 SDS5 STI11B SSI10 SKS5 SCD5 (3,100)	RLI8	RLR9

WEEK 16
(Recovery)

This week's goal: Fully absorb your recent training and have a solid Olympic-distance triathlon performance on Sunday if you have the opportunity.

	Tuesday	Wednesday	Thursday	Friday	Saturday	Sunday
Level 8	SWU4 SDS5 SBI5 SLI11 SCD4 (2,200)	SWU4 SDS7 SBI17 SCD4 (2,400)	CFR5	CLI2	CRR1 or BRW9*	Olympic- Distance Triathlon or SWU2 SBI26 SCD2 (2,000)*

	Tuesday	Wednesday	Thursday	Friday	Saturday	Sunday
Level 8 (cont.)	CTR9	RTR8	RLI6	SWU4 SDS5 STI4 SSI1 SCD4 (2,100)		RFR9*
Level 9	SWU5 SDS5 SBI5 SLI11 SCD5 (2,300)	SWU4 SDS7 SBI21 SCD4 (2,600)	CFR5	CLI2	CRR1 or BRW9*	Olympic-Distance Triathlon or SWU3 SBI26 SCD3 (2,100)*
	CTR10	RTR9	RLI7	SWU5 SDS5 STI4 SSI1 SCD5 (2,200)		RLR1*
Level 10	SWU5 SDS5 SBI6 SLI11 SCD5 (2,400)	SWU4 SDS7 SBI15 SBI6 SCD4 (2,700)	CFR5	CLI2	CRR1 or BRW10*	Olympic-Distance Triathlon or SWU4 SBI26 SCD4 (2,200)*
	CTR11	RTR10	RLI9	SWU5 SDS5 STI4 SSI5 SCD5 (2,300)		RLR2*

*If not racing

WEEK 17

This week's goal: Dig deep in Friday's challenging long hill climbs on the bike.

	Tuesday	Wednesday	Thursday	Friday	Saturday	Sunday
Level 8	SWU4 SDS5 SBI8 SLI15 SKS5 SCD4 (2,950)	SWU4 SDS7 SBI17 SBI5 SCD4 (3,000)	BRW9A	CLH6	CLR10	SWU3 SBI29 SCD3 (3,000)
	CTR14	RTR14		SWU4 SDS5 STI13 SSI14 SKS5 SCD4 (2,900)	RLI10	RLR8
Level 9	SWU5 SDS5 SBI7 SLI16 SKS5 SCD5 (3,100)	SWU4 SDS7 SBI17 SBI5 SCD4 (3,000)	BRW9A	CLH7	CLR11	SWU3 SBI30 SCD3 (3,200)
	CTR15	RTR15		SWU5 SDS5 STI13 SSI14 SKS5 SCD5 (3,000)	RLI11	RLR9
Level 10	SWU5 SDS5 SBI7 SLI17 SKS5 SCD5 (3,250)	SWU4 SDS7 SBI17 SBI6 SCD4 (3,100)	BRW11A	CLH8	CLR12	SWU3 SBI31 SCD3 (3,400)
	CTR16	RTR16		SWU5 SDS5 STI14 SSI10 SKS5 SCD5 (3,200)	RLI12	RLR10

WEEK 18

This week's goal: Go all out in Sunday's race-simulation swim time trial.

	Tuesday	Wednesday	Thursday	Friday	Saturday	Sunday
Level 8	SWU4 SDS5 SBI8 SLI15A SKS5 SCD4 (2,950)	SWU4 SDS7 SBI17 SBI5 SCD4 (3,000)	CSS2	CLI5	BRW15	SWU1 STT4 SCD1 (2,512)
	CTR15	RTR15	RLI11	SWU4 SDS5 STI13A SSI14 SKS5 SCD4 (2,900)		RLR1
Level 9	SWU5 SDS5 SBI7 SLI16A SKS5 SCD5 (3,100)	SWU4 SDS7 SBI17 SBI6 SCD4 (3,100)	CSS3	CLI6	BRW15	SWU2 STT4 SCD2 (2,612)
	CTR16	RTR16	RLI12	SWU5 SDS5 STI13A SSI14 SKS5 SCD5 (3,000)		RLR2
Level 10	SWU5 SDS5 SBI7 SLI17A SKS5 SCD5 (3,250)	SWU4 SDS7 SBI17 SBI7 SCD4 (3,200)	CSS3	CLI7	BRW15	SWU3 STT4 SCD3 (2,712)

	Tuesday	Wednesday	Thursday	Friday	Saturday	Sunday
Level 10 *(cont.)*	CTR17	RTR16	RLI13	SWU5 SDS5 STI14A SSI10 SKS5 SCD5 (3,200)		RLR3

QUICK TIP:

Consciously monitor your form periodically in every swim, bike, and run workout. You should have a feel for the elements of proper form and use your body awareness to correct any lapses you sense as you go. Form flaws are bad habits, and bad habits die hard—you must address them every time you plunge into the pool, mount the bike, or lace up your shoes.

WEEK 19
(Half Taper)
This week's goal: Hang in there through Wednesday's workouts—the next 10 days are a tapering period.

	Tuesday	Wednesday	Thursday	Friday	Saturday	Sunday
Level 8	SWU4 SDS5 SBI8 SLI15B SKS5 SCD4 (2,950)	SWU4 SDS7 SBI17 SBI4 SCD4 (2,900)	BRW8	CLH3	CLR3	SWU3 SBI27 SCD3 (2,400)
	CTR14	RTR13		SWU4 SDS5 STI13B SSI10 SKS5 SCD4 (2,700)	RLI6	RLR3

	Tuesday	Wednesday	Thursday	Friday	Saturday	Sunday
Level 9	SWU5 SDS5 SBI7 SLI16B SKS5 SCD5 (3,100)	SWU4 SDS7 SBI17 SBI5 SCD4 (3,000)	BRW8A	CLH4	CLR4	SWU3 SBI28 SCD3 (2,600)
	CTR15	RTR14		SWU5 SDS5 STI13B SSI10 SKS5 SCD5 (2,800)	RLI6	RLR4
Level 10	SWU5 SDS5 SBI7 SLI17B SKS5 SCD5 (3,250)	SWU4 SDS7 SBI17 SBI6 SCD4 (3,100)	BRW8A	CLH5	CLR5	SWU1 SBI29 SCD1 (2,800)
	CTR16	RTR15		SWU5 SDS5 STI14B SSI1 SKS5 SCD5 (3,100)	RLI6	RLR5

WEEK 20

This week's goal: Have a great half-Ironman on Sunday!

	Tuesday	Wednesday	Thursday	Friday	Saturday	Sunday
Level 8	SWU4 SDS5 SBI5 SLI10 SCD4 (2,100)	SWU4 SDS7 SBI15 SCD4 (2,000)	CFR2	SWU3 STI2 SSI10 SCD3 (1,400)	CRR1	Half-Ironman Triathlon
	CTR9	RTR7	RFR3 + RSS3			

	Tuesday	Wednesday	Thursday	Friday	Saturday	Sunday
Level 9	SWU5 SDS5 SBI5 SLI10 SCD5 (2,200)	SWU4 SDS7 SBI15 SCD4 (2,000)	CFR2	SWU3 STI2 SSI10 SCD3 (1,400)	CRR1	Half-Ironman Triathlon
	CTR10	RTR8	RFR3 + RSS3			
Level 10	SWU5 SDS5 SBI5 SLI11 SCD5 (2,300)	SWU4 SDS7 SBI15 SCD4 (2,000)	CFR2	SWU3 STI2 SSI10 SCD3 (1,400)	CRR1	Half-Ironman Triathlon
	CTR11	RTR8	RFR3 + RSS3			

Chapter 12

IRONMAN TRIATHLON
TRAINING PLANS
Levels 1–3

One of the very first triathlons ever staged was also the very first Ironman, which took place on the Big Island of Hawaii back in 1978. Most of its participants were not superathletes, but just guys (they were all guys) who liked to play outdoors. As the sport of triathlon became popular, the Hawaii Ironman, and the other Ironman races that began popping up, became more competitive, but only at the top level. The dream of finishing an Ironman has continued to draw thousands of everyday men and women to these events, and when they start, they almost always do finish.

If you think of yourself as an everyday athlete, and you have a dream of finishing an Ironman, one of the three plans in this chapter is your ticket to the finish line. It takes a lot of swimming, cycling, and running to prepare for a successful Ironman finish, but with the right approach it doesn't take as much training as some people fear. The training plans in this chapter feature nine workouts per week, with relatively short workouts during the week and all of the long ones crammed into the weekends. In the odd-numbered weeks you'll do three swims, three rides, and three runs. In Weeks 2, 6, and so forth, you will do a brick workout instead of a ride on Saturday, which effectively adds a fourth run to your schedule. In Weeks 4, 8, and so forth, you will do a brick workout on Sunday instead of a run, which effectively adds a fourth ride to the schedule.

The plans are 24 weeks long, which I consider the optimal amount of specific preparation time for an Ironman. Each phase—base, build, and peak—is eight weeks long. Every fourth week is a recovery week and the final two weeks constitute a tapering period. There are three optional tune-up races scheduled: a sprint in Week 12, an Olympic-distance event in Week 16, and a half-Ironman in Week 20.

Level 1

This plan offers the minimal training you need for a successful Ironman finish. And by successful I mean finishing strong, not limping across the line and falling on your face! The plan begins with 4,300 yards of swimming, 2 hours and 45 minutes of cycling, and 1 hour and 51 minutes of running in Week 1. It peaks with 8,600 yards of swimming, 8 hours and 50 minutes of cycling, and 2 hours and 45 minutes of running in Week 22. (Note that, including the brick workout, this is a week with four rides and three runs, so the total cycling time is higher and the running time lower than in Weeks 21 and 23.)

Level 2

Like the Level 2 training plans for shorter distances, this plan offers a small training "cushion" so you can start your Ironman with a little more certainty that you're prepared to finish strong. It begins with 4,500 yards of swimming, 3 hours and 5 minutes of cycling, and 2 hours and 1 minute of running in Week 1. It peaks with 9,100 yards of swimming, 9 hours and 30 minutes of cycling, and 2 hours and 47 minutes of running in Week 22. (Note that, including the brick workout, this is a week with four rides and three runs, so the total cycling time is higher and the running time lower than in Weeks 21 and 23.)

Level 3

This plan is a good fit if you want to prepare for an Ironman on a schedule of nine workouts per week, but you're prepared to handle nine fairly challenging workouts. It begins with 4,900 yards of swimming, 3 hours and 30 minutes of cycling, and 2 hours and 11 minutes of running in Week 1. It peaks with 9,600 yards of swimming, 10 hours and 20 minutes of cycling, and 2 hours and 54 minutes of running in Week 22. (Note that, including the brick workout, this is a week with four rides and three runs, so the total cycling time is higher and the running time lower than in Weeks 21 and 23.)

Quick Reference Guide to Workout Codes for Ironman Triathlon Training Plans Levels 1-3

Code Prefix	Workout Type	Brief Description	Levels
BRW	Brick Workout	Bike ride followed by immediate run, both @ moderate aerobic intensity	BRW3: 45 min/10 min BRW4: 45 min/15 min BRW5: 1 hr/20 min BRW6: 1 hr/30 min BRW8: 1 hr 15 min/30 min BRW9: 1 hr 30 min/30 min BRW10: 1 hr 30 min/45 min BRW11: 1 hr 45 min/45 min BRW12: 1 hr 45 min/50 min BRW13: 2 hr/50 min BRW14: 2 hr 15 min/55 min BRW15: 2 hr 30 min/55 min BRW16: 3 hr/1 hr BRW17: 3 hr 30 min/1 hr BRW18: 4 hr/1 hr
CFR	Foundation Bike	Steady ride @ moderate aerobic intensity	CFR2: 45 min CFR3: 1 hr CFR4: 1 hr 15 min CFR5: 1 hr 30 min CFR6: 1 hr 45 min CFR7: 2 hr
CLH	Bike Long Hill Climbs	5-minute climbing intervals @ threshold/VO_2 max intensity w/ 3-minute active recoveries; warm up and cool down long enough to reach total time	CLH2: 3 x 5 min (1 hr 5 min total) CLH3: 4 x 5 min (1 hr 10 min) CLH4: 5 x 5 min (1 hr 15 min) CLH5: 6 x 5 min (1 hr 20 min)
CLI	Bike Lactate Intervals	3-minute intervals @ VO_2 max intensity w/ 3-minute active recoveries; warm up and cool down long enough to reach total time	CLI2: 3 x 3 min (1 hr 10 min total) CLI3: 4 x 3 min (1 hr 15 min) CLI4: 5 x 3 min (1 hr 20 min) CLI5: 6 x 3 min (1 hr 25 min)
CLR	Long Bike Ride	Long steady ride @ moderate aerobic intensity	CLR2: 2 hr 15 min CLR3: 2 hr 30 min CLR4: 2 hr 45 min CLR5: 3 hr

Code Prefix	Workout Type	Brief Description	Levels
CLR (cont.)			CLR6: 3 hr 15 min CLR7: 3 hr 30 min CLR8: 3 hr 45 min CLR9: 4 hr CLR10: 4 hr 15 min CLR11: 4 hr 30 min CLR12: 4 hr 45 min CLR13: 5 hr CLR14: 5 hr 15 min CLR15: 5 hr 30 min CLR16: 5 hr 45 min CLR17: 6 hr
CPI	Bike Power Intervals	20-second intervals done in a high gear @ speed intensity w/ 2-minute active recoveries; warm up and cool down long enough to reach total time	CPI1: 4 x 20 sec (45 min total) CPI2: 5 x 20 sec (50 min) CPI3: 6 x 20 sec (1 hr) CPI4: 7 x 20 sec (1 hr 10 min) CPI5: 8 x 20 sec (1 hr 20 min)
CRR	Recovery Bike	Steady ride @ recovery intensity	CRR3: 45 min CRR4: 1 hr CRR5: 1 hr 15 min CRR6: 1 hr 30 min
CSI	Bike Speed Intervals	1-minute intervals @ speed intensity w/ 2-minute active recoveries or 1.5-minute intervals @ speed intensity w/ 3-minute active recoveries; warm up and cool down long enough to reach total time	CSI3: 6 x 1 min (55 min total) CSI4: 7 x 1 min (1 hr) CSI5: 8 x 1 min (1 hr 5 min) CSI10: 4 x 1 min 30 sec (1 hr 30 min) CSI11: 5 x 1 min 30 sec (1 hr 35 min) CSI12: 6 x 1 min 30 sec (1 hr 40 min) CSI13: 7 x 1 min 30 sec (1 hr 45 min) CSI14: 8 x 1 min 30 sec (1 hr 50 min)
CSH	Bike Short Hill Climbs	1-minute hill climbs @ VO_2 max/speed intensity w/ 2-minute active recoveries; warm up and cool down long enough to reach total time	CSH3: 6 x 1 min (55 min total) CSH4: 7 x 1 min (1 hr) CSH5: 8 x 1 min (1 hr 5 min) CSH6: 9 x 1 min (1 hr 10 min) CSH7: 10 x 1 min (1 hr 15 min)

Code Prefix	Workout Type	Brief Description	Levels
CSS	Steady-State Ride	Steady ride @ high aerobic intensity	CSS1: 1 hr 10 min CSS2: 1 hr 15 min CSS3: 1 hr 30 min
CTR	Tempo Bike Ride	One or two blocks of riding @ threshold intensity (10-minute active recovery when threshold-intensity riding is divided into two blocks); warm up and cool down long enough to reach total time	CTR3: 22 min (55 min total) CTR4: 2 x 12 min (1 hr) CTR5: 24 min (1 hr 5 min) CTR8: 28 min (1 hr 20 min) CTR9: 30 min (1 hr 25 min) CTR10: 2 x 16 min (1 hr 30 min) CTR11: 32 min (1 hr 35 min) CTR12: 34 min (1 hr 40 min) CTR13: 2 x 18 min (1 hr 45 min) CTR14: 36 (1 hr 50 min) CTR15: 38 min (1 hr 55 min) CTR16: 2 x 20 min (2 hr) CTR17: 40 min (2 hr 5 min)
RFL	Fartlek Run	Foundation run with 30-second bursts @ VO_2 max/speed intensity	RFL3: 6 x 30 sec (35 min total) RFL4: 8 x 30 sec (35 min) RFL5: 6 x 30 sec (40 min) RFL6: 8 x 30 sec (40 min) RFL7: 6 x 30 sec (45 min) RFL8: 8 x 30 sec (45 min)
RFR	Foundation Run	Steady run @ moderate aerobic intensity	RFR3: 30 min RFR4: 35 min RFR5: 40 min RFR6: 45 min RFR7: 50 min RFR8: 55 min RFR9: 1 hr
RHR	Run Hill Repeats	1-minute uphill running intervals @ speed intensity w/ 2-minute active recoveries; warm up and cool down long enough to reach total time	RHR6: 4 x 1 min (34 min total) RHR7: 6 x 1 min (38 min) RHR8: 8 x 1 min (44 min)
RLI	Run Lactate Intervals	1–3-minute intervals run @ VO_2 max intensity w/ active recoveries equal in duration to intervals; warm up and cool down long enough to reach total time	RLI6: 8 x 1 min (36 min total) RLI7: 10 x 1 min (40 min) RLI8: 12 x 1 min (44 min) RLI9: 3 x 3 min (38 min) RLI10: 4 x 3 min (44 min)

Code Prefix	Workout Type	Brief Description	Levels
RLR	Long Run	Long, steady-pace run @ moderate aerobic intensity	RLR1: 1 hr 5 min RLR2: 1 hr 10 min RLR3: 1 hr 20 min RLR4: 1 hr 30 min RLR5: 1 hr 40 min RLR6: 1 hr 50 min RLR7: 2 hr RLR8: 2 hr 10 min RLR9: 2 hr 20 min RLR10: 2 hr 30 min RLR11: 2 hr 40 min
RRR	Recovery Run	Short run @ recovery intensity	RRR3: 30 min RRR4: 35 min RRR5: 40 min
RSS	Running Strides	20-second "relaxed sprints" @ speed intensity w/ 40-second active recoveries	RSS1: 2 x 20 sec RSS2: 4 x 20 sec RSS3: 6 x 20 sec
RTR	Tempo Run	Steady run @ threshold intensity; warm up and cool down long enough to reach total time	RTR2: 12 min (32 min total) RTR3: 14 min (34 min) RTR4: 16 min (36 min) RTR5: 18 min (38 min) RTR6: 20 min (40 min) RTR7: 22 min (42 min) RTR8: 24 min (44 min) RTR9: 26 min (46 min) RTR10: 28 min (48 min) RTR11: 30 min (50 min)
SBI	Swim Base Intervals	100-yard intervals swum @ moderate aerobic intensity w/ 5-second rest periods or 200-yard intervals swum @ moderate aerobic intensity w/ 10-second rest periods or single longer swims @ moderate aerobic intensity	SBI1: 2 x 100 SBI2: 3 x 100 SBI3: 4 x 100 SBI4: 5 x 100 SBI5: 6 x 100 SBI6: 7 x 100 SBI7: 8 x 100 SBI13: 3 x 200 SBI14: 4 x 200 SBI24: 1,000 SBI25: 1,200

Code Prefix	Workout Type	Brief Description	Levels
SBI (cont.)			SBI26: 1,500 SBI27: 1,800 SBI28: 2,000 SBI29: 2,400 SBI30: 2,600 SBI31: 2,800 SBI32: 3,000 SBI33: 3,200
SCD	Swim Cool-Down	Easy swim @ recovery intensity	SCD1: 200 SCD2: 250 SCD3: 300 SCD4: 350 SCD5: 400
SDS	Swim Drill Set	25-yard intervals of mixed form drills w/ 10-second rest periods	SDS3: 8 x 25
SFI	Swim Fartlek Intervals	100–200-yard intervals with easy/hard or build/descend format (hard = threshold intensity, easy = moderate aerobic intensity) w/ rest periods of 10–20 seconds	SFI1: 4 x 100 (25 easy/25 hard...), 10-sec rest SFI2: 6 x 100 (25 easy/25 hard...), 10-sec rest SFI2A: 6 x 100 (25 build/25 descend...), 10-sec rest SFI3: 8 x 100 (25 easy/25 hard...), 10-sec rest SFI3A: 8 x 100 (25 build/25 descend...), 10-sec rest SFI4: 4 x 150 (50 easy/25 hard...), 15-sec rest SFI4A: 4 x 150 (50 build/25 descend...), 15-sec rest SFI5: 5 x 150 (50 easy/25 hard...), 15-sec rest SFI5A: 5 x 150 (50 build/25 descend...), 15-sec rest SFI6: 6 x 150 (50 easy/25 hard...), 15-sec rest SFI6A: 6 x 150 (50 build/25 descend...), 15-sec rest SFI8: 4 x 200 (50 easy/50 hard...), 20-sec rest

Code Prefix	Workout Type	Brief Description	Levels
SFI (cont.)			SFI8A: 4 x 200 (50 build/50 descend...), 20-sec rest
			SFI9: 5 x 200 (50 easy/50 hard...), 20-sec rest
			SFI9A: 5 x 200 (50 build/50 descend...), 20-sec rest
			SFI10: 6 x 200 (50 easy/50 hard...), 20-sec rest
			SFI10A: 6 x 200 (50 build/50 descend...), 20-sec rest
SKS	Swim Kick Set	25-yard intervals kicking only w/ 15-second rest periods	SKS3: 8 x 25
SLI	Swim Lactate Intervals	75–150-yard intervals swum @ VO$_2$ max intensity with rest periods of 30 seconds to 1 min 15 seconds	SLI2: 5 x 75, 45-sec rest
			SLI3: 6 x 75, 45-sec rest
			SLI4: 7 x 75, 45-sec rest
			SLI5: 8 x 75, 45-sec rest
			SLI6: 9 x 75, 45-sec rest
			SLI8: 3 x 100, 1-min rest
			SLI9: 4 x 100, 1-min rest
			SLI11: 6 x 100, 1-min rest
			SLI11A: 6 x 100, 45-sec rest
			SLI11B: 6 x 100, 30-sec rest
			SLI12: 7 x 100, 1-min rest
			SLI12A: 7 x 100, 45-sec rest
			SLI12B: 7 x 100, 30-sec rest
			SLI13: 8 x 100, 1-min rest
			SLI13A: 8 x 100, 45-sec rest
			SLI13B: 8 x 100, 30-sec rest
			SLI14: 4 x 150, 1-min 15-sec rest
			SLI15: 5 x 150, 1-min 15-sec rest
			SLI15A: 5 x 150, 1-min rest
			SLI16: 6 x 150, 1-min 15-sec rest
			SLI16A: 6 x 150, 1-min rest
			SLI17: 7 x 150, 1-min 15-sec rest
			SLI17A: 7 x 150 1-min rest
SSI	Swim Sprint Intervals	25–50-yard intervals swum @ speed intensity w/ 20-second rest periods, except "A" suffix = 10-second rest, "B" suffix = 5-second rest	SSI1: 4 x 25
			SSI3: 6 x 25
			SSI4: 7 x 25
			SSI5: 8 x 25
			SSI6: 9 x 25

Code Prefix	Workout Type	Brief Description	Levels
SSI (cont.)			SSI7: 10 x 25
			SSI9: 12 x 25
			SSI10: 4 x 50
			SSI11: 5 x 50
			SSI12: 6 x 50
			SSI12A: 6 x 50
			SSI12B: 6 x 50
			SSI13A: 7 x 50
			SSI13B: 7 x 50
			SSI14: 8 x 50
			SSI14A: 8 x 50
			SSI15: 9 x 50
			SSI15A: 9 x 50
			SSI16: 10 x 50
			SSI17: 11 x 50
STI	Swim Threshold Intervals	200–400-yard intervals swum @ threshold intensity w/ rest periods of 20–45 seconds	STI1: 2 x 200, 45-sec rest
			STI1A: 2 x 200, 30-sec rest
			STI1B: 2 x 200, 20-sec rest
			STI2: 3 x 200, 45-sec rest
			STI2A: 3 x 200, 30-sec rest
			STI2B: 3 x 200, 20-sec rest
			STI3: 4 x 200, 45-sec rest
			STI3A: 4 x 200, 30-sec rest
			STI3B: 4 x 200, 20-sec rest
			STI4: 5 x 200, 45-sec rest
			STI4A: 5 x 200, 30-sec rest
			STI4B: 5 x 200, 20-sec rest
			STI5: 6 x 200, 45-sec rest
			STI5A: 6 x 200, 30-sec rest
			STI5B: 6 x 200, 20-sec rest
STT	Swim Time Trial	Designated distance swum @ maximum effort	STT3: 1,650
			STT4: 1.2 miles (2,112)
			STT5: 3,200
SWU	Swim Warm-Up	Easy swim @ recovery intensity	SWU1: 200
			SWU2: 250
			SWU3: 300
			SWU4: 350
			SWU5: 400

General Schedule

	Tuesday	Wednesday	Thursday	Friday	Saturday	Sunday
BASE PHASE						
Week 1	Bike Power Intervals	Swim Base Intervals / Foundation Run + Strides	Foundation Bike	Swim Fartlek Intervals / Foundation Run + Strides	Foundation Bike	Swim Base Intervals / Foundation Run
Week 2	Bike Power Intervals	Swim Base Intervals / Foundation Run + Strides	Foundation Bike	Swim Fartlek Intervals / Foundation Run + Strides	Brick Workout	Swim Base Intervals / Foundation Run
Week 3	Bike Power Intervals	Swim Base Intervals / Foundation Run + Strides	Foundation Bike	Swim Fartlek Intervals / Foundation Run + Strides	Foundation Bike	Swim Base Intervals / L1: Foundation Run L2–3: Long Run
Week 4 (Recovery)	Bike Power Intervals	Swim Base Intervals / Foundation Run + Strides	Recovery Bike	Swim Fartlek Intervals / Recovery Run + Strides	Foundation Bike	Swim Base Intervals / Brick Workout
Week 5	Bike Short Hills	Swim Base + Sprint Intervals / Fartlek Run	Foundation Bike	Swim Fartlek + Sprint Intervals / Foundation Run + Strides	Long Bike	Swim Base Intervals / Long Run
Week 6	Bike Short Hills	Swim Base + Sprint Intervals / Fartlek Run	Foundation Bike	Swim Fartlek + Sprint Intervals / Foundation Run + Strides	Brick Workout	Swim Time Trial / Foundation Run
Week 7	Bike Short Hills	Swim Base + Sprint Intervals / Fartlek Run	Foundation Bike	Swim Fartlek + Sprint Intervals / Foundation Run + Strides	Long Bike	Swim Base Intervals / Long Run

	Tuesday	Wednesday	Thursday	Friday	Saturday	Sunday
Week 8 (Recovery)	Bike Short Hills	Swim Base + Sprint Intervals	Recovery Bike	Swim Fartlek + Sprint Intervals	Foundation Bike	Swim Base Intervals
		Fartlek Run		Foundation Run + Strides		Brick Workout
BUILD PHASE						
Week 9	Bike Speed Intervals	Swim Base + Sprint Intervals	Foundation Bike	Swim Fartlek + Sprint Intervals	Long Bike	Swim Base Intervals
		Run Hill Repeats		Foundation Run + Strides		Long Run
Week 10	Bike Speed Intervals	Swim Base + Sprint Intervals	Foundation Bike	Swim Fartlek + Sprint Intervals	Long Bike	Swim Base Intervals
		Run Hill Repeats		Foundation Run + Strides		Long Run
Week 11	Bike Speed Intervals	Swim Base + Sprint Intervals	Foundation Bike	Swim Fartlek + Sprint Intervals	Long Bike	Swim Time Trial
		Run Hill Repeats		Foundation Run + Strides		Long Run
Week 12 (Recovery)	Bike Speed Intervals	Swim Base + Sprint Intervals	Recovery Bike	Swim Fartlek + Sprint Intervals	Recovery Bike or Foundation Bike	Sprint Triathlon or Swim Base Intervals
		Run Hill Repeats		Recovery Run + Strides		Sprint Triathlon or Brick Workout
Week 13	Bike Long Hills	Swim Base + Threshold Intervals	Foundation Bike	Swim Base + Lactate + Sprint Intervals	Long Bike	Swim Base Intervals
		Run Lactate Intervals		Foundation Run + Strides		Long Run

	Tuesday	Wednesday	Thursday	Friday	Saturday	Sunday
Week 14	Bike Lactate Intervals	Swim Base + Threshold Intervals	Foundation Bike	Swim Base + Lactate + Sprint Intervals	Long Bike	Swim Base Intervals
		Run Lactate Intervals		Foundation Run + Strides		Brick Workout
Week 15	Bike Long Hills	Swim Base + Threshold Intervals	Foundation Bike	Swim Base + Lactate + Sprint Intervals	Long Bike	Swim Base Intervals
		Run Lactate Intervals		Foundation Run + Strides		Long Run
Week 16 (Recovery)	Bike Long Hills	Swim Base + Threshold Intervals	Recovery Bike	Swim Base + Lactate + Sprint Intervals	Recovery Bike or Foundation Bike	Olympic-Distance Triathlon or Swim Base Intervals
		Run Lactate Intervals		Recovery Run + Strides		Olympic-Distance Triathlon or Brick Workout
PEAK PHASE						
Week 17	Tempo Bike	Swim Base + Threshold Intervals	Foundation Bike	Swim Base + Lactate + Sprint Intervals	Long Bike	Swim Base Intervals
		Tempo Run		Foundation Run + Strides		Long Run
Week 18	Tempo Bike	Swim Base + Threshold Intervals	Foundation Bike	Swim Base + Lactate + Sprint Intervals	Brick Workout	Swim Time Trial
		Tempo Run		Foundation Run + Strides		Long Run
Week 19	Tempo Bike	Swim Base + Threshold Intervals	L1–2: Foundation Bike L3: Steady-State Bike	Swim Base + Lactate + Sprint Intervals	Long Bike	Swim Base Intervals
		Tempo Run		Foundation Run + Strides		Long Run

	Tuesday	Wednesday	Thursday	Friday	Saturday	Sunday
Week 20 (Recovery)	Tempo Bike	Swim Base + Threshold Intervals	Recovery Bike	Swim Base + Lactate + Sprint Intervals	Recovery Bike or Foundation Bike	Half-Ironman Triathlon or Swim Base Intervals
		Tempo Run		Recovery Run + Strides		Half-Ironman Triathlon or Brick Workout
Week 21	Tempo Bike	Swim Base + Threshold Intervals	Steady-State Bike	Swim Base + Lactate + Sprint Intervals	Long Bike	Swim Base Intervals
		Tempo Run		Foundation Run + Strides		Long Run
Week 22	Tempo Bike	Swim Base + Threshold Intervals	Steady-State Bike	Swim Base + Lactate + Sprint Intervals	Long Bike	Swim Base Intervals
		Tempo Run		Foundation Run + Strides		Brick Workout
Week 23 (Taper)	Tempo Bike	Swim Base + Threshold	Foundation Bike Intervals	Swim Base + Lactate + Sprint Intervals	Long Bike Intervals	Swim Base
		Tempo Run		Foundation Run + Strides		Long Run
Week 24 (Taper)	Tempo Bike	Swim Base + Threshold Intervals	Foundation Bike	Swim Lactate + Sprint Intervals	Recovery Bike	Ironman Triathlon
		Tempo Run		Foundation Run + Strides		

Week-by-Week Schedule

Base Phase

Far and away the most important aspect of training for an Ironman is developing the endurance to exercise for 9 to 17 hours nonstop. So the primary focus of this eight-week base phase is to build endurance steadily with long weekend workouts and plenty of moderate aerobic-intensity training during the week as well. There's a small amount of high-intensity work to enhance your efficiency and prepare your body for the build phase.

WEEK 1

This week's goal: Get accustomed to your new workout schedule.

	Tuesday	Wednesday	Thursday	Friday	Saturday	Sunday
Level 1	CPI1	SWU3 SDS3 SBI3 SKS3 SCD3 (1,400)	CFR2	SWU3 SDS3 SFI1 SKS3 SCD3 (1,400)	CFR4	SWU2 SBI24 SCD2 (1,500)
		RFR3 + RSS1		RFR3 + RSS1		RFR6
Level 2	CPI2	SWU3 SDS3 SBI4 SKS3 SCD3 (1,500)	CFR2	SWU3 SDS3 SFI1 SKS3 SCD3 (1,400)	CFR5	SWU3 SBI24 SCD3 (1,600)
		RFR4 + RSS1		RFR3 + RSS1		RFR7
Level 3	CPI3	SWU3 SDS3 SBI5 SKS3 SCD3 (1,600)	CFR2	SWU3 SDS3 SFI2 SKS3 SCD3 (1,600)	CFR6	SWU2 SBI25 SCD2 (1,700)
		RFR5 + RSS1		RFR3 + RSS1		RFR8

WEEK 2

This week's goal: Gather momentum by completing all scheduled workouts as prescribed.

292

		Tuesday	Wednesday	Thursday	Friday	Saturday	Sunday
Level 1		CPI2	SWU3 SDS3 SBI4 SKS3 SCD3 (1,500)	CFR2	SWU3 SDS3 SFI2A SKS3 SCD3 (1,600)	BRW3	SWU3 SBI24 SCD3 (1,600)
			RFR4 + RSS2		RFR3 + RSS2		RFR5
Level 2		CPI3	SWU3 SDS3 SBI5 SKS3 SCD3 (1,600)	CFR2	SWU3 SDS3 SFI3A SKS3 SCD3 (1,800)	BRW4	SWU2 SBI25 SCD2 (1,700)
			RFR5 + RSS2		RFR3 + RSS2		RFR6
Level 3		CPI4	SWU3 SDS3 SBI6 SKS3 SCD3 (1,700)	CFR3	SWU3 SDS3 SFI6A SKS3 SCD3 (1,900)	BRW4	SWU3 SBI25 SCD3 (1,800)
			RFR6 + RSS2		RFR4 + RSS2		RFR7

QUICK TIP:

If you can spare the time and cash, consider getting a weekly sports massage from an experienced sports massage therapist. This can help prevent injuries by loosening trigger points (areas of extreme tightness in muscles) and revealing potential injury spots before they become painful during training.

WEEK 3

This week's goal: If you find yourself feeling flat toward the end of the week, hang in there—you have a recovery week coming up.

	Tuesday	Wednesday	Thursday	Friday	Saturday	Sunday
Level 1	CPI3	SWU3 SDS3 SBI5 SKS3 SCD3 (1,600)	CFR2	SWU3 SDS3 SFI2 SKS3 SCD3 (1,600)	CFR3	SWU2 SBI25 SCD2 (1,700)
		RFR5 + RSS3		RFR4 + RSS3		RFR9
Level 2	CPI4	SWU3 SDS3 SBI6 SKS3 SCD3 (1,700)	CFR3	SWU3 SDS3 SFI3 SKS3 SCD3 (1,800)	CFR3	SWU3 SBI25 SCD3 (1,800)
		RFR6 + RSS3		RFR4 + RSS3		RLR1
Level 3	CPI5	SWU3 SDS3 SBI7 SKS3 SCD3 (1,800)	CFR3	SWU3 SDS3 SFI6 SKS3 SCD3 (1,900)	CFR4	SWU2 SBI26 SCD2 (2,000)
		RFR6 + RSS3		RFR4 + RSS3		RLR2

WEEK 4
(Recovery)

This week's goal: Fully absorb your recent training and finish the week feeling rested and ready to return to harder training next week.

	Tuesday	Wednesday	Thursday	Friday	Saturday	Sunday
Level 1	CPI1	SWU3 SDS3 SBI3 SCD3 (1,200)	CRR3	SWU3 SDS3 SFI1 SCD3 (1,200)	CFR3	SWU3 SBI24 SCD3 (1,600)
		RFR3 + RSS2		RRR3 + RSS1		BRW4

	Tuesday	Wednesday	Thursday	Friday	Saturday	Sunday
Level 2	CPI2	SWU3 SDS3 SBI4 SCD3 (1,300)	CRR3	SWU3 SDS3 SFI4 SCD3 (1,400)	CFR4	SWU2 SBI25 SCD2 (1,700)
		RFR4 + RSS2		RRR3 + RSS1		BRW4
Level 3	CPI3	SWU3 SDS3 SBI5 SCD3 (1,400)	CRR3	SWU3 SDS3 SFI5 SCD3 (1,550)	CFR5	SWU3 SBI25 SCD3 (1,800)
		RFR4 + RSS2		RRR4 + RSS1		BRW5

WEEK 5

This week's goal: Pedal hard but relaxed in Tuesday's short cycling hill climbs.

	Tuesday	Wednesday	Thursday	Friday	Saturday	Sunday
Level 1	CSH3	SWU3 SDS3 SBI5 SSI10 SKS3 SCD3 (1,800)	CFR3	SWU3 SDS3 SFI4A SSI3 SKS3 SCD3 (1,750)	CLR2	SWU2 SBI26 SCD2 (2,000)
		RFL3		RFR4 + RSS3		RLR3
Level 2	CSH4	SWU3 SDS3 SBI6 SSI11 SKS3 SCD3 (1,950)	CFR3	SWU3 SDS3 SFI5A SSI3 SKS3 SCD3 (1,900)	CLR3	SWU3 SBI26 SCD3 (2,100)
		RFL3		RFR4 + RSS3		RLR3

	Tuesday	Wednesday	Thursday	Friday	Saturday	Sunday
Level 3	CSH5	SWU3 SDS3 SBI7 SSI11 SKS3 SCD3 (2,050)	CFR4	SWU3 SDS3 SFI6A SSI3 SKS3 SCD3 (2,050)	CLR4	SWU2 SBI27 SCD2 (2,300)
		RFL5		RFR5 + RSS3		RLR3

WEEK 6

This week's goal: Go all out to get a good sense of your current swimming performance level in Sunday's swim time trial.

	Tuesday	Wednesday	Thursday	Friday	Saturday	Sunday
Level 1	CSH4	SWU3 SDS3 SBI5 SSI11 SKS3 SCD3 (1,850)	CFR3	SWU3 SDS3 SFI4 SSI5 SKS3 SCD3 (1,800)	BRW4	SWU3 STT3 SCD3 (2,250)
		RFL4		RFR4 + RSS3		RFR3
Level 2	CSH5	SWU3 SDS3 SBI6 SSI12 SKS3 SCD3 (2,000)	CFR4	SWU3 SDS3 SFI5 SSI5 SKS3 SCD3 (1,950)	BRW5	SWU3 STT3 SCD3 (2,250)
		RFL4		RFR5 + RSS3		RFR4
Level 3	CSH6	SWU3 SDS3 SBI7 SSI12 SKS3 SCD3 (2,100)	CFR4	SWU3 SDS3 SFI6 SSI5 SKS3 SCD3 (2,100)	BRW6	SWU4 STT3 SCD4 (2,350)
		RFL6		RFR5 + RSS3		RFR5

WEEK 7

This week's goal: Finish strong in Saturday's long ride.

	Tuesday	Wednesday	Thursday	Friday	Saturday	Sunday
Level 1	CSH5	SWU3 SDS3 SBI5 SSI12 SKS3 SCD3 (1,900)	CFR4	SWU3 SDS3 SFI8A SSI5 SKS3 SCD3 (2,000)	CLR3	SWU3 SBI26 SCD3 (2,100)
		RFL6		RFR5 + RSS3		RLR3
Level 2	CSH6	SWU3 SDS3 SBI6 SSI13 SKS3 SCD3 (2,050)	CFR4	SWU3 SDS3 SFI6A SSI5 SKS3 SCD3 (2,100)	CLR4	SWU2 SBI27 SCD2 (2,300)
		RFL6		RFR5 + RSS3		RLR3
Level 3	CSH7	SWU3 SDS3 SBI7 SSI13 SKS3 SCD3 (2,150)	CFR4	SWU3 SDS3 SFI9A SSI9 SKS3 SCD3 (2,300)	CLR5	SWU3 SBI27 SCD3 (2,400)
		RFL8		RFR5 + RSS3		RLR4

QUICK TIP:

It's a good idea to participate in an online message board for your upcoming Ironman event to learn more about the course and get all of your other event-related questions answered. Just click on the "Forum" or "Message Board" tab on the official Web site of your event and then look for the relevant discussion thread.

WEEK 8
(Recovery)

This week's goal: Fully absorb your recent training and finish the week feeling rested and ready to return to harder training next week.

	Tuesday	Wednesday	Thursday	Friday	Saturday	Sunday
Level 1	CSH3	SWU3 SDS3 SBI4 SSI10 SCD3 (1,500)	CRR3	SWU3 SDS3 SFI4 SSI3 SCD3 (1,550)	CFR6	SWU3 SBI25 SCD3 (1,800)
		RFL5		RRR4 + RSS1		BRW5
Level 2	CSH4	SWU3 SDS3 SBI5 SSI10 SCD3 (1,600)	CRR4	SWU3 SDS3 SFI4 SSI5 SCD3 (1,600)	CFR7	SWU2 SBI26 SCD2 (2,000)
		RFL5		RRR4 + RSS1		BRW6
Level 3	CSH5	SWU3 SDS3 SBI6 SSI10 SCD3 (1,700)	CRR4	SWU3 SDS3 SFI5 SSI5 SCD3 (1,750)	CFR8	SWU1 SBI27 SCD1 (2,200)
		RFL7		RRR5 + RSS1		BRW6

Build Phase

In this eight-week phase the top priority remains the same: building raw endurance in swimming, cycling, and running. But you will also do some tough high-intensity workouts (e.g., running hill repeats) to maximize your aerobic capacity and efficiency, which will also boost your ability to go long.

WEEK 9

This week's goal: Do Wednesday's running hill repeats at the fastest pace you can maintain through the end of the last interval without slowing.

	Tuesday	Wednesday	Thursday	Friday	Saturday	Sunday
Level 1	CSI10	SWU3 SDS3 SBI13 SSI12 SKS3 SCD3 (1,900) RHR6	CFR4	SWU3 SDS3 SFI5A SSI3 SKS3 SCD3 (1,900) RFR5 + RSS3	CLR5	SWU3 SBI27 SCD3 (2,400) RLR4
Level 2	CSI11	SWU3 SDS3 SBI14 SSI12 SKS3 SCD3 (2,100) RHR7	CFR4	SWU3 SDS3 SFI8A SSI5 SKS3 SCD3 (2,000) RFR5 + RSS3	CLR6	SWU3 SBI28 SCD3 (2,600) RLR5
Level 3	CSI12	SWU3 SDS3 SBI14 SSI14 SKS3 SCD3 (2,200) RHR8	CFR5	SWU3 SDS3 SFI9A SSI5 SKS3 SCD3 (2,200) RFR6 + RSS3	CLR7	SWU1 SBI29 SCD1 (2,800) RLR6

WEEK 10

This week's goal: Find your running legs quickly in Saturday's bike-run brick workout.

	Tuesday	Wednesday	Thursday	Friday	Saturday	Sunday
Level 1	CSI11	SWU3 SDS3 SBI13 SSI13 SKS3 SCD3 (1,950) RHR7	CFR4	SWU3 SDS3 SFI8 SSI5 SKS3 SCD3 (2,000) RFR5 + RSS3	BRW6	SWU3 SBI28 SCD3 (2,600) RFR5

	Tuesday	Wednesday	Thursday	Friday	Saturday	Sunday
Level 2	CSI12	SWU3 SDS3 SBI14 SSI14 SKS3 SCD3 (2,200)	CFR5	SWU3 SDS3 SFI9 SSI5 SKS3 SCD3 (2,200)	BRW8	SWU1 SBI29 SCD1 (2,800)
		RHR8		RFR6 + RSS3		RFR6
Level 3	CSI13	SWU3 SDS3 SBI14 SSI16 SKS3 SCD3 (2,300)	CFR5	SWU3 SDS3 SFI10 SSI5 SKS3 SCD3 (2,400)	BRW9	SWU3 SBI29 SCD3 (3,000)
		RHR8		RFR6 + RSS3		RFR7

WEEK 11

This week's goal: Go all out in Sunday's longer swim time trial to simulate the demands of racing.

	Tuesday	Wednesday	Thursday	Friday	Saturday	Sunday
Level 1	CSI12	SWU3 SDS3 SBI13 SSI14 SKS3 SCD3 (2,000)	CFR5	SWU3 SDS3 SFI8A SSI5 SKS3 SCD3 (2,000)	CLR6	SWU1 STT4 SCD1 (2,512)
		RHR8		RFR6 + RSS3		RLR5
Level 2	CSI13	SWU3 SDS3 SBI14 SSI15 SKS3 SCD3 (2,250)	CFR5	SWU3 SDS3 SFI9A SSI5 SKS3 SCD3 (2,200)	CLR7	SWU2 STT4 SCD2 (2,612)
		RHR8		RFR6 + RSS3		RLR6

	Tuesday	Wednesday	Thursday	Friday	Saturday	Sunday
Level 3	CSI14	SWU3 SDS3 SBI14 SSI17 SKS3 SCD3 (2,350)	CFR5	SWU3 SDS3 SFI10A SSI5 SKS3 SCD3 (2,400)	CLR8	SWU3 STT4 SCD3 (2,712)
		RHR9		RFR6 + RSS3		RLR7

WEEK 12
(Recovery)

This week's goal: Fully absorb your recent training and have a solid sprint triathlon performance on Sunday if you have the opportunity.

	Tuesday	Wednesday	Thursday	Friday	Saturday	Sunday
Level 1	CSI3	SWU3 SDS3 SBI4 SSI10 SCD3 (1,500)	CRR4	SWU3 SDS3 SFI4 SSI3 SCD3 (1,550)	CRR1 or CFR5*	Sprint Triathlon or SWU3 SBI26 SCD3 (2,100)*
		RHR6		RRR4 + RSS1		BRW8*
Level 2	CSI4	SWU3 SDS3 SBI5 SSI10 SCD3 (1,600)	CRR4	SWU3 SDS3 SFI5 SSI3 SCD3 (1,700)	CRR1 or CFR6*	Sprint Triathlon or SWU2 SBI27 SCD2 (2,300)*
		RHR6		RRR5 + RSS1		BRW9*
Level 3	CSI5	SWU3 SDS3 SBI6 SSI10 SCD3 (1,700)	CRR4	SWU3 SDS3 SFI3 SSI5 SCD3 (1,800)	CRR1 or CFR6*	Sprint Triathlon or SWU3 SBI27 SCD3 (2,400)*
		RHR7		RRR5 + RSS1		BRW10*

*If not racing

QUICK TIP:

Prescription running shoe orthotics are helpful in treating 60 percent of the injuries for which they are prescribed. If you have a running injury or a history of running injuries, make an appointment with a podiatrist with experience in treating runners and find out whether prescription running shoe orthotics might be right for you.

WEEK 13

This week's goal: Dig deep in Tuesday's long cycling hill climbs.

	Tuesday	Wednesday	Thursday	Friday	Saturday	Sunday
Level 1	CLH2	SWU3 SDS3 SBI2 STI1 SKS3 SCD3 (1,700)	CFR5	SWU3 SDS3 SBI2 SLI2 SSI3 SKS3 SCD3 (1,825)	CLR7	SWU3 SBI28 SCD3 (2,600)
		RLI6		RFR6 + RSS3		RLR7
Level 2	CLH3	SWU3 SDS3 SBI4 STI1 SKS3 SCD3 (1,900)	CFR5	SWU3 SDS3 SBI2 SLI3 SSI3 SKS3 SCD3 (1,900)	CLR8	SWU1 SBI29 SCD1 (2,800)
		RLI7		RFR6 + RSS3		RLR7
Level 3	CLH4	SWU3 SDS3 SBI6 STI1 SKS3 SCD3 (2,100)	CFR6	SWU3 SDS3 SBI3 SLI4 SSI4 SKS3 SCD3 (2,100)	CLR9	SWU3 SBI29 SCD3 (3,000)
		RLI9		RFR7 + RSS3		RLR8

WEEK 14

This week's goal: Find a steady groove at threshold intensity (8–8.5 RPE) in Wednesday's threshold swim intervals set.

	Tuesday	Wednesday	Thursday	Friday	Saturday	Sunday
Level 1	CLI3	SWU3 SDS3 SBI4 STI1A SKS3 SCD3 (1,900)	CFR5	SWU3 SDS3 SBI2 SLI3 SSI3 SKS3 SCD3 (1,900)	CLR2	SWU1 SBI29 SCD1 (2,800)
		RLI7		RFR6 + RSS3		BRW11
Level 2	CLI4	SWU3 SDS3 SBI6 STI1A SKS3 SCD3 (2,100)	CFR6	SWU3 SDS3 SBI3 SLI4 SSI4 SKS3 SCD3 (2,100)	CLR3	SWU3 SBI29 SCD3 (3,000)
		RLI8		RFR7 + RSS3		BRW12
Level 3	CLI5	SWU3 SDS3 SBI6 STI2 SKS3 SCD3 (2,300)	CFR6	SWU3 SDS3 SBI4 SLI5 SSI5 SKS3 SCD3 (2,300)	CLR4	SWU3 SBI30 SCD3 (3,200)
		RLI10		RFR7 + RSS3		BRW13

WEEK 15

This week's goal: Finish strong in Saturday's very long ride.

	Tuesday	Wednesday	Thursday	Friday	Saturday	Sunday
Level 1	CLH3	SWU3 SDS3 SBI5 STI1B	CFR6	SWU3 SDS3 SBI2 SLI4	CLR9	SWU3 SBI29 SCD3 (3,000)

	Tuesday	Wednesday	Thursday	Friday	Saturday	Sunday
Level 1 *(cont.)*		SKS3 SCD3 (2,000)		SSI4 SKS3 SCD3 (2,000)		
		RLI8		RFR7 + RSS3		RLR8
Level 2	CLH4	SWU3 SDS3 SBI5 STI2 SKS3 SCD3 (2,200)	CFR6	SWU3 SDS3 SBI3 SLI5 SSI5 SKS3 SCD3 (2,200)	CLR10	SWU3 SBI30 SCD3 (3,200)
		RLI10		RFR7 + RSS3		RLR8
Level 3	CLH5	SWU3 SDS3 SBI6 STI2A SKS3 SCD3 (2,300)	CFR6	SWU3 SDS3 SBI3 SLI6 SSI6 SKS3 SCD3 (2,300)	CLR11	SWU3 SBI31 SCD3 (3,400)
		RLI10		RFR7 + RSS3		RLR9

WEEK 16
(Recovery)

This week's goal: Fully absorb your recent training and have a solid Olympic-distance triathlon performance if you have the opportunity.

	Tuesday	Wednesday	Thursday	Friday	Saturday	Sunday
Level 1	CLI2	SWU3 SDS3 SBI1 STI1 SCD3 (1,400)	CRR4	SWU3 SDS3 SLI3 SSI5 SCD3 (1,450)	CRR1 or CLR4*	Olympic-Distance Triathlon or SWU2 SBI27 SCD2 (2,300)*
		RLI6		RRR5 + RSS1		BRW13*

*If not racing

	Tuesday	Wednesday	Thursday	Friday	Saturday	Sunday
Level 2	CLI2	SWU3 SDS3 SBI2 STI1 SCD3 (1,500)	CRR4	SWU3 SDS3 SLI4 SSI6 SCD3 (1,550)	CRR1 or CLR5*	Olympic- Distance Triathlon or SWU3 SBI27 SCD3 (2,400)*
		RLI6		RRR5 + RSS1		BRW14*
Level 3	CLI3	SWU3 SDS3 SBI3 STI1 SCD3 (1,600)	CRR5	SWU3 SDS3 SLI4 SSI6 SCD3 (1,550)	CRR1 or CLR6*	Olympic- Distance Triathlon or SWU2 SBI28 SCD2 (2,500)*
		RLI9		RRR5 + RSS1		BRW15*

*If not racing

Peak Phase

In this eight-week phase you will develop that last bit of endurance you need. You will also do some longer workouts at high aerobic and threshold intensity to ratchet up the pace you are able to maintain over long distance. Your training load will steadily decline over the final two weeks to ensure you're rested and ready to go on race day.

WEEK 17

This week's goal: Find a steady groove at threshold intensity (8–8.5 RPE) in Wednesday's tempo run.

	Tuesday	Wednesday	Thursday	Friday	Saturday	Sunday
Level 1	CTR8	SWU3 SDS3 SBI5 STI2 SKS3 SCD3 (2,200)	CFR6	SWU3 SDS3 SBI2 SLI11 SSI12 SKS3 SCD3 (2,200)	CLR11	SWU3 SBI29 SCD3 (3,000)
		RTR5		RFR7 + RSS3		RLR9

	Tuesday	Wednesday	Thursday	Friday	Saturday	Sunday
Level 2	CTR9	SWU3 SDS3 SBI5 STI3 SKS3 SCD3 (2,400)	CFR6	SWU3 SDS3 SBI3 SLI12 SSI12 SKS3 SCD3 (2,400)	CLR12	SWU3 SBI30 SCD3 (3,200)
		RTR6		RFR7 + RSS3		RLR9
Level 3	CTR10	SWU3 SDS3 SBI5 STI4 SKS3 SCD3 (2,600)	CFR7	SWU3 SDS3 SBI4 SLI13 SSI12 SKS3 SCD3 (2,600)	CLR13	SWU3 SBI31 SCD3 (3,400)
		RTR7		RFR8 + RSS3		RLR10

WEEK 18

This week's goal: Go all out for a great race-specific workout in Sunday's swim time trial.

	Tuesday	Wednesday	Thursday	Friday	Saturday	Sunday
Level 1	CTR10	SWU3 SDS3 SBI5 STI2A SKS3 SCD3 (2,200)	CFR6	SWU3 SDS3 SBI2 SLI11A SSI12A SKS3 SCD3 (2,200)	BRW14	SWU1 STT5 SCD1 (3,600)
		RTR6		RFR7 + RSS3		RFR6
Level 2	CTR11	SWU3 SDS3 SBI5 STI3A SKS3 SCD3 (2,400)	CFR7	SWU3 SDS3 SBI3 SLI12A SSI12A SKS3 SCD3 (2,400)	BRW15	SWU2 STT5 SCD2 (3,700)
		RTR7		RFR8 + RSS3		RFR7

	Tuesday	Wednesday	Thursday	Friday	Saturday	Sunday
Level 3	CTR12	SWU3 SDS3 SBI5 STI4A SKS3 SCD3 (2,600)	CFR7	SWU3 SDS3 SBI4 SLI13A SSI12A SKS3 SCD3 (2,600)	BRW16	SWU3 STT5 SCD3 (3,800)
		RTR8		RFR8 + RSS3		RFR8

QUICK TIP:

The diet of the average American is deficient in essential omega-3 fatty acids. These vital nutrients are not only necessary for such things as healthy cell membranes, but they also benefit triathletes by contributing to the formation of anti-inflammatory prostaglandins, which help you recover faster from workouts. Get the omega-3 fats you need by taking a daily fish oil or flaxseed oil supplement.

WEEK 19

Pace yourself as evenly as possible through Sunday's long swim.

	Tuesday	Wednesday	Thursday	Friday	Saturday	Sunday
Level 1	CTR12	SWU3 SDS3 SBI5 STI2B SKS3 SCD3 (2,200)	CFR7	SWU3 SDS3 SBI2 SLI11B SSI12B SKS3 SCD3 (2,200)	CLR13	SWU3 SBI31 SCD3 (3,400)
		RTR7		RFR8 + RSS3		RLR10
Level 2	CTR13	SWU3 SDS3 SBI5 STI3B SKS3	CFR7	SWU3 SDS3 SBI3 SLI12B SSI12B	CLR14	SWU3 SBI32 SCD3 (3,600)

	Tuesday	Wednesday	Thursday	Friday	Saturday	Sunday
Level 2 (cont.)		SCD3 (2,400)		SKS3 SCD3 (2,400)		
		RTR8		RFR8 + RSS3		RLR10
Level 3	CTR14	SWU3 SDS3 SBI5 STI4B SKS3 SCD3 (2,600)	CSS1	SWU3 SDS3 SBI4 SLI13B SSI12B SKS3 SCD3 (2,600)	CLR15	SWU3 SBI33 SCD3 (3,800)
		RTR9		RFR9 + RSS3		RLR10

WEEK 20
(Recovery)

This week's goal: Fully absorb your recent training and have a solid half-Ironman triathlon performance on Sunday if you have the opportunity.

	Tuesday	Wednesday	Thursday	Friday	Saturday	Sunday
Level 1	CTR8	SWU3 SDS3 SBI1 STI1 SCD3 (1,400)	CRR5	SWU3 SDS3 SLI9 SSI1 SCD3 (1,300)	CRR1 or CFR3*	Half-Ironman Triathlon or SWU3 SBI28 SCD3 (2,600)*
		RTR4		RRR5 + RSS1		BRW16*
Level 2	CTR9	SWU3 SDS3 SBI2 STI1 SCD3 (1,500)	CRR5	SWU3 SDS3 SLI9 SSI10 SCD3 (1,400)	CRR1 or CFR3*	Half-Ironman Triathlon or SWU1 SBI29 SCD1 (2,800)*
		RTR5		RRR5 + RSS1		BRW17*

*If not racing

	Tuesday	Wednesday	Thursday	Friday	Saturday	Sunday
Level 3	CTR10	SWU3 SDS3 SBI1 STI2 SCD3 (1,600)	CRR6	SWU3 SDS3 SBI1 SLI11 SSI10 SCD3 (1,600)	CRR1 or CFR3*	Half-Ironman Triathlon or SWU3 SBI29 SCD3 (3,000)*
		RTR6		RRR6 + RSS1		BRW18*

*If not racing

WEEK 21

This week's goal: Finish strong in Saturday's long ride—the longest in this training plan.

	Tuesday	Wednesday	Thursday	Friday	Saturday	Sunday
Level 1	CTR14	SWU3 SDS3 SBI5 STI3 SKS3 SCD3 (2,400)	CSS1	SWU3 SDS3 SBI2 SLI15 SSI13 SKS3 SCD3 (2,400)	CLR15	SWU3 SBI33 SCD3 (3,800)
		RTR8		RFR8 + RSS3		RLR11
Level 2	CTR15	SWU3 SDS3 SBI5 STI4 SKS3 SCD3 (2,600)	CSS1	SWU3 SDS3 SBI2 SLI16 SSI14 SKS3 SCD3 (2,600)	CLR16	SWU4 SBI33 SCD4 (3,900)
		RTR9		RFR9 + RSS3		RLR11
Level 3	CTR16	SWU3 SDS3 SBI5 STI5 SKS3 SCD3 (2,800)	CSS1	SWU3 SDS3 SBI2 SLI17 SSI15 SKS3 SCD3 (2,800)	CLR17	SWU5 SBI33 SCD5 (4,000)
		RTR10		RFR9 + RSS3		RLR11

WEEK 22

This week's goal: Hang in there: This is your peak training week; your prerace taper begins next Monday.

	Tuesday	Wednesday	Thursday	Friday	Saturday	Sunday
Level 1	CTR15	SWU3 SDS3 SBI5 STI3A SKS3 SCD3 (2,400)	CSS1	SWU3 SDS3 SBI2 SLI15A SSI13A SKS3 SCD3 (2,400)	CLR9	SWU3 SBI33 SCD3 (3,800)
		RTR9		RFR9 + RSS3		BRW12
Level 2	CTR16	SWU3 SDS3 SBI5 STI4A SKS3 SCD3 (2,600)	CSS2	SWU3 SDS3 SBI2 SLI16A SSI14A SKS3 SCD3 (2,600)	CLR10	SWU4 SBI33 SCD4 (3,900)
		RTR10		RFR9 + RSS3		BRW13
Level 3	CTR17	SWU3 SDS3 SBI5 STI5A SKS3 SCD3 (2,800)	CSS3	SWU3 SDS3 SBI2 SLI17A SSI15A SKS3 SCD3 (2,800)	CLR11	SWU5 SBI33 SCD5 (4,000)
		RTR11		RFR9 + RSS3		BRW14

WEEK 23
(Taper)

This week's goal: Gain confidence for next weekend's big event by feeling your fitness begin to peak during this week's workouts.

	Tuesday	Wednesday	Thursday	Friday	Saturday	Sunday
Level 1	CTR12	SWU3 SDS3 SBI5 STI3B SKS3 SCD3 (2,400)	CFR4	SWU3 SDS3 SBI2 SLI14 SSI10 SKS3 SCD3 (2,100)	CLR4	SWU3 SBI28 SCD3 (2,600)
		RTR8		RFR6 + RSS2		RLR4
Level 2	CTR13	SWU3 SDS3 SBI5 STI4B SKS3 SCD3 (2,600)	CFR5	SWU3 SDS3 SBI3 SLI14 SSI10 SKS3 SCD3 (2,200)	CLR5	SWU1 SBI29 SCD1 (2,800)
		RTR9		RFR7 + RSS2		RLR4
Level 3	CTR14	SWU3 SDS3 SBI5 STI5B SKS3 SCD3 (2,800)	CFR5	SWU3 SDS3 SBI3 SLI15 SSI11 SKS3 SCD3 (2,400)	CLR6	SWU3 SBI29 SCD3 (3,000)
		RTR10		RFR7 + RSS2		RLR5

QUICK TIP:

Resist the temptation to keep training hard during the final two weeks of this training plan. Research has shown time and again that drastically cutting back on training during the final week to two weeks before a long race is the best way to ensure optimal performance in the race. You would actually fare better by not training at all during the final week than by training normally.

WEEK 24
(Taper)

This week's goal: Have a great Ironman on Sunday!

	Tuesday	Wednesday	Thursday	Friday	Saturday	Sunday
Level 1	CTR3	SWU3 SDS3 STI2 SCD3 (1,400) RTR2	CFR3	SWU3 SLI8 SSI1 SCD3 (1,000) RSS3	CRR1	Ironman Triathlon
Level 2	CTR4	SWU3 SDS3 STI3 SCD3 (1,600) RTR3	CFR3	SWU3 SLI8 SSI1 SCD3 (1,000) RSS3	CRR1	Ironman Triathlon
Level 3	CTR5	SWU3 SDS3 STI4 SCD3 (1,800) RTR4	CFR3	SWU3 SLI8 SSI10 SCD3 (1,100) RSS3	CRR1	Ironman Triathlon

Chapter 13

IRONMAN TRIATHLON
TRAINING PLANS
Levels 4–6

*T*he three training plans presented in this chapter are custom-made for those who want to do more than just finish an Ironman. Perhaps you are returning to an Ironman event you have done in the past and you want to better your time. Or maybe you even have an ambition to earn a qualifying slot for the Hawaii Ironman World Championship. These training plans will help you achieve such goals in a time-efficient way that still allows you to please your boss and enjoy your family.

All three plans feature 10 weekly workouts: three swims, three rides, three runs, and a bike-run brick workout. The bricks are scheduled on Thursday in odd-numbered weeks and on Saturday in even-numbered weeks.

Each plan is 24 weeks long. The base, build, and peak phases last eight weeks apiece. Every fourth week is a recovery week and the final two weeks constitute a tapering period. There are three optional tune-up races scheduled: a sprint in Week 12, an Olympic-distance event in Week 16, and a half-Ironman in Week 20.

Level 4

Choose this training plan if you are not accustomed to a training load of 10 workouts per week (including a bike-run brick) but feel you are ready for such a schedule now. The plan begins with 4,700 yards of swimming, 4 hours and 45 minutes of cycling, and 2 hours and 23 minutes of running in Week 1. It peaks with 10,375 yards of swimming, 8 hours and 40 minutes of cycling, and 3 hours and 45 minutes of running in Week 22.

Level 5

This training plan provides the perfect balance of challenging training and time efficiency. It begins with 5,400 yards of swimming, 5 hours and 10 minutes of cycling, and 2 hours and 33 minutes of running in Week 1. It peaks with 10,825 yards of swimming, 9 hours and 30 minutes of cycling, and 3 hours and 52 minutes of running in Week 22.

Level 6

If you are not *quite* willing and able to take on the 11-workouts-per-week schedules in the next chapter, try this plan. It packs a lot of focused training into 10 weekly workouts. It begins with 5,850 yards of swimming, 5 hours and 50 minutes of cycling, and 2 hours and 53 minutes of running in Week 1. It peaks with 11,175 yards of swimming, 10 hours and 20 minutes of cycling, and 3 hours and 59 minutes of running in Week 22.

Quick Reference Guide to Workout Codes for Ironman Triathlon Training Plans Levels 4–6

Code Prefix	Workout Type	Brief Description	Levels
BRW	Brick Workout	Bike ride followed by immediate run, both @ moderate aerobic intensity, except "A" suffix = run @ threshold intensity or bike and run @ high aerobic intensity, as indicated	BRW3: 45 min/10 min BRW4: 45 min/15 min BRW5: 1 hr/20 min BRW5A: 1 hr/20 min (run @ threshold) BRW6: 1 hr/30 min BRW6A: 1 hr/30 min (run @ threshold) BRW7: 1 hr 15 min/20 min BRW7A: 1 hr 15 min/20 min (bike and run @ high aerobic) BRW8: 1 hr 15 min/30 min BRW8A: 1 hr 15 min/30 min (bike and run @ high aerobic) BRW9: 1 hr 30 min/30 min BRW9A: 1 hr 30 min/30 min (bike and run @ high aerobic) BRW10: 1 hr 30 min/45 min BRW10A: 1 hr 30 min/45 min (bike and run @ high aerobic)

Code Prefix	Workout Type	Brief Description	Levels
BRW (cont.)			BRW11: 1 hr 45 min/45 min BRW12: 1 hr 45 min/50 min BRW13: 2 hr/50 min BRW14: 2 hr 15 min/55 min BRW15: 2 hr 30 min/55 min BRW16: 3 hr/1 hr BRW17: 3 hr 30 min/1 hr BRW18: 4 hr/1 hr
CFR	Foundation Bike	Steady ride @ moderate aerobic intensity	CFR3: 1 hr CFR4: 1 hr 15 min CFR5: 1 hr 30 min CFR6: 1 hr 45 min CFR7: 2 hr
CLH	Bike Long Hill Climbs	5-minute climbing intervals @ threshold/VO_2 max intensity w/ 3-minute active recoveries; warm up and cool down long enough to reach total time	CLH4: 5 x 5 min (1 hr 15 min total) CLH5: 6 x 5 min (1 hr 20 min) CLH6: 7 x 5 min (1 hr 30 min) CLH7: 8 x 5 min (1 hr 35 min)
CLI	Bike Lactate Intervals	3-minute intervals @ VO_2 max intensity w/ 3-minute active recoveries; warm up and cool down long enough to reach total time	CLI3: 4 x 3 min (1 hr 15 min total) CLI4: 5 x 3 min (1 hr 20 min) CLI5: 6 x 3 min (1 hr 25 min) CLI6: 7 x 3 min (1 hr 30 min) CLI7: 8 x 3 min (1 hr 35 min)
CLR	Long Bike Ride	Long steady ride @ moderate aerobic intensity	CLR2: 2 hr 15 min CLR3: 2 hr 30 min CLR4: 2 hr 45 min CLR5: 3 hr CLR6: 3 hr 15 min CLR7: 3 hr 30 min CLR8: 3 hr 45 min CLR9: 4 hr CLR10: 4 hr 15 min CLR11: 4 hr 30 min CLR12: 4 hr 45 min CLR13: 5 hr CLR14: 5 hr 15 min CLR15: 5 hr 30 min CLR16: 5 hr 45 min CLR17: 6 hr

Code Prefix	Workout Type	Brief Description	Levels
CPI	Bike Power Intervals	20-second intervals done in a high gear @ speed intensity w/ 2-minute active recoveries; warm up and cool down long enough to reach total time	CPI3: 6 x 20 sec (1 hr total) CPI4: 7 x 20 sec (1 hr 10 min) CPI5: 8 x 20 sec (1 hr 20 min) CPI6: 9 x 20 sec (1 hr 25 min) CPI7: 10 x 20 sec (1 hr 30 min)
CRR	Recovery Bike	Steady ride @ recovery intensity	CRR1: 20 min
CSI	Bike Speed Intervals	1-minute intervals @ speed intensity w/ 2-minute active recoveries or 1.5-minute intervals @ speed intensity w/ 3-minute active recoveries; warm up and cool down long enough to reach total time	CSI5: 8 x 1 min (1 hr 5 min total) CSI6: 9 x 1 min (1 hr 10 min) CSI7: 10 x 1 min (1 hr 15 min) CSI12: 6 x 1 min 30 sec (1 hr 40 min) CSI13: 7 x 1 min 30 sec (1 hr 45 min) CSI14: 8 x 1 min 30 sec (1 hr 50 min) CSI15: 9 x 1 min 30 sec (1 hr 55 min) CSI16: 10 x 1 min 30 sec (2 hr)
CSH	Bike Short Hill Climbs	1-minute hill climbs @ VO_2 max/speed intensity w/ 2-minute active recoveries; warm up and cool down long enough to reach total time	CSH3: 6 x 1 min (55 min total) CSH4: 7 x 1 min (1 hr) CSH5: 8 x 1 min (1 hr 5 min) CSH6: 9 x 1 min (1 hr 10 min) CSH7: 10 x 1 min (1 hr 15 min) CSH8: 11 x 1 min (1 hr 20 min) CSH9: 12 x 1 min (1 hr 25 min)
CSS	Steady-State Ride	Steady ride @ high aerobic intensity	CSS1: 1 hr 10 min CSS2: 1 hr 15 min CSS3: 1 hr 30 min CSS4: 1 hr 45 min
CTR	Tempo Bike Ride	One or two blocks of riding @ threshold intensity (10-minute active recovery when threshold-intensity riding is divided into two blocks); warm up and cool down long enough to reach total time	CTR5: 24 min (1 hr 5 min total) CTR9: 30 min (1 hr 25 min) CTR10: 2 x 16 min (1 hr 30 min) CTR11: 32 min (1 hr 35 min) CTR12: 34 min (1 hr 40 min) CTR13: 2 x 18 min (1 hr 45 min) CTR14: 36 (1 hr 50 min) CTR15: 38 min (1 hr 55 min) CTR16: 2 x 20 min (2 hr) CTR17: 40 min (2 hr 5 min)

Code Prefix	Workout Type	Brief Description	Levels
RFL	Fartlek Run	Foundation run with 30-second bursts @ VO_2 max/speed intensity	RFL5: 6 x 30 sec (40 min) RFL6: 8 x 30 sec (40 min) RFL7: 6 x 30 sec (45 min) RFL8: 8 x 30 sec (45 min) RFL9: 6 x 30 sec (50 min) RFL10: 8 x 30 sec (50 min)
RFR	Foundation Run	Steady run @ moderate aerobic intensity	RFR3: 30 min RFR4: 35 min RFR5: 40 min RFR6: 45 min RFR7: 50 min RFR8: 55 min RFR9: 1 hr
RHR	Run Hill Repeats	30-second uphill running intervals @ speed intensity w/ 1-minute active recoveries or 1-minute uphill running intervals @ speed intensity w/ 2-minute active recoveries; warm up and cool down long enough to reach total time	RHR5: 12 x 30 sec (38 min total) RHR6: 4 x 1 min (34 min) RHR7: 6 x 1 min (38 min) RHR8: 8 x 1 min (44 min) RHR9: 10 x 1 min (50 min) RHR10: 12 x 1 min (56 min)
RLI	Run Lactate Intervals	1–3-minute intervals run @ VO_2 max intensity w/ active recoveries equal to intervals in duration; warm up and cool down long enough to reach total time	RLI6: 8 x 1 min (36 min total) RLI7: 10 x 1 min (40 min) RLI8: 12 x 1 min (44 min) RLI10: 4 x 3 min (44 min) RLI11: 5 x 3 min (50 min)
RLR	Long Run	Long, steady-pace run @ moderate aerobic intensity	RLR1: 1 hr 5 min RLR2: 1 hr 10 min RLR3: 1 hr 20 min RLR4: 1 hr 30 min RLR5: 1 hr 40 min RLR6: 1 hr 50 min RLR7: 2 hr RLR8: 2 hr 10 min RLR9: 2 hr 20 min RLR10: 2 hr 30 min RLR11: 2 hr 40 min RLR12: 2 hr 50 min RLR13: 3 hr

IRONMAN TRIATHLON TRAINING PLANS • LEVELS 4–6

Code Prefix	Workout Type	Brief Description	Levels
RRR	Recovery Run	Short run @ recovery intensity	RRR2: 25 min RRR3: 30 min RRR4: 35 min RRR5: 40 min RRR6: 45 min
RSS	Running Strides	20-second "relaxed sprints" @ speed intensity w/ 40-second active recoveries	RSS1: 2 x 20 sec RSS2: 4 x 20 sec RSS3: 6 x 20 sec
RTR	Tempo Run	Steady run @ threshold intensity; warm up and cool down long enough to reach total time	RTR4: 16 min (36 min total) RTR5: 18 min (38 min) RTR6: 20 min (40 min) RTR7: 22 min (42 min) RTR8: 24 min (44 min) RTR9: 26 min (46 min) RTR10: 28 min (48 min) RTR11: 30 min (50 min) RTR12: 32 min (52 min)
SBI	Swim Base Intervals	100-yard intervals swum @ moderate aerobic intensity w/ 5-second rest periods or 200-yard intervals swum @ moderate aerobic intensity w/ 10-second rest periods or single longer swims @ moderate aerobic intensity	SBI2: 3 x 100 SBI3: 4 x 100 SBI4: 5 x 100 SBI5: 6 x 100 SBI6: 7 x 100 SBI7: 8 x 100 SBI8: 9 x 100 SBI9: 10 x 100 SBI10: 11 x 100 SBI14: 4 x 200 SBI15: 5 x 200 SBI16: 6 x 200 SBI24: 1,000 SBI25: 1,200 SBI26: 1,500 SBI27: 1,800 SBI28: 2,000 SBI29: 2,400 SBI30: 2,600 SBI31: 2,800 SBI32: 3,000 SBI33: 3,200 SBI34: 3,500 SBI35: 3,800

Code Prefix	Workout Type	Brief Description	Levels
SCD	Swim Cool-Down	Easy swim @ recovery intensity	SCD1: 200 SCD2: 250 SCD3: 300 SCD4: 350 SCD5: 400
SDS	Swim Drill Set	25-yard intervals of mixed form drills w/ 10-second rest periods	SDS3: 8 x 25 SDS4: 10 x 25
SFI	Swim Fartlek Intervals	100–200-yard intervals with easy/hard or build/descend format (hard = threshold intensity, easy = moderate aerobic intensity) w/ rest periods of 10–20 seconds	SFI1: 4 x 100 (25 easy/25 hard…), 10-sec rest SFI1A: 4 x 100 (25 build/25 descend…), 10-sec rest SFI2: 6 x 100 (25 easy/25 hard…), 10-sec rest SFI2A: 6 x 100 (25 build/25 descend…), 10-sec rest SFI3A: 8 x 100 (25 build/25 descend…), 10-sec rest SFI4: 4 x 150 (50 easy/25 hard…), 15-sec rest SFI4A: 4 x 150 (50 build/25 descend…), 15-sec rest SFI5: 5 x 150 (50 easy/25 hard…), 15-sec rest SFI5A: 5 x 150 (50 build/25 descend…), 15-sec rest SFI6: 6 x 150 (50 easy/25 hard…), 15-sec rest SFI6A: 6 x 150 (50 build/25 descend…), 15-sec rest SFI9: 5 x 200 (50 easy/50 hard…), 20-sec rest SFI9A: 5 x 200 (50 build/50 descend…), 20-sec rest SFI10: 6 x 200 (50 easy/50 hard…), 20-sec rest
SKS	Swim Kick Set	25-yard intervals kicking only w/ 15-second rest periods	SKS3: 8 x 25 SKS4: 10 x 25

Code Prefix	Workout Type	Brief Description	Levels
SLI	Swim Lactate Intervals	75–150-yard intervals swum @ VO_2 max intensity w/ rest periods of 20 seconds to 1 min 15 seconds	SLI3: 6 x 75, 45-sec rest SLI4: 7 x 75, 45-sec rest SLI5: 8 x 75, 45-sec rest SLI6: 9 x 75, 45-sec rest SLI6A: 9 x 75, 30-sec rest SLI6B: 9 x 75, 20-sec rest SLI7: 10 x 75, 45-sec rest SLI7A: 10 x 75, 30-sec rest SLI7B: 10 x 75, 20-sec rest SLI8: 3 x 100, 1-min rest SLI12: 7 x 100, 1-min rest SLI12A: 7 x 100, 45-sec rest SLI12B: 7 x 100, 30-sec rest SLI13: 8 x 100, 1-min rest SLI13A: 8 x 100, 45-sec rest SLI13B: 8 x 100, 30-sec rest SLI14: 4 x 150, 1-min 15-sec rest SLI15: 5 x 150, 1-min 15-sec rest SLI15A: 5 x 150, 1-min rest SLI16: 6 x 150, 1-min 15-sec rest SLI16A: 6 x 150, 1-min rest SLI16B: 6 x 150, 45-sec rest SLI17: 7 x 150, 1-min 15-sec rest SLI17A: 7 x 150, 1-min rest SLI18: 8 x 150, 1-min 15-sec rest SLI18A: 8 x 150, 1-min rest
SSI	Swim Sprint Intervals	25–50-yard intervals swum @ speed intensity w/ 20-second rest periods, except "A" suffix = 10-second rest, "B" suffix = 5-second rest	SSI3: 6 x 25 SSI5: 8 x 25 SSI6A: 9 x 25 SSI6B: 9 x 25 SSI7: 10 x 25 SSI9: 12 x 25 SSI10: 4 x 50 SSI11: 5 x 50 SSI12: 6 x 50 SSI12A: 6 x 50 SSI12B: 6 x 50 SSI13: 7 x 50 SSI14: 8 x 50 SSI15: 9 x 50 SSI15A: 9 x 50

Code Prefix	Workout Type	Brief Description	Levels
SSI (cont.)			SSI16: 10 x 50 SSI17: 11 x 50 SSI18: 12 x 50
STI	Swim Threshold Intervals	200–400-yard intervals swum @ threshold intensity w/ rest periods of 20–45 seconds	STI1: 2 x 200, 45-sec rest STI2: 3 x 200, 45-sec rest STI2A: 3 x 200, 30-sec rest STI2B: 3 x 200, 20-sec rest STI3: 4 x 200, 45-sec rest STI3A: 4 x 200, 30-sec rest STI3B: 4 x 200, 20-sec rest STI4: 5 x 200, 45-sec rest STI4A: 5 x 200, 30-sec rest STI4B: 5 x 200, 20-sec rest STI5: 6 x 200, 45-sec rest STI5A: 6 x 200, 30-sec rest STI5B: 6 x 200, 20-sec rest STI6: 7 x 200, 45-sec rest STI6A: 7 x 200, 30-sec rest STI6B: 7 x 200, 20-sec rest
STT	Swim Time Trial	Designated distance swum @ maximum effort	STT3: 1,650 yards STT4: 1.2 miles (2,112) STT5: 3,200 STT6: 2.4 miles (4,225)
SWU	Swim Warm-Up	Easy swim @ recovery intensity	SWU1: 200 SWU2: 250 SWU3: 300 SWU4: 350 SWU5: 400

General Schedule

	Tuesday	Wednesday	Thursday	Friday	Saturday	Sunday
BASE PHASE						
Week 1	Swim Base Intervals	Foundation Run + Strides	Brick Workout	Foundation Bike	Long Bike	Swim Base Intervals
	Bike Power Intervals			Swim Fartlek Intervals	Recovery Run	Long Run
Week 2	Swim Base Intervals	Foundation Run + Strides	Foundation Bike	Foundation Bike	Brick Workout	Swim Base Intervals
	Bike Power Intervals		Foundation Run	Swim Fartlek Intervals		Foundation Run
Week 3	Swim Base Intervals	Foundation Run + Strides	Brick Workout	Foundation Bike	Long Bike	Swim Base Intervals
	Bike Power Intervals			Swim Fartlek Intervals	Recovery Run	Long Run
Week 4 (Recovery)	Swim Base Intervals	Foundation Run + Strides	Foundation Bike	Foundation Bike	Brick Workout	Swim Base Intervals
	Bike Power Intervals		Foundation Run	Swim Fartlek Intervals		Foundation Run
Week 5	Swim Base + Sprint Intervals	Fartlek Run	Brick Workout	Foundation Bike	Long Bike	Swim Base Intervals
	Bike Short Hills			Swim Fartlek + Sprint Intervals	Recovery Run	Long Run
Week 6	Swim Base + Sprint Intervals	Fartlek Run	Foundation Bike	Foundation Bike	Brick Workout	Swim Time Trial
	Bike Short Hills		Foundation Run	Swim Fartlek + Sprint Intervals		Foundation Run
Week 7	Swim Base + Sprint Intervals	Fartlek Run	Brick Workout	Foundation Bike	Long Bike	Swim Base Intervals
	Bike Short Hills			Swim Fartlek + Sprint Intervals	Recovery Run	Long Run

	Tuesday	Wednesday	Thursday	Friday	Saturday	Sunday
Week 8 (Recovery)	Swim Base + Sprint Intervals	Fartlek Run	Foundation Bike	Foundation Bike	Brick Workout	Swim Base Intervals
	Bike Short Hills		Foundation Run	Swim Fartlek + Sprint Intervals		Foundation Run
BUILD PHASE						
Week 9	Swim Base + Sprint Intervals	Run Hill Repeats	Brick Workout	Steady-State Bike	Long Bike	Swim Base Intervals
	Bike Speed Intervals			Swim Fartlek + Sprint Intervals	Recovery Run	Long Run
Week 10	Swim Base + Sprint Intervals	Run Hill Repeats	Foundation Bike	Steady-State Bike	Brick Workout	Swim Base Intervals
	Bike Speed Intervals		Foundation Run	Swim Fartlek + Sprint Intervals		Foundation Run
Week 11	Swim Base + Sprint Intervals	Run Hill Repeats	Brick Workout	Steady-State Bike	Long Bike	Swim Time Trial
	Bike Speed Intervals			Swim Fartlek + Sprint Intervals	Recovery Run	Long Run
Week 12 (Recovery)	Swim Base + Sprint Intervals	Run Hill Repeats	Foundation Bike	Steady-State Bike	Recovery Bike or Brick Workout	Sprint Triathlon or Swim Base Intervals
	Bike Speed Intervals		Foundation Run	Swim Fartlek + Sprint Intervals		Sprint Triathlon or Foundation Run
Week 13	Swim Base + Threshold Intervals	Run Lactate Intervals	Brick Workout	Steady-State Bike	Long Bike	Swim Base Intervals

	Tuesday	Wednesday	Thursday	Friday	Saturday	Sunday
Week 13 (cont.)	Bike Long Hills			Swim Base + Lactate + Sprint Intervals	Recovery Run	Long Run
Week 14	Swim Base + Threshold Intervals	Run Lactate Intervals	Foundation Bike	Steady-State Bike	Brick Workout	Swim Base Intervals
	Bike Lactate Intervals		Foundation Run	Swim Base + Lactate + Sprint Intervals		Foundation Run
Week 15	Swim Base + Threshold Intervals	Run Lactate Intervals	Brick Workout	Steady-State Bike	Long Bike	Swim Base Intervals
	Bike Long Hills			Swim Base + Lactate + Sprint Intervals	Recovery Run	Long Run
Week 16 (Recovery)	Swim Base + Threshold Intervals	Run Lactate Intervals	Foundation Bike	Foundation Bike	Recovery Bike or Brick Workout	Olympic-Distance Triathlon or Swim Base Intervals
	Bike Lactate Intervals		Foundation Run	Swim Base + Lactate + Sprint Intervals		Olympic-Distance Triathlon or Foundation Run

PEAK PHASE

	Tuesday	Wednesday	Thursday	Friday	Saturday	Sunday
Week 17	Swim Base + Threshold Intervals	Tempo Run	Brick Workout	Steady-State Bike	Long Bike	Swim Base Intervals
	Tempo Bike			Swim Base + Lactate + Sprint Intervals	Recovery Run	Long Run
Week 18	Swim Base + Threshold Intervals	Tempo Run	Foundation Bike	Steady-State Bike	Brick Workout	Swim Time Trial

	Tuesday	Wednesday	Thursday	Friday	Saturday	Sunday
Week 18 (cont.)	Tempo Bike		Foundation Run	Swim Base + Lactate + Sprint Intervals		L4: Foundation Run L5–6: Long Run
Week 19	Swim Base + Threshold Intervals	Tempo Run	Brick Workout	Steady-State Bike	Long Bike	Swim Base Intervals
	Tempo Bike			Swim Base + Lactate + Sprint Intervals	Recovery Run	Long Run
Week 20 (Recovery)	Swim Base + Threshold Intervals	Tempo Run	Foundation Bike	Steady-State Bike	Recovery Bike or Brick Workout	Half-Ironman Triathlon or Swim Base Intervals
	Tempo Bike		Foundation Run	Swim Base + Lactate + Sprint Intervals		Half-Ironman Triathlon or Foundation Run
Week 21	Swim Base + Threshold Intervals	Tempo Run	Brick Workout	Steady-State Bike	Long Bike	Swim Base Intervals
	Tempo Bike			Swim Base + Lactate + Sprint Intervals	Recovery Run	Long Run
Week 22	Swim Base + Threshold Intervals	Tempo Run	Foundation Bike	Steady-State Bike	Brick Workout	Swim Time Trial
	Tempo Bike		Foundation Run	Swim Base + Lactate + Sprint Intervals		L4–5: Foundation Run L6: Long Run

	Tuesday	Wednesday	Thursday	Friday	Saturday	Sunday
Week 23 (Taper)	Swim Base + Threshold Intervals	Tempo Run	Brick Workout	Foundation Bike	Long Bike	Swim Base Intervals
	Tempo Bike			Swim Base + Lactate + Sprint Intervals	Recovery Run	Long Run
Week 24 (Taper)	Swim Base + Threshold Intervals	Tempo Run	Foundation Bike	Swim Lactate + Sprint Intervals	Recovery Bike	Ironman Triathlon
	Tempo Bike		Foundation Run + Strides			

Week-by-Week Schedule

Base Phase

The conditioning priorities in this eight-week phase are developing aerobic capacity and building endurance. The key workouts are base and fartlek swim intervals and foundation and long rides and runs. You will also do a small amount of high-intensity work (e.g., running strides) to gain efficiency and prepare your body to handle the high-intensity workouts of the build phase.

WEEK 1

This week's goal: Get accustomed to your new workout schedule.

	Tuesday	Wednesday	Thursday	Friday	Saturday	Sunday
Level 4	SWU4 SDS3 SBI4 SKS3 SCD4 (1,600)	RFR5 + RSS1	BRW3	CFR3	CLR1	SWU1 SBI25 SCD1 (1,600)
	CPI3			SWU4 SDS3 SFI1 SKS3 SCD4 (1,500)	RRR2	RLR1

	Tuesday	Wednesday	Thursday	Friday	Saturday	Sunday
Level 5	SWU4 SDS4 SBI5 SKS4 SCD4 (1,800)	RFR5 + RSS1	BRW4	CFR3	CLR2	SWU3 SBI25 SCD3 (1,800)
	CPI4			SWU4 SDS4 SFI2 SKS4 SCD4 (1,800)	RRR2	RLR2
Level 6	SWU4 SDS4 SBI6 SKS4 SCD4 (1,900)	RFR6 + RSS1	BRW5	CFR3	CLR3	SWU2 SBI26 SCD2 (2,000)
	CPI5			SWU4 SDS4 SFI5 SKS4 SCD4 (1,950)	RRR2	RLR3

WEEK 2

This week's goal: Gather momentum by completing all scheduled workouts as prescribed.

	Tuesday	Wednesday	Thursday	Friday	Saturday	Sunday
Level 4	SWU4 SDS3 SBI5 SKS3 SCD4 (1,700)	RFR6 + RSS2	CFR3	CFR3	BRW4	SWU2 SBI25 SCD2 (1,700)
	CPI4		RFR5	SWU4 SDS3 SFI2A SKS3 SCD4 (1,700)		RFR6

	Tuesday	Wednesday	Thursday	Friday	Saturday	Sunday
Level 5	SWU4 SDS4 SBI6 SKS4 SCD4 (1,900)	RFR6 + RSS2	CFR3	CFR4	BRW5	SWU4 SBI25 SCD4 (1,900)
	CPI5		RFR5	SWU4 SDS4 SFI5A SKS4 SCD4 (1,950)		RFR6
Level 6	SWU4 SDS4 SBI7 SKS4 SCD4 (2,000)	RFR6 + RSS2	CFR3	CFR4	BRW5	SWU3 SBI26 SCD3 (2,100)
	CPI6		RFR5	SWU4 SDS4 SFI6A SKS4 SCD4 (2,100)		RFR7

QUICK TIP:

Dynamic stretching is a special type of stretching that takes your joints through a full range of motion in sport-specific movements. Regular dynamic stretching allows you to swim, bike, and run more efficiently by reducing internal resistance in your muscles. For guidelines on dynamic stretching, see Chapter 17.

WEEK 3

This week's goal: Find your running legs quickly in Thursday's brick workout.

	Tuesday	Wednesday	Thursday	Friday	Saturday	Sunday
Level 4	SWU4 SDS3 SBI6 SKS3 SCD4 (1,800)	RFR6 + RSS3	BRW4	CFR4	CLR2	SWU3 SBI25 SCD3 (1,800)
	CPI5			SWU4 SDS3 SFI4 SKS3 SCD4 (1,700)	RRR3	RLR2
Level 5	SWU4 SDS4 SBI7 SKS4 SCD4 (2,000)	RFR6 + RSS3	BRW5	CFR4	CLR3	SWU2 SBI26 SCD2 (2,000)
	CPI6			SWU4 SDS4 SFI5 SKS4 SCD4 (1,950)	RRR3	RLR3
Level 6	SWU4 SDS4 SBI8 SKS4 SCD4 (2,100)	RFR7 + RSS3	BRW6	CFR4	CLR4	SWU4 SBI26 SCD4 (2,200)
	CPI7			SWU4 SDS4 SFI6 SKS4 SCD4 (2,100)	RRR3	RLR4

WEEK 4
(Recovery)

This week's goal: Fully absorb your recent training and finish the week feeling rested and ready to return to harder training next week.

	Tuesday	Wednesday	Thursday	Friday	Saturday	Sunday
Level 4	SWU4 SDS3 SBI4 SCD4 (1,400)	RFR3 + RSS2	CFR3	CFR3	BRW5	SWU1 SBI24 SCD1 (1,400)
	CPI3		RFR4	SWU4 SDS3 SFI1A SCD4 (1,300)		RFR6
Level 5	SWU4 SDS4 SBI5 SCD4 (1,550)	RFR5 + RSS2	CFR3	CFR3	BRW6	SWU3 SBI24 SCD3 (1,600)
	CPI4		RFR4	SWU4 SDS4 SFI4A SCD4 (1,550)		RFR7
Level 6	SWU4 SDS4 SBI6 SCD4 (1,650)	RFR5 + RSS2	CFR3	CFR3	BRW7	SWU3 SBI25 SCD3 (1,800)
	CPI5		RFR4	SWU4 SDS4 SFI5A SCD4 (1,700)		RFR8

WEEK 5

This week's goal: Run hard but relaxed at VO_2 max intensity (9 RPE) in Wednesday's fartlek running intervals.

	Tuesday	Wednesday	Thursday	Friday	Saturday	Sunday
Level 4	SWU4 SDS3 SBI6 SSI11 SKS3 SCD4 (2,050)	RFL5	BRW6	CFR4	CLR4	SWU3 SBI26 SCD3 (2,100)
	CSH5			SWU4 SDS3 SFI6 SSI3 SKS3 SCD4 (2,150)	RRR3	RLR3
Level 5	SWU4 SDS4 SBI7 SSI11 SKS4 SCD4 (2,250)	RFL7	BRW7	CFR4	CLR5	SWU2 SBI27 SCD2 (2,300)
	CSH6			SWU4 SDS4 SFI6 SSI5 SKS4 SCD4 (2,300)	RRR3	RLR4
Level 6	SWU4 SDS4 SBI9 SSI11 SKS4 SCD4 (2,450)	RFL7	BRW8	CFR5	CLR6	SWU4 SBI27 SCD4 (2,500)
	CSH7			SWU4 SDS4 SFI9 SSI7 SKS4 SCD4 (2,450)	RRR3	RLR5

WEEK 6

This week's goal: Go all out to get a good sense of your current swimming performance level in Sunday's swim time trial.

	Tuesday	Wednesday	Thursday	Friday	Saturday	Sunday
Level 4	SWU4 SDS3 SBI7 SSI12 SKS3 SCD4 (2,200)	RFL6	CFR4	CFR4	BRW6	SWU1 STT3 SCD1 (2,050)
	CSH6		RFR6	SWU4 SDS3 SFI6A SSI5 SKS3 SCD4 (2,200)		RFR6
Level 5	SWU4 SDS4 SBI8 SSI12 SKS4 SCD4 (2,400)	RFL8	CFR4	CFR5	BRW7	SWU2 STT3 SCD2 (2,150)
	CSH7		RFR6	SWU4 SDS4 SFI6A SSI7 SKS4 SCD4 (2,350)		RFR6
Level 6	SWU4 SDS4 SBI10 SSI12 SKS4 SCD4 (2,600)	RFL9	CFR4	CFR5	BRW8	SWU3 STT3 SCD3 (2,250)

	Tuesday	Wednesday	Thursday	Friday	Saturday	Sunday
Level 6 (cont.)	CSH8		RFR6	SWU4 SDS4 SFI9A SSI9 SKS4 SCD4 (2,500)		RFR7

WEEK 7

This week's goal: Finish strong in Saturday's long ride.

	Tuesday	Wednesday	Thursday	Friday	Saturday	Sunday
Level 4	SWU4 SDS3 SBI7 SSI13 SKS3 SCD4 (2,250)	RFL8	BRW7	CFR5	CLR5	SWU2 SBI27 SCD2 (2,300)
	CSH7			SWU4 SDS3 SFI6 SSI9 SKS3 SCD4 (2,300)	RRR3	RLR4
Level 5	SWU4 SDS4 SBI8 SSI13 SKS4 SCD4 (2,450)	RFL8	BRW8	CFR5	CLR6	SWU4 SBI27 SCD4 (2,500)
	CSH8			SWU4 SDS4 SFI9 SSI9 SKS4 SCD4 (2,500)	RRR3	RLR5

	Tuesday	Wednesday	Thursday	Friday	Saturday	Sunday
Level 6	SWU4 SDS4 SBI10 SSI13 SKS4 SCD4 (2,650)	RFL10	BRW9	CFR5	CLR7	SWU4 SBI28 SCD4 (2,700)
	CSH9			SWU4 SDS4 SFI10 SSI9 SKS4 SCD4 (2,700)	RRR3	RLR6

WEEK 8
(Recovery)

This week's goal: Fully absorb your recent training and finish the week feeling rested and ready to return to harder training next week.

	Tuesday	Wednesday	Thursday	Friday	Saturday	Sunday
Level 4	SWU4 SDS3 SBI5 SSI10 SCD4 (1,700)	RFL5	CFR3	CFR3	BRW4	SWU1 SBI25 SCD1 (1,600)
	CSH3		RFR4	SWU4 SDS3 SFI2A SSI3 SCD4 (1,650)		RFR6
Level 5	SWU4 SDS4 SBI6 SSI10 SCD4 (1,850)	RFL7	CFR3	CFR3	BRW5	SWU3 SBI25 SCD3 (1,800)

	Tuesday	Wednesday	Thursday	Friday	Saturday	Sunday
Level 5 (cont.)	CSH4		RFR4	SWU4 SDS4 SFI3A SSI3 SCD4 (1,900)		RFR7
Level 6	SWU4 SDS4 SBI7 SSI11 SCD4 (2,000)	RFL7	CFR3	CFR3	BRW6	SWU2 SBI26 SCD2 (2,000)
	CSH5		RFR4	SWU4 SDS4 SFI6A SSI3 SCD4 (2,000)		RFR7

QUICK TIP:

There is no magical proportion of carbs, fats, and proteins that you need to maintain in your diet. Most triathletes are able to perform equally well on either a moderate-carb or a high-carb diet, while others fare better on one or the other. You may need to experiment to find the proportions that work best for you.

Build Phase

Because you are training for a very long race, your primary conditioning objective in this eight-week build phase remains endurance development, which you will achieve through your long weekend workouts. But you will also maximize your aerobic capacity and build high-intensity fatigue resistance and efficiency through challenging high-intensity workouts including swim sprint intervals, cycling speed intervals, and running hill repetitions.

WEEK 9

This week's goal: Use the perceived exertion guidelines from Chapter 2 to find the appropriate intensity for the high-intensity segments of this week's new workouts.

	Tuesday	Wednesday	Thursday	Friday	Saturday	Sunday
Level 4	SWU4 SDS3 SBI14 SSI14 SKS3 SCD4 (2,300)	RHR8	BRW5A	CSS1	CLR7	SWU4 SBI28 SCD4 (2,700)
	CSI12			SWU4 SDS3 SFI9 SSI10 SKS3 SCD4 (2,300)	RRR3	RLR6
Level 5	SWU4 SDS4 SBI15 SSI14 SKS4 SCD4 (2,600)	RHR8	BRW6A	CSS1	CLR8	SWU2 SBI29 SCD2 (2,900)
	CSI13			SWU4 SDS4 SFI9 SSI12 SKS4 SCD4 (2,500)	RRR3	RLR7
Level 6	SWU4 SDS4 SBI16 SSI13 SKS4 SCD4 (2,750)	RHR8	BRW7A	CSS1	CLR9	SWU4 SBI29 SCD4 (3,100)

	Tuesday	Wednesday	Thursday	Friday	Saturday	Sunday
Level 6 (cont.)	CSI14			SWU4 SDS4 SFI10 SSI12 SKS4 SCD4 (2,700)	RRR4	RLR8

WEEK 10

This week's goal: Swim Tuesday's sprint intervals at the fastest pace you can maintain through the end of the last interval.

	Tuesday	Wednesday	Thursday	Friday	Saturday	Sunday
Level 4	SWU4 SDS3 SBI14 SSI16 SKS3 SCD4 (2,400)	RHR8	CFR5	CSS1	BRW10	SWU2 SBI29 SCD2 (2,900)
	CSI13		RFR7	SWU4 SDS3 SFI9A SSI12 SKS3 SCD4 (2,400)		RFR7
Level 5	SWU4 SDS4 SBI15 SSI16 SKS4 SCD4 (2,700)	RHR9	CFR5	CSS1	BRW11	SWU4 SBI29 SCD4 (3,100)
	CSI14		RFR7	SWU4 SDS4 SFI9A SSI14 SKS4 SCD4 (2,600)		RFR7

	Tuesday	Wednesday	Thursday	Friday	Saturday	Sunday
Level 6	SWU4 SDS4 SBI16 SSI15 SKS4 SCD4 (2,850)	RHR9	CFR5	CSS2	BRW12	SWU4 SBI30 SCD4 (3,300)
	CSI15		RFR7	SWU4 SDS4 SFI10A SSI14 SKS4 SCD4 (2,800)		RFR8

WEEK 11

This week's goal: Find a steady groove at threshold intensity (8–8.5 RPE) in the run segment of Thursday's brick workout.

	Tuesday	Wednesday	Thursday	Friday	Saturday	Sunday
Level 4	SWU4 SDS3 SBI14 SSI17 SKS3 SCD4 (2,450)	RHR9	BRW7A	CSS2	CLR8	SWU1 STT4 SCD1 (2,512)
	CSI14			SWU4 SDS3 SFI9 SSI14 SKS3 SCD4 (2,500)	RRR3	RLR6
Level 5	SWU4 SDS4 SBI15 SSI15 SKS4 SCD4 (2,650)	RHR9	BRW8A	CSS2	CLR9	SWU2 STT4 SCD2 (2,612)

	Tuesday	Wednesday	Thursday	Friday	Saturday	Sunday
Level 5 (cont.)	CSI15			SWU4 SDS4 SFI9 SSI16 SKS4 SCD4 (2,700)	RRR4	RLR8
Level 6	SWU4 SDS4 SBI15 SSI18 SKS4 SCD4 (2,800)	RHR10	BRW9A	CSS2	CLR10	SWU3 STT3 SCD3 (2,712)
	CSI16			SWU4 SDS4 SFI10 SSI14 SKS4 SCD4 (2,800)	RRR4	RLR8

WEEK 12
(Recovery)

This week's goal: Fully absorb your recent training and have a solid sprint triathlon performance on Sunday if you have the opportunity.

	Tuesday	Wednesday	Thursday	Friday	Saturday	Sunday
Level 4	SWU4 SDS3 SBI5 SSI10 SCD4 (1,700)	RHR5	CFR4	CFR3	CRR1 or BRW8*	Sprint Triathlon or SWU3 SBI25 SCD3 (1,800)*
	CSI5		RFR5	SWU4 SDS3 SFI2A SSI5 SCD4 (1,700)		RFR7*

*If not racing

339

	Tuesday	Wednesday	Thursday	Friday	Saturday	Sunday
Level 5	SWU4 SDS4 SBI6 SSI10 SCD4 (1,850)	RHR6	CFR4	CFR3	CRR1 or BRW9*	Sprint Triathlon or SWU2 SBI26 SCD2 (2,000)*
	CSI6		RFR5	SWU4 SDS4 SFI5A SSI5 SCD4 (1,900)		RFR7*
Level 6	SWU4 SDS4 SBI7 SSI11 SCD4 (2,000)	RHR7	CFR4	CFR3	CRR1 or BRW10*	Sprint Triathlon or SWU4 SBI26 SCD4 (2,200)*
	CSI7		RFR5	SWU4 SDS4 SFI6A SSI5 SCD4 (2,050)		RFR8*

*If not racing

QUICK TIP:

If you begin to experience pain in your heel during the first steps of your runs, and perhaps also first thing in the morning, you might be developing a case of plantar fasciitis. This injury could curtail your running for many weeks if you don't treat it aggressively. The most effective treatments are switching to running shoes with more cushioning, prescription orthotics, and wearing a night splint.

WEEK 13

This week's goal: Finish strong in Sunday's long swim.

	Tuesday	Wednesday	Thursday	Friday	Saturday	Sunday
Level 4	SWU4 SDS3 SBI6 STI2 SKS3 SCD4 (2,400)	RLI6	BRW7	CSS2	CLR9	SWU2 SBI29 SCD2 (2,900)
	CLH4			SWU4 SDS3 SBI4 SLI5 SSI5 SKS3 SCD4 (2,400)	RRR4	RLR7
Level 5	SWU4 SDS4 SBI7 STI2 SKS4 SCD4 (2,600)	RLI7	BRW8	CSS2	CLR10	SWU4 SBI29 SCD4 (3,100)
	CLH5			SWU4 SDS4 SBI4 SLI6 SSI5 SKS4 SCD4 (2,575)	RRR4	RLR8
Level 6	SWU4 SDS4 SBI7 STI3 SKS4 SCD4 (2,800)	RLI8	BRW9	CSS2	CLR11	SWU4 SBI30 SCD4 (3,300)

	Tuesday	Wednesday	Thursday	Friday	Saturday	Sunday
Level 6 (cont.)	CLH6			SWU4 SDS4 SBI5 SLI7 SSI5 SKS4 SCD4 (2,750)	RRR4	RLR9

WEEK 14

This week's goal: Try to swim this week's threshold and lactate intervals at the same pace you did last week despite the shorter rest periods.

	Tuesday	Wednesday	Thursday	Friday	Saturday	Sunday
Level 4	SWU4 SDS3 SBI6 STI2A SKS3 SCD4 (2,400)	RLI7	CFR6	CSS2	BRW12	SWU2 SBI30 SCD2 (3,100)
	CLI5		RFR8	SWU4 SDS3 SBI3 SLI6A SSI6A SKS3 SCD4 (2,400)		RFR8
Level 5	SWU4 SDS4 SBI7 STI2A SKS4 SCD4 (2,600)	RLI8	CFR6	CSS3	BRW13	SWU2 SBI31 SCD2 (3,300)
	CLI6		RFR8	SWU4 SDS4 SBI3 SLI7A SSI6A SKS4 SCD4 (2,575)		RFR8

	Tuesday	Wednesday	Thursday	Friday	Saturday	Sunday
Level 6	SWU4 SDS4 SBI7 STI3A SKS4 SCD4 (2,800)	RLI10	CFR6	CSS3	BRW14	SWU4 SBI31 SCD4 (3,500)
	CLI7		RFR8	SWU4 SDS4 SBI4 SLI13A SSI6A SKS4 SCD4 (2,725)		RFR9

WEEK 15

This week's goal: Don't be discouraged if you feel general fatigue beginning to mount as this week progresses—just concentrate on getting the work done and on the coming recovery week.

	Tuesday	Wednesday	Thursday	Friday	Saturday	Sunday
Level 4	SWU4 SDS3 SBI6 STI2B SKS3 SCD4 (2,400)	RLI8	BRW8	CSS3	CLR11	SWU3 SBI30 SCD3 (3,200)
	CLH5			SWU4 SDS3 SBI3 SLI6B SSI6B SKS3 SCD4 (2,400)	RRR4	RLR9
Level 5	SWU4 SDS4 SBI7 STI2B	RLI10	BRW9	CSS3	CLR12	SWU3 SBI31 SCD3 (3,400)

	Tuesday	Wednesday	Thursday	Friday	Saturday	Sunday
Level 5 (cont.)	SKS4 SCD4 (2,600)					
	CLH6			SWU4 SDS4 SBI3 SLI7B SSI6B SKS4 SCD4 (2,575)	RRR4	RLR10
Level 6	SWU4 SDS4 SBI7 STI3B SKS4 SCD4 (2,800)	RLI11	BRW10	CSS3	CLR13	SWU3 SBI32 SCD3 (3,600)
	CLH7			SWU4 SDS4 SBI4 SLI13B SSI6B SKS4 SCD4 (2,725)	RRR5	RLR10

WEEK 16
(Recovery)

This week's goal: Fully absorb your recent training and have a solid Olympic-distance triathlon on Sunday if you have the opportunity.

	Tuesday	Wednesday	Thursday	Friday	Saturday	Sunday
Level 4	SWU4 SDS3 SBI2 STI1 SKS3 SCD4 (1,800)	RLI6	CFR4	CFR3	CRR1 or BRW13*	Olympic-Distance Triathlon or SWU3 SBI26 SCD3 (2,100)*

*If not racing

	Tuesday	Wednesday	Thursday	Friday	Saturday	Sunday
Level 4 (cont.)	CLI3		RFR6	SWU4 SDS3 SLI3 SSI6 SKS3 SCD4 (1,775)		RFR8*
Level 5	SWU4 SDS4 SBI3 STI1 SKS4 SCD4 (2,000)	RLI6	CFR5	CFR3	CRR1 or BRW14*	Olympic-Distance Triathlon or SWU2 SBI27 SCD2 (2,300)*
	CLI4		RFR6	SWU4 SDS4 SLI4 SSI6 SKS4 SCD4 (1,950)		RFR9*
Level 6	SWU4 SDS4 SBI3 STI2 SKS4 SCD4 (2,200)	RLI6	CFR5	CFR3	CRR1 or BRW15*	Olympic-Distance Triathlon or SWU4 SBI27 SCD4 (2,500)*
	CLI5		RFR7	SWU4 SDS4 SLI5 SSI6 SKS4 SCD4 (2,025)		RLR1*

*If not racing

Peak Phase

You're already fit. It's time to get race fit in this eight-week peak phase. You'll do this by completing your longest swims, rides, runs, and brick workouts, to maximize your endurance. You will also do longer workouts at high aerobic intensity and threshold intensity to enhance your ability to sustain a relatively fast pace.

WEEK 17

This week's goal: Concentrate on maintaining a realistic Ironman race pace in Friday's steady-state ride.

	Tuesday	Wednesday	Thursday	Friday	Saturday	Sunday
Level 4	SWU4 SDS3 SBI5 STI4 SKS3 SCD4 (2,700)	RTR5	BRW9	CSS1	CLR13	SWU2 SBI31 SCD2 (3,300)
	CTR10			SWU4 SDS3 SBI5 SLI12 SSI12 SKS3 SCD4 (2,700)	RRR4	RLR9
Level 5	SWU4 SDS4 SBI6 STI4 SKS4 SCD4 (2,900)	RTR6	BRW10	CSS2	CLR14	SWU2 SBI32 SCD2 (3,500)
	CTR11			SWU4 SDS4 SBI5 SLI13 SSI12 SKS4 SCD4 (2,900)	RRR5	RLR10

	Tuesday	Wednesday	Thursday	Friday	Saturday	Sunday
Level 6	SWU4 SDS4 SBI6 STI5 SKS4 SCD4 (3,100)	RTR7	BRW11	CSS3	CLR15	SWU4 SBI32 SCD4 (3,700)
	CTR12			SWU4 SDS4 SBI5 SLI16 SSI12 SKS4 SCD4 (3,000)	RRR5	RLR11

QUICK TIP:

If possible, do some of your long Sunday swims in open water. Swimming in open water—with the lack of lane lines, the wave chop, and lack of walls to rest on—is very different from swimming in a pool. Practicing in open water is essential to being able to swim comfortably and effectively in this type of environment in races.

WEEK 18

This week's goal: Go all out for an excellent race-specific workout in Sunday's swim time trial.

	Tuesday	Wednesday	Thursday	Friday	Saturday	Sunday
Level 4	SWU4 SDS3 SBI5 STI4A SKS3 SCD4 (2,700)	RTR6	CFR6	CSS2	BRW14	SWU1 STT5 SCD1 (3,600)

	Tuesday	Wednesday	Thursday	Friday	Saturday	Sunday
Level 4 (cont.)	CTR11		RFR8	SWU4 SDS3 SBI5 SLI12A SSI12A SKS3 SCD4 (2,700)		RFR9
Level 5	SWU4 SDS4 SBI6 STI4A SKS4 SCD4 (2,900)	RTR7	CFR7	CSS3	BRW15	SWU2 STT5 SCD2 (3,700)
	CTR12		RFR8	SWU4 SDS4 SBI5 SLI13A SSI12A SKS4 SCD4 (2,900)		RLR1
Level 6	SWU4 SDS4 SBI6 STI5A SKS4 SCD4 (3,100)	RTR8	CFR7	CSS4	BRW16	SWU3 STT5 SCD3 (3,800)
	CTR13		RFR9	SWU4 SDS4 SBI5 SLI16A SSI12A SKS4 SCD4 (3,000)		RLR2

WEEK 19

This week's goal: Dig deep in Tuesday's challenging tempo ride.

	Tuesday	Wednesday	Thursday	Friday	Saturday	Sunday
Level 4	SWU4 SDS3 SBI5 STI4B SKS3 SCD4 (2,700)	RTR7	BRW8A	CSS4	CLR14	SWU2 SBI33 SCD2 (3,700)
	CTR13			SWU4 SDS3 SBI5 SLI12B SSI12B SKS3 SCD4 (2,700)	RRR5	RLR10
Level 5	SWU4 SDS4 SBI6 STI4B SKS4 SCD4 (2,900)	RTR8	BRW9A	CSS4	CLR15	SWU4 SBI33 SCD4 (3,900)
	CTR14			SWU4 SDS4 SBI5 SLI13B SSI12B SKS4 SCD4 (2,900)	RRR5	RLR11
Level 6	SWU4 SDS4 SBI6 STI5B SKS4 SCD4 (3,100)	RTR9	BRW10A	CSS4	CLR16	SWU3 SBI34 SCD3 (4,100)

	Tuesday	Wednesday	Thursday	Friday	Saturday	Sunday
Level 6 (cont.)	CTR15			SWU4 SDS4 SBI5 SLI16B SSI12B SKS4 SCD4 (3,000)	RRR6	RLR12

WEEK 20

This week's goal: Fully absorb your recent training and have a solid half-Ironman performance on Sunday if you have the opportunity.

	Tuesday	Wednesday	Thursday	Friday	Saturday	Sunday
Level 4	SWU4 SDS3 SBI2 STI1 SKS3 SCD4 (1,800)	RTR6	CFR4	CFR3	CRR1 or BRW16*	Half- Ironman Triathlon or SWU4 SBI26 SCD4 (2,200)*
	CTR9		RFR6	SWU4 SDS3 SBI1 SLI8 SSI10 SKS3 SCD4 (1,800)		RFR7*
Level 5	SWU4 SDS4 SBI3 STI1 SKS4 SCD4 (2,000)	RTR7	CFR5	CFR3	CRR1 or BRW17*	Half- Ironman Triathlon or SWU3 SBI27 SCD3 (2,400)*
	CTR10		RFR6	SWU4 SDS4 SBI1		RFR8*

	Tuesday	Wednesday	Thursday	Friday	Saturday	Sunday
Level 5 (cont.)				SLI9 SSI10 SKS4 SCD4 (2,000)		
Level 6	SWU4 SDS4 SBI3 STI2 SKS4 SCD4 (2,200)	RTR8	CFR5	CFR3	CRR1 or BRW17*	Half- Ironman Triathlon or SWU3 SBI28 SCD3 (2,600)*
	CTR11		RFR7	SWU4 SDS4 SBI2 SLI10 SSI10 SKS4 SCD4 (2,200)		RFR9*

*If not racing

WEEK 21

This week's goal: Pace yourself evenly through Sunday's very long run.

	Tuesday	Wednesday	Thursday	Friday	Saturday	Sunday
Level 4	SWU4 SDS3 SBI5 STI5 SKS3 SCD4 (2,900)	RTR10	BRW9A	CSS3	CLR15	SWU4 SBI33 SCD4 (3,900)
	CTR14			SWU4 SDS3 SBI3 SLI16 SSI15 SKS3 SCD4 (2,850)	RRR5	RLR11

351

	Tuesday	Wednesday	Thursday	Friday	Saturday	Sunday
Level 5	SWU4 SDS4 SBI6 STI5 SKS4 SCD4 (3,100)	RTR11	BRW9A	CSS4	CLR16	SWU3 SBI34 SCD3 (4,100)
	CTR15			SWU4 SDS4 SBI3 SLI17 SSI15 SKS4 SCD4 (3,100)	RRR6	RLR12
Level 6	SWU4 SDS4 SBI6 STI6 SKS4 SCD4 (3,300)	RTR12	BRW9A	CSS5	CLR17	SWU2 SBI35 SCD2 (4,300)
	CTR16			SWU4 SDS4 SBI3 SLI18 SSI15 SKS4 SCD4 (3,250)	RRR6	RLR13

WEEK 22

This week's goal: Put your best effort into each of this week's work-outs—your prerace taper begins next week!

	Tuesday	Wednesday	Thursday	Friday	Saturday	Sunday
Level 4	SWU4 SDS3 SBI5 STI5A	RTR11	CFR7	CSS4	BRW16	SWU1 STT6 SCD1 (4,625)

	Tuesday	Wednesday	Thursday	Friday	Saturday	Sunday
Level 4 *(cont.)*	SKS3 SCD4 (2,900)					
	CTR15		RFR9	SWU4 SDS3 SBI3 SLI16A SSI15A SKS3 SCD4 (2,850)		RFR8
Level 5	SWU4 SDS4 SBI6 STI5A SKS4 SCD4 (3,100)	RTR12	CFR7	CSS5	BRW17	SWU1 STT6 SCD1 (4,625)
	CTR16		RFR9	SWU4 SDS4 SBI3 SLI17A SSI15A SKS4 SCD4 (3,100)		RFR9
Level 6	SWU4 SDS4 SBI6 STI6A SKS4 SCD4 (3,300)	RTR13	CFR7	CSS6	BRW18	SWU1 STT6 SCD1 (4,625)
	CTR17		RFR9	SWU4 SDS4 SBI3 SLI18A SSI15A SKS4 SCD4 (3,250)		RLR1

QUICK TIP:

One of the most common mistakes in long-distance triathlons is consuming too much nutrition during the latter portion of the bike leg. Due to the stomach jostling involved during running, athletes are not able to tolerate as much nutrition in the stomach while running as they can on the bike. For this reason, triathletes who take in too much on the bike develop gastrointestinal problems early in the run. To spare yourself this misery, consume only fluids and energy gels in modest amounts during the last 30–45 minutes of cycling.

WEEK 23
(Taper)

This week's goal: Gain confidence by feeling your fitness begin to peak in this week's workouts.

	Tuesday	Wednesday	Thursday	Friday	Saturday	Sunday
Level 4	SWU4 SDS3 SBI3 STI5B SKS3 SCD4 (2,700)	RTR10	BRW5	CFR4	CLR3	SWU2 SBI29 SCD2 (2,900)
	CTR14			SWU4 SDS3 SBI3 SLI14 SSI11 SKS3 SCD4 (2,350)	RRR4	RLR3
Level 5	SWU4 SDS4 SBI4 STI5B SKS4 SCD4 (2,900)	RTR11	BRW6	CFR4	CLR4	SWU2 SBI30 SCD2 (3,100)

	Tuesday	Wednesday	Thursday	Friday	Saturday	Sunday
Level 5 (cont.)	CTR14			SWU4 SDS4 SBI3 SLI15 SSI11 SKS4 SCD4 (2,600)	RRR4	RLR4
Level 6	SWU4 SDS4 SBI4 STI6B SKS4 SCD4 (3,100)	RTR12	BRW7	CFR4	CLR5	SWU4 SBI30 SCD4 (3,300)
	CTR14			SWU4 SDS4 SBI3 SLI16 SSI11 SKS4 SCD4 (2,750)	RRR5	RLR5

WEEK 24

This week's goal: Have a great Ironman on Sunday!

	Tuesday	Wednesday	Thursday	Friday	Saturday	Sunday
Level 4	SWU4 SDS3 STI4 SCD4 (1,900)	RTR4	CFR1	SWU4 SLI8 SSI10 SCD4 (1,200)	CRR1	Ironman Triathlon
	CTR5		RFR1 + RSS3			
Level 5	SWU4 SDS3 STI4 SCD4 (1,900)	RTR4	CFR1	SWU4 SLI8 SSI10 SCD4 (1,200)	CRR1	Ironman Triathlon
	CTR5		RFR1 + RSS3			

	Tuesday	Wednesday	Thursday	Friday	Saturday	Sunday
Level 6	SWU4 SDS3 STI4 SCD4 (1,900)	RTR4	CFR1	SWU4 SLI8 SSI10 SCD4 (1,200)	CRR1	Ironman Triathlon
	CTR5		RFR1 + RSS3			

Chapter 14

IRONMAN TRIATHLON TRAINING PLANS
Levels 7–10

When I first got hooked on triathlons my goals were never more than a pace or two in front of me. I was content just to improve, bit by bit. But after improving bit by bit for a while I started to wonder about the ultimate limit of my endurance potential, and I dreamed about fully realizing it. At last, when the time was right, I took the plunge and trained for an Ironman like it was my job. The training plan I created for myself looked a lot like the training plans in this chapter. You'll be happy to know that in following it I became fitter than I had ever dreamed I could be, and I had a great race.

The four training plans in this chapter will have you swimming, cycling, and running each four times a week. This weekly workout schedule includes a bike-run brick workout, which takes place on Thursday in odd-numbered weeks and on Saturday in even-numbered weeks. While you may have seen Ironman plans that entail higher volume than these plans do, I doubt you will find plans that are more effective, as there is absolutely no waste in these schedules. What they may lack in volume they more than make up for with specificity, workout variation, carefully orchestrated progression, and optimal recovery.

Each plan is 24 weeks long. The base, build, and peak phases last eight weeks apiece. Every fourth week is a recovery week and the final two weeks constitute a tapering period. There are three optional tune-up races scheduled: a sprint in Week 12, an Olympic-distance event in Week 16, and a half-Ironman in Week 20.

Level 7

This is essentially the plan I used to train for my first Ironman. It prepared me for a strong performance but was efficient enough to leave me plenty of time to coach, write, and hang out with my wife. The plan begins with 7,300 yards of swimming, 5 hours and 15 minutes of cycling, and 2 hours and 38 minutes of running in Week 1. It peaks with 13,625 yards of swimming, 10 hours and 20 minutes of cycling, and 4 hours and 44 minutes of running in Week 22.

Level 8

Choose this plan if you are experienced at the Ironman distance and want to take your performance to the next level. The plan begins with 8,100 yards of swimming, 5 hours and 40 minutes of cycling, and 2 hours and 48 minutes of running in Week 1. It peaks with 14,325 yards of swimming, 10 hours and 35 minutes of cycling, and 4 hours and 58 minutes of running in Week 22.

Level 9

When training toward the upper limits of what the human body can handle it's all too easy to become overtrained. Choose this plan if you feel you could train as hard as anyone but want to be careful you don't overtrain. The plan begins with 8,500 yards of swimming, 6 hours and 10 minutes of cycling, and 3 hours and 3 minutes of running in Week 1. It peaks with 14,625 yards of swimming, 11 hours and 5 minutes of cycling, and 5 hours and 14 minutes of running in Week 22.

Level 10

If your goal is to win an Ironman, or you wish to train as well as those who do win Ironmans, use this plan. It begins with 9,300 yards of swimming, 6 hours and 40 minutes of cycling, and 3 hours and 13 minutes of running in Week 1. It peaks with 15,275 yards of swimming, 11 hours and 20 minutes of cycling, and 5 hours and 30 minutes of running in Week 22.

Quick Reference Guide to Workout Codes for Ironman Triathlon Training Plans Levels 7–10

Code Prefix	Workout Type	Brief Description	Levels
BRW	Brick Workout	Bike ride followed by immediate run, both @ moderate aerobic intensity, except "A" and "B" suffix = run @ threshold intensity	BRW4: 45 min/15 min BRW4A: 45 min/15 min (run @ threshold) BRW5: 1 hr/20 min BRW5A: 1 hr/20 min (run @ threshold) BRW6: 1 hr/30 min BRW6A: 1 hr/30 min (run @ threshold) BRW7: 1 hr 15 min/20 min BRW7B: 1 hr 15 min/20 min (run @ threshold) BRW8: 1 hr 15 min/30 min BRW8B: 1 hr 15 min/30 min (run @ threshold) BRW9: 1 hr 30 min/30 min BRW9B: 1 hr 30 min/30 min (run @ threshold) BRW10: 1 hr 30 min/45 min BRW11: 1 hr 45 min/45 min BRW12: 1 hr 45 min/50 min BRW13: 2 hr/50 min BRW14: 2 hr 15 min/55 min BRW15: 2 hr 30 min/55 min BRW16: 3 hr/1 hr BRW17: 3 hr 30 min/1 hr BRW18: 4 hr/1 hr
CFR	Foundation Bike	Steady ride @ moderate aerobic intensity	CFR3: 1 hr CFR4: 1 hr 15 min CFR5: 1 hr 30 min CFR6: 1 hr 45 min CFR7: 2 hr CFR8: 2 hr 15 min
CLH	Bike Long Hill Climbs	5–8-minute climbing intervals @ threshold/VO$_2$ max intensity w/ 3-minute active recoveries; warm up and cool down long enough to reach total time	CLH3: 4 x 5 min (1 hr 10 min total) CLH5: 6 x 5 min (1 hr 20 min) CLH7: 10 x 1 min (1 hr 15 min) CLH10: 4 x 8 min (1 hr 50 min) CLH11: 5 x 8 min (2 hr)

Code Prefix	Workout Type	Brief Description	Levels
CLI	Bike Lactate Intervals	3–5-minute intervals @ VO_2 max intensity w/ 3-minute active recoveries; warm up and cool down long enough to reach total time	CLI3: 4 x 3 min (1 hr 15 min total) CLI5: 6 x 3 min (1 hr 25 min) CLI6: 7 x 3 min (1 hr 30 min) CLI7: 8 x 3 min (1 hr 35 min) CLI10: 4 x 5 min (1 hr 50 min) CLI11: 5 x 5 min (2 hr)
CLR	Long Bike Ride	Long steady ride @ moderate aerobic intensity	CLR3: 2 hr 30 min CLR4: 2 hr 45 min CLR5: 3 hr CLR6: 3 hr 15 min CLR7: 3 hr 30 min CLR8: 3 hr 45 min CLR9: 4 hr CLR10: 4 hr 15 min CLR11: 4 hr 30 min CLR12: 4 hr 45 min CLR13: 5 hr CLR14: 5 hr 15 min CLR15: 5 hr 30 min CLR16: 5 hr 45 min CLR17: 6 hr CLR18: 6 hr 15 min CLR19: 6 hr 30 min CLR20: 6 hr 45 min CLR21: 7 hr
CPI	Bike Power Intervals	20-second intervals done in a high gear @ speed intensity w/ 2-minute active recoveries; warm up and cool down long enough to reach total time	CPI3: 6 x 20 sec (1 hr total) CPI4: 7 x 20 sec (1 hr 10 min) CPI5: 8 x 20 sec (1 hr 20 min) CPI6: 9 x 20 sec (1 hr 25 min)
CRR	Recovery Bike	Steady ride @ recovery intensity	CRR1: 20 min
CSI	Bike Speed Intervals	1-minute intervals @ speed intensity w/ 2-minute active recoveries or 1.5-minute intervals @ speed intensity w/ 3-minute active recoveries; warm up and cool down long enough to reach total time	CSI5: 8 x 1 min (1 hr 5 min total) CSI6: 9 x 1 min (1 hr 10 min) CSI7: 10 x 1 min (1 hr 15 min) CSI8: 11 x 1 min (1 hr 20 min) CSI9: 12 x 1 min (1 hr 25 min) CSI14: 8 x 1 min 30 sec (1 hr 50 min) CSI15: 9 x 1 min 30 sec (1 hr 55 min)

Code Prefix	Workout Type	Brief Description	Levels
CSI *(cont.)*			CSI16: 10 x 1 min 30 sec (2 hr)
			CSI17: 17 x 1 min 30 sec (2 hr 5 min)
			CSI18: 12 x 1 min 30 sec (2 hr 10 min)
CSH	Bike Short Hill Climbs	1-minute hill climbs @ VO_2 max/speed intensity w/ 2-minute active recoveries or 1.5-minute hill climbs @ VO_2 max/speed intensity w/ 3-minute active recoveries; warm up and cool down long enough to reach total time	CSH5: 8 x 1 min (1 hr 5 min total)
			CSH6: 9 x 1 min (1 hr 10 min)
			CSH7: 10 x 1 min (1 hr 15 min)
			CSH8: 11 x 1 min (1 hr 20 min)
			CSH9: 12 x 1 min (1 hr 25 min)
			CSH14: 8 x 1 min 30 sec (1 hr 50 min)
			CSH15: 9 x 1 min 30 sec (1 hr 55 min)
			CSH16: 10 x 1 min 30 sec (2 hr)
			CSH17: 11 x 1 min 30 sec (2 hr 5 min)
			CSH18: 12 x 1 min 30 sec (2 hr 10 min)
CSS	Steady-State Ride	Steady ride @ high aerobic intensity	CSS2: 1 hr 15 min
			CSS3: 1 hr 30 min
			CSS4: 1 hr 45 min
			CSS5: 2 hr
			CSS6: 2 hr 15 min
			CSS7: 2 hr 30 min
			CSS8: 2 hr 45 min
			CSS9: 3 hr
CTR	Tempo Bike Ride	One or two blocks of riding @ threshold intensity (10-minute active recovery when threshold-intensity riding is divided into two blocks); warm up and cool down long enough to reach total time	CTR5: 24 min (1 hr 5 min total)
			CTR6: 26 min (1 hr 10 min)
			CTR7: 2 x 14 min (1 hr 15 min)
			CTR8: 28 min (1 hr 20 min)
			CTR9: 30 min (1 hr 25 min)
			CTR10: 2 x 16 min (1 hr 30 min)
			CTR11: 32 min (1 hr 35 min)
			CTR12: 34 min (1 hr 40 min)
			CTR13: 2 x 18 min (1 hr 45 min)
			CTR14: 36 (1 hr 50 min)
			CTR15: 38 min (1 hr 55 min)
			CTR16: 2 x 20 min (2 hr)
			CTR17: 40 min (2 hr 5 min)

Code Prefix	Workout Type	Brief Description	Levels
RFL	Fartlek Run	Foundation run with 30-second bursts @ VO_2 max/speed intensity	RFL3: 6 x 30 sec (35 min total) RFL5: 6 x 30 sec (40 min) RFL7: 6 x 30 sec (45 min) RFL8: 8 x 30 sec (45 min) RFL9: 6 x 30 sec (50 min) RFL10: 8 x 30 sec (50 min)
RFR	Foundation Run	Steady run @ moderate aerobic intensity	RFR3: 30 min RFR4: 35 min RFR5: 40 min RFR6: 45 min RFR7: 50 min RFR8: 55 min RFR9: 1 hr
RHR	Run Hill Repeats	1-minute uphill running intervals @ speed intensity w/ 2-minute active recoveries; warm up and cool down long enough to reach total time	RHR7: 6 x 1 min (38 min total) RHR8: 8 x 1 min (44 min) RHR9: 10 x 1 min (50 min) RHR10: 12 x 1 min (56 min)
RLI	Run Lactate Intervals	3–4-minute intervals run @ VO_2 max intensity w/ 3-minute active recoveries; warm up and cool down long enough to reach total time	RLI9: 3 x 3 min (38 min total) RLI10: 4 x 3 min (44 min) RLI11: 5 x 3 min (50 min) RLI12: 6 x 3 min (56 min) RLI13: 5 x 4 min (1 hr)
RLR	Long Run	Long, steady-pace run @ moderate aerobic intensity	RLR1: 1 hr 5 min RLR2: 1 hr 10 min RLR3: 1 hr 20 min RLR4: 1 hr 30 min RLR5: 1 hr 40 min RLR6: 1 hr 50 min RLR7: 2 hr RLR8: 2 hr 10 min RLR9: 2 hr 20 min RLR10: 2 hr 30 min RLR11: 2 hr 40 min RLR12: 2 hr 50 min RLR13: 3 hr

Code Prefix	Workout Type	Brief Description	Levels
RRR	Recovery Run	Short run @ recovery intensity	RRR2: 25 min RRR3: 30 min RRR4: 35 min RRR5: 40 min RRR6: 45 min
RSI	Running Speed Intervals	1-minute intervals run @ speed intensity w/ 3-minute active recoveries; warm up and cool down long enough to reach total time	RSI12: 6 x 1 min (47 min total) RSI13: 7 x 1 min (50 min) RSI14: 8 x 1 min (57 min) RSI15: 9 x 1 min (1 hr 1 min) RSI16: 10 x 1 min (1 hr 5 min) RSI17: 11 x 1 min (1 hr 9 min) RSI18: 12 x 1 min (1 hr 12 min)
RSS	Running Strides	20-second "relaxed sprints" @ speed intensity w/ 40-second active recoveries	RSS1: 2 x 20 sec RSS2: 4 x 20 sec RSS3: 6 x 20 sec
RTR	Tempo Run	Steady run @ threshold intensity; warm up and cool down long enough to reach total time	RTR3: 14 min (34 min total) RTR4: 16 min (36 min) RTR5: 18 min (38 min) RTR6: 20 min (40 min) RTR7: 22 min (42 min) RTR10: 28 min (48 min) RTR11: 30 min (50 min) RTR12: 32 min (52 min) RTR13: 34 min (54 min) RTR14: 36 min (56 min) RTR15: 38 min (58 min) RTR16: 40 min (1 hr)
SBI	Swim Base Intervals	100-yard intervals swum @ moderate aerobic intensity w/ 5-second rest periods or 200-yard intervals swum @ moderate aerobic intensity w/ 10-second rest periods or single longer swims @ moderate aerobic intensity	SBI1: 2 x 100 SBI2: 3 x 100 SBI3: 4 x 100 SBI4: 5 x 100 SBI5: 6 x 100 SBI6: 7 x 100 SBI7: 8 x 100 SBI8: 9 x 100 SBI9: 10 x 100 SBI10: 11 x 100 SBI11: 12 x 100

Code Prefix	Workout Type	Brief Description	Levels
SBI *(cont.)*			SBI14: 4 x 200
			SBI15: 5 x 200
			SBI16: 6 x 200
			SBI17: 7 x 200
			SBI25: 1,200
			SBI26: 1,500
			SBI27: 1,800
			SBI28: 2,000
			SBI29: 2,400
			SBI30: 2,600
			SBI31: 2,800
			SBI32: 3,000
			SBI33: 3,200
			SBI34: 3,500
			SBI35: 3,800
SCD	Swim Cool-Down	Easy swim @ recovery intensity	SCD1: 200
			SCD2: 250
			SCD3: 300
			SCD4: 350
			SCD5: 400
SDS	Swim Drill Set	25–50-yard intervals of mixed form drills w/ 10-second rest periods	SDS3: 8 x 25
			SDS4: 10 x 25
			SDS5: 12 x 25
			SDS7: 6 x 50
SFI	Swim Fartlek Intervals	100–200-yard intervals with easy/hard or build/descend format (hard = threshold intensity, easy = moderate aerobic intensity) w/ rest periods of 10–20 seconds	SFI2A: 6 x 100 (25 build/25 descend…), 10-sec rest
			SFI3: 8 x 100 (25 build/25 descend…), 10-sec rest
			SFI3A: 8 x 100 (25 build/25 descend…), 10-sec rest
			SFI4: 4 x 150 (50 easy/25 hard…), 15-sec rest
			SFI5: 5 x 150 (50 easy/25 hard…), 15-sec rest
			SFI5A: 5 x 150 (50 build/25 descend…), 15-sec rest
			SFI6: 6 x 150 (50 easy/25 hard…), 15-sec rest
			SFI6A: 6 x 150 (50 build/25 descend…), 15-sec rest

Code Prefix	Workout Type	Brief Description	Levels
SFI *(cont.)*			SFI8: 4 x 200 (50 easy/50 hard...), 20-sec rest
			SFI8A: 4 x 200 (50 build/50 descend...), 20-sec rest
			SFI9: 5 x 200 (50 easy/50 hard...), 20-sec rest
			SFI9A: 5 x 200 (50 build/50 descend...), 20-sec rest
			SFI10: 6 x 200 (50 easy/50 hard...), 20-sec rest
			SFI10A: 6 x 200 (50 build/50 descend...), 20-sec rest
SKS	Swim Kick Set	25-yard intervals kicking only w/ 15-second rest periods	SKS3: 8 x 25
			SKS4: 10 x 25
			SKS5: 12 x 25
SLI	Swim Lactate Intervals	75–150-yard intervals swum @ VO_2 max intensity with rest periods of 20 seconds to 1 min 15 seconds	SLI4: 7 x 75, 45-sec rest
			SLI5: 8 x 75, 45-sec rest
			SLI5A: 8 x 75, 30-sec rest
			SLI5B: 8 x 75, 20-sec rest
			SLI6: 9 x 75, 45-sec rest
			SLI6A: 9 x 75, 30-sec rest
			SLI6B: 9 x 75, 20-sec rest
			SLI8: 3 x 100, 1-min rest
			SLI9: 4 x 100, 1-min rest
			SLI10: 5 x 100, 1-min rest
			SLI12: 7 x 100, 1-min rest
			SLI12A: 7 x 100, 45-sec rest
			SLI12B: 7 x 100, 30-sec rest
			SLI13: 8 x 100, 1-min rest
			SLI13A: 8 x 100, 45-sec rest
			SLI13B: 8 x 100, 30-sec rest
			SLI14: 4 x 150, 1-min 15-sec rest
			SLI15: 5 x 150, 1-min 15-sec rest
			SLI16: 6 x 150, 1-min 15-sec rest
			SLI16A: 6 x 150, 1-min rest
			SLI16B: 6 x 150, 45-sec rest
			SLI17: 7 x 150, 1-min 15-sec rest
			SLI17A: 7 x 150, 1-min rest
			SLI17B: 7 x 150, 45-sec rest
			SLI18: 8 x 150, 1-min 15-sec rest
			SLI18A: 8 x 150, 1-min rest

Code Prefix	Workout Type	Brief Description	Levels
SSI	Swim Sprint Intervals	25–50-yard intervals swum @ speed intensity w/ 20-second rest periods, except "A" suffix = 10-second rest, "B" suffix = 5-second rest	SSI3: 6 x 25 SSI4: 7 x 25 SSI5: 8 x 25 SSI5A: 8 x 25 SSI5B: 8 x 25 SSI6A: 9 x 25 SSI6B: 9 x 25 SSI7: 10 x 25 SSI8: 11 x 25 SSI9: 12 x 25 SSI10: 4 x 50 SSI11: 5 x 50 SSI12: 6 x 50 SSI12A: 6 x 50 SSI12B: 6 x 50 SSI13: 7 x 50 SSI14: 8 x 50 SSI15: 9 x 50 SSI15A: 9 x 50 SSI16: 10 x 50 SSI17: 11 x 50
STI	Swim Threshold Intervals	200-yard intervals swum @ threshold intensity w/ rest periods of 20–45 seconds	STI1: 2 x 200, 45-sec rest STI2: 3 x 200, 45-sec rest STI2A: 3 x 200, 30-sec rest STI2B: 3 x 200, 20-sec rest STI3: 4 x 200, 45-sec rest STI3A: 4 x 200, 30-sec rest STI3B: 4 x 200, 20-sec rest STI5: 6 x 200, 45-sec rest STI5A: 6 x 200, 30-sec rest STI5B: 6 x 200, 20-sec rest STI6: 7 x 200, 45-sec rest STI6A: 7 x 200, 30-sec rest STI6B: 7 x 200, 20-sec rest STI7: 8 x 200, 45-sec rest STI7A: 8 x 200, 30-sec rest STI7B: 8 x 200, 20-sec rest
STT	Swim Time Trial	Designated distance swum @ maximum effort	STT3: 1,650 STT4: 1.2 miles (2,112) STT5: 3,200 STT6: 2.4 miles (4,225)

Code Prefix	Workout Type	Brief Description	Levels
SWU	Swim Warm-Up	Easy swim @ recovery intensity	SWU1: 200 SWU2: 250 SWU3: 300 SWU4: 350 SWU5: 400

General Schedule						
	Tuesday	Wednesday	Thursday	Friday	Saturday	Sunday
BASE PHASE						
Week 1	Swim Base Intervals	Swim Base Intervals	Brick Workout	Bike Power Intervals	Long Bike	Swim Base Intervals
	Foundation Bike	Foundation Run + Strides		Swim Fartlek Intervals	Recovery Run	Long Run
Week 2	Swim Base Intervals	Swim Base Intervals	Foundation Bike	Bike Power Intervals	Brick Workout	Swim Base Intervals
	Foundation Bike	Foundation Run + Strides	Foundation Run	Swim Fartlek Intervals		Foundation Run
Week 3	Swim Base Intervals	Swim Base Intervals	Brick Workout	Bike Power Intervals	Long Bike	Swim Base Intervals
	Foundation Bike	Foundation Run + Strides		Swim Fartlek Intervals	Recovery Run	Long Run
Week 4 (Recovery)	Swim Base Intervals	Swim Base Intervals	Foundation Bike	Bike Power Intervals	Brick Workout	Swim Base Intervals
	Foundation Bike	Foundation Run + Strides	Foundation Run	Swim Fartlek Intervals		Foundation Run
Week 5	Swim Base + Sprint Intervals	Swim Base Intervals	Brick Workout	Bike Short Hills	Long Bike	Swim Base Intervals
	Foundation Bike	Fartlek Run		Swim Fartlek + Sprint Intervals	Recovery Run	Long Run
Week 6	Swim Base + Sprint Intervals	Swim Base Intervals	Foundation Bike	Bike Short Hills	Brick Workout	Swim Time Trial

	Tuesday	Wednesday	Thursday	Friday	Saturday	Sunday
Week 6 (cont.)	Foundation Bike	Fartlek Run	Foundation Run	Swim Fartlek + Sprint Intervals		L7–9: Foundation Run L10: Long Run
Week 7	Swim Base + Sprint Intervals	Swim Base Intervals	Brick Workout	Bike Short Hills	Long Bike	Swim Base Intervals
	Foundation Bike	Fartlek Run		Swim Fartlek + Sprint Intervals	Recovery Run	Long Run
Week 8 (Recovery)	Swim Base + Sprint Intervals	Swim Base Intervals	Foundation Bike	Bike Short Hills	Brick Workout	Swim Base Intervals
	Foundation Bike	Fartlek Run	Foundation Run	Swim Fartlek + Sprint Intervals		L7–9: Foundation Run L10: Long Run
BUILD PHASE						
Week 9	Swim Base + Sprint Intervals	Swim Base Intervals	Brick Workout	Bike Speed Intervals	Long Bike	Swim Base Intervals
	Steady-State Bike	Run Hill Repeats		Swim Fartlek + Sprint Intervals	Recovery Run	Long Run
Week 10	Swim Base + Sprint Intervals	Swim Base Intervals	Foundation Bike	Bike Speed Intervals	Brick Workout	Swim Base Intervals
	Steady-State Bike	Run Hill Repeats	Foundation Run	Swim Fartlek + Sprint Intervals		L7–8: Foundation Run L9–10: Long Run
Week 11	Swim Base + Sprint Intervals	Swim Base Intervals	Brick Workout	Bike Speed Intervals	Long Bike	Swim Time Trial
	Steady-State Bike	Run Hill Repeats		Swim Fartlek + Sprint Intervals	Recovery Run	Long Run

	Tuesday	Wednesday	Thursday	Friday	Saturday	Sunday
Week 12 (Recovery)	Swim Base + Sprint Intervals	Swim Base Intervals	Foundation Bike	Bike Speed Intervals	Recovery Bike or Brick Workout	Sprint Triathlon or Swim Base Intervals
	Steady-State Bike	Run Hill Repeats	Foundation Run	Swim Fartlek + Sprint Intervals		Sprint Triathlon or L7–8: Foundation Run L9–10: Long Run
Week 13	Swim Base + Threshold Intervals	Swim Base Intervals	Brick Workout (w/ tempo run)	Bike Lactate Intervals	Long Bike	Swim Base Intervals
	Tempo Bike	Run Speed Intervals		Swim Base + Lactate + Sprint Intervals	Recovery Run	Long Run
Week 14	Swim Base + Threshold Intervals	Swim Base Intervals	Foundation Bike	Bike Long Hills	Brick Workout	Swim Base Intervals
	Tempo Bike	Run Speed Intervals	Tempo Run	Swim Base + Lactate + Sprint Intervals		L7: Foundation Run L8–10: Long Run
Week 15	Swim Base + Threshold Intervals	Swim Base Intervals	Brick Workout (w/ tempo run)	Bike Lactate Intervals	Long Bike	Swim Base Intervals
	Tempo Bike	Run Speed Intervals		Swim Base + Lactate + Sprint Intervals	Recovery Run	Long Run
Week 16 (Recovery)	Swim Base + Threshold Intervals	Swim Base Intervals	Foundation Bike	Bike Long Hills	Recovery Bike or Brick Workout	Olympic-Distance Triathlon or Swim Base Intervals

	Tuesday	Wednesday	Thursday	Friday	Saturday	Sunday
Week 16 (cont.)	Tempo Bike	Run Speed Intervals	Tempo Run	Swim Base + Lactate + Sprint Intervals		Olympic-Distance Triathlon or Long Run
PEAK PHASE						
Week 17	Swim Base + Threshold Intervals	Swim Base Intervals	Brick Workout (w/ tempo run)	Bike Lactate Intervals	Long Bike	Swim Base Intervals
	Tempo Bike	Run Lactate Intervals		Swim Base + Lactate + Sprint Intervals	Recovery Run	Long Run
Week 18	Swim Base + Threshold Intervals	Swim Base Intervals	Foundation Bike	Bike Long Hills	Brick Workout	Swim Time Trial
	Tempo Bike	Run Lactate Intervals	Tempo Run	Swim Base + Lactate + Sprint Intervals		Long Run
Week 19	Swim Base + Threshold Intervals	Swim Base Intervals	Brick Workout (w/ tempo run)	Bike Lactate Intervals	Long Bike	Swim Base Intervals
	Tempo Bike	Run Lactate Intervals		Swim Base + Lactate + Sprint Intervals	Recovery Run	Long Run
Week 20 (Recovery)	Swim Base + Threshold Intervals	Swim Base Intervals	Foundation Bike	Bike Long Hills	Recovery Bike or Brick Workout	Half-Ironman Triathlon or Swim Base Intervals
	Tempo Bike	Run Lactate Intervals	Tempo Run	Swim Base + Lactate + Sprint Intervals		Half-Ironman Triathlon or Long Run
Week 21	Swim Base + Threshold Intervals	Swim Base Intervals	Brick Workout (w/ tempo run)	Steady-State Bike	Long Bike	Swim Base Intervals

	Tuesday	Wednesday	Thursday	Friday	Saturday	Sunday
Week 21 (cont.)	Tempo Bike	Run Lactate Intervals		Swim Base + Lactate + Sprint Intervals	Recovery Run	Long Run
Week 22	Swim Base + Threshold Intervals	Swim Base Intervals	Foundation Bike	Foundation Bike	Brick Workout	Swim Base Intervals
	Tempo Bike	Run Lactate Intervals	Tempo Run	Swim Base + Lactate + Sprint Intervals		Long Run
Week 23 (Taper)	Swim Base + Threshold Intervals	Swim Base Intervals	Brick Workout (w/ tempo run)	Steady-State Bike	Long Bike	Swim Base Intervals
	Tempo Bike	Run Lactate Intervals		Swim Base + Lactate + Sprint Intervals	Recovery Run	Long Run
Week 24 (Taper)	Swim Base + Threshold Intervals	Swim Base Intervals	Foundation Bike	Swim Lactate + Sprint Intervals	Recovery Bike	Ironman Triathlon
	Tempo Bike	Run Lactate Intervals	Tempo Run			

Week-by-Week Schedule

Base Phase

In this eight-week phase you will build your aerobic capacity with lots of workouts at moderate aerobic intensity, build endurance with long workouts on the weekends, and, secondarily, develop power and efficiency with stimuli including swim sprint sets, cycling power intervals, and running strides.

WEEK 1

This week's goal: Get accustomed to your new workout schedule.

	Tuesday	Wednesday	Thursday	Friday	Saturday	Sunday
Level 7	SWU4 SDS4 SBI5 SKS4 SCD4 (1,800)	SWU4 SDS4 SBI8 SCD4 (1,850)	BRW4	CPI3	CLR3	SWU3 SBI25 SCD3 (1,800)
	CFR3	RFR6 + RSS1		SWU4 SDS4 SFI4 SKS4 SCD4 (1,800)	RRR2	RLR1
Level 8	SWU4 SDS5 SBI6 SKS5 SCD4 (2,000)	SWU4 SDS5 SBI9 SCD4 (2,000)	BRW4	CPI4	CLR4	SWU2 SBI26 SCD2 (2,000)
	CFR3	RFR6 + RSS1		SWU4 SDS5 SFI5 SKS5 SCD4 (2,050)	RRR3	RLR2
Level 9	SWU5 SDS5 SBI6 SKS5 SCD5 (2,100)	SWU5 SDS5 SBI9 SCD5 (2,100)	BRW5	CPI4	CLR5	SWU3 SBI26 SCD3 (2,100)
	CFR3	RFR6 + RSS1		SWU5 SDS5 SFI5 SKS5 SCD5 (2,150)	RRR3	RLR3
Level 10	SWU5 SDS5 SBI8 SKS5 SCD5 (2,300)	SWU5 SDS5 SBI11 SCD5 (2,300)	BRW6	CPI4	CLR6	SWU5 SBI26 SCD5 (2,300)

	Tuesday	Wednesday	Thursday	Friday	Saturday	Sunday
Level 10 (cont.)	CFR4	RFR7 + RSS1		SWU5 SDS5 SBI1 SFI5 SKS5 SCD5 (2,350)	RRR3	RLR4

QUICK TIP:

Recent studies of the effects of the herb ginseng on post-exercise recovery have produced promising results. Spanish researchers found that ginseng supplementation reduced muscle damage and inflammation in rats following eccentric exercise. You might want to consider taking a daily ginseng supplement. The standard dosage is 1 to 2 grams per day.

WEEK 2

This week's goal: Gather momentum by completing all scheduled workouts as prescribed.

	Tuesday	Wednesday	Thursday	Friday	Saturday	Sunday
Level 7	SWU4 SDS4 SBI6 SKS4 SCD4 (1,900)	SWU4 SDS4 SBI9 SCD4 (1,950)	CFR3	CPI4	BRW5	SWU1 SBI26 SCD1 (1,900)
	CFR3	RFR6 + RSS2	RFR6	SWU4 SDS4 SFI5A SKS4 SCD4 (1,950)		RFR7

	Tuesday	Wednesday	Thursday	Friday	Saturday	Sunday
Level 8	SWU4 SDS5 SBI7 SKS5 SCD4 (2,100)	SWU4 SDS5 SBI10 SCD4 (2,100)	CFR3	CPI4	BRW6	SWU3 SBI26 SCD3 (2,100)
	CFR4	RFR6 + RSS2	RFR6	SWU4 SDS5 SFI8A SKS5 SCD4 (2,100)		RFR8
Level 9	SWU5 SDS5 SBI7 SKS5 SCD5 (2,200)	SWU5 SDS5 SBI10 SCD5 (2,200)	CFR4	CPI5	BRW7	SWU4 SBI26 SCD4 (2,200)
	CFR4	RFR7 + RSS2	RFR7	SWU5 SDS5 SFI6A SKS5 SCD5 (2,300)		RFR8
Level 10	SWU5 SDS5 SBI9 SKS5 SCD5 (2,400)	SWU5 SDS5 SBI17 SCD5 (2,500)	CFR4	CPI5	BRW8	SWU3 SBI27 SCD3 (2,400)
	CFR4	RFR7 + RSS2	RFR7	SWU5 SDS5 SBI1 SFI6A SKS5 SCD5 (2,500)		RFR9

WEEK 3

Find your running legs quickly in Thursday's brick workout.

	Tuesday	Wednesday	Thursday	Friday	Saturday	Sunday
Level 7	SWU4 SDS4 SBI7 SKS4 SCD4 (2,000)	SWU4 SDS4 SBI10 SCD4 (2,050)	BRW5	CPI5	CLR4	SWU3 SBI26 SCD3 (2,100)
	CFR4	RFR7 + RSS3		SWU4 SDS4 SFI5 SKS4 SCD4 (1,950)	RRR3	RLR2
Level 8	SWU4 SDS5 SBI8 SKS5 SCD4 (2,200)	SWU4 SDS5 SBI11 SCD4 (2,200)	BRW6	CPI5	CLR5	SWU4 SBI26 SCD4 (2,200)
	CFR4	RFR7 + RSS3		SWU4 SDS5 SFI8 SKS5 SCD4 (2,100)	RRR4	RLR3
Level 9	SWU5 SDS5 SBI8 SKS5 SCD5 (2,300)	SWU5 SDS5 SBI11 SCD5 (2,300)	BRW7	CPI5	CLR6	SWU2 SBI27 SCD2 (2,300)
	CFR4	RFR7 + RSS3		SWU5 SDS5 SFI6 SKS5 SCD5 (2,300)	RRR4	RLR4

	Tuesday	Wednesday	Thursday	Friday	Saturday	Sunday
Level 10	SWU5 SDS5 SBI10 SKS5 SCD5 (2,500)	SWU5 SDS5 SBI17 SCD5 (2,500)	BRW8	CPI6	CLR7	SWU4 SBI27 SCD4 (2,500)
	CFR4	RFR7 + RSS3		SWU5 SDS5 SBI1 SFI6 SKS5 SCD5 (2,500)	RRR4	RLR5

WEEK 4
(Recovery)

This week's goal: Fully absorb your recent training and finish the week feeling rested and ready to return to harder training next week.

	Tuesday	Wednesday	Thursday	Friday	Saturday	Sunday
Level 7	SWU4 SDS4 SBI5 SCD4 (1,550)	SWU4 SDS4 SBI8 SCD4 (1,850)	CFR3	CPI3	BRW6	SWU3 SBI25 SCD3 (1,800)
	CFR3	RFR4 + RSS2	RFR4	SWU4 SDS4 SFI4A SCD4 (1,550)		RFR8
Level 8	SWU4 SDS5 SBI6 SCD4 (1,700)	SWU4 SDS5 SBI9 SCD4 (2,000)	CFR3	CPI3	BRW7	SWU2 SBI26 SCD2 (2,000)
	CFR3	RFR4	RFR4	SWU4 SDS5 SFI5A SCD4 (1,750)		RFR9

	Tuesday	Wednesday	Thursday	Friday	Saturday	Sunday
Level 9	SWU5 SDS5 SBI6 SCD5 (1,800)	SWU5 SDS5 SBI9 SCD5 (2,100)	CFR3	CPI3	BRW8	SWU3 SBI26 SCD3 (2,100)
	CFR3	RFR5	RFR5	SWU5 SDS5 SFI3A SCD5 (1,900)		RLR1
Level 10	SWU5 SDS5 SBI8 SCD5 (2,000)	SWU5 SDS5 SBI11 SCD5 (2,300)	CFR4	CPI3	BRW9	SWU5 SBI26 SCD5 (2,300)
	CFR3	RFR5	RFR5	SWU5 SDS5 SBI1 SFI3A SCD5 (2,100)		RLR2

WEEK 5

This week's goal: Do Friday's short cycling hill climbs at the fastest speed you can maintain through the end of the last climb without slowing.

	Tuesday	Wednesday	Thursday	Friday	Saturday	Sunday
Level 7	SWU4 SDS4 SBI7 SSI11 SKS4 SCD4 (2,250)	SWU4 SDS4 SBI10 SCD4 (2,050)	BRW5	CSH6	CLR6	SWU2 SBI27 SCD2 (2,300)
	CFR4	RFL7		SWU4 SDS4 SFI6 SSI3 SKS4 SCD4 (2,250)	RRR3	RLR3

	Tuesday	Wednesday	Thursday	Friday	Saturday	Sunday
Level 8	SWU4 SDS5 SBI8 SSI11 SKS5 SCD4 (2,450)	SWU4 SDS5 SBI11 SCD4 (2,200)	BRW6	CSH7	CLR7	SWU4 SBI27 SCD4 (2,500)
	CFR4	RFL7		SWU4 SDS5 SBI1 SFI8 SSI3 SKS5 SCD4 (2,450)	RRR3	RLR4
Level 9	SWU5 SDS5 SBI8 SSI11 SKS5 SCD5 (2,550)	SWU5 SDS5 SBI11 SCD5 (2,300)	BRW7	CSH8	CLR8	SWU3 SBI28 SCD3 (2,600)
	CFR4	RFL7		SWU5 SDS5 SBI2 SFI8 SSI3 SKS5 SCD5 (2,650)	RRR4	RLR5
Level 10	SWU5 SDS5 SBI10 SSI11 SKS5 SCD5 (2,750)	SWU5 SDS5 SBI17 SCD5 (2,500)	BRW8	CSH9	CLR9	SWU5 SBI28 SCD5 (2,800)
	CFR5	RFL7		SWU5 SDS5 SBI2 SFI9	RRR4	RLR6

	Tuesday	Wednesday	Thursday	Friday	Saturday	Sunday
Level 10 (cont.)				SSI3 SKS5 SCD5 (2,850)		

WEEK 6

This week's goal: Go all out to get a good sense of your current swim performance level in Sunday's swim time trial.

	Tuesday	Wednesday	Thursday	Friday	Saturday	Sunday
Level 7	SWU4 SDS4 SBI7 SSI12 SKS4 SCD4 (2,300)	SWU4 SDS4 SBI6 SBI5 SCD4 (2,250)	CFR5	CSH14	BRW8	SWU2 STT3 SCD2 (2,150)
	CFR4	RFL8	RFR8	SWU4 SDS4 SFI6A SSI5 SKS4 SCD4 (2,300)		RFR7
Level 8	SWU4 SDS5 SBI8 SSI12 SKS5 SCD4 (2,500)	SWU4 SDS5 SBI6 SBI6 SCD4 (2,400)	CFR5	CSH15	BRW9	SWU3 STT3 SCD3 (2,250)
	CFR4	RFL8	RFR8	SWU4 SDS5 SBI1 SFI8A SSI5 SKS5 SCD4 (2,500)		RFR8

	Tuesday	Wednesday	Thursday	Friday	Saturday	Sunday
Level 9	SWU5 SDS5 SBI8 SSI12 SKS5 SCD5 (2,600)	SWU5 SDS5 SBI6 SBI6 SCD5 (2,500)	CFR5	CSH16	BRW10	SWU4 STT3 SCD4 (2,350)
	CFR5	RFL8	RFR9	SWU5 SDS5 SBI2 SFI8A SSI5 SKS5 SCD5 (2,700)		RFR9
Level 10	SWU5 SDS5 SBI10 SSI12 SKS5 SCD5 (2,800)	SWU5 SDS5 SBI7 SBI7 SCD5 (2,700)	CFR6	CSH17	BRW11	SWU5 STT3 SCD5 (2,450)
	CFR5	RFL9	RFR9	SWU5 SDS5 SBI2 SFI9A SSI5 SKS5 SCD5 (2,900)		RLR1

WEEK 7

This week's goal: Finish strong in Sunday's long run.

	Tuesday	Wednesday	Thursday	Friday	Saturday	Sunday
Level 7	SWU4 SDS4 SBI7 SSI13 SKS4 SCD4 (2,350)	SWU4 SDS7 SBI15 SBI3 SCD4 (2,400)	BRW6	CSH15	CLR7	SWU2 SBI28 SCD2 (2,500)

	Tuesday	Wednesday	Thursday	Friday	Saturday	Sunday
Level 7 *(cont.)*	CFR5	RFL8		SWU4 SDS4 SFI9 SSI5 SKS4 SCD4 (2,400)	RRR3	RLR4
Level 8	SWU4 SDS5 SBI8 SSI13 SKS5 SCD4 (2,550)	SWU4 SDS7 SBI16 SBI4 SCD4 (2,700)	BRW7	CSH16	CLR8	SWU4 SBI28 SCD4 (2,700)
	CFR5	RFL10		SWU4 SDS5 SBI1 SFI9 SSI5 SKS5 SCD4 (2,700)	RRR3	RLR5
Level 9	SWU5 SDS5 SBI8 SSI13 SKS5 SCD5 (2,650)	SWU5 SDS7 SBI16 SBI4 SCD5 (2,800)	BRW8	CSH17	CLR9	SWU1 SBI29 SCD1 (2,800)
	CFR5	RFL10		SWU5 SDS5 SBI1 SFI9 SSI5 SKS5 SCD5 (2,800)	RRR3	RLR6
Level 10	SWU5 SDS5 SBI10 SSI13	SWU5 SDS7 SBI16 SBI6	BRW9	CSH18	CLR10	SWU3 SBI29 SCD3 (3,000)

	Tuesday	Wednesday	Thursday	Friday	Saturday	Sunday
Level 10 (cont.)	SKS5 SCD5 (2,850)	SCD5 (3,000)				
	CFR5	RFL10		SWU5 SDS5 SBI2 SFI9 SSI5 SKS5 SCD5 (2,900)	RRR4	RLR7

QUICK TIP:

If you experience pain along your shinbones during running, you are probably developing a tibial bone strain (a.k.a. shin splints). The primary cause of this injury is increasing your running mileage too quickly. You can usually correct it by reducing your running volume until the pain goes away and then ramping back up more slowly.

WEEK 8
(Recovery)

This week's goal: Fully absorb your recent training and finish the week feeling rested and ready to return to harder training next week.

	Tuesday	Wednesday	Thursday	Friday	Saturday	Sunday
Level 7	SWU4 SDS4 SBI6 SSI10 SCD4 (1,850)	SWU4 SDS7 SBI14 SBI3 SCD4 (2,200)	CFR4	CSH5	BRW6	SWU1 SBI27 SCD1 (2,200)
	CFR3	RFL3	RFR5	SWU4 SDS4 SFI3A SSI3 SCD4 (1,900)		RFR7

	Tuesday	Wednesday	Thursday	Friday	Saturday	Sunday
Level 8	SWU4 SDS5 SBI7 SSI10 SCD4 (2,000)	SWU4 SDS7 SBI15 SBI3 SCD4 (2,400)	CFR5	CSH5	BRW7	SWU3 SBI27 SCD3 (2,400)
	CFR3	RFL3	RFR5	SWU4 SDS5 SFI3A SSI3 SCD4 (1,950)		RFR8
Level 9	SWU5 SDS5 SBI7 SSI10 SCD5 (2,100)	SWU5 SDS7 SBI15 SBI3 SCD5 (2,500)	CFR5	CSH5	BRW8	SWU4 SBI27 SCD4 (2,500)
	CFR4	RFL5	RFR6	SWU5 SDS5 SFI3A SSI3 SCD5 (2,050)		RFR9
Level 10	SWU5 SDS5 SBI9 SSI10 SCD5 (2,300)	SWU5 SDS7 SBI15 SBI5 SCD5 (2,700)	CFR5	CSH5	BRW9	SWU4 SBI28 SCD4 (2,700)
	CFR4	RFL5	RFR5	SWU5 SDS5 SFI6A SSI3 SCD5 (2,150)		RLR1

Build Phase

In this eight-week phase the top priority remains the same: building raw endurance in swimming, cycling, and running. But you will also do some tough high-intensity workouts (e.g. running hill repeats) to maximize your aerobic capacity and efficiency, which will also boost your capacity to go long.

WEEK 9

This week's goal: Be sure to perform the high-intensity segments of this week's new workouts at the appropriate intensities.

	Tuesday	Wednesday	Thursday	Friday	Saturday	Sunday
Level 7	SWU4 SDS4 SBI14 SSI14 SKS4 SCD4 (2,400)	SWU4 SDS7 SBI15 SBI3 SCD4 (2,400)	BRW8	CSI6	CLR8	SWU2 SBI29 SCD2 (2,900)
	CSS2	RHR7		SWU4 SDS4 SBI1 SFI6 SSI7 SKS4 SCD4 (2,550)	RRR4	RLR5
Level 8	SWU4 SDS5 SBI15 SSI14 SKS5 SCD4 (2,700)	SWU4 SDS7 SBI16 SBI4 SCD4 (2,700)	BRW8	CSI7	CLR9	SWU4 SBI29 SCD4 (3,100)
	CSS3	RHR8		SWU4 SDS5 SBI1 SFI9 SSI7 SKS5 SCD4 (2,750)	RRR4	RLR6

	Tuesday	Wednesday	Thursday	Friday	Saturday	Sunday
Level 9	SWU5 SDS5 SBI15 SSI14 SKS5 SCD5 (2,800)	SWU5 SDS7 SBI16 SBI4 SCD5 (2,800)	BRW9	CSI8	CLR10	SWU3 SBI30 SCD3 (3,200)
	CSS3	RHR8		SWU5 SDS5 SBI1 SFI9 SSI7 SKS5 SCD5 (2,850)	RRR5	RLR7
Level 10	SWU5 SDS5 SBI16 SSI14 SKS5 SCD5 (3,000)	SWU5 SDS7 SBI16 SBI6 SCD5 (3,000)	BRW10	CSI9	CLR11	SWU5 SBI30 SCD5 (3,400)
	CSS4	RHR9		SWU5 SDS5 SBI1 SFI10 SSI7 SKS5 SCD5 (3,050)	RRR5	RLR8

WEEK 10

This week's goal: Do Tuesday's steady-state ride at your Ironman goal speed.

	Tuesday	Wednesday	Thursday	Friday	Saturday	Sunday
Level 7	SWU4 SDS4 SBI14 SSI16 SKS4 SCD4 (2,500)	SWU4 SDS7 SBI15 SBI4 SCD4 (2,500)	CFR6	CSI14	BRW10	SWU2 SBI30 SCD2 (3,100)

	Tuesday	Wednesday	Thursday	Friday	Saturday	Sunday
Level 7 (cont.)	CSS2	RHR8	RFR8	SWU4 SDS4 SBI1 SFI6A SSI7 SKS4 SCD4 (2,550)		RFR8
Level 8	SWU4 SDS5 SBI15 SSI16 SKS5 SCD4 (2,800)	SWU4 SDS7 SBI16 SBI5 SCD4 (2,800)	CFR6	CSI15	BRW11	SWU2 SBI31 SCD2 (3,300)
	CSS3	RHR8	RFR9	SWU4 SDS5 SBI1 SFI9A SSI7 SKS5 SCD4 (2,750)		RFR9
Level 9	SWU5 SDS5 SBI15 SSI16 SKS5 SCD5 (2,900)	SWU5 SDS7 SBI16 SBI5 SCD5 (2,900)	CFR7	CSI16	BRW12	SWU3 SBI31 SBI31 SBI31 (3,400)
	CSS4	RHR9	RFR9	SWU5 SDS5 SBI2 SFI9A SSI7 SKS5 SCD5 (2,950)		RLR1

	Tuesday	Wednesday	Thursday	Friday	Saturday	Sunday
Level 10	SWU5 SDS5 SBI16 SSI16 SKS5 SCD5 (3,100)	SWU5 SDS7 SBI16 SBI7 SCD5 (3,100)	CFR7	CSI17	BRW13	SWU5 SBI31 SCD5 (3,600)
	CSS5	RHR10	RFR9	SWU5 SDS5 SBI2 SFI10A SSI7 SKS5 SCD5 (3,150)		RLR2

WEEK 11

This week's goal: Try to maintain the same pace in Sunday's longer swim time trial as you did in Week 6's shorter swim time trial.

	Tuesday	Wednesday	Thursday	Friday	Saturday	Sunday
Level 7	SWU4 SDS4 SBI14 SSI17 SKS4 SCD4 (2,550)	SWU4 SDS7 SBI16 SBI4 SCD4 (2,700)	BRW8	CSI15	CLR10	SWU2 STT4 SCD2 (2,612)
	CSS4	RHR9		SWU4 SDS4 SBI1 SFI6A SSI9 SKS4 SCD4 (2,600)	RRR4	RLR6
Level 8	SWU4 SDS5 SBI15 SSI17 SKS5 SCD4 (2,850)	SWU4 SDS7 SBI17 SBI5 SCD4 (3,000)	BRW9	CSI16	CLR11	SWU3 STT4 SCD3 (2,712)

	Tuesday	Wednesday	Thursday	Friday	Saturday	Sunday
Level 8 (cont.)	CSS4	RHR10		SWU4 SDS5 SBI1 SFI9 SSI9 SKS5 SCD4 (2,800)	RRR4	RLR7
Level 9	SWU5 SDS5 SBI15 SSI17 SKS5 SCD5 (2,950)	SWU5 SDS7 SBI17 SBI5 SCD5 (3,100)	BRW10	CSI17	CLR12	SWU4 STT4 SCD4 (2,812)
	CSS5	RHR10		SWU5 SDS5 SBI2 SFI9 SSI9 SKS5 SCD5 (3,000)	RRR5	RLR8
Level 10	SWU5 SDS5 SBI16 SSI17 SKS5 SCD5 (3,150)	SWU5 SDS7 SBI17 SBI7 SCD5 (3,300)	BRW11	CSI18	CLR13	SWU4 STT4 SCD4 (2,812)
	CSS5	RHR10		SWU5 SDS5 SBI2 SFI10 SSI9 SKS5 SCD5 (3,200)	RRR5	RLR9

WEEK 12
(Recovery)

This week's goal: Fully absorb your recent training and have a solid sprint triathlon performance on Sunday if you have the opportunity.

	Tuesday	Wednesday	Thursday	Friday	Saturday	Sunday
Level 7	SWU4 SDS4 SBI6 SSI10 SCD4 (1,850)	SWU4 SDS7 SBI14 SBI3 SCD4 (2,200)	CFR5	CSI5	CRR1 or BRW7*	Sprint Triathlon or SWU2 SBI28 SCD2 (2,500)*
	CFR4	RHR7	RFR5	SWU4 SDS4 SFI2A SSI5 SCD4 (1,750)		RFR8*
Level 8	SWU4 SDS5 SBI7 SSI10 SCD4 (2,000)	SWU4 SDS7 SBI15 SBI4 SCD4 (2,500)	CFR5	CSI5	CRR1 or BRW8*	Sprint Triathlon or SWU4 SBI28 SCD4 (2,700)*
	CFR4	RHR7	RFR5	SWU4 SDS5 SFI3A SSI5 SCD4 (2,000)		RFR9*
Level 9	SWU5 SDS5 SBI7 SSI10 SCD5 (2,100)	SWU5 SDS7 SBI15 SBI4 SCD5 (2,600)	CFR6	CSI5	CRR1 or BRW9*	Sprint Triathlon or SWU1 SBI29 SCD1 (2,800)*

*If not racing

	Tuesday	Wednesday	Thursday	Friday	Saturday	Sunday
Level 9 (cont.)	CFR5	RHR7	RFR5	SWU5 SDS5 SFI5A SSI5 SCD5 (2,050)		RLR1*
Level 10	SWU5 SDS5 SBI9 SSI10 SCD5 (2,300)	SWU5 SDS7 SBI15 SBI6 SCD5 (2,800)	CFR6	CSI5	CRR1 or BRW10*	Sprint Triathlon or SWU3 SBI29 SCD3 (3,000)*
	CFR5	RHR7	RFR6	SWU5 SDS5 SFI6 SSI5 SCD5 (2,200)		RLR2*

*If not racing

WEEK 13

This week's goal: Pace yourself evenly through Sunday's long run.

	Tuesday	Wednesday	Thursday	Friday	Saturday	Sunday
Level 7	SWU4 SDS4 SBI6 STI2 SKS4 SCD4 (2,500)	SWU4 SDS7 SBI17 SBI3 SCD4 (2,800)	BRW5A	CLI6	CLR12	SWU2 SBI30 SCD2 (3,100)
	CTR9	RSI13		SWU4 SDS4 SBI4 SLI5 SSI5 SKS4 SCD4 (2,500)	RRR4	RLR7

390

	Tuesday	Wednesday	Thursday	Friday	Saturday	Sunday
Level 8	SWU4 SDS5 SBI7 STI2 SKS5 SCD4 (2,700)	SWU4 SDS7 SBI17 SBI5 SCD4 (3,000)	BRW6A	CLI6	CLR13	SWU4 SBI30 SCD4 (3,300)
	CTR10	RSI14		SWU4 SDS5 SBI5 SLI5 SSI5 SKS5 SCD4 (2,700)	RRR5	RLR8
Level 9	SWU5 SDS5 SBI7 STI2 SKS5 SCD5 (2,800)	SWU5 SDS7 SBI17 SBI5 SCD5 (3,100)	BRW7B	CLI7	CLR14	SWU3 SBI31 SCD3 (3,400)
	CTR10	RSI15		SWU5 SDS5 SBI5 SLI5 SSI5 SKS5 SCD5 (2,800)	RRR5	RLR9
Level 10	SWU5 SDS5 SBI7 STI3 SKS5 SCD5 (3,000)	SWU5 SDS7 SBI17 SBI7 SCD5 (3,300)	BRW8B	CLI7	CLR15	SWU5 SBI31 SCD5 (3,600)

	Tuesday	Wednesday	Thursday	Friday	Saturday	Sunday
Level 10 (cont.)	CTR11	RSI16		SWU5 SDS5 SBI6 SLI6 SSI6 SKS5 SCD5 (3,000)	RRR6	RLR10

QUICK TIP:

If you would like to know exactly how far you've run and how fast you're running in real time, consider purchasing a speed and distance device for runners such as a Timex BodyLink or a Garmin Forerunner 305. These devices use GPS technology to give you an extremely accurate readout of your distance and pace on your sports watch. It makes your run training a lot less approximate. These devices cost in the neighborhood of $300 and are available at many triathlon specialty shops.

WEEK 14

This week's goal: Try to swim Tuesday's threshold intervals at the same pace you did last week, despite the shorter rest periods.

	Tuesday	Wednesday	Thursday	Friday	Saturday	Sunday
Level 7	SWU4 SDS4 SBI6 STI2A SKS4 SCD4 (2,500)	SWU4 SDS7 SBI17 SBI4 SCD4 (2,900)	CFR6	CLH5	BRW11	SWU2 SBI31 SCD2 (3,300)
	CTR10	RSI14	RTR10	SWU4 SDS4 SBI3 SLI6A SSI6A SKS4 SCD4 (2,500)		RFR9

	Tuesday	Wednesday	Thursday	Friday	Saturday	Sunday
Level 8	SWU4 SDS5 SBI7 STI2A SKS5 SCD4 (2,700)	SWU4 SDS7 SBI17 SBI6 SCD4 (3,100)	CFR6	CLH6	BRW12	SWU4 SBI31 SCD4 (3,500)
	CTR11	RSI15	RTR11	SWU4 SDS5 SBI5 SLI5A SSI5A SKS5 SCD4 (2,700)		RLR1
Level 9	SWU5 SDS5 SBI7 STI2A SKS5 SCD5 (2,800)	SWU5 SDS7 SBI17 SBI6 SCD5 (3,200)	CFR6	CLH6	BRW13	SWU3 SBI32 SCD3 (3,600)
	CTR11	RSI16	RTR12	SWU5 SDS5 SBI5 SLI5A SSI5A SKS5 SCD5 (2,800)		RLR2
Level 10	SWU5 SDS5 SBI7 STI3A SKS5 SCD5 (3,000)	SWU5 SDS7 SBI17 SBI8 SCD5 (3,400)	CFR7	CLH7	BRW14	SWU5 SBI32 SCD5 (3,800)

	Tuesday	Wednesday	Thursday	Friday	Saturday	Sunday
Level 10 (cont.)	CTR12	RSI17	RTR13	SWU5 SDS5 SBI6 SLI6A SSI6A SKS5 SCD5 (3,000)		RLR3

WEEK 15

This week's goal: Finish strong in Saturday's long ride.

	Tuesday	Wednesday	Thursday	Friday	Saturday	Sunday
Level 7	SWU4 SDS4 SBI6 STI2B SKS4 SCD4 (2,500)	SWU4 SDS7 SBI17 SBI4 SCD4 (2,900)	BRW7B	CLI7	CLR14	SWU1 SBI32 SCD1 (3,400)
	CTR11	RSI15		SWU4 SDS4 SBI3 SLI6B SSI6B SKS4 SCD4 (2,500)	RRR5	RLR9
Level 8	SWU4 SDS5 SBI7 STI2B SKS5 SCD4 (2,700)	SWU4 SDS7 SBI17 SBI6 SCD4 (3,100)	BRW8B	CLI7	CLR15	SWU3 SBI32 SCD3 (3,600)
	CTR11	RSI16		SWU4 SDS5 SBI5 SLI5B SSI5B SKS5 SCD4 (2,700)	RRR5	RLR9

	Tuesday	Wednesday	Thursday	Friday	Saturday	Sunday
Level 9	SWU5 SDS5 SBI7 STI2B SKS5 SCD5 (2,800)	SWU5 SDS7 SBI17 SBI6 SCD5 (3,200)	BRW9B	CLI7	CLR16	SWU4 SBI32 SCD4 (3,700)
	CTR12	RSI17		SWU5 SDS5 SBI5 SLI5B SSI5B SKS5 SCD5 (2,800)	RRR6	RLR10
Level 10	SWU5 SDS5 SBI7 STI3B SKS5 SCD5 (3,000)	SWU5 SDS7 SBI17 SBI8 SCD5 (3,400)	BRW10A	CLI7	CLR17	SWU4 SBI32 SCD4 (3,900)
	CTR13	RSI18		SWU5 SDS5 SBI5 SLI6B SSI6B SKS5 SCD5 (2,900)	RRR6	RLR11

WEEK 16
(Recovery)

This week's goal: Fully absorb your recent training and have a solid Olympic-distance triathlon performance on Sunday if you have the opportunity.

	Tuesday	Wednesday	Thursday	Friday	Saturday	Sunday
Level 7	SWU4 SDS4 SBI3 STI1 SCD4 (1,750)	SWU4 SDS7 SBI15 SBI2 SCD4 (2,300)	CFR4	CLH3	CRR1 or BRW8*	Olympic-Distance Triathlon or SWU4 SBI28 SCD4 (2,700)*
	CTR6	RSI12	RTR4	SWU4 SDS4 SLI4 SSI4 SCD4 (1,650)		RLR1*
Level 8	SWU4 SDS5 SBI4 STI1 SCD4 (1,900)	SWU4 SDS7 SBI15 SBI4 SCD4 (2,500)	CFR4	CLH3	CRR1 or BRW9*	Olympic-Distance Triathlon or SWU1 SBI29 SCD1 (2,800)*
	CTR7	RSI12	RTR5	SWU4 SDS5 SLI4 SSI6 SCD4 (1,750)		RLR2*
Level 9	SWU5 SDS5 SBI4 STI1 SCD5 (2,000)	SWU5 SDS7 SBI15 SBI4 SCD5 (2,600)	CFR5	CLH3	CRR1 or BRW10*	Olympic-Distance Triathlon or SWU2 SBI29 SCD2 (2,900)*
	CTR7	RSI13	RTR6	SWU5 SDS5 SLI4 SSI6 SCD5 (1,850)		RLR3*

*If not racing

	Tuesday	Wednesday	Thursday	Friday	Saturday	Sunday
Level 10	SWU5 SDS5 SBI4 STI2 SCD5 (2,200)	SWU5 SDS7 SBI15 SBI5 SCD5 (2,700)	CFR5	CLH3	CRR1 or BRW11*	Olympic-Distance Triathlon or SWU3 SBI29 SCD3 (3,000)*
	CTR8	RSI13	RTR7	SWU5 SDS5 SLI6 SSI8 SCD5 (2,050)		RLR4*

*If not racing

Peak Phase

In this eight-week peak phase you will transform the all-around triathlon fitness you developed in the previous two phases into race fitness. You'll do this by completing your longest swims, rides, runs, and brick workouts, to maximize your endurance. You will also do longer workouts at high aerobic intensity and threshold intensity to enhance your ability to sustain a relatively fast pace.

WEEK 17

This week's goal: Find a steady groove at threshold intensity (8–8.5 RPE) in both the bike and run segments of Thursday's brick workout.

	Tuesday	Wednesday	Thursday	Friday	Saturday	Sunday
Level 7	SWU4 SDS4 SBI4 STI5 SKS4 SCD4 (2,900)	SWU4 SDS7 SBI17 SBI4 SCD4 (2,900)	BRW8B	CLI10	CLR15	SWU2 SBI32 SCD2 (3,500)
	CTR12	RLI9		SWU4 SDS4 SBI3 SLI16 SSI12 SKS4 SCD4 (2,800)	RRR5	RLR10

	Tuesday	Wednesday	Thursday	Friday	Saturday	Sunday
Level 8	SWU4 SDS5 SBI5 STI5 SKS5 SCD4 (3,100)	SWU4 SDS7 SBI17 SBI6 SCD4 (3,100)	BRW9B	CLI10	CLR16	SWU4 SBI32 SCD4 (3,700)
	CTR13	RLI10		SWU4 SDS5 SBI4 SLI16 SSI12 SKS5 SCD4 (3,000)	RRR6	RLR11
Level 9	SWU5 SDS5 SBI5 STI5 SKS5 SCD5 (3,200)	SWU5 SDS7 SBI17 SBI6 SCD5 (3,200)	BRW10A	CLI10	CLR17	SWU3 SBI33 SCD3 (3,800)
	CTR13	RLI10		SWU5 SDS5 SBI4 SLI16 SSI12 SKS5 SCD5 (3,100)	RRR6	RLR11
Level 10	SWU5 SDS5 SBI5 STI6 SKS5 SCD5 (3,400)	SWU5 SDS7 SBI17 SBI8 SCD5 (3,400)	BRW11A	CLI11	CLR18	SWU5 SBI33 SCD5 (4,000)

	Tuesday	Wednesday	Thursday	Friday	Saturday	Sunday
Level 10 (cont.)	CTR14	RLI11		SWU5 SDS5 SBI5 SLI17 SSI12 SKS5 SCD5 (3,350)	RRR6	RLR12

WEEK 18

This week's goal: Go all out for a great race-specific workout in Sunday's swim time trial.

	Tuesday	Wednesday	Thursday	Friday	Saturday	Sunday
Level 7	SWU4 SDS4 SBI4 STI5A SKS4 SCD4 (2,900)	SWU4 SDS7 SBI17 SBI4 SCD4 (2,900)	CFR7	CLH10	BRW13	SWU1 STT5 SCD1 (3,600)
	CTR13	RLI10	RTR12	SWU4 SDS4 SBI3 SLI16A SSI12A SKS4 SCD4 (2,800)		RLR2
Level 8	SWU4 SDS5 SBI5 STI5A SKS5 SCD4 (3,100)	SWU4 SDS7 SBI17 SBI6 SCD4 (3,100)	CFR7	CLH10	BRW14	SWU2 STT5 SCD2 (3,700)
	CTR13	RLI11	RTR13	SWU4 SDS5 SBI4 SLI16A SSI12A SKS5 SCD4 (3,000)		RLR3

	Tuesday	Wednesday	Thursday	Friday	Saturday	Sunday
Level 9	SWU5 SDS5 SBI5 STI5A SKS5 SCD5 (3,200)	SWU5 SDS7 SBI17 SBI6 SCD5 (3,200)	CFR7	CLH11	BRW15	SWU3 STT5 SCD3 (3,800)
	CTR14	RLI11	RTR14	SWU5 SDS5 SBI4 SLI16A SSI12A SKS5 SCD5 (3,100)		RLR4
Level 10	SWU5 SDS5 SBI5 STI6A SKS5 SCD5 (3,400)	SWU5 SDS7 SBI17 SBI8 SCD5 (3,400)	CFR8	CLH11	BRW16	SWU4 STT5 SCD4 (3,900)
	CTR15	RLI12	RTR15	SWU5 SDS5 SBI5 SLI17A SSI12A SKS5 SCD5 (3,350)		RLR5

QUICK TIP:

Glutamine is an important amino acid that is used at a high rate during exercise. Glutamine levels are often chronically low in endurance athletes. This can leave you susceptible to illness and compromise your recovery from workouts, as glutamine is a key fuel for immune cells. To ensure your body gets all the glutamine it needs, consider using a post-workout recovery drink containing whey protein, such as Endurox R[4], after workouts. Whey protein is high in glutamine.

WEEK 19

This week's goal: Dig deep in Friday's tough cycling lactate intervals workout.

	Tuesday	Wednesday	Thursday	Friday	Saturday	Sunday
Level 7	SWU4 SDS4 SBI4 STI5B SKS4 SCD4 (2,900)	SWU4 SDS7 SBI17 SBI4 SCD4 (2,900)	BRW8B	CLI11	CLR17	SWU3 SBI32 SCD3 (3,600)
	CTR14	RLI11		SWU4 SDS4 SBI3 SLI16B SSI12B SKS4 SCD4 (2,800)	RRR6	RLR11
Level 8	SWU4 SDS5 SBI5 STI5B SKS5 SCD4 (3,100)	SWU4 SDS7 SBI17 SBI6 SCD4 (3,100)	BRW9B	CLI11	CLR18	SWU3 SBI33 SCD3 (3,800)
	CTR15	RLI12		SWU4 SDS5 SBI4 SLI16B SSI12B SKS5 SCD4 (3,000)	RRR6	RLR12
Level 9	SWU5 SDS5 SBI5 STI5B SKS5 SCD5 (3,200)	SWU5 SDS7 SBI17 SBI6 SCD5 (3,200)	BRW10A	CLI11	CLR19	SWU4 SBI33 SCD4 (3,900)

	Tuesday	Wednesday	Thursday	Friday	Saturday	Sunday
Level 9 (cont.)	CTR15	RLI12		SWU5 SDS5 SBI4 SLI16B SSI12B SKS5 SCD5 (3,100)	RRR6	RLR12
Level 10	SWU5 SDS5 SBI5 STI6B SKS5 SCD5 (3,400)	SWU5 SDS7 SBI17 SBI7 SCD5 (3,300)	BRW11A	CLI11	CLR20	SWU3 SBI34 SCD3 (4,100)
	CTR16	RLI13		SWU5 SDS5 SBI4 SLI17B SSI12B SKS5 SCD5 (3,250)	RRR6	RLR12

WEEK 20

This week's goal: Fully absorb your recent training and have a solid half-Ironman triathlon performance on Sunday if you have the opportunity.

	Tuesday	Wednesday	Thursday	Friday	Saturday	Sunday
Level 7	SWU4 SDS4 SBI3 STI1 SCD4 (1,750)	SWU4 SDS7 SBI14 SCD4 (1,800)	CFR3	CLI3	CRR1 or BRW12*	Half-Ironman Triathlon or SWU1 SBI28 SCD1 (2,400)*

*If not racing

	Tuesday	Wednesday	Thursday	Friday	Saturday	Sunday
Level 7 (cont.)	CTR7	RLI9	RTR9	SWU4 SDS4 SBI1 SLI9 SSI10 SCD4 (1,750)		RFR9*
Level 8	SWU4 SDS5 SBI4 STI1 SCD4 (1,900)	SWU4 SDS7 SBI15 SCD4 (2,000)	CFR3	CLI3	CRR1 or BRW13*	Half-Ironman Triathlon or SWU3 SBI28 SCD3 (2,600)*
	CTR8	RLI9	RTR10	SWU4 SDS5 SBI2 SLI9 SSI10 SCD4 (1,900)*		RLR1
Level 9	SWU5 SDS5 SBI4 STI1 SCD5 (2,000)	SWU5 SDS7 SBI15 SCD5 (2,100)	CFR4	CLI3	CRR1 or BRW14*	Half-Ironman Triathlon or SWU4 SBI28 SCD4 (2,700)*
	CTR8	RLI10	RTR10	SWU5 SDS5 SBI2 SLI9 SSI10 SCD5 (2,000)		RLR2*

*If not racing

	Tuesday	Wednesday	Thursday	Friday	Saturday	Sunday
Level 10	SWU5 SDS5 SBI4 STI2 SCD5 (2,200)	SWU5 SDS7 SBI16 SCD5 (2,300)	CFR4	CLI3	CRR1 or BRW15*	Half- Ironman Triathlon or SWU2 SBI29 SCD2 (2,900)*
	CTR9	RLI10	RTR11	SWU5 SDS5 SBI2 SLI10 SSI10 SCD5 (2,100)		RLR3*

*If not racing

WEEK 21

This week's goal: Finish strong in Saturday's very long ride.

	Tuesday	Wednesday	Thursday	Friday	Saturday	Sunday
Level 7	SWU4 SDS4 SBI4 STI6 SKS4 SCD4 (3,100)	SWU4 SDS7 SBI17 SBI5 SCD4 (3,000)	BRW9B	CSS5	CLR18	SWU3 SBI34 SCD3 (4,100)
	CTR16	RTR13		SWU4 SDS4 SBI2 SLI17 SSI15 SKS4 SCD4 (3,000)	RRR6	RLR13
Level 8	SWU4 SDS5 SBI5 STI6 SKS5 SCD4 (3,300)	SWU4 SDS7 SBI17 SBI7 SCD4 (3,200)	BRW10A	CSS6	CLR19	SWU2 SBI35 SCD2 (4,300)

	Tuesday	Wednesday	Thursday	Friday	Saturday	Sunday
Level 8 *(cont.)*	CTR16	RTR14		SWU4 SDS5 SBI3 SLI17 SSI15 SKS5 SCD4 (3,200)	RRR6	RLR13
Level 9	SWU5 SDS5 SBI5 STI6 SKS5 SCD5 (3,400)	SWU5 SDS7 SBI17 SBI7 SCD5 (3,300)	BRW10A	CSS7	CLR20	SWU3 SBI35 SCD3 (4,400)
	CTR16	RTR15		SWU5 SDS5 SBI3 SLI17 SSI15 SKS5 SCD5 (3,300)	RRR6	RLR13
Level 10	SWU5 SDS5 SBI5 STI7 SKS5 SCD5 (3,600)	SWU5 SDS7 SBI17 SBI9 SCD5 (3,500)	BRW11A	CSS8	CLR21	SWU5 SBI35 SCD5 (4,600)
	CTR17	RTR16		SWU5 SDS5 SBI4 SLI18 SSI15 SKS5 SCD5 (3,550)	RRR6	RLR13

WEEK 22

This week's goal: Approach this week—the hardest training week in this entire plan—as one final challenge to overcome before your pre-race taper begins next week.

	Tuesday	Wednesday	Thursday	Friday	Saturday	Sunday
Level 7	SWU4 SDS4 SBI4 STI6A SKS4 SCD4 (3,100)	SWU4 SDS7 SBI17 SBI4 SCD4 (2,900)	CFR7	CSS6	BRW18	SWU1 STT6 SCD1 (4,625)
	CTR17	RLI11	RTR13	SWU4 SDS4 SBI2 SLI17A SSI15A SKS4 SCD4 (3,000)		RLR7
Level 8	SWU4 SDS5 SBI5 STI6A SKS5 SCD4 (3,300)	SWU4 SDS7 SBI17 SBI7 SCD4 (3,200)	CFR7	CSS7	BRW18	SWU1 STT6 SCD1 (4,625)
	CTR17	RLI12	RTR14	SWU4 SDS5 SBI3 SLI17A SSI15A SKS5 SCD4 (3,200)		RLR8
Level 9	SWU5 SDS5 SBI5 STI6A SKS5 SCD5 (3,400)	SWU5 SDS7 SBI17 SBI7 SCD5 (3,300)	CFR8	CSS8	BRW18	SWU1 STT6 SCD1 (4,625)

	Tuesday	Wednesday	Thursday	Friday	Saturday	Sunday
Level 9 (cont.)	CTR17	RLI13 SDS5 SBI3 SLI17A SSI15A SKS5 SCD5 (3,300)	RTR15	SWU5		RLR9
Level 10	SWU5 SDS5 SBI5 STI7A SKS5 SCD5 (3,600)	SWU5 SDS7 SBI17 SBI9 SCD5 (3,500)	CFR8	CSS9	BRW18	SWU1 STT6 SCD1 (4,625)
	CTR17	RLI13	RTR16	SWU5 SDS5 SBI4 SLI18A SSI15A SKS5 SCD5 (3,550)		RLR10

QUICK TIP:

Should you carbo-load (eat large amounts of carbohydrates) in the final days before a long race? Research shows that carbo-loading has little effect on endurance performance in athletes who take in adequate carbohydrate during the race itself. Carbo-loading won't hurt, but fueling your body properly during the race is more important.

WEEK 23
(Taper)

This week's goal: Gain confidence for next week's race by feeling your fitness begin to peak during this week's workouts.

	Tuesday	Wednesday	Thursday	Friday	Saturday	Sunday
Level 7	SWU4 SDS4 SBI4 STI6B SKS4 SCD4 (3,100)	SWU4 SDS7 SBI16 SBI4 SCD4 (2,700)	BRW4A	CFR4	CLR4	SWU1 SBI29 SCD1 (2,800)
	CTR8	RLI9		SWU4 SDS4 SBI1 SLI14 SSI10 SKS4 SCD4 (2,200)	RRR5	RLR4
Level 8	SWU4 SDS5 SBI5 STI6B SKS5 SCD4 (3,300)	SWU4 SDS7 SBI16 SBI5 SCD4 (2,800)	BRW5A	CFR5	CLR5	SWU3 SBI29 SCD3 (3,000)
	CTR9	RLI9		SWU4 SDS5 SBI1 SLI14 SSI11 SKS5 SCD4 (2,350)	RRR5	RLR5
Level 9	SWU5 SDS5 SBI5 STI6AB SKS5 SCD5 (3,400)	SWU5 SDS7 SBI16 SBI5 SCD5 (2,900)	BRW5A	CFR5	CLR6	SWU2 SBI30 SCD2 (3,100)
	CTR10	RLI10		SWU5 SDS5 SBI1 SLI14	RRR5	RLR6

	Tuesday	Wednesday	Thursday	Friday	Saturday	Sunday
Level 9 (cont.)				SSI11 SKS5 SCD5 (2,450)		
Level 10	SWU5 SDS5 SBI5 STI7AB SKS5 SCD5 (3,600)	SWU5 SDS7 SBI17 SBI5 SCD5 (3,100)	BRW7B	CFR6	CLR7	SWU4 SBI30 SCD4 (3,300)
	CTR11	RLI10		SWU5 SDS5 SBI1 SLI15 SSI11 SKS5 SCD5 (2,600)	RRR5	RLR7

WEEK 24
(Taper)

This week's goal: Have a great Ironman on Sunday!

	Tuesday	Wednesday	Thursday	Friday	Saturday	Sunday
Level 7	SWU4 SDS3 STI4 SKS3 SCD4 (2,100)	SWU4 SDS7 SBI15 SCD4 (2,000)	CFR3	SWU4 SLI8 SSI10 SCD4 (1,200)	CRR1	Ironman Triathlon
	CTR5	RFR3 + RSS3	RTR3			
Level 8	SWU4 SDS3 STI4 SKS3 SCD4 (2,100)	SWU4 SDS7 SBI15 SCD4 (2,000)	CFR3	SWU4 SLI8 SSI10 SCD4 (1,200)	CRR1	Ironman Triathlon
	CTR5	RFR3 + RSS3	RTR3			

	Tuesday	Wednesday	Thursday	Friday	Saturday	Sunday
Level 9	SWU4 SDS3 STI4 SKS3 SCD4 (2,100)	SWU4 SDS7 SBI15 SCD4 (2,000)	CFR3	SWU4 SLI8 SSI10 SCD4 (1,200)	CRR1	Ironman Triathlon
	CTR5	RFR3 + RSS3	RTR3			
Level 10	SWU4 SDS3 STI4 SKS3 SCD4 (2,100)	SWU4 SDS7 SBI15 SCD4 (2,000)	CFR3	SWU4 SLI8 SSI10 SCD4 (1,200)	CRR1	Ironman Triathlon
	CTR5	RFR3 + RSS3	RTR3			

Chapter 15

OFF-SEASON TRAINING PLANS

Almost every sport is seasonal, and triathlon is no exception. For the typical triathlete, the triathlon season begins in the spring and lasts until the fall, with most races taking place during the summer. The late fall and winter months constitute the off-season period. What sort of training should you do during the off-season? The short answer: transition-phase training. Now for the long answer.

As you've seen, each of the training plans presented in the preceding chapters comprises three phases: base, build, and peak. Together, these three phases make up a complete training cycle that culminates in a peak race. There is a fourth training phase, called the transition phase, which falls between training cycles. The purpose of the transition phase is twofold: It allows you to recover from the recently completed training cycle, and it prepares you for the next.

It is not always necessary to insert a transition phase between training cycles. Often, when you wrap up a training cycle in the heat of the racing season, you can simply take a few days off after completing a peak race and then immediately begin the next training plan without suffering any consequences. But at least once a year you should complete a transition phase lasting 8 to 12 weeks. The most logical time to do so is during the winter off-season, when there are no triathlons taking place.

A winter transition phase should begin with one to two weeks of complete rest. Feel free to go for long walks or hikes, play a little basketball, or get some exercise in other ways that are fun and informal, but stay out of the pool and off the bike and leave your running shoes in the closet. (These nonstructured activities are designated by the code "NSA" in the transition phase training plans that follow.) Taking a real, honest-to-goodness break will allow your body to recover from the wear and tear that comes from all of the swimming, cycling, and running you do during the rest of the year and, just as important, give you a mental vacation from these activities. By the time you resume them after a couple of weeks you should feel free of aches and pains and eager for workouts in those old, familiar triathlon disciplines.

The major conditioning priorities of the transition phase are to develop injury resistance and improve your swimming, cycling, and running technique. These two goals go hand-in-hand, because improving your technique will itself increase your injury resistance. The rationale for focusing on these two types of training during the transition phase is that each of them prepares you for the higher volume endurance training that necessarily becomes the focus when you begin a new base phase. Good technique is the true foundation of performance in swimming, cycling, and running, so it only makes sense to make technique development your first priority in the training calendar. Also, as your training volume increases, so do your chances of developing an overuse injury such as runner's knee or swimmer's shoulder. The primary causes of most triathlon overuse injuries are technique flaws and muscular imbalances, so it's important to proactively minimize these factors during the transition phase.

There are three types of training that will help you achieve the objectives of the transition phase: technique workouts, drills, and functional strength training. Most if not all of your transition-phase workouts should involve these three types of training.

Technique Workouts

In so-called skill sports such as golf and tennis, participants are accustomed to improving their technique by repetitively practicing specific movement patterns copied from the best players. As a triathlete, you can and should improve your swimming, cycling, and running technique in the same way.

The first step is to identify a specific flaw in your technique or, put another way, to identify an aspect of correct technique that is missing from your own. This may require the assistance of a coach or other observer. One example of a common and correctable technique flaw is pronounced heel striking in running.

Step two is to incorporate this technique modification into your swim stroke, pedal stroke, or running stride. Our example of pronounced heel striking results from allowing the foot to land too far ahead of the body during running. If you have this flaw, you'll want to practice running with your entire body angled slightly forward, so that your foot is more or less forced to land flat underneath your body instead of heel first out ahead of your body.

Once you've gotten a basic feel for the new technique you have chosen to work on, your task is to repeat this improved movement pattern as exactly as possible with every single stroke or stride until it has become automatic. This will probably take several weeks.

The process of incorporating a technique improvement requires great concentration and focus. Therefore I recommend that you work on just one technique modification at a time in each discipline. It's also important to swim, bike, and run for only short periods of time when trying to groove a technique change. If you go too long, fatigue (which will come more quickly than usual, as you're using some muscles in new ways) and/or inattention will cause you to revert back to old habits.

Choose one technique correction per discipline to work on during any single transition phase. Altering the deeply ingrained neuromotor patterns that control your swimming, cycling, and running is never easy, and it becomes nearly impossible when you try to effect two or more changes simultaneously. The good news is that one change can go a long way. Here are suggestions for your next off-season transition phase.

Swimming Fixes

If you're like a lot of triathletes, you routinely work on any of a number of common components of good freestyle technique. That's wonderful, but for your transition phase, select the *one* technique component that will do you the most good to master and practice it exclusively. In each workout, focus your full attention on executing it correctly and integrating it properly into your overall stroke with *every* stroke. Do only those drills that serve to develop this particular component.

Recruit your masters swim coach, if possible, or another technique authority to watch you in action initially and let you know when you're making the change correctly and when you're not. Try to memorize how it feels and looks to do it right so you can continue doing it right even when you're unobserved. Paying attention to the *rhythm* of the correct movement as it fits into the overall stroke is also helpful, as are verbal cues. For example, if your chosen correction is to finish your stroke better, you might concentrate on scraping your thumb against your upper thigh at this point of the stroke and chant in your head, "and *scrape*, and *scrape*, and *scrape*," etc. to the "beat" of the stroke.

Here are a few suggested swim technique improvements to focus on in your next off-season transition phase.

SWIM DOWNHILL

It's important to float high in the water, as it minimizes drag. Beginners tend to allow their hips and legs to sink, a flaw that is sometimes referred to as "swimming uphill." It's a lot more efficient to swim downhill. To do so, concentrate on pushing your chest toward the bottom of the pool. This will naturally cause your hips and legs to rise. The Chest Press drill (p. 11) described in Chapter 2 promotes a downhill body position.

ROTATE

By rotating your entire body from side to side with each stroke, you swim more narrowly and can slice through the water with less drag. As you extend your leading arm ahead of you, rotate your body about 60 degrees toward the opposite side (as though you're reaching to pluck an item off a high shelf). Be sure to keep your neck and head neutral, however. The Side Kicking drill (p. 12) promotes better body rotation.

MAKE A BIGGER PADDLE

Once you've reached full extension with your leading arm, rotate your shoulder and elbow so that your hand and forearm form a single long "paddle" that pulls backward toward your feet. A proper high elbow pull is often described as feeling like "reaching over a barrel." The Fist drill (p. 13) helps swimmers make a bigger paddle.

LENGTHEN YOUR STROKE

Long strokes mean more distance traveled per stroke. Be sure to pull all the way back until your arm is fully extended toward your foot. Your hand should exit the water next to your upper thigh. The Count-Stroke drill (p. 12) and the Thumb Scrape drill (p. 13) promote a longer stroke.

TIGHTEN YOUR KICK

Kicking too hard will create more drag than it does propulsion, so concentrate on making a tight, small, "flicking" kick that uses minimal energy. The proper motion is similar to that of kicking a ball, but you're moving your foot only six inches in either direction. Forget about your arms for a while and swim while concentrating entirely on creating this tight, efficient kick. The Side Kicking drill (p. 12) promotes a tighter kick.

BREATHE BILATERALLY

Most triathletes have a highly asymmetrical swim stroke. They are substantially more efficient when stroking on one side (left or right) versus the other. Most triathletes are also able to breathe on only one side or the other. This limitation is a major cause of the asymmetries that reduce their efficiency on one side of the body versus the other. By learning to breathe comfortably on both left and right sides, you will naturally make your swim stroke more symmetrical, improving your overall efficiency. It's frustrating at first, but with patience and discipline, anyone can do it. You simply have to force yourself.

Cycling Fixes

To the uninitiated, every cycling pedal stroke looks the same. Every cyclist turns the pedals around and around with the feet and legs. The idea of improving one's pedaling form seems as odd as that of improving one's automobile driving form. You're just operating a machine, right? Wrong. Although the differences are relatively subtle as compared to those between, say, the best and worst swimmers, a superior pedal stroke nevertheless produces far more power with far less energy. Here are three ways to enhance the efficiency of your cycling.

ELIMINATE YOUR DEAD SPOT

In both cycling and running some of the most common technique flaws are caused by muscular laziness. Certain muscles try to catch little rests when they should be doing their share of the work. As a result, other muscles have to do more than their share and the overall amount of work required to maintain a given level of power output, or pace, is increased.

In cycling the classic moment of muscular laziness is the dead spot between 6:00 and 9:00 for the right leg (between 6:00 and 3:00 for the left leg) of the pedal stroke. In this quadrant of the stroke cycle your hamstrings should be actively contracting, pulling your heel toward your butt and the pedal with it. Instead, most of us pull only weakly while putting most of our energy into pushing down on the pedal with the opposite leg.

To do away with this dead spot, focus your full attention on actively pulling your heel toward your butt with every pedal stroke of every ride throughout your technique focus period. Forget about everything else. You will probably find that your hamstrings tire quickly (and your mind will want to wander, causing you to revert to laziness), so keep your rides relatively short.

PEDAL IN CIRCLES

In an efficient pedal stroke, the foot leads the pedal in a circle. In other words, the foot moves with the pedal in a neat circular motion instead of working against the pedal by pulling or pushing it in a direction it does not want to go. This requires a high degree of fine neuromuscular coordination, because instinctively we tend to push and pull things in relatively straight lines. This is precisely what less efficient cyclists tend to do, and what even advanced cyclists tend to do as they become fatigued: pedal in squares, more or less.

Of course, it's not possible to actually pedal in squares, as the pedal crank is totally inflexible and therefore it always wins. But if you watch closely you can see a subtle difference in the way different cyclists turn the pedals. Better cyclists clearly lead the pedal in a circle, whereas lesser cyclists (and fatigued ones) seem to pull straight back, then straight up, then push straight forward and finally straight down, therefore fighting the pedal the whole way. Put another way, efficient cyclists would pedal in circles even if the pedals disappeared, whereas inefficient cyclists really would make squares if the pedals weren't there to enforce circles. You get more speed from less effort when you lead the pedal in circles, so practice doing so with each and every turn of the crank until it becomes second nature.

LOOSEN YOUR ANKLES

Another form discrepancy that exists between more and less efficient cyclists is in the ankles. Better cyclists pedal with loose ankles. At the bottom of the pedal stroke the ankle dorsiflexes (i.e., the heel comes down toward the ground), and at the top of the pedal stroke the ankle plantar flexes (i.e., the heel comes up toward the seat). The advantage of pedaling with loose ankles is that it allows the muscles of your lower leg to contribute more pedal power. When you keep your ankles locked, these muscles are not able to contribute as much pedal power. So work on getting a feel for pedaling with loose ankles and repeat it with every pedal stroke until it's automatic.

Running Fixes

Most runners believe that, for better or worse, the stride you're "born with" is the stride you're stuck with. Not so. It is more difficult to improve your running form than, say, your golf swing, because the former is learned at an earlier age and repeated with much greater frequency. But with a little knowledge and some discipline, a variety of small but crucial adjustments are feasible. It's worth the effort, because making even small improvements in your stride can increase your efficiency (the energy cost of running at any given pace) and reduce your risk of injuries.

It's a two-step process. Step one is to select one specific alteration to your stride that makes it either more efficient or more stable, or both. Step two is to re-create this new pattern conscientiously with every single stride of every run until it's second nature. Allow at least three weeks for this to happen. Then you can make another change. Here are six basic technique changes to work on.

REDUCE YOUR STANCE PAUSE
One of the key features of the stride of the most efficient runners is the lack, or near total lack, of any pause during the stance phase of the stride. The stance phase is when the foot is flat or almost flat on the ground, between the foot strike and toe-off phases. To reduce your stance pause, begin to retract your leg just before your foot lands with each stride, so that you're already thrusting backward when your foot makes ground contact.

RUN TALL
Many runners tend to "collapse" at the hips and pelvis when their foot comes into contact with the ground. This wastes energy and can lead to a variety of overuse injuries. To overcome this type of collapsing, concentrate on running more erectly. Imagine wires attached to your shoulders and pulling gently upward. Thrust your hips forward just a bit and gently engage the muscles of your lower abdomen to keep your pelvis neutral.

RELAX YOUR UPPER BODY
Most runners run with unnecessary tension in their arms, shoulders, neck, and even their faces, especially when running hard. All of this tension equals wasted energy. Practice running with your fingers, forearms, and upper arms loose, and with no hunch in your shoulders and a placid facial expression.

LAND ON THE MIDFOOT
Landing heel first is like driving with the emergency brake engaged. Not every heel striker can transform himself or herself into a midfoot striker, but many can. A good way to begin the process is to practice running with a very slight forward lean of the whole body (that is, from the ankles up, not from the waist up).

USE YOUR BIG TOE

The metatarsal phalangeal (MP) joint at the ball of the foot was designed to actively plantar flex (flex downward) during the push-off phase of the running stride. The rigidity of running shoes inhibits the MP joint from actively plantar flexing, reducing the power of your stride. You can get some of it back by consciously pushing off the ground with your big toe, beginning at its origin at the midfoot-forefoot juncture.

BOUNCE LESS

Runners need to push themselves upward slightly in order to float between foot strikes. By becoming airborne you can take longer strides than you do when you walk. Faster runners in fact spend more time airborne and less time in contact with the ground than slower runners. But as much as possible you want to float *forward,* not upward, and indeed faster runners tend to keep the top of their head closer to the ground (relative to their height) than slower runners. Practice this "scooting" style of running.

Form Drills

The difference between technique workouts and drills is that, in the former, you swim, ride, or run normally while consciously controlling one specific component of the movement, whereas in the latter, you break down the normal swim stroke, pedal stroke, or stride into basic components and work on developing proper technique in each, one at a time.

Drills are, of course, common in swimming. In a typical swim workout, a drill set is sandwiched between the warm-up and the main set. During your technique focus period, the drill set should become your main set. Increase the variety and volume of drills you do and scrap the intervals altogether. I covered a selection of swim drills in Chapter 2.

It's important that you also do cycling and running drills during your technique focus period. Here are some suggestions:

Running Drills

HIGH KNEES

Run with a fast cadence and highly exaggerated knee lift, bringing your thighs up parallel to the ground with each stride. Continue for 30 seconds.

FAST FEET

This drill is the same as High Knees except you do it as fast as you can, and keep it up for only 15 to 20 seconds.

BUTT KICKS

Run in place or slowly forward while keeping your thighs perpendicular to the ground and trying to kick yourself in the butt with your heels. Continue for 30 seconds.

LEAP RUNNING

Run with the longest, leaping strides you can achieve (like the first two jumps in a track-and-field triple jump). Continue for 30 seconds.

GOOSE STEP

Walk forward by kicking your legs as high as possible in front of you with minimal knee bend. Extend your arms straight ahead of you, zombie-style, and try to touch your toe to your palm with each step. Continue for 30 seconds. In the following transition phase training plans, the code RDR indicates a running drill set. RDR1 is two drills performed for 30 seconds each; RDR2 is three drills, etc.

Cycling Drills

SINGLE-LEG PEDALING

On a wind trainer or a stationary bike, pedal in a low gear (low resistance level) with a single leg while keeping your other leg out of the way (e.g., on a chair). Go for one minute and then switch legs. Repeat the drill a few times more.

SPINNING OUT

Gradually increase your pedaling cadence over the course of several minutes, in a very low gear, until you reach your maximum pedaling speed. Maintain it for 30 to 60 seconds. Try to keep your butt from bouncing in the saddle.

MASHING

On a flat road or slight incline, shift into your highest gear and pedal as hard as you can, keeping your butt on the seat and your upper body relaxed. Keep it up for 30 seconds.

In addition to drills, there are special tools you can use to improve your pedal stroke. Two that I recommend for the technique focus period are CompuTrainer's Spin Scan (www.computrainer.com), which allows you to watch a real-time, graphic representation of your pedal stroke during an indoor ride, and Power Cranks (www.power-cranks.com), a special type of pedal crank that forces you to pedal with a perfectly symmetrical stroke. In the following transition phase training plans, the code CDS indicates a cycling drill set. CDS1 is two drills; CDS2 is three drills, etc. (You may repeat the same drill or do different ones.)

Strength Training

Various muscular imbalances contribute to technique flaws and the overuse injuries that result from them. For example, weak hip abductors can cause the pelvis to tilt laterally on impact during running, placing stress on the hips and knees. All the drills and conscious technique modification in the world won't allow you to swim, bike, and run correctly if you don't have the right musculature to support good form.

Strength training can give you the muscle balance and joint stability you need to improve your technique. A little strength training can go a long way for triathletes, but a technique focus period is the best time to do the greatest amount of this type of training. I recommend three sessions per week lasting 20 to 40 minutes apiece. In the following chapter I will show you specific exercises to do and workout formats to follow. Here is a list of strength workout formats. A circuit entails completing each exercise one time. In a two-circuit strength workout you complete each exercise once and then go back and complete each a second time. In a three-circuit workout you extend the same pattern.

Code	Format
WST1	6 exercises, 1 circuit
WST2	8 exercises, 1 circuit
WST3	10 exercises, 1 circuit
WST4	8 exercises, 2 circuits
WST5	10 exercises, 2 circuits
WST6	8 exercises, 3 circuits
WST7	10 exercises, 3 circuits

Low-Volume Transition Phase Training Plan

This 12-week plan is appropriate for less advanced triathletes and those who prefer a lighter off-season training load, for whatever reason. Following a week of complete rest and a week of optional nonstructured activity (NSA), it begins with a single workout in each of the three triathlon disciplines and three short strength workouts. It builds up to two workouts per week in each triathlon discipline plus three strength workouts. Monday is always an off day.

The T at the end of a workout code (as in CFR2T) indicates a technique workout (or a technique set, in the case of swimming). Swim, ride, or run these sessions with total focus on practicing the specific technique improvement you have selected for this off-season transition phase. SPS stands for Swim Pull Set, which entails swimming without kicking, preferably with swim-hand paddles to build strength. Level 1 (SPS) is four times 25 yards with 10-second rest periods. Each subsequent level adds two more intervals.

	Tuesday	Wednesday	Thursday	Friday	Saturday	Sunday
Week 1	Off	Off	Off	Off	Off	Off
Week 2	Off or NSA	Off or NSA	Off or NSA	Off or NSA	Off or NSA	Off or NSA
Week 3	WST1	SWU2T SDS1 SBI1T SKS1 SPS1 SCD2T	WST1	CFR1T CDS1	WST1	RFR1T RDR1
Week 4	WST2	SWU2T SDS2 SBI2T SKS2 SPS2 SCD2T	WST2	CFR2T CDS2	WST2	RFR2T RDR2
Week 5	WST3	SWU2T SDS3 SBI3T SKS2 SPS2 SCD2T	WST2	CFR2T CDS3	WST2	RFR2T RDR3
Week 6	WST3	SWU3T SDS3 SBI3T SKS2 SPS2 SCD3T	WST2	CFR2T CDS3	WST2	RFR3T RDR3

	Tuesday	Wednesday	Thursday	Friday	Saturday	Sunday
Week 7	WST3 CFR2T CDS3	SWU3T SDS3 SBI3T SKS3 SPS3 SCD3T	WST2	CFR2T CDS3	WST3	RFR3T RDR4
Week 8	WST3 CFR3T CDS3	SWU3T SDS4 SBI3T SKS3 SPS3 SCD3T	WST3 RFR4T RDR4	CFR3T CDS3	WST3	RFR3T RDR4
Week 9	WST3 CFR3T CDS3	SWU3T SDS5 SBI5T SKS4 SPS4 SCD3T	WST3 RFR4T RDR4	CFR3T CDS3	WST3 SWU3T SDS5 SBI5T SKS4 SPS4 SCD3T	RFR4T RDR4
Week 10	WST3 CFR4T CDS4	SWU3T SDS5 SBI5T SKS5 SPS4 SCD3T	WST3 RFR4T RDR4	CFR3T CDS3	WST3 SWU3T SDS5 SBI5T SKS5 SPS4 SCD3T	RFR5T RDR4
Week 11	WST3 CFR4T CDS4	SWU3T SDS5 SBI5T SKS5 SPS5 SCD3T	WST3 RFR5T RDR4	CFR4T CDS4	WST3 SWU3T SDS5 SBI5T SKS5 SPS5 SCD3T	RFR5T RDR4
Week 12	WST3 CFR4T CDS4	SWU3T SDS5 SBI5T SKS5 SPS5 SCD3T	WST3 RFR5T RDR4	CFR4T CDS4	WST3 SWU3T SDS5 SBI5T SKS5 SPS5 SCD3T	RFR5T RDR4

Higher Volume Transition Phase Training Plan

Like the low-volume transition phase training plan described above, this higher volume plan lasts 12 weeks and begins with a week of total rest followed by a week of optional unstructured exercise. It also entails three strength workouts per week beginning in Week 3, but these workouts become longer and more challenging than they do in the lower volume plan. Formal training starts with two swims, two rides, and two runs per week in Week 3 and builds up to three swims, rides, and runs.

	Tuesday	Wednesday	Thursday	Friday	Saturday	Sunday
Week 1	Off	Off	Off	Off	Off	Off
Week 2	Off or NSA	Off or NSA	Off or NSA	Off or NSA	Off or NSA	Off or NSA
Week 3	WST1 CFR1T CDS1	SWU3T SDS3 SBI3T SKS2 SPS2 SCD3T	WST1 RFR1T RDR1	CFR1T CDS1	WST1 SWU3T SDS3 SBI3T SKS2 SPS2 SCD3T	RFR1T RDR1
Week 4	WST2 CFR1T CDS2	SWU3T SDS3 SBI3T SKS3 SPS2 SCD3T	WST1 RFR1T RDR2	CFR1T CDS2	WST2 SWU3T SDS3 SBI3T SKS3 SPS2 SCD3T	RFR1T RDR2
Week 5	WST2 CFR2T CDS2	SWU3T SDS3 SBI3T SKS3 SPS3 SCD3T	WST2 RFR2T RDR2	CFR2T CDS2	WST2 SWU3T SDS3 SBI3T SKS3 SPS3 SCD3T	RFR5T RFR2T RDR2

	Tuesday	Wednesday	Thursday	Friday	Saturday	Sunday
Week 6	WST3	SWU3T SDS3 SBI4T SKS3 SPS3 SCD3T	WST2	CFR2T CDS3	WST2	RFR2T RDR3
	CFR2T CDS3		RFR2T RDR3		SWU3T SDS3 SBI4T SKS3 SPS3 SCD3T	CDS2 CFR1T CDS2
Week 7	WST3	SWU3T SDS4 SBI4T SKS3 SPS3 SCD3T	WST3	CFR3T CDS3	WST3	RFR3T RDR3
	CFR3T CDS3		RFR3T RDR3	SWU3T SDS4 SKS4 SPS4 SCD3T	SWU3T SDS4 SBI4T SKS3 SPS3 SCD3T	CDS2 CFR2T CDS2
Week 8	WST4	SWU3T SDS4 SBI4T SKS4 SPS3 SCD3T	WST3	CFR3T CDS3	WST3	RFR3T RDR4
	CFR3T CDS3	RDR2 RFR1T RDR2	RFR3T RDR4	SWU4T SDS5 SKS4 SPS4 SCD4T	SWU3T SDS4 SBI4T SKS4 SPS3 SCD3T	CDS3 CFR2T CDS2
Week 9	WST4	SWU3T SDS4 SBI4T SKS4 SPS4 SCD3T	WST3	CFR4T CDS3	WST4	RFR4T RDR4
	CFR4T CDS3	RDR2 RFR2T RDR2	RFR4T RDR4	SWU3T SBI6T SCD3T	SWU3T SDS4 SBI4T SKS4 SPS4 SCD3T	CDS3 CFR2T CDS3

	Tuesday	Wednesday	Thursday	Friday	Saturday	Sunday
Week 10	WST4	SWU3T SDS4 SBI5T SKS4 SPS4 SCD3T	WST4	CFR4T CDS3	WST4	RFR4T RDR4
	CFR4T CDS3	RDR3 RFR2T RDR2	RFR4T RDR4	SWU4T SDS5 SKS5 SPS4 SCD4T	SWU3T SDS4 SBI5T SKS4 SPS4 SCD3T	CDS3 CFR3T CDS3
Week 11	WST4	SWU3T SDS4 SBI6T SKS4 SPS4 SCD3T	WST4	CFR5T CDS3	WST4	RFR5T RDR4
	CFR5T CDS3	RDR3 RFR2T RDR3	RFR5T RDR4	SWU3T SBI7T SCD3T	SWU3T SDS4 SBI6T SKS4 SPS4 SCD3T	CDS4 CFR3T CDS3
Week 12	WST4	SWU3T SDS4 SBI7T SKS4 SPS4 SCD3T	WST4	CFR5T CDS3	WST4	RFR5T RDR4
	CFR5T CDS3	RDR3 RFR3T RDR3	RFR5T RDR4	SWU4T SDS5 SKS5 SPS5 SCD4T	SWU3T SDS4 SBI7T SKS4 SPS4 SCD3T	CDS4 CFR3T CDS4

Chapter 16

STRENGTH EXERCISES

*A*s if you aren't busy enough trying to fit in all of your swim, bike, and run workouts, I also recommend that you perform strength workouts two or three times a week throughout the year. But fear not: These workouts require minimal time and can be done right at home while you watch television or keep an eye on your kids. And the rewards are significant. By strength training properly and consistently you will substantially reduce the number of injuries you experience and enhance your performance in all three triathlon disciplines.

There are many types of strength training. More than one type of strength training can be beneficial to triathletes, but the one type I consider to be essential for triathletes is stability strength training. As the name suggests, stability exercises serve to increase the stability of your joints, including your knees, hips, spine, and shoulders. Inadequate stability in the major joints is a primary cause of most overuse injuries. Stability exercises are therefore an excellent way to prevent such injuries. Improving the stability of your joints will also allow you to swim, ride, and run with greater efficiency.

Stability exercises enhance your ability to activate certain key stabilizing muscles, such as the hip abductors on the outside of the hip, that are underused and underdeveloped in most of us. The key muscles to focus on are those involved in stabilizing the shoulders, the lower spine, the pelvis, the hips, the knees, and the ankles. (Exercises designed to enhance the stability of the lower spine, pelvis, and hips are better known are "core strength" exercises.)

Do three strength workouts a week during the winter transition phase, when your endurance training is greatly reduced and you have plenty of time to "hit the gym." Strength training twice a week is adequate throughout the rest of the year, but you may enjoy additional benefits if you continue to do it three times a week.

In this chapter I include 13 of my favorite stability exercises. There are many other effective stability exercises that are not included. After you've mastered my suggested exercises, expand your repertoire by trying others. Variation is important to continued progress in strength training. Just be sure to learn new exercises from a good source, such as a licensed personal trainer with lots of experience in working with endurance athletes.

Your strength workouts should include at least one exercise for each of the above-mentioned joints, and at least six total exercises. Many exercises affect more than one joint. There is no need to do strength workouts including more than a dozen or so exercises. Start with one set of each exercise and advance to two sets (i.e., repeat each exercise in the workout a second time) if you wish.

Some of these exercises require the use of basic equipment items, including a wobble board, an exercise bench or other similar support, and a chin-up bar. Required equipment is identified within the exercise descriptions.

Stability Exercises

Do at least six of these exercises in each strength workout, and as many as all 13. Start with one circuit (i.e., do each exercise once). After several sessions move to two complete circuits (i.e., do each exercise once, then go back and do each one a second time) if you wish. Do not rest between exercises any longer than is necessary to move unhurriedly from one to the next.

The recommended number of repetitions for each exercise is included in the exercise descriptions. For exercises using nonbody-weight resistance, choose a resistance such that the last repetition of the exercise is very challenging, but you're still able to maintain perfect form.

Hip Abduction
Hip stability

Lay on your right side with your legs straight, ankles together, and your head supported on the palm of your right hand. Lift your left leg as high as you can and slowly return it to the starting position. Complete 15 to 30 lifts and switch sides. For a greater challenge, loop an elastic strap such as a Thera-Band around your ankles.

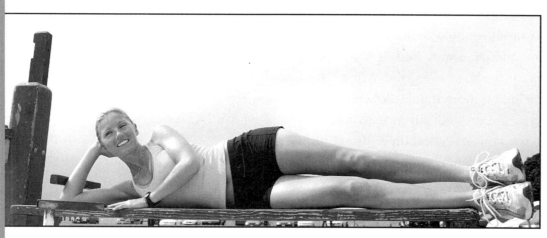

Push-up Plus
Shoulder stability

Assume a standard push-up position with your hands placed slightly more than shoulder-width apart, your body forming a perfectly straight line, and your head facing forward. Lower your chest to within an inch of the floor and then push back upward to the starting position. Pause for 2 to 3 seconds and then thrust your shoulders forward, arching your upper back and thereby creating another inch or two of distance between your chest and the floor. Pause again for 2 or 3 seconds and return to the starting position. That's one complete Push-up

Plus. Do as many repetitions as you can with perfect form, up to a maximum of 30.

If you cannot complete 10 Push-ups Plus with perfect form, modify your starting position so that your knees are in contact with the floor instead of your feet.

Supine Bridge Progression
Lower spine and pelvic stability

A. SUPINE BRIDGE

Lay faceup with your knees flexed 90 degrees, your feet flat on the floor, and your arms relaxed at your sides, palms down. Now raise your hips upward until your body forms a perfectly straight line from

neck to knees. Activate your abdominal muscles to prevent any sagging. Hold this position for 30 seconds. Begin with one bridge and advance to two and then three bridges as it becomes easier to hold it. Once you can comfortably hold three 30-second bridges, advance to the Supine Bridge with Leg Extension.

B. SUPINE BRIDGE WITH LEG EXTENSION

Assume a Supine Bridge Position as described above, but this time lift your left foot and extend your left leg completely so that it comes in line with your torso. Push into the floor with your right heel to keep your hips high. Hold this position for 15 seconds and then lower your

left foot to the floor; extend your right leg and hold for 15 seconds. Begin with one set of this exercise and advance to two and then three sets as it becomes easier to hold it. Once you can comfortably complete three sets of the Supine Bridge with Leg Extension, advance to the Supine Bridge and March.

C. SUPINE BRIDGE AND MARCH

Assume a Supine Bridge position. Keeping the 90-degree bend in your right leg, lift it until your left heel is 8 to 12 inches above the floor. Hold this position for 5 seconds, return to the starting position, and then repeat on the opposite side. Complete a total of five 5-second holds with each leg. Start with one set and advance to two and then three sets as it gets easier.

Scapular Dip
Shoulder stability

Place your hands shoulder-width apart on the edge of an exercise bench; position your heels on the floor in front of the bench, and suspend your body in the air between these points of contact. Your legs are fully extended; your elbows are locked, and your torso is perpendicular to the floor. Now dip your buttocks toward the floor by relaxing the muscles of your shoulders. This movement is only a few inches. Return to the starting position and then use your shoulder muscles to push your palms into the bench and raise your head another inch or two higher. Pause for one second at the top of this movement and return again to the starting position. Complete 8–15 repetitions.

VMO Dip
Knee stability

Stand normally on a stable support such as an exercise step that's 6 to 12 inches high, your toes even with an edge. Shift your full weight onto your right foot and reach down toward the floor in front of the step with your left foot. Touch your left heel to the floor without putting any weight on it and return to the starting position. Complete 10–12 repetitions and repeat with the right leg.

Back Extension
Spinal stability

Lay facedown on the floor with your arms outstretched in front of you, like Superman in flight. Contract the muscles of your lower back and lift your upper body and your legs as high above the floor as possible. Only your lower abdomen is now in contact with the floor. Hold for one second at the top of the movement and relax. Complete 10–15 repetitions.

Balance Board

Ankle stability

Balance on a balance board such as the Reebok Core Board or Fitter First balance board. Keep the edges of the board from touching the floor as long as possible. Spend a total of 2–3 minutes balancing.

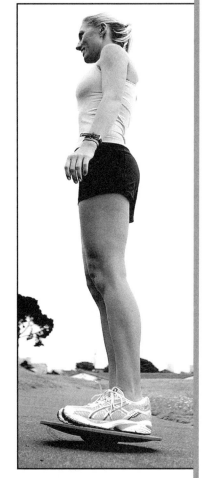

Single Leg Squat

Pelvic, hip, and knee stability

Stand on your right foot with an exercise bench or similar support 3 feet behind you. Reach back with your left leg and rest the top of your left foot on the bench. Your right foot should now be about 12–15 inches ahead of your body. Squat down until your right thigh is parallel to the floor and then thrust back upward to the starting position. Keep most of your weight on the heel of your right foot throughout this movement. Complete 10–12 repetitions and then reverse your position to work your left leg.

Stick Crunch
Lower spine and pelvic stability

Lay on your back, bend your knees, and draw them as close to your chest as possible. Grasp any type of stick or rod (such as a broom handle) with both hands, positioned shoulder-width apart. Begin with your arms extended straight toward your toes. Now squeeze your abdominal muscles and reach forward with the stick until it passes beyond your toes. Pause for one second and relax. Do 15–30 repetitions.

Pull-up
Shoulder stability

Grip a chin-up bar with your hands placed shoulder-width apart. You may use either an overhand or underhand grip, and indeed you should mix both grips as you repeat this exercise. Begin in a free hanging position with your knees flexed 90 degrees and your ankles crossed. Pull your body upward by bending and retracting your arms until your chin is level with the bar, then slowly return to a hanging position. Do as many repetitions as you can, up to a maximum of 20. If you are able to do only five or fewer Pull-ups, have an assistant help you or do the Modified Pull-up described below.

Modified Pull-up: In order to do this exercise you need to have some sort of sturdy rod secured 3 to 4 feet above the floor. A broom handle laid across a pair of barstools will do the trick. Sit under the bar and grab it underhand with your hands positioned at shoulder-width. Raise your hips up and form a straight line with your whole body. You are now "hanging" from the bar with only your heels touching the floor. Pull your chest to the bar and then return slowly to a hanging position. Do 12–18 repetitions.

Bend and Reach

Lower spine, pelvic, hip, and knee stability

Stand on your left foot with your right knee slightly bent and your right foot elevated a few inches above the floor. Bend your left leg and reach with your right hand to touch a spot on the floor located 10 to 16 inches in front of your left foot. Your left arm and right leg will naturally reach behind your body for balance. Return to the starting position. Do 10–12 repetitions and then repeat with your right foot planted.

Side Step-up

Hip and knee stability

Stand with your left side next to a 12- to 18-inch platform (such as a weight bench or tall aerobics step). Place your left foot on the platform and keep your right foot on the floor (your left knee is now sharply bent and your right leg is straight). Shift your weight onto your left leg and extend it, lifting your entire body 12 to 18 inches. Pause briefly with your right foot unsupported in the air next to your left foot, then bend your left knee again and slowly lower your right foot back down to the floor. Do 10–12 repetitions and then switch legs.

Lower Abdominal Squeeze
Lower spine and pelvic stability

Lay faceup with your arms relaxed at your sides and your legs extended straight toward the ceiling, heels together. Now contract the muscles of your lower abdomen and, by doing so, try to lift your heels ever so slightly toward the ceiling. (This is a very small movement). Hold the contraction for 1 second, then relax for 1 second. Do 10–12 repetitions.

Chapter 17

STRETCHES FOR TRIATHLETES

*T*riathlon is not a sport that requires supernormal all-around flexibility, as do some sports including figure skating and gymnastics. But triathletes do need to stretch. For triathletes, there are four distinct goals of stretching.

1. Increase the range of motion in particular joints.

While you don't need supernormal all-around flexibility as a triathlete, you do need a wide range of motion in particular joints. Top swimmers tend to have greater than average range of motion in their shoulder joints. This allows them to create longer strokes and cover more distance per stroke. Likewise, better runners tend to have greater than normal range of motion in the hips, which helps them take longer strides. So it's a good idea for you to work at increasing the range of motion in your shoulders and hips through stretching.

2. Increase dynamic flexibility.

Whenever you perform a sports action such as running, your working muscles have to overcome a certain amount of resistance from other, nonactive muscles. Dynamic flexibility is the ability of nonactive muscles to relax and stretch during sports actions so that they present minimal resistance to the working muscles, thereby enhancing the efficiency of the movement.

The best way to increase dynamic flexibility is by doing dynamic stretches. Dynamic stretches are movements that mimic the way your muscles and connective tissues actually stretch during running. An example is the leg swing (described on p. 446). Dynamic stretching reduces internal resistance in your swimming, cycling, and running movements so you can do them with less energy cost.

3. Prevent and rehabilitate injuries.

Abnormally tight and/or unnaturally shortened muscles and tendons contribute to several common overuse injuries. Loosening and lengthening the most problematic muscles and tendons is an effective way to prevent such injuries from occurring, or recurring. For example, unnaturally shortened calves and Achilles tendons (which most of us have, because it's caused by wearing shoes—*any* shoes) are known to contribute to plantar fasciitis, shin splints, Achilles tendonitis, and calf muscle strains. Stretching the calves and Achilles tendons regularly will reduce your risk of experiencing these injuries. Other muscles and tendons that usually require "corrective" stretching are the hamstrings, hip flexors (the muscles that lift your thighs), and the iliotibial band.

4. Warm up for workouts.

Dynamic stretches, in addition to increasing dynamic flexibility, are excellent warm-up exercises. They warm, lubricate, and loosen the muscles to prepare them for activity. Dynamic stretches are essential before high-intensity running to prevent acute muscle strains in the hamstrings and calves. I also recommend doing them before every swim, to prepare your shoulders to make long strokes without straining.

There are two types of stretches you should do. Corrective stretches help increase range of motion and lengthen and loosen muscles and tendons that are unnaturally shortened and/or abnormally tight. Dynamic stretches increase dynamic flexibility and are good warm-up exercises.

Corrective Stretches

Do these stretches at least three times a week at any time of day except first thing in the morning, when the spine in particular is less flexible. Stretch any "problem" muscles and tendons daily, and as often as three times a day. For example, I stretch my hip flexors three times a day to prevent the recurrence of tendonitis in my groin area, which is often caused by tight hip flexors.

Chest Stretch

Lift your arms straight to the sides, palms forward, and press them backward until you feel a stretch in your chest muscles. Hold this positions for 15 seconds.

Biceps and Front-Shoulder Stretch

Stand with your arms at your sides and your palms turned inward. Raise your arms behind your body until you feel a stretch in the front of your shoulders and in your biceps. Hold this position for 15 seconds.

Rotator Cuff Stretches

To stretch your internal shoulder rotators: Raise your arms in a "Don't shoot" position and press your elbows backward until you feel a stretch in your shoulders. Hold this position for 15 seconds.

To stretch your external shoulder rotators: From the "Don't shoot" position, rotate your hands 180 degrees so that your fingers are now pointing toward the floor and your palms are facing backward. Again, press your elbows backward until you feel a stretch in your shoulders. Hold this position for 15 seconds.

Triceps Stretch

Raise your right arm straight upward and bend it fully, touching the fingers to your upper spine. Grab your right elbow with your left hand and pull gently backward until you feel a stretch in your right triceps. Hold this position for 15 seconds and then stretch your left triceps.

Back Stretch

Reach your arms straight overhead and lace your fingers together. Lean to the left until you feel a stretch in the right side of your back. Hold this position for 15 seconds and then lean to the right.

Hip Flexors Stretch

Kneel on your left knee and place your right foot on the floor well in front of your body. Draw your navel toward your spine and roll your

pelvis backward. Now put your weight forward into the lunge until you feel a good stretch in your left hip flexors (located where your thigh joins your pelvis). You can extend the stretch to your psoas (a pair of hip flexor muscles connecting your pelvis and spine) by raising your left arm over your head and actively reaching toward the ceiling. Hold the stretch for 20 seconds and then repeat on the right side.

Hamstrings Stretch

Lay on your back with both legs bent. Begin with one foot resting flat on the floor and the other leg elevated so that the thigh is perpendicular to the floor and the shin is parallel to the floor. Loop a strap or rope around the bottom of this foot and grasp the two segments together in your stretching-side hand next to your knee. By contracting your quadriceps, straighten the rope-looped leg completely. Pull toward your head on the rope until you feel a good stretch in your hamstrings. Hold it for 1–2 seconds and relax. Repeat this stretch a total of 10 times, then stretch the opposite leg.

Iliotibial Band Stretch

Stand with your legs crossed so that your left foot is planted several inches to the right of your right foot. Sink your weight into your right hip socket and tip your torso to the left (but remain facing forward). You should begin to feel a stretch at the top of your iliotibial band, just beneath your hipbone. Hold this stretch for 20 seconds and then cross your right leg over your left to stretch the left IT band. Now repeat the stretch on both sides.

Calf Stretch

Stand on the edge of a step. Place the ball of your left foot at the very edge so that your heel is unsupported. Drop your left heel toward the floor while keeping your leg straight. Hold this stretch for 20 seconds. This will stretch the gastrocnemius, which is the larger, more visible muscle in your calf. Now bend your knee slightly and feel the stretch migrate downward into your soleus muscle. Hold this stretch for 20 seconds. Now stretch the right side.

Achilles Tendon Stretch

Stand in a split stance, one foot a step ahead of the other, with both feet flat on the ground and both knees slightly bent. Now bend your back leg a little more and concentrate on trying to "sink" your butt straight down toward the heel of that foot. Keep your torso upright. You should begin to feel a stretch in your Achilles tendon. You may have to fiddle with your position before you find it. When you do, hold it for 10–12 seconds, relax, and then stretch it a couple more times.

Dynamic Stretches

Do at least the first three of these stretches before jumping in the pool for swim workouts. Do at least the last five before high-intensity running. You can always do all eight of these stretches before either type of workout if you wish, or at any other time except first thing in the morning.

Arm Circles

Raise your arms straight to the sides and swing them in giant circles. Do six forward rotations and six backward rotations.

Side Bend

This stretch is identical to the Back Stretch, except you move continuously from side to side instead of holding the stretch for 15 seconds on each side. Stand with your arms raised straight overhead and your hands together. Bend to the right from the waist until you feel a stretch in the left side of your back. Now bend to the left. Bend to each side six times.

Trunk Rotation

Raise your arms straight out to the sides. Twist your torso as far as you can to the right. Without pausing, reverse direction and twist over to the left. Repeat 10 times.

Lunge Walk

Take 10 giant steps forward with each foot, lunging as far forward as you can each time.

Lateral Lunge

From a standing position, take a large step to the right with your right foot and lower yourself into a deep squat. Return immediately to a standing position and lunge to the left. Lunge five times to each side.

Forward Leg Swing

Stand on your right foot and swing your left leg backward and forward in an exaggerated kicking motion. Complete 10 swings and repeat with the right leg.

Lateral Leg Swing

Stand facing a wall; lean toward it slightly from the waist up, and brace the fingers of both hands against it. Swing your

fully extended right leg left to the right in wide arcs between your body and the wall. After completing 10 swings, swing your left leg.

Heel Bounce

Lean forward against a wall with your feet close together and flat on the ground. Raise both heels as high as possible and then lower them to the ground. Without pausing, return to the starting position. Immediately begin the next "bounce." Repeat 20 times.

Appendix

24-WEEK TRAINING LOG

Keeping a training log is essential to getting the most out of your training. The human memory is faulty. You can't rely on your memory to keep an accurate and complete record of your training. But you can always rely on a training log (unless you exaggerate your performances when you record them, like a golfer!). Having such a record available whenever you need it offers several benefits. First of all, it helps ensure that you are actually training according to plan. A training log also helps you identify patterns that you can use to make changes when necessary. For example, if you develop an injury you can look at your training log to see if your training changed in the days preceding its onset. A training log also provides the purely psychological benefit of enhancing motivation and confidence. I always get a big confidence boost from looking back at all the training I have accomplished as a big race approaches.

Following is a basic 24-week training log to get you started. You can photocopy pages to take your log beyond 24 weeks, or you can create your own on the computer, or buy one of the several training logbooks on the market. If you would like to keep an online training log with bells and whistles including the ability to download data to your log straight from your heart-rate monitor and bike computer, you can rent log space at www.trainingpeaks.com for a small monthly fee. You can even purchase online versions of the individual training plans contained in this book, so you can follow your training plan and log it online with special features including the ability to create graphs and track the mileage on your running shoes.

Week of: _____

	Swim	Bike	Run	Notes
Monday _____ **Date**				
Tuesday _____ **Date**				
Wednesday _____ **Date**				
Thursday _____ **Date**				
Friday _____ **Date**				
Saturday _____ **Date**				
Sunday _____ **Date**				
Weekly Summary				

Week of: _____

	Swim	Bike	Run	Notes
Monday _____ **Date**				
Tuesday _____ **Date**				
Wednesday _____ **Date**				
Thursday _____ **Date**				
Friday _____ **Date**				
Saturday _____ **Date**				
Sunday _____ **Date**				
Weekly Summary				

Week of: _____

	Swim	Bike	Run	Notes
Monday _____ **Date**				
Tuesday _____ **Date**				
Wednesday _____ **Date**				
Thursday _____ **Date**				
Friday _____ **Date**				
Saturday _____ **Date**				
Sunday _____ **Date**				
Weekly Summary				

Week of: _____

	Swim	Bike	Run	Notes
Monday _____ **Date**				
Tuesday _____ **Date**				
Wednesday _____ **Date**				
Thursday _____ **Date**				
Friday _____ **Date**				
Saturday _____ **Date**				
Sunday _____ **Date**				
Weekly Summary				

Week of: _____

	Swim	Bike	Run	Notes
Monday _____ **Date**				
Tuesday _____ **Date**				
Wednesday _____ **Date**				
Thursday _____ **Date**				
Friday _____ **Date**				
Saturday _____ **Date**				
Sunday _____ **Date**				
Weekly Summary				

Week of: _____

	Swim	Bike	Run	Notes
Monday _____ **Date**				
Tuesday _____ **Date**				
Wednesday _____ **Date**				
Thursday _____ **Date**				
Friday _____ **Date**				
Saturday _____ **Date**				
Sunday _____ **Date**				
Weekly Summary				

Week of: _____

	Swim	Bike	Run	Notes
Monday _____ **Date**				
Tuesday _____ **Date**				
Wednesday _____ **Date**				
Thursday _____ **Date**				
Friday _____ **Date**				
Saturday _____ **Date**				
Sunday _____ **Date**				
Weekly Summary				

Week of: _____

	Swim	Bike	Run	Notes
Monday _____ **Date**				
Tuesday _____ **Date**				
Wednesday _____ **Date**				
Thursday _____ **Date**				
Friday _____ **Date**				
Saturday _____ **Date**				
Sunday _____ **Date**				
Weekly Summary				

Week of: _____

	Swim	Bike	Run	Notes
Monday _____ **Date**				
Tuesday _____ **Date**				
Wednesday _____ **Date**				
Thursday _____ **Date**				
Friday _____ **Date**				
Saturday _____ **Date**				
Sunday _____ **Date**				
Weekly Summary				

Week of: _____

	Swim	Bike	Run	Notes
Monday _____ **Date**				
Tuesday _____ **Date**				
Wednesday _____ **Date**				
Thursday _____ **Date**				
Friday _____ **Date**				
Saturday _____ **Date**				
Sunday _____ **Date**				
Weekly Summary				

Week of: _____

	Swim	Bike	Run	Notes
Monday _____ **Date**				
Tuesday _____ **Date**				
Wednesday _____ **Date**				
Thursday _____ **Date**				
Friday _____ **Date**				
Saturday _____ **Date**				
Sunday _____ **Date**				
Weekly Summary				

Week of: _____

	Swim	Bike	Run	Notes
Monday _____ **Date**				
Tuesday _____ **Date**				
Wednesday _____ **Date**				
Thursday _____ **Date**				
Friday _____ **Date**				
Saturday _____ **Date**				
Sunday _____ **Date**				
Weekly Summary				

Week of: _____

	Swim	Bike	Run	Notes
Monday _____ **Date**				
Tuesday _____ **Date**				
Wednesday _____ **Date**				
Thursday _____ **Date**				
Friday _____ **Date**				
Saturday _____ **Date**				
Sunday _____ **Date**				
Weekly Summary				

Week of: _____

	Swim	Bike	Run	Notes
Monday _____ **Date**				
Tuesday _____ **Date**				
Wednesday _____ **Date**				
Thursday _____ **Date**				
Friday _____ **Date**				
Saturday _____ **Date**				
Sunday _____ **Date**				
Weekly Summary				

Week of: _____

	Swim	Bike	Run	Notes
Monday _____ **Date**				
Tuesday _____ **Date**				
Wednesday _____ **Date**				
Thursday _____ **Date**				
Friday _____ **Date**				
Saturday _____ **Date**				
Sunday _____ **Date**				
Weekly Summary				

Week of: _____

	Swim	Bike	Run	Notes
Monday _____ **Date**				
Tuesday _____ **Date**				
Wednesday _____ **Date**				
Thursday _____ **Date**				
Friday _____ **Date**				
Saturday _____ **Date**				
Sunday _____ **Date**				
Weekly Summary				

Week of: _____

	Swim	Bike	Run	Notes
Monday _____ **Date**				
Tuesday _____ **Date**				
Wednesday _____ **Date**				
Thursday _____ **Date**				
Friday _____ **Date**				
Saturday _____ **Date**				
Sunday _____ **Date**				
Weekly Summary				

Week of: _____

	Swim	Bike	Run	Notes
Monday _____ **Date**				
Tuesday _____ **Date**				
Wednesday _____ **Date**				
Thursday _____ **Date**				
Friday _____ **Date**				
Saturday _____ **Date**				
Sunday _____ **Date**				
Weekly Summary				

Week of: _____

	Swim	Bike	Run	Notes
Monday _____ **Date**				
Tuesday _____ **Date**				
Wednesday _____ **Date**				
Thursday _____ **Date**				
Friday _____ **Date**				
Saturday _____ **Date**				
Sunday _____ **Date**				
Weekly Summary				

Week of: _____

	Swim	Bike	Run	Notes
Monday _____ **Date**				
Tuesday _____ **Date**				
Wednesday _____ **Date**				
Thursday _____ **Date**				
Friday _____ **Date**				
Saturday _____ **Date**				
Sunday _____ **Date**				
Weekly Summary				

Week of: _____

	Swim	Bike	Run	Notes
Monday _____ **Date**				
Tuesday _____ **Date**				
Wednesday _____ **Date**				
Thursday _____ **Date**				
Friday _____ **Date**				
Saturday _____ **Date**				
Sunday _____ **Date**				
Weekly Summary				

Week of: _____

	Swim	Bike	Run	Notes
Monday _____ **Date**				
Tuesday _____ **Date**				
Wednesday _____ **Date**				
Thursday _____ **Date**				
Friday _____ **Date**				
Saturday _____ **Date**				
Sunday _____ **Date**				
Weekly Summary				

Week of: _____

	Swim	Bike	Run	Notes
Monday _____ **Date**				
Tuesday _____ **Date**				
Wednesday _____ **Date**				
Thursday _____ **Date**				
Friday _____ **Date**				
Saturday _____ **Date**				
Sunday _____ **Date**				
Weekly Summary				

Week of: _____

	Swim	Bike	Run	Notes
Monday _____ **Date**				
Tuesday _____ **Date**				
Wednesday _____ **Date**				
Thursday _____ **Date**				
Friday _____ **Date**				
Saturday _____ **Date**				
Sunday _____ **Date**				
Weekly Summary				